1985

Texts and Monographs in Computer Science

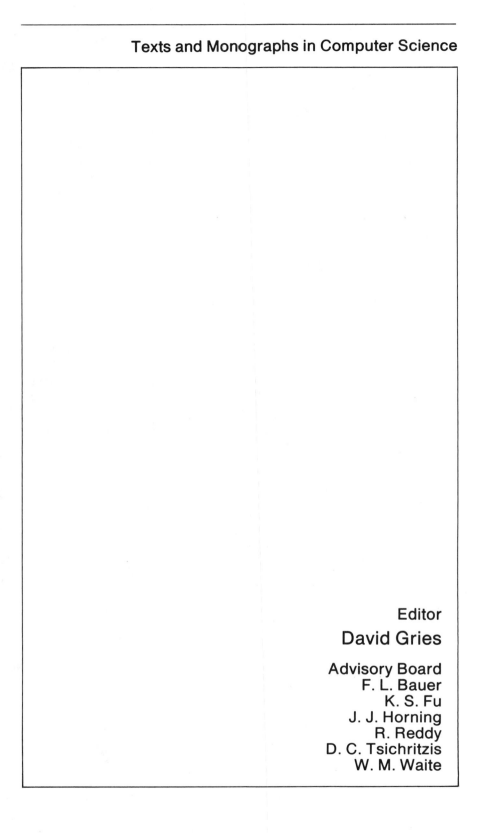

Compiler Construction

William M. Waite
Gerhard Goos

With 196 Figures

Springer-Verlag
New York Berlin Heidelberg Tokyo

William M. Waite
Department of Electrical
Engineering
University of Colorado
Boulder, CO 80309
U.S.A.

Gerhard Goos
Institut für Informatik II
Universität Karlsruhe
7500 Karlsruhe 1
Postfach 6380
West Germany

Series Editor

David Gries
Department of Computer Science
Cornell University
Upson Hall
Ithaca, NY 14853
U.S.A.

AMS Subject Classification 68B99
(C.R.) Computer Classification: D2

Library of Congress Cataloging in Publication Data
Waite, W. M. (William McCastline)
    Compiler construction.
    (Texts and monographs in computer science)
    1. Compiling (Electronic computers) I.
Goos, Gerhard, 1937-   II. Title. III. Series.
QA76.6.W3195   1983   001.64'25   83-14714

Media conversion by House of Equations Inc., Newton, New Jersey.
Printed and bound by R.R. Donnelley & Sons, Harrisonburg, Virginia.
Printed in the United States of America.

9 8 7 6 5 4 3 2 1

ISBN 0-387-90821-8 Springer-Verlag New York Berlin Heidelberg Tokyo
ISBN 3-540-90821-8 Springer-Verlag Berlin Heidelberg New York Tokyo

To all who know more than one language

Preface

Compilers and operating systems constitute the basic interfaces between a programmer and the machine for which he is developing software. In this book we are concerned with the construction of the former. Our intent is to provide the reader with a firm theoretical basis for compiler construction and sound engineering principles for selecting alternate methods, implementing them, and integrating them into a reliable, economically viable product. The emphasis is upon a clean decomposition employing modules that can be re-used for many compilers, separation of concerns to facilitate team programming, and flexibility to accommodate hardware and system constraints. A reader should be able to understand the questions he must ask when designing a compiler for language X on machine Y, what tradeoffs are possible, and what performance might be obtained. He should not feel that any part of the design rests on whim; each decision must be based upon specific, identifiable characteristics of the source and target languages or upon design goals of the compiler.

The vast majority of computer professionals will never write a compiler. Nevertheless, study of compiler technology provides important benefits for almost everyone in the field.

- It focuses attention on the basic relationships between languages and machines. Understanding of these relationships eases the inevitable transitions to new hardware and programming languages and improves a person's ability to make appropriate tradeoffs in design and implementation.

- It illustrates application of software engineering techniques to the solution of a significant problem. The problem is understandable to most users of computers, and involves both combinatorial and data processing aspects.

- Many of the techniques used to construct a compiler are useful in a wide variety of applications involving symbolic data. In particular, every man-machine interface constitutes a form of programming language and the handling of input involves these techniques.

We believe that software tools will be used increasingly to support many aspects of compiler construction. Much of Chapters 7 and 8 is therefore devoted to parser generators and analyzers for attribute grammars. The details of this discussion are only interesting to those who must construct such tools; the general outlines must be known to all who use them. We also realize that construction of compilers by hand will remain an important alternative, and thus we have presented manual methods even for those situations where tool use is recommended.

Virtually every problem in compiler construction has a vast number of possible solutions. We have restricted our discussion to the methods that are most useful today, and make no attempt to give a comprehensive survey. Thus, for example, we treat only the LL and LR parsing techniques and provide references to the literature for other approaches. Because we do not constantly remind the reader that alternative solutions are available, we may sometimes appear overly dogmatic although that is not our intent.

Chapters 5 and 8, and Appendix B, state most theoretical results without proof. Although this makes the book unsuitable for those whose primary interest is the theory underlying a compiler, we felt that emphasis on proofs would be misplaced. Many excellent theoretical texts already exist; our concern is reduction to practice.

A compiler design is carried out in the context of a particular language/machine pair. Although the principles of compiler construction are largely independent of this context, the detailed design decisions are not. In order to maintain a consistent context for our major examples, we therefore need to choose a particular source language and target machine. The source language that we shall use is defined in Appendix A. We chose not to use an existing language for several reasons, the most important being that a new language enabled us to control complexity: Features illustrating significant questions in compiler design could be included while avoiding features that led to burdensome but obvious detail. It also allows us to illustrate how a compiler writer derives information about a language, and provides an example of an informal but relatively precise language definition.

We chose the machine language of the IBM 370 and its imitators as our target. This architecture is widely used, and in many respects it is a difficult one to deal with. The problems are representative of many computers, the important exceptions being those (such as the Intel 8086) without a set of general registers. As we discuss code generation and assembly strategies we shall point out simplifications for more uniform architectures like those of the DEC PDP11 and Motorola 68000.

We assume that the reader has a minimum of one year of experience with a block-structured language, and some familiarity with computer organization. Chapters 5 and 8 use notation from logic and set theory, but the material itself is straightforward. Several important algorithms are based upon results from graph theory summarized in Appendix B.

This book is based upon many compiler projects and upon the lectures given by the authors at the Universität Karlsruhe and the University of Colorado. For self-study, we recommend that a reader with very little background begin with Section 1.1, Chapters 2 and 3, Section 12.1 and Appendix A. His objective should be to thoroughly understand the relationships between typical programming languages and typical machines, relationships that define the task of the compiler. It is useful to examine the machine code produced by existing compilers while studying this material. The remainder of Chapter 1 and all of Chapter 4 give an overview of the organization of a compiler and the properties of its major data structures, while Chapter 14 shows how three production compilers have been structured. From this material the reader should gain an appreciation for how the various subtasks relate to one another, and the important characteristics of the interfaces between them.

Chapters 5, 6 and 7 deal with the task of determining the structure of the source program. This is perhaps the best-understood of all compiler tasks, and the one for which the most theoretical background is available. The theory is summarized in Chapter 5, and applied in Chapters 6 and 7. Readers who are not theoretically inclined, and who are not concerned with constructing parser generators, should skim Chapter 5. Their objectives should be to understand the notation for describing grammars, to be able to deal with finite automata, and to understand the concept of using a stack to resolve parenthesis nesting. These readers should then concentrate on Chapter 6, Section 7.1 and the recursive descent parse algorithm of Section 7.2.2.

The relationship between Chapter 8 and Chapter 9 is similar to that between Chapter 5 and Chapter 7, but the theory is less extensive and less formal. This theory also underlies parts of Chapters 10 and 11. We suggest that the reader who is actually engaged in compiler construction devote more effort to Chapters 8-11 than to Chapters 5-7. The reason is that parser generators can be obtained "off the shelf" and used to construct the lexical and syntactic analysis modules quickly and reliably. A compiler designer must typically devote most of his effort to specifying and implementing the remainder of the compiler, and hence familiarity with Chapters 8-11 will have a greater effect on his productivity.

The lecturer in a one-semester, three-hour course that includes exercises is compelled to restrict himself to the fundamental concepts. Details of programming languages (Chapter 2), machines (Chapter 3) and formal languages and automata theory (Chapter 5) can only be covered in a cursory fashion or must be assumed as background. The specific techniques for parser development and attribute grammar analysis, as well as the whole of Chapter 13, must be reserved for a separate course. It seems best to present theoretical concepts from Chapter 5 in close conjunction with the specific methods of Chapters 6 and 7, rather than as a single topic. A typical outline is:

1. The Nature of the Problem   4 hours
    1.1.   Overview of compilation (Chapter 1)
    1.2.   Languages and machines (Chapters 2 and 3)
2. Compiler Data Structures (Chapter 4)   4 hours
3. Structural Analysis   10 hours
    3.1.   Formal Systems (Chapter 5)
    3.2.   Lexical analysis (Chapter 6)
    3.3.   Parsing (Chapter 7)
Review and Examination   2 hours
4. Consistency Checking   10 hours
    4.1.   Attribute grammars (Chapter 8)
    4.2.   Semantic analysis (Chapter 9)
5. Code Generation (Chapter 10)   8 hours
6. Assembly (Chapter 11)   2 hours
7. Error Recovery (Chapter 12)   3 hours
Review   2 hours

The students do *not* write a compiler during this course. For several years it has been run concurrently with a practicum in which the students implement the essential parts of a LAX compiler. They are given the entire compiler, with stubs replacing the parts they are to write. In contrast to project courses in which the students must write a complete compiler, this approach has the advantage that they need not be concerned with unimportant organizational tasks. Since only the central problems need be solved, one can deal with complex language properties. At the same time, students are forced to read the environment programs and to adhere to interface specifications. Finally, if a student cannot solve a particular problem it does not cause his entire project to fail since he can take the solution given by the instructor and proceed.

Acknowledgments

This book is the result of many years of collaboration. The necessary research projects and travel were generously supported by our respective universities, the Deutsche Forschungsgemeinschaft and the National Science Foundation.

It is impossible to list all of the colleagues and students who have influenced our work. We would, however, like to specially thank four of our doctoral students, Lynn Carter, Bruce Haddon, Uwe Kastens and Johannes Röhrich, for both their technical contributions and their willingness to read the innumerable manuscripts generated during the book's gestation. Mae Jean Ruehlman and Gabriele Sahr also have our gratitude for learning more than they ever wanted to know about computers and word processing as they produced and edited those manuscripts.

Contents

CHAPTER 1
Introduction and Overview

The term *compilation* denotes the conversion of an algorithm expressed in a human-oriented *source language* to an equivalent algorithm expressed in a hardware-oriented *target language*. We shall be concerned with the *engineering* of compilers — their organization, algorithms, data structures and user interfaces.

1.1. Translation and Interpretation

Programming languages are tools used to construct formal descriptions of finite computations (algorithms). Each computation consists of operations that transform a given *initial state* into some *final state*. A programming language provides essentially three components for describing such computations:

- Data types, objects and values with operations defined upon them.
- Rules fixing the chronological relationships among specified operations.
- Rules fixing the (static) structure of a program.

These components together constitute the *level of abstraction* on which we can formulate algorithms in the language. We shall discuss abstractions for programming languages in detail in Chapter 2.

The collection of objects existing at a given point in time during the computation constitutes the state, s, of the computation at that time. The set, S, of all states that could occur during computations expressed in the language is called the *state space* of the language. The *meaning* of an algorithm is the (partially-defined) function $f: S \rightarrow S$ by which it transforms initial states to final states.

1

Figure 1.1 illustrates the concept of a state. Figure 1.1a is a fragment of a program written in Pascal. Since this fragment does not declare the identifiers i and j, we add the fact that both are integer variables. The values of i and j before the given fragment begins to execute constitute the initial state; their values after execution ceases constitute the final state. Figure 1.1b illustrates the state transformations carried out by the fragment, starting from a particular initial state.

Let f be the function defined by the state transformation of some particular algorithm A. If we are to preserve the meaning of A when compiling it

while $i \neq j$ **do**
  if $i > j$ **then** $i := i - j$ **else** $j := j - i$;

a) An algorithm

Initial: $i = 36$ $j = 24$
              $i = 12$ $j = 24$
Final: $i = 12$ $j = 12$

b) A particular sequence of states

Figure 1.1 Algorithms and States

to a new language then the state transformation function f' of the translated algorithm A' must, in some sense, 'agree' with f. Since the state space, S', of the target language may differ from that of the source language, we must first decide upon a function, M, to map each state $s \in S$ to a subset $M(s)$ of S'. The function f' then preserves the meaning of f if $f'(M(s))$ is a subset of $M(f(s))$ for all allowable initial states $s \in S$.

For example, consider the language of a simple computer with a single accumulator and two data locations called I and J respectively (Exercise 1.3). Suppose that M maps a particular state of the algorithm given in Figure 1.1a to a set of machine states in which I contains the value of the variable i, J contains the value of the variable j, and the accumulator contains any arbitrary value. Figure 1.2a shows a translation of Figure 1.1a for this machine; a partial state sequence is given in Figure 1.2b.

In determining the state sequence of Figure 1.1b, we used only the concepts of Pascal as specified by the language definition. For every programming language, *PL*, we can define an *abstract machine*: The operations, data structures and control structures of *PL* become the memory elements and instructions of the machine. A 'Pascal machine' is therefore an imaginary computer with Pascal operations as its machine instructions and the data objects possible in Pascal as its memory elements. Execution of an algorithm written in *PL* on such a machine is called *interpretation*; the abstract machine is an *interpreter*.

A *pure* interpreter analyzes the character form of each source language instruction every time that instruction is executed. If the given instruction is only to be executed once, pure interpretation is the least expensive method of all. Hence it is often used for job control languages and the 'immediate commands' of interactive languages. When instructions are to be executed

```
LOOP    LOAD    I
        SUB     J
        JZERO   EXIT
        JNEG    SUBI
        STORE   I
        JUMP    LOOP
SUBI    LOAD    J
        SUB     I
        STORE   J
        JUMP    LOOP
EXIT
```

a) An algorithm

```
Initial:   I = 36   J = 24   ACC = ?
           I = 36   J = 24   ACC = 36
           I = 36   J = 24   ACC = 12
             .        .        .
             .        .        .
             .        .        .
Final:     I = 12   J = 12   ACC = 0
```

b) A sequence of states corresponding to Figure 1.1b

Figure 1.2 A Translation of Figure 1.1

repeatedly, a better approach is to analyze the character form of the source program only once, replacing it with a sequence of symbols more amenable to interpretation. This analysis is simply a translation of the source language into some target language, which is then interpreted.

The translation from the source language to the target language can take place as each instruction of the program is executed for the first time (*interpretation with substitution*). Thus only that part of the program actually executed will be translated; during testing this may be only a fraction of the entire program. Also, the character form of the source program can often be stored more compactly than the equivalent target program. The disadvantage of interpretation with substitution is that both the compiler and interpreter must be available during execution. In practice, however, a system of this kind should not be significantly larger than a pure interpreter for the same language.

Examples may be found of virtually all levels of interpretation. At one extreme are the systems in which the compiler merely converts constants to internal form, fixes the meaning of identifiers and perhaps transforms infix notation to postfix (APL and SNOBOL4 are commonly implemented this way); at the other are the systems in which the hardware, assisted by a small run-time system, forms the interpreter (FORTRAN and Pascal implementations usually follow this strategy).

1.2. The Tasks of a Compiler

A compilation is usually implemented as a sequence of transformations $(SL, L_1), (L_1, L_2), ..., (L_k, TL)$, where SL is the source language and TL is the target language. Each language L_i is called an *intermediate language*. Intermediate languages are conceptual tools used in decomposing the task of compiling from the source language to the target language. The design of a particular compiler determines which (if any) intermediate language programs actually appear as concrete text or data structures during compilation.

Any compilation can be broken down into two major tasks:

• Analysis: Discover the structure and primitives of the source program, determining its meaning.
• Synthesis: Create a target program equivalent to the source program.

This breakdown is useful because it separates our concerns about the source and target languages.

The analysis concerns itself solely with the properties of the source language. It converts the program text submitted by the programmer into an abstract representation embodying the essential properties of the algorithm. This abstract representation may be implemented in many ways, but it is usually conceptualized as a tree. The structure of the tree represents the control and data flow aspects of the program, and additional information is attached to the nodes to describe other aspects vital to the compilation. In Chapter 2 we review the general characteristics of source languages, pointing out the properties relevant for the compiler writer. Figure 1.3 illustrates the general idea with an abstraction of the algorithm of Figure 1.1a.

Figure 1.3a describes the control and data flow of the algorithm by means of the 'k^{th} descendant of' relation. For example, to carry out the algorithm described by a subtree rooted in a **while** node we first evaluate the expression described by the subtree that is the first descendant of the **while** node. If this expression yields *true* then we carry out the algorithm described by the subtree that is the second descendant. Similarly, to evaluate the expression described by an expression subtree, we evaluate the first and third descendants and then apply the operator described by the second descendant to the results.

The algorithm of Figure 1.1a is not completely characterized by Figure 1.3a. Information must be added (Figure 1.3b) to complete the description. Note that some of this information (the actual identifier for each *idn*) is taken directly form the source text. The remainder is obtained by process-

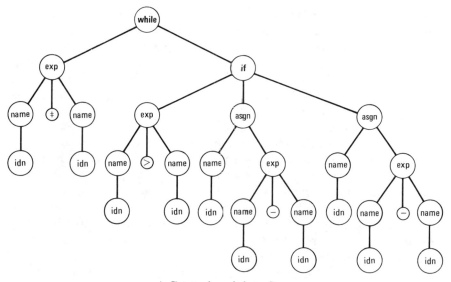

a) Control and data flow

Node	Additional Information
idn	identifier corresponding declaration
name	type of the variable
exp	type of the expression value

b) Additional information about the source program

Node	Additional Information
name	corresponding data location
if	address of code to carry out the **else** part
while	address of the expression evaluation code

c) Additional information about the target program

Figure 1.3 An Abstract Program Fragment

ing the tree. For example, the type of the expression value depends upon the operator and the types of the operands.

Synthesis proceeds from the abstraction developed during analysis. It augments the tree by attaching additional information (Figure 1.3c) that reflects the source-to-target mapping discussed in the previous section. For example, the access function for the variable *i* in Figure 1.1a would become the address of data location I according to the mapping *M* assumed by Figure 1.2. Similarly, the address of the **else** part of the conditional was represented by the label SUBI. Chapter 3 discusses the general characteristics of machines, highlighting properties that are important in the development of source-to-target mappings.

Formal definitions of the source language and the source-to-target mapping determine the structure of the tree and the computation of the additional information. The compiler simply implements the indicated transformations, and hence the abstraction illustrated in Figure 1.3 forms the basis for the entire compiler design. In Chapter 4 we discuss this abstraction in detail, considering possible intermediate languages and the auxiliary data structures used in transforming between them.

Analysis is the more formalized of the two major compiler tasks. It is generally broken down into two parts, the *structural analysis* to determine the static structure of the source program, and the *semantic analysis* to fix the additional information and check its consistency. Chapter 5 summarizes some results from the theory of formal languages and shows how they are used in the structural analysis of a program. Two subtasks of the structural analysis are identified on the basis of the particular formalisms employed: *Lexical analysis* (Chapter 6) deals with the basic symbols of the source program, and is described in terms of finite-state automata; *syntactic analysis*, or *parsing*, (Chapter 7) deals with the static structure of the program, and is described in terms of pushdown automata. Chapter 8 extends the theoretical treatment of Chapter 5 to cover the additional information attached to the components of the structure, and Chapter 9 applies the resulting formalism (attribute grammars) to semantic analysis.

There is little in the way of formal models for the entire synthesis process, although algorithms for various subtasks are known. We view synthesis as consisting of two distinct subtasks, *code generation* and *assembly*. Code generation (Chapter 10) transforms the abstract source program appearing at the analysis/synthesis interface into an equivalent target machine program. This transformation is carried out in two steps: First we map the algorithm from source concepts to target concepts, and then we select a specific sequence of target machine instructions to implement that algorithm.

Assembly (Chapter 11) resolves all target addressing and converts the target machine instructions into an appropriate output format. We should stress that by using the term 'assembly' we do not imply that the code generator will produce symbolic assembly code for input to the assembly task. Instead, it delivers an internal representation of target instructions in which most addresses remain unresolved. This representation is similar to that resulting from analysis of symbolic instructions during the first pass of a normal symbolic assembler. The output of the assembly task should be in the format accepted by the standard link editor or loader on the target machine.

Errors may appear at any time during the compilation process. In order to detect as many errors as possible in a single run, repairs must be made such that the program is consistent, even though it may not reflect the programmer's intent. Violations of the rules of the source language should be detected and reported during analysis. If the source algorithm uses concepts of the source language for which no target equivalent has been defined in a particular implementation, or if the target algorithm exceeds limitations of a specific target language interpreter (e.g. requires more memory than a specific computer provides), this should be reported during synthesis. Finally, errors must be reported if any storage limits of the compiler itself are violated.

In addition to the actual *error handling*, it is useful for the compiler to provide extra information for run-time error detection and debugging. This task is closely related to error handling, and both are discussed in Chapter 12.

A number of strategies may be followed in an attempt to improve the target program relative to some specified measure of cost. (Code size and execution speed are typical cost measures.) These strategies may involve deeper analysis of the source program, more complex mapping functions, and transformations of the target program. We shall treat the first two in our discussions of analysis and code generation respectively; the third is the subject of Chapter 13.

1.3. Data Management in a Compiler

As with other large programs, data management and access account for many of the problems to be solved by the design of a compiler. In order to control complexity, we separate the functional aspects of a data object from the implementation aspects by regarding it as an instance of an *abstract data type*. (An abstract data type is defined by a set of creation, assignment and access operators and their interaction; no mention is made of the concrete implementation technique.) This enables us to concentrate upon the relationships between tasks and data objects without becoming enmeshed in details of resource allocation that reflect the machine upon which the compiler is running (the *compiler host*) rather than the problem of compilation.

A particular implementation is chosen for a data object on the basis of the relationship between its pattern of usage and the resources provided by the compiler host. Most of the basic issues involved become apparent if we distinguish three classes of data:

- Local data of compiler tasks
- Program text in various intermediate representations
- Tables containing information that represents context-dependence in the program text

Storage for local data can be allocated statically or managed via the normal stacking mechanisms of a block-structured language. Such strategies are not useful for the program text, however, or for the tables containing contextual information. Because of memory limitations, we can often hold only a small segment of the program text in directly-accessible storage. This constrains us to process the program sequentially, and prevents us from representing it directly as a linked data structure. Instead, a linear notation that represents a specific traversal of the data structure (e.g. prefix or postfix) is often employed. Information to be used beyond the immediate vicinity of the place where it was obtained is stored in tables. Conceptually, this information is a component of the program text; in practice it often occupies different data structures because it has different access patterns. For example, tables must often be accessed randomly. In some cases it is necessary to search them, a process that may require a considerable fraction of the total compilation time. For this reason we do not usually consider the possibility of spilling tables to a file.

The size of the program text and that of most tables grows linearly with the *length* of the original source program. Some data structures (e.g. the parse stack) only grow with the *complexity* of the source program. (Complexity is generally related to nesting of constructs such as procedures and loops. Thus long, straight-line programs are not particularly complex.) Specification of bounds on the size of any of these data structures leads automatically to restrictions on the class of translatable programs. These restrictions may not be onerous to a human programmer but may seriously limit programs generated by pre-processors.

1.4. Compiler Structure

A decomposition of any problem identifies both tasks and data structures. For example, in Section 1.2 we discussed the analysis and synthesis tasks. We mentioned that the analyzer converted the source program into an abstract representation and that the synthesizer obtained information from this abstract representation to guide its construction of the target algorithm. Thus we are led to recognize a major data object, which we call the *structure tree*, in addition to the analysis and synthesis tasks.

We define one *module* for each task and each data structure identified during the decomposition. A module is specified by an interface that defines the objects and actions it makes available, and the global data and operations it uses. It is implemented (in general) by a collection of procedures accessing a common data structure that embodies the state of the module. Modules fall into a spectrum with single procedures at one end and simple data objects at the other. Four points on this spectrum are important for our purposes:

- Procedure: An abstraction of a single 'memoryless' action (i.e. an action with no internal state). It may be invoked with parameters, and its effect depends only upon the parameter values. (Example – A procedure to calculate the square root of a real value.)
- Package: An abstraction of a collection of actions related by a common internal state. The declaration of a package is also its instantiation, and hence only one instance is possible. (Example – The analysis or structure tree module of a compiler.)

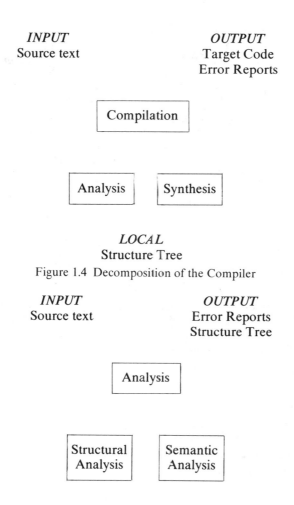

Figure 1.4 Decomposition of the Compiler

Figure 1.5 Decomposition of the Analysis Task

- Abstract data type: An abstraction of a data object on which a number of actions can be performed. Declaration is separate from instantiation, and hence many instances may exist. (Example — A stack abstraction providing the operations *push, pop, top,* etc.)
- Variable: An abstraction of a data object on which exactly two operations, *fetch* and *store,* can be performed. (Example — An integer variable in most programming languages.)

Abstract data types can be implemented via packages: The package defines a data type to represent the desired object, and procedures for all operations on the object. Objects are then instantiated separately. When an operation

INPUT   *OUTPUT*
Source text   Error Reports
                                                Connection Sequence

```
          ┌─────────────┐
          │ Structural  │
          │ Analysis    │
          └─────────────┘


    ┌───────────┐    ┌───────────┐
    │ Lexical   │    │           │
    │ Analysis  │    │ Parsing   │
    └───────────┘    └───────────┘
```

LOCAL
Token Sequence

Figure 1.6 Decomposition of the Structural Analysis Task

INPUT   *OUTPUT*
Structure Tree   Error Reports
                                                Target Code

```
          ┌─────────────┐
          │  Synthesis  │
          └─────────────┘


    ┌───────────┐    ┌───────────┐
    │  Code     │    │           │
    │Generation │    │ Assembly  │
    └───────────┘    └───────────┘
```

LOCAL
Target Tree

Figure 1.7 Decomposition of the Synthesis Task

is invoked, the particular object to which it should be applied is passed as a parameter to the operation procedure.

The overall compiler structure that we shall use in this book is outlined in Figures 1.4 through 1.8. Each of these figures describes a single step in the decomposition. The central block of the figure specifies the problem being decomposed at this step. To the left are the data structures from which information is obtained, and to the right are those to which information is delivered. Below is the decomposition of the problem, with boxes represent-

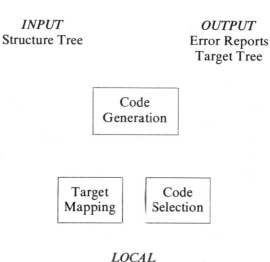

Figure 1.8 Decomposition of the Code Generation Task

ing subtasks. Data structures used for communication among these subtasks are listed at the bottom of the figure. Each box and each entry in any of the three data lists corresponds to a module of the compiler. It is important to note that Figures 1.4 through 1.8 reflect *only* the overall structure of the compiler; they are not flowcharts and they do not specify module interfaces.

Our decomposition is based upon our understanding of the compilation problem and our perception of the best techniques currently available for its solution. The choice of precise boundaries is driven by control and data flow considerations, primarily minimization of flow at interfaces. Specific criteria that influenced our decisions will be discussed throughout the text.

The decomposition is virtually independent of the underlying implementation, and of the specific characteristics of the source language and target machine. Clearly these factors influence the complexity of the modules that we have identified, in some cases reducing them to trivial stubs, but the overall structure remains unchanged.

Independence of the modules from the concrete implementation is obtained by assuming that each module is implemented on its own abstract machine, which provides the precise operations needed by the module. The local data structures of Figures 1.4-1.8 are thus components of the abstract machine on which the given subproblem is solved.

One can see the degree of freedom remaining in the implementation by noting that our diagrams never prescribe the time sequence of the subproblem solutions. Thus, for example, analysis and synthesis might run sequentially. In this case the structure tree must be completely built as a linked data structure during analysis, written to a file if necessary, and then processed during synthesis. Analysis and synthesis might, however, run concurrently and interact as coroutines: As soon as the analyzer has extracted an element of the structure tree, the synthesizer is activated to process this element further. In this case the structure tree will never be built as a concrete object, but is simply an abstract data structure; only the element being processed exists in concrete form.

In particular, our decomposition has nothing to do with the possible division of a compiler into *passes*. (We consider a pass to be a single, sequential scan of the entire text in either direction. A pass either transforms the program from one internal representation to another or performs specified changes while holding the representation constant.) The pass structure commonly arises from storage constraints in main memory and from input/output considerations, rather than from any logical necessity to divide the compiler into several sequential steps. One module is often split across several passes, and/or tasks belonging to several modules are carried out in the same pass. Possible criteria will be illustrated by concrete examples in Chapter 14. Proven programming methodologies indicate that it is best to regard pass structure as an implementation question. This permits development of program families with the same modular decomposition but different pass organization. The above consideration of coroutines and other implementation models illustrates such a family.

1.5. Notes and References

Compiler construction is one of the areas of computer science that early workers tried to consider systematically. Knuth [1962] reports some of those efforts. Important sources from the first half of the 60's are an issue of the *Communications of the ACM* [1961], the report of a conference sponsored by the International Computing Centre [ICC 1962] and the collection of papers edited by Rosen [1967]. Finally, *Annual Review in Automatic Programming* contains a large number of fundamental papers in compiler construction.

The idea of an algorithmic conversion of expressions to a machine-oriented form originated in the work of Rutishauser [1952]. Although most of our current methods bear only a distant resemblance to those of the 50's and early 60's, we have inherited a view of the description of programming languages that provides the foundation of compiler construction today: Intermediate languages were first proposed as interfaces in the compilation process by a SHARE committee [Mock 1958]; the extensive theory of formal languages, first developed by the linguist Noam Chomsky [1956], was employed in the definition of ALGOL 60 [Naur 1963]; the use of pushdown automata as models for syntax analysis appears in the work of Samelson and Bauer [1960].

The book by Randell and Russell [1964] remains a useful guide for a quick implementation of ALGOL 60 that does not depend upon extensive tools. Grau, Hill and Langmaack [1967] describe an ALGOL 60 implementation in an extended version of ALGOL 60. The books by Gries [1971], Aho and Ullman [1972, 1977a] and Bauer and Eickel [1976] represent the state of the art in the mid 1970's.

Recognition that parsing can be understood via models from the theory of formal languages led to a plethora of work in this area and provided the strongest motivation for the further development of that theory. From time to time the impression arises that parsing is the only relevant component of compiler construction. Parsing unquestionably represents one of the most important control mechanisms of a compiler. However, while just under one third of the papers collected in Pollack's 1972 bibliography are devoted to parsing, there was not one reference to the equally important topic of code generation. Measurements [Lalonde 1972] have shown that parsing represents approximately 9% of a compiler's code and 11% of the total compilation time. On the other hand, code generation and optimization account for 50-70% of the compiler. Certainly this discrepancy is due, in part, to the great advances made in the theory of parsing; the value of this work should not be underestimated. We must stress, however, that a more balanced viewpoint is necessary if progress is to be maintained.

Modular decomposition [Parnas 1972, Parnas 1976] is a design technique in which intermediate stages are represented by specifications of the external behavior (interfaces) of program modules. The technique of data-driven decomposition was discussed by Liskov and Zilles [1974], and a summary of program module characteristics was given by Goos and Kastens [1978]. This latter paper shows how the various kinds of program modules are constructed in several programming languages. Our diagrams depicting single decompositions are loosely based upon some ideas of Stevens, Myers and Constantine [1974].

EXERCISES

1.1. Consider the Pascal algorithm of Figure 1.1a.
    a. What are the elementary objects and operations?
    b. What are the rules for chronological relations?
    c. What composition rules are used to construct the static program?

1.2. Determine the state transformation function, f, for the algorithm of Figure 1.1a. What initial states guarantee termination? How do you characterize the corresponding final states?

1.3. Consider a simple computer with an accumulator and two data locations. The instruction set is:

LOAD	d:	Copy the contents of data location d to the accumulator.
STORE	d:	Copy the contents of the accumulator to data location d.
SUB	d:	Subtract the contents of data location d from the accumulator, leaving the result in the accumulator. (Ignore any possibility of overflow.)
JUMP	i:	Execute instruction i next.

JZERO   i: Execute instruction i next if the accumulator contents are
                   zero.
JNEG   i: Execute instruction i next if the accumulator contents are
                   less than zero.

a. What are the elementary objects?
b. What are the elementary actions?
c. What composition rules are used?
d. Complete the state sequence of Figure 1.2b.

CHAPTER 2
Properties of Programming Languages

Programming languages are often described by stating the meaning of the constructs (expressions, statements, clauses, etc.) interpretively. This description implicitly defines an interpreter for an abstract machine whose machine language is the programming language.

The output of the analysis task is a representation of the program to be compiled in terms of the operations and data structures of this abstract machine. By means of code generation and the run-time system, these elements are modeled by operation sequences and data structures of the computer and its basic software (operating system, etc.)

In this chapter we explore the properties of programming languages that determine the construction and possible forms of the associated abstract machines, and demonstrate the correspondence between the elements of the programming language and the abstract machine. On the basis of this discussion, we select the features of our example source language, LAX. A complete definition of LAX is given in Appendix A.

2.1. Overview

The basis of every language implementation is a language definition. (See the Bibliography for a list of the language definitions that we shall refer to in this book.) Users of the language read the definition as a user manual: What is the practical meaning of the primitive elements? How can they be meaningfully used? How can they be combined in a meaningful way? The compiler writer, on the other hand, is interested in the question of which constructions are *permitted*. Even if he cannot at the moment see any useful application of a construct, or if the construct leads to serious implementation difficulties, he must implement it exactly as specified by the language definition. Descriptions such as programming textbooks, which are oriented towards the meaningful applications of the language elements, do not clearly define the boundaries between what is permitted and what is prohibited. Thus it is difficult to make use of such descriptions as bases for the construction of a compiler. (Programming textbooks are also informal, and often cover only a part of the language.)

2.1.1. Syntax, Semantics and Pragmatics   The syntax of a language determines which character strings constitute well-formed programs in the language and which do not. The semantics of a language describe the meaning of a program in terms of the basic concepts of the language. Pragmatics relate the basic concepts of the language to concepts outside the language (to concepts of mathematics or to the objects and operations of a computer, for example).

Semantics include properties that can be deduced without executing the program as well as those only recognizable during execution. Following Griffiths [1973], we denote these properties *static* and *dynamic* semantics respectively. The assignment of a particular property to one or the other of these classes is partially a design decision by the compiler writer. For example, some implementations of ALGOL 60 assign the distinction between integer and real to the dynamic semantics, although this distinction can normally be made at compile time and thus could belong to the static semantics.

Pragmatic considerations appear in language definitions as unelaborated statements of existence, as references to other areas of knowledge, as appeals to intuition, or as explicit statements. Examples are the statements '[Boolean] values are the truth values denoted by the identifiers true and false' (Pascal Report, Section 6.1.2), 'their results are obtained in the sense of numerical analysis' (ALGOL 68 Revised Report, Section 2.1.3.1.e) or 'decimal numbers have their conventional meaning' (ALGOL 60 Report, Section 2.5.3). Most pragmatic properties are hinted at through a suggestive choice of words that are not further explained. Statements that certain constructs only have a defined meaning under specified conditions also belong to the pragmatics of a language. In such cases the compiler writer is usually free to fix the meaning of the construct under other conditions. The richer the pragmatics of a language, the more latitude a compiler writer has for efficient implementation and the heavier the burden on the user to write his program to give the same answers regardless of the implementation.

We shall set the following goals for our analysis of a language definition:

● Stipulation of the syntactic rules specifying construction of programs.
● Stipulation of the static semantic rules. These, in conjunction with the syntactic rules, determine the form into which the analysis portion of the compiler transforms the source program.

- Stipulation of the dynamic semantic rules and differentiation from pragmatics. These determine the objects and operations of the language-oriented abstract machine, which can be used to describe the interface between the analysis and synthesis portions of the compiler: The analyzer translates the source program into an abstract target program that could run on the abstract machine.
- Stipulation of the mapping of the objects and operations of the abstract machine onto the objects and operations of the hardware and operating system, taking the pragmatic meanings of these primitives into account. This mapping will be carried out partly by the code generator and partly by the run-time system; its specification is the basis for the decisions regarding the partitioning of tasks between these two phases.

2.1.2. Syntactic Properties

The syntactic rules of a language belong to distinct levels according to their meaning. The lowest level contains the 'spelling rules' for basic symbols, which describe the construction of keywords, identifiers and special symbols. These rules determine, for example, whether keywords have the form of identifiers (*begin*) or are written with special delimiters ('BEGIN', .BEGIN), whether lower case letters are permitted in addition to upper case, and which spellings ($< =$, .LE., 'NOT' 'GREATER') are permitted for symbols such as $\leqslant$ that cannot be reproduced on all I/O devices. A common property of these rules is that they do not affect the meaning of the program being represented. (In this book we have distinguished keywords by using boldface type. This convention is used only to enhance readability, and does not imply anything about the actual representation of keywords in program text.)

The second level consists of the rules governing representation and interpretation of constants, for example rules about the specification of exponents in floating point numbers or the allowed forms of integers (decimal, hexadecimal, etc.) These rules affect the meanings of programs insofar as they specify the possibilities for direct representation of constant values. The treatment of both of these syntactic classes is the task of lexical analysis, discussed in Chapter 6.

The third level of syntactic rules is termed the *concrete syntax*. Concrete syntax rules describe the composition of language contructs such as expressions and statements from basic symbols. Figure 2.1a shows the *parse tree* (a graphical representation of the application of concrete syntax rules) of the Pascal statement 'if *a* or *b* and *c* then $\cdots$ else $\cdots$'. Because the goal of the compiler's analysis task is to determine the meaning of the source program, semantically irrelevant complications such as operator precedence and certain keywords can be suppressed. The language constructs are described by an *abstract syntax* that specifies the compositional structure of a program while leaving open some aspects of its concrete representation as a string of basic symbols. Application of the abstract syntax rules can be illustrated by a *structure tree* (Figure 2.1b).

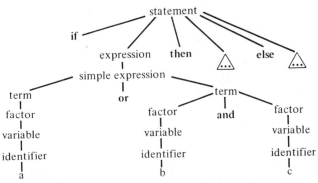

a) Parse tree (application of concrete syntax rules)

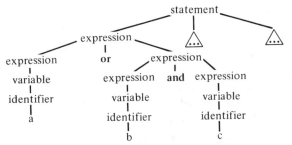

b) Structure tree (application of abstract syntax rules)

Figure 2.1. Concrete and Abstract Syntax

2.1.3. Semantic Properties

Most current programming languages specify algorithms *operationally*, in contrast to 'very high level' languages that allow the user to formally describe a problem and leave the implementation to the compiler. Essential semantic elements of operational languages are -

- Data objects and structures upon which operations take place
- Operations and construction rules for expressions and other operative statements
- Constructs providing flow of control, the dynamic composition of program fragments

Data objects appear as explicit constants, as values of variables and as results of operations. At any point in the execution of a program the totality of variable values represents the *state* of the abstract machine. This state constitutes the environment for execution of further operations.

Included in the set of operations are the access functions such as indexing of an array or selection of a field of a record, and operations such as the addition or comparison of two values. These operations do not alter the state of the abstract machine. Assignment is an example of an operation with a *side effect* that alters the contents of a variable, a component of the state of the abstract machine. Most programming languages contain a large number of such state-changing operations, all of which may be regarded as assignment combined with other operations. Usually these operations are formulated as statements without results. Most COBOL 'verbs' designate such statements. Finally, operations include block entry and exit, procedure call and return, and creation of variables. These operations, which we associate with control of the state, change the state by creating and deleting objects (variables, parameters, etc.) and altering the allowable access functions.

Flow of control includes conditional expressions or statements, case selection, iteration, jumps and so forth. These elements appear in various forms in most programming languages, and frequently take into account some special implementation possibility or practice. For example, the conditional statement

> **if** *truth_value* **then** s_1 **else** s_2;

and the case selection

> **case** *truth_value* **of** *true*: s_1; *false*: s_2 **end**;

have identical effects in Pascal. As we shall see later, however, the two constructs would probably be implemented differently.

In considering semantic properties, it is important for the compiler writer to systematically collect the countless details such as properties of data objects, operations and side effects, possibilities for iteration, and so forth, into some schema. The clarity and adequacy of this schema determines the quality of the compiler because the compiler structure is derived from it. A shoddy schema makes well-nigh impossible a convincing argument that the compiler translates the source language fully and completely.

For many languages, including ALGOL 60, ALGOL 68, Pascal and Ada, good schemata are comparatively easy to obtain because the language definitions are suitably structured. Other language definitions take the form of a collection of language element descriptions with many exception rules; a systematic treatment of such languages is often impossible.

2.2. Data Objects and Operations

The most important characteristics of a programming language are the available data objects and the operations that may be executed upon them. The term 'object' means a concrete instance of an abstract value. Many such instances of the same value may exist at the same time. The set of values possible in a language, such as numbers, character strings, records and so forth, is usually infinite although a given program naturally uses only a finite number of them.

Objects and values may be classified according to many criteria. For example, their internal (to the computer) or external representation, the algorithm used to access them, or the access rights might be used. Each such classification leads to an attribute of the object. The most important classification is a partition of the set of values according to the applicable operations; the corresponding attribute is called the *type* or *mode* of the value. Examples are the numeric types *integer* and *real*, to which the basic arithmetic operations may be applied. (The special role of zero in division is not covered by this classification.)

A rough subdivision of object types can be made on the basis of the possible access functions. If an object can be accessed only in its entirety we say that its type is *elementary*. If, however, the object consists of a collection of distinct components, which may be altered individually, then we say that its type is *composite*. Thus if a programming language were to explain floating point operations in terms of updating operations on fraction and exponent individually, floating point values would be composite. This is not usually done; the floating point operations can only yield complete floating numbers, and hence *real* is an elementary type.

Every operation interprets its operands in a specified manner. The assignment of a type to a value fixes this interpretation and admits only those operations for which this interpretation is meaningful. As usual with such attributes, there are many possible choices for the *binding time* — the point at which a particular attribute is ascribed to a particular object: If the type is first fixed upon execution of an operation, and if practically any operation can be applied to any object (so long as its length is appropriate), then we term the language *typeless* or *type-free*; otherwise it is called a *typed* language. If the type of an object can be determined explicitly from the program text, we speak of *manifest* type; the type is *latent* if it cannot be determined until the program is executed. (A language whose types are manifest throughout is sometimes called a *strongly-typed* language, while one whose types are latent is called *weakly-typed*.) Objects with latent types must be provided with an explicit type indication during execution. Most assembly languages are examples of typeless languages. In contrast, ALGOL 60, FORTRAN and COBOL are languages with manifest types: All variables are declared (either explicitly or implicitly) to have values of a certain type, and there are different forms of denotation for constants of different types. SNOBOL4 has neither declarations nor implied type specifications for its variables; on the contrary, the type may change during execution. Thus SNOBOL4 has latent types. The union modes in ALGOL 68 and the variant records of Pascal and Ada take an intermediate position. A variable of such a 'discriminated union' has a latent type, but the possible value types may only be drawn from an explicitly-stated set.

In a typeless language, the internal representation ('coding') of an object is the concern of the programmer; the implementor of a typed language can fix the coding because he is fully aware of all desired interpretations. Erroneous coding by the programmer is thus impossible. Further, inconsistent creation or use of a data object can be detected automatically and hence the class of automatically-detected errors is broadened. With manifest types such errors appear during compilation, with latent types they are first detected during execution. Moreover, in a language with latent types the erroneous creation of an object is only detected upon subsequent use and the necessary dynamic type checking increases the computation time.

2.2.1. Elementary Types   Our purpose in this section and the next is to give an overview of the types usually found in programming languages and explore their 'normal' properties. The reader should note in particular how these properties may be deduced from the language definition.

The elementary types can be partitioned according to the (theoretical) size of their value sets. A type is called *finite* if only a fixed number of values of this type exist; otherwise the type is (potentially) *infinite*.

Finite types can be defined by enumeration of all of the values of the type. Examples are the type *Boolean* whose value set is $\{true, false\}$ and the type *character*, with the entire set of characters permitted by an implementation as its value set. Almost all operations and properties of a type with n values can be defined giving a 1-1 correspondence with the natural numbers $0, \ldots, n - 1$ and then defining operations using these ordinal numbers. This possibility does not imply that such a mapping is actually specified in every language; on the contrary, finite types are introduced primarily to represent value sets for which a numerical interpretation is meaningless. For example, the revised ALGOL 68 report defines no correspondence between truth values and the integers 0 and 1. It asserts that such a correspondence exists for character values, but leaves its precise specification to the implementor: '... this relationship is defined only to the extent that different characters have different integral equivalents, and that there exists a "largest integral equivalent"' (Section 2.1.3.1.g). This specification permits gaps in the sequence of corresponding integers, an important point in many implementations.

In principle the value set of a finite type is unordered. If an ordering is needed, say to define relational operators or a successor function, the ordering induced by the mapping to natural numbers is used. For example, Pascal specifies that the relation $false < true$ holds and thus demands the mapping $false \to 0$, $true \to 1$ (although the ordering of Boolean values is really irrelevant). Often the mere existence of an ordering is sufficient. For example, the ALGOL 68 specification of character values permits the use of sorted tables or trees to speed up searching, even though the user could not guarantee a *particular* ordering. Many applications demand that some particular ordering (*collating sequence*) be defined on the set of characters; the task of lexicographic ordering in a telephone book is a common example. Different collating sequences may be appropriate for different problems. COBOL recognizes this fact by allowing the user to provide different collating sequences for different programs or for different operations within the same program.

The integers and floating point numbers belong to the class of infinite types. Most language definitions rely upon the mathematical intuition of the reader for the definition of these types. Some of our mathematical intuition is invalidated, however, because the machine representations of these types are necessarily finite.

The important characteristics of *integer* type are that a successor function is defined on the values, and that exact arithmetic is available. In contrast, a *real* value has no defined successor (although a total ordering is defined) and arithmetic is inexact. Some of the familiar axioms fail — for example, associativity is lost. In the representation of a floating point number as a pair (s,e) such that $v = s*b^e$ is stored in a single word, additional range is obtained at the cost of decreased precision. In comparison to the integer representation, the number of significant digits in s has been shortened to obtain space for the exponent e. The radix b is usually 2, 8, 10 or 16. Both a range and a precision must be specified to characterize the floating point domain, while a range alone suffices for the integer domain. The specifications for the two domains are independent of one another. In particular, it is often impossible to represent all valid integers exactly as floating point numbers because s is not large enough to hold all integer values.

The number of significant digits and the size of the exponent (and similar properties of other types) vary from computer to computer and implementation to implementation. Since an algorithm's behavior may depend upon the particular values of such parameters, the values should be accessible. For this purpose many languages provide *environment inquiries*; some languages, Ada for example, allow specifications for the range and precision of numbers in the form of minimum requirements.

Restriction of the integer domain and similar specification of subranges of finite types is often erroneously equated to the concept of a type. ALGOL 68, for example, distinguishes an infinity of 'sizes' for integer and real values. Although these sizes define different modes in the ALGOL 68 sense, the Standard Environment provides identical operators for each; thus they are indistinguishable according to the definition of type given at the beginning of Section 2.2. The distinction can only be understood by examination of the internal coding.

The basic arithmetic operations are usually defined by recourse to the reader's mathematical intuition. Only integer division involving negative operands requires a more exact stipulation in a language definition. Number theorists recognize two kinds of integer division, one truncating toward zero (-3 divided by 2 yields -1) and the other truncating toward negative infinity (-3 divided by 2 yields -2). ALGOL 60 uses the first definition, which also forms the basis for most hardware realizations.

We have already seen that a correspondence between the values of a finite type and a subset of the natural numbers can be defined. This correspondence may be specified by the language definition, or it may be described but its definition left to the implementor. As a general principle, similar relationships are possible between the value sets of other types. For example, the ALGOL 68 Revised Report asserts that for every integer of a given length there is an equivalent real of that length; the FORTRAN Standard implies a relation between integer and real values by its definition of assignment, but does not define it precisely.

Even if two values of different types (say 2 and 2.0) are logically equivalent, they must be distinguished because different operations may be applied to them. If a programmer is to make use of the equivalence, the abstract machine must provide appropriate *transfer* (*conversion*) operations. This is often accomplished by overloading the assignment operator. For example, Section 4.2.4 of the ALGOL 60 Report states that 'if the the type of the arithmetic expression [in an assignment] differs from that associated with the variables and procedure identifiers [making up the left part list], appropriate transfer functions are understood to be automatically invoked'. Another way of achieving this effect is to say that the operator indication ':=' stands for one of a number of assignment operations, just as '+' stands for either integer or real addition.

The meaning of ':=' must be determined from the context in the above example. Another approach to the conversion problem is to use the context to determine the type of value directly, and allow the compiler to insert a transfer operation if necessary. We say that the compiler *coerces* the value to a type appropriate for the context; the inserted transfer operation is a *coercion*.

Coercions are most frequently used when the conversion is defined for all values of the type being converted. If this is not the case, the programmer may be required to write an explicit transfer function. In Pascal, for example, a coercion is provided from integer to real but not from real to integer. The programmer must use one of the two explicit transfer functions *trunc* or *round* in the latter case.

Sometimes coercions are restricted to certain syntactic positions. ALGOL 68 has elaborate rules of this kind, dividing the complete set of available coercions into four classes and allowing different classes in different positions. The particular rules are chosen to avoid ambiguity in the program. Ada provides a set of coercions, but does not restrict their use. Instead, the language definition requires simply that each construct be unambiguously interpretable.

LAX provides Boolean, integer and real as elementary types. We omitted characters and programmer-defined finite types because they do not raise any additional significant issues. Integer division is defined to truncate towards zero to match the behavior of most hardware. Coercion from integer to real is defined, but there is no way to convert in the opposite direction. Again, the reason for this omission is that no new issues are raised by it.

2.2.2. Composite Types   Composite objects are constructed from a finite number of *components*, each of which may be accessed by a *selector*. A composite type is formed from the types of the components by a *type constructor*, which also defines the selectors. Programming languages usually provide two sorts of composite objects: *records* (also known as *structures*) and *arrays*.

Records are composite objects with a fixed number of components called *fields*. Identifiers, which cannot be computed by the program, are used as field selectors. The type of the composite object is given by enumeration of the types and selectors of the fields. In some languages (such as COBOL and PL/1) the description of a record type is bound to a single object.

A record is used to collect related items, for example the name, address, profession and other data about a single person. Often the number or form of the data may vary in such cases. For example, the location of a point in space could be given in terms of rectangular (x, y, z) or cylindrical (r, phi, z) coordinates. In a record of type 'point', variations in the form of the data are thus possible. Pascal allows such a *record with variants* to be constructed:

```
type
   coordinates = (rectangular, cylindrical);
   point = record
     z : real;
     case c : coordinates of
       rectangular : (x, y : real);
       cylindrical : (r, phi: real);
   end;
```

The fields appearing in every record of the type are written first, followed by alternative sets of fields; the c appearing in the case construct describes which alternative set is actually present.

A union mode in ALGOL 68 is a special case of a variant record, in which every variant consists of exactly one field and the fixed part consists only of the variant selector. Syntactically, the construct is not described as a record and the variant selector is not given explicitly. In languages such as APL or SNOBOL4, essentially *all* objects are specified in this manner. An important question about such objects is whether the variant is fixed for the lifetime of a particular object, or whether it forms a part of the state and may be changed.

Arrays differ from records in that their components may be selected via a computable, one-to-one function whose domain is some finite set (such as any finite type or a subrange $p \leqslant i \leqslant q$ of the integers). In languages with manifest types, all elements of an array have the same type. The operation $a[e]$ ('select the component of a corresponding to e') is called *indexing*. Most programming languages also permit multi-dimensional rectangular arrays, in which the index set represents a Cartesian product $I_1 \times I_2 \times \cdots \times I_n$ over a collection of index domains. Depending upon the time at which the number of elements is bound, we speak of *static* (fixed at compile time), *dynamic* (fixed at the time the object is created) or *flexible* (variable by assignment) arrays (cf. Section 2.5.3).

One-dimensional arrays of Boolean values (*bit vectors*) may also be regarded as tabular encodings of characteristic functions over the index set *I*. Every value of an array *c* corresponds to $\{i \mid c[i] = true\}$. In Pascal such arrays are introduced as 'sets' with type **set of** *index_set*; in Ada they are described as here, as Boolean arrays. In both cases, the operations union (represented by + or **or**), intersection (*, **and**), set difference (-), equality (= and < >), inclusion (<, < =, >, > =) and membership (**in**) are defined on such sets. Difficulties arise in specifying set constants: The element type can, of course be determined by looking at the elements of the constant. But if sets can be defined over a subrange of a type, it is not usually possible to determine the appropriate subrange just by looking at the elements. In Pascal the problem is avoided by regarding all sets made up of elements of a particular scalar type to be of the same type, regardless of the subrange specified as the index set. (Sets of integers are regarded as being over an implementation-defined subrange.) In Ada the index set is determined by the context.

Only a few programming languages provide operations (other than set operations) that may be applied to a composite object as a whole. (APL has the most comprehensive collection of such operations.) Processing of composite objects is generally carried out componentwise, with field selection, indexing and component assignment used as access operations on the composite objects. It may also be possible to describe groups of array elements, for example entire rows or columns or even arbitrary rectangular index domains ($a[i_1:i_2, j_1:j_2]$ in ALGOL 68); this process is called *slicing*.

2.2.3. Strings   Strings are exceptional cases in most programming languages. In ALGOL 60, strings are permitted only as arguments to procedures and can thus ultimately be used only as data for code procedures (normally I/O routines). ALGOL 68 considers strings as flexible arrays, and in FORTRAN 77 or PL/1 the size can increase only to a maximum value fixed when the object is created. In both languages, single characters may be extracted by indexing; in addition, comparison and concatenation may be carried out on strings whose length is known. These latter operations consider the entire string as a single unit. In SNOBOL4 strings are always considered to be single units: Assignment, concatenation, conversion to a pattern, pattern matching and replacement are elementary operations of the language.

We omitted strings from LAX because they do not lead to any unique problems in compiler construction.

2.2.4. Pointers   Records, arrays and strings are composite objects constructed as contiguous sequences of elements. Composition according to the model of a directed graph is possible using pointers, with which one node can point to another. In all languages providing arrays, pointers can be represented by indices in an array. Some languages (such as ALGOL 68,

Pascal and PL/1) define pointers as a new kind of type. In PL/1 the type of the object pointed to is not specified, and hence one can place an arbitrary interpretation upon the target node of the pointer. In the other languages mentioned, however, the pointer type carries the type of the object pointed to.

Pointers have the advantage of security over indices in an array: Indices can be confused with other uses of integers, pointers cannot. Above all, however, pointers can be used to reference anonymous objects that are created dynamically. The number of objects thus created need not be known ahead of time. With indices the array bounds fix the maximum number of objects (except when the array is flexible).

Pascal pointers can reference only anonymous objects, whereas in ALGOL 68 either named or anonymous objects may be referenced. When named objects have at most a bounded lifetime, it is possible that a pointer to an object could outlive the object to which it points. Such *dangling references* will be discussed in Section 2.5.2.

In addition to the technical questions of pointer implementation, the compiler writer should be concerned with special testing aids (such as printing programs that can traverse a structure, outputting links in some reasonable way). The reason is that programs containing pointers are usually more difficult to debug than those not containing pointers.

2.2.5. Type Equivalence   Whenever we use an object in a typed language (e.g. as an operand of an operation), we must verify that the type of the object satisfies the requirements of the context and is thus admissible. To do this we need a technique to compare types with one another and to determine whether they are equivalent.

The question of type equivalence is easy to answer as long as there are no type declarations, and no subranges of a type are treated as types. Under such circumstances we use *textual equivalence*: Two types are equivalent if their external representations are the same. Thus for the elementary types Boolean, character, integer and real the same symbol is required. Array types are equivalent if they have equivalent element types and the same number of dimensions; the values of the bounds are compared only in languages with static arrays. Pointers must point to objects of equivalent type. Procedures must have the same number of parameters, and corresponding parameter and result types must be equivalent. For records, it is usually required that both types and field selectors be equivalent and appear in the same order. Therefore the following records are all of different types:

> **record** *a* : *real* ; *b* : *integer* **end**
> **record** *x* : *real* ; *y* : *integer* **end**
> **record** *y* : *integer* ; *x* : *real* **end**

When type declarations and pointers are both allowed, textual equivalence is no longer a useful criterion. Attempting to extend the above definitions to *recursive types* leads to a cycle in the test. For example, the equivalence of the following types depends upon the equivalence of the second field which, in turn, depends upon the equivalence of the original types:

type
> m = **record** x : *real*; y : $\uparrow m$ **end**;
> p = **record** x : *real*; y : $\uparrow p$ **end**;

To break the cycle, we may generalize textual equivalence to either *structural equivalence* or *name equivalence*.

Structural equivalence is used in ALGOL 68. In this case, each type identifier (*mode indication*) is assumed to be a shorthand notation for the right side of the type declaration. Two types are equivalent if they are textually equivalent after all type identifiers have been replaced by the right hand sides of their declarations. This process may introduce other type identifiers, and the substitution must be repeated; clearly a recursive type has an infinite textual representation. In order to test for structural equivalence, these infinite representations must be compared. In Section 9.2 we shall see that a practical decision procedure using finite representations and working in polynomial time is available.

Name equivalence states that two types are equivalent if and only if they are denoted by the same identifier, which identifies the same definition in each case. M and p above are different types under this definition, since m and p are distinct identifiers. The right hand sides of the declarations of m and p are automatically different, since they are not type identifiers. Name equivalence is obviously easy to check, since it only involves fixing the identity of type declarations.

Name equivalence seldom appears in pure form. On the one hand it leads to a flood of type declarations, and on the other to problems in linking to library procedures that have array parameters. However, name equivalence is the basis for the definition of abstract data types, where type declarations that carry the details of the representation are not revealed outside the declaration. This is exactly the effect of name equivalence, whereas structural equivalence has the opposite result. Most programming languages that permit type declarations use an intermediate strategy. Euclid uses structural equivalence locally; as soon as a type is 'exported', it is known only by a type identifier and hence name equivalence applies.

If the language allows subranges of the basic types (such as a subrange of integers in Pascal) the question of whether or not this subrange is a distinct type arises. Ada allows both: The subrange can be defined as a *subtype* or as a new type. In the second case, the pre-defined operations of the base type will be taken over but later procedures requiring parameters of the base type cannot be passed arguments of the new type.

The type equivalence rules of LAX embody a representative compromise. They require textual equivalence as discussed above, but whenever a type is denoted by an identifier it is considered elementary. (In other words, if the compiler is comparing two type specifications for equality and an identifier appears in one then the same identifier must appear in the same position in the other.) Implementation of these rules illustrate the compiler mechanisms needed to handle both structure and name equivalence.

2.3. Expressions

Expressions (or *formulas*) are examples of composite operations. Their structure resembles that of composite objects: They consist of a simple operation with operands, which are either ordinary data objects or further expressions. In other words, an expression is a tree with operations as interior nodes and data objects as leaves.

An expression written in linear infix notation may lead to distinct trees when interpreted according to different language definitions (Figure 2.2). In low-level languages modeled upon PL/360, the operators are strictly left-associative with no operator precedence, and parentheses are prohibited; APL uses right-associativity with no precedence, but permits grouping by parentheses. Most higher-level languages employ the normal precedence

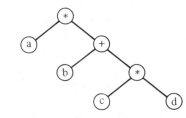

a) Left-associative (e.g. PL/360)

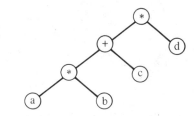

b) Right-associative (e.g. APL)

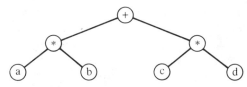

c) Normal precedence rules

Figure 2.2. Trees for $a*b+c*d$

rules of mathematics and associate operators of the same precedence to the left. FORTRAN 77 (Section 6.6.4) is an exception: 'Once [a tree] has been established in accordance with [the precedence, association and parenthesization] rules, the processor may evaluate any mathematically equivalent expression, provided that the integrity of parentheses is not violated.' The phrase 'mathematically equivalent' implies that a FORTRAN compiler may assume that addition is associative, even though this is not true for computer implementation of floating point arithmetic. (The programmer can, however, always indicate the correct sequence by proper use of parentheses.)

The leaves of an expression tree represent activities that can be carried out independently of all other nodes of the tree. Interior nodes, on the other hand, depend upon the values returned by their descendants. The entire tree may thus be evaluated by the following algorithm:

repeat
    Select an arbitrary leaf and carry out its designated activity (access to
        an object or execution of an operation);
    if the selected leaf is the root **then** terminate;
    Transmit the result to the parent of the leaf and delete the leaf;
until termination

This evaluation algorithm performs the operations in some sequence permitted by the data flow constraints embodied in the tree, but does not specify the order in which operands are evaluated. It is based upon a principle known as *referential transparency* [Quine 1960] that holds in mathematics: The value of an expression can be determined solely from the values of its subexpressions, and if any subexpression is replaced by an arbitrary expression with the same value then the value of the entire expression remains unchanged.

In programming languages, evaluation of an expression may additionally alter the state of the underlying abstract machine through a *side effect*. If the altered state is used in another part of the expression then the principle of referential transparency does not hold, and different evaluation orders may yield different results.

Side effects are generally undesirable because they complicate program verification and optimization. Unfortunately, it is often impossible to mechanically guarantee that no side effects are present. In Euclid an attempt was made to restrict the possibilities to the point where the compiler could perform such a check safely. These restrictions include prohibition of assignments to result parameters and global variables in functions, and prohibition of I/O operations in functions.

Some side effects do not destroy referential transparency, and are thus somewhat less dangerous. Section 6.6 of the FORTRAN 77 Standard formulates the weakest useful restrictions: 'The execution of a function reference in a statement may not alter the value of any other entity within the statement in which the function reference appears.'

In some expressions the value of a subexpression determines that of the entire expression. Examples are:

a **and** $(\cdots)$ when $a = false$

b **or** $(\cdots)$ when $b = true$

$c * (\cdots)$ when $c = 0$

If the remainder of the expression has no side effect, only the subexpression determining the value need be computed. The FORTRAN 77 Standard allows this *short circuit* evaluation regardless of side effects; the description is such that the program is undefined if side effects are present, and hence it is immaterial whether the remainder of the expression is evaluated or not in that case. The wording (Section 6.6.1) is: 'If a statement contains a function reference in a part of an expression that need not be evaluated, all entities that would have become defined in the execution of that reference become undefined at the completion of evaluation of the expression containing the function reference.'

ALGOL 60, ALGOL 68 and many other languages require, in principle, the evaluation of all operands and hence preclude such optimization unless the compiler can guarantee that no side effects are possible. Pascal permits short circuit evaluation, but only in Boolean expressions (User Manual, Section 4a): 'The rules of Pascal neither require nor forbid the evaluation of the second part [of a Boolean expression, when the first part fixes the value]'. Ada provides two sets of Boolean operators, one (**and**, **or**) prohibiting short circuit evaluation and the other (**and then**, **or else**) requiring it.

LAX requires complete evaluation of operands for all operators except **and** and **or**. The order of evaluation is constrained only by data flow considerations, so the compiler may assume referential transparency. This simplifies the treatment of optimization. By requiring a specific short circuit evaluation for **and** and **or**, we illustrate other optimization techniques and also show how the analysis of an expression is complicated by evaluation order rules.

2.4. Control Structures

There are three possibilities for the composition of several actions: *serial, collateral* and *parallel*. Serial execution is implied by any dependence of two actions upon one another. Such dependence occurs when (say) one action uses the result of another; more generally, it occurs in any case where the outcome depends upon the sequence in which the actions occur. If the actions may be carried out serially or in parallel, or can be interleaved in time, then we speak of collateral execution. Finally, we use the term parallel when either simultaneous or interleaved execution is required.

When actions are composed serially, the sequence may be prescribed either implicitly or explicitly. Most programming languages use the sequence in which the statements are written as an implicit serial order. The semicolon separating two successive statements in ALGOL 60 and its successors is thus often called the 'sequence operator'. For explicit control, we have the following possibilities:

- Conditional clause
- Case clause
- Iteration (with or without a count)
- Jump, exit, etc.
- Procedure call

Conditional clauses make the execution of a component S dependent upon fulfillment of a Boolean condition. In many languages S may only take on one of a restricted number of forms — in the extreme case, S may only be a jump.

The case clause is a generalization of the conditional clause in which the distinct values of an expression are associated with distinct statements. The correspondence is either implicit as in ALGOL 68 (the statements correspond successively to the values 1,2,3,...), or explicit as in Pascal (the value is used as a case label for the corresponding statement). The latter construct allows one statement to correspond with more than one value and permits gaps in the list of values. It also avoids counting errors and enhances program readability.

Several syntactically distinct iteration constructs appear in many programming languages: with or without counters, test at the beginning or end, etc. The inefficient ALGOL 60 rules requiring the (arbitrarily complex) step and limit expressions to be re-evaluated for each iteration have been replaced in newer languages by the requirement that these expressions be evaluated exactly once. Another interesting point is whether the value of the counter may be altered by assignment within the body of the iteration (as in ALGOL 60), or whether it must remain constant (as in ALGOL 68). This last is important for many optimizations of iterations, as is the usual prohibition on jumps into an iteration.

Many programming languages allow jumps with variable targets. Examples are the use of indexing in an array of labels (the ALGOL 60 *switch*) and the use of label variables (the FORTRAN assigned GOTO). While COBOL or FORTRAN jumps control only the succession of statements, jumps out of blocks or procedures in ALGOL-like languages influence the program state (see Section 2.5). Procedure calls also influence the state.

The ALGOL 60 and ALGOL 68 definitions explain the operation of procedure calls by substitution of the procedure body for the call (*copy rule*). This copying process could form the basis for an implementation (*open subroutines*), if the procedure is not recursive. Recursion requires that the procedure be implemented as a closed subroutine, a model on which many other language definitions are based. Particular difficulties await the writer of compilers for languages such as COBOL, which do not distinguish the beginning and end of the procedure body in the code. This means that, in addition to the possibility of invoking the procedure by means of a call (PERFORM in COBOL), the statements could be executed sequentially as a part of the main program.

Parallel execution of two actions is required if both begin from the same initial state and alter this state in incompatible ways. A typical example is the parallel assignment $x, y := y, x$, in which the values are exchanged. To represent this in a sequential program, the compiler must first extend the state so that the condition 'identical starting states for both actions' can be preserved. This can be done here by introducing an auxiliary variable t, to which x is assigned.

Another case of parallel execution of two actions arises when explicit synchronization is embedded in these actions to control concurrent execution. The compiler must fall back upon coroutines or parallel processing facilities in the operating system in order to achieve such synchronization; we shall not discuss this further.

Collateral execution of two actions means that the compiler need not fix their sequence according to source language constraints. It can, for example, exchange actions if this will lead to a more efficient program. If both actions contain identical sub-actions then it suffices to carry out this sub-action only once; this has the same effect as the (theoretically possible) perfectly-synchronized parallel execution of the two identical sub-actions. If a language specifies collateral evaluation, the question of whether the evaluation of $f(x)$ in the assignment $a[i+1] := f(x) + a[i+1]$ can influence the address calculation for $a[i+1]$ by means of a side effect is irrelevant. The compiler need only compute the address of $a[i+1]$ once, even if i were the following function procedure:

function i : *integer* ; **begin** $k := k+1; i := k$ **end**;

In this case k will be incremented only once.

2.5. Program Environments and Abstract Machine States

The operations of a programming language are applied to states of the abstract machine for this language and transform those states. The state is represented by the combination of the data objects and values existing at a particular point in time, the hierarchy of procedure calls not yet completed, and the representation of the next operation in the program text. The set of data objects belonging to a state (independent of their values), together with the procedure call hierarchy, constitute the *environment* (present in that state). We can thus distinguish three distinct schemata for state transitions:

• Specify a new successor operation (e.g. by means of a jump).

- Change the value of an existing data object by means of an assignment.
- Change the size of the state.

We have already discussed the first possibility in Section 2.4.

2.5.1. Constants, Variables and Assignment

The data objects in a programming language either have constant values or are variable. Constants are either specified by denotations (numbers, characters, strings) or are made to correspond to identifiers by giving a declaration. The latter are called *symbolic constants*, and contain the *manifest constants* as a subclass. The value of a manifest constant is permanently fixed and can be determined at compile time. A compiler could replace each occurrence of a manifest constant identifier by its value, and then forget the identifier completely. (The constant declarations of Pascal, for example, create manifest constants.) In addition to manifest constants, a language may permit *dynamic constants*. These can be treated by the compiler as variables to which a value is assigned when the variable is declared, and to which further assignments are prohibited. The following ALGOL 68 identity declaration creates a dynamic constant c:

$$\textbf{int } c \ = \ \textbf{if } p \ \textbf{then } 3{*}x \ \textbf{else } y + 1 \ \textbf{fi};$$

(If p, x and y are really manifest constants then the compiler could optimize by evaluating the conditional statement and then treating c as a manifest constant as well. This optimization is called *folding* — see Chapter 13.)

In the simplest case, variables are data objects with the following properties:

- They are identified either by an identifier or a composite access path such as a pair (*identifier, index*).
- They possess a value (from a domain determined by their type).
- There exists an access function to use their value as an operand.
- There exists an access function/assignment to alter their value.

This model of an *elementary variable* explains the variable concepts in FORTRAN, COBOL, ALGOL 60, and partially explains that of Pascal.

In many languages, the only assignment permitted to a variable of composite type is an assignment to a component. For example, ALGOL 60 does not allow assignment of an entire composite object and also prohibits composite objects as results of function procedures. A composite object must, however, be considered basically as a unit. Thus any assignment to a component is an assignment to the entire object.

A variable does not always retain the last assigned value until a new value is assigned. Typical examples are the control variables in ALGOL 60 and FORTRAN iterations, whose values are undefined upon normal termination of the iteration. These rules permit the compiler to advance the control variable either before or after the termination test. (Clearly the two possibilities lead to different results and hence the value of the controlled variable cannot be guaranteed. ALGOL 68 avoids this problem because the control variable is local to the iteration body.) Another example is the undefinition of a COBOL record by the write operation. This permits implementation of the write operation by either changing the buffer pointer or by transferring data. The FORTRAN 66 Standard gives (in Section 10.2.3.1) a further list of situations in which variables become undefined. A compiler writer should carefully examine the language definition for such rules, since they normally lead to optimization possibilities.

The pointer objects discussed in Section 2.2.4 provide access paths to other objects. By using pointers, an arbitrary number of access paths to a given object can be created. In the special case of parameter transmission, additional access paths can be created even without pointers (see Section 2.5.3). The following identity declaration from ALGOL 68 is an example of the general case:

ref m x = $\cdots$;

Here the right hand side must give an access path to an object; x then identifies a new access path to this object. In contrast to the ALGOL 60 name parameter, the identity of the object is fixed at the time the identity declaration is executed. Some languages permit creation of access paths with limited access rights: Assignments may be forbidden over certain access paths or in certain contexts. For example, assignments to global parameters are forbidden in Euclid functions. If such restrictions exist, adherence to them must be verified by the compiler during semantic analysis.

Existence of several access paths to the same object complicates the data flow analysis (analysis of assignment and use patterns) required to verify certain semantic constraints and to check for the applicability of certain optimizations. If the compiler writer wishes to delay an assignment, for example, he must be certain that an access to the new value will not be attempted over a different access path. This complication is termed the *aliasing problem*.

The LAX identity declaration allows creation of an arbitrary number of new access paths to any variable. It is, however, the *only* mechanism by which new access paths can be created. This allows us to illustrate the aliasing problem in its full generality in one place, rather than having it appear in several different constructs with possibly different constraints.

2.5.2. The Environment   The environment of a program fragment specifies not only which objects exist, but also the access paths by which they may be reached. Changes in the accessibility (or *visibility*) of objects are generally associated with procedure call and return, and for this reason the procedure call hierarchy forms a part of the environment. We shall now consider questions of lifetime and visibility; the related topic of procedure parameter transmission will be deferred to Section 2.5.3.

That part of the execution history of a program during which an object exists is called the *extent* of the object. The extent rules of most programming languages classify objects as follows:

- Static: The extent of the object is the entire execution history of the program.
- Automatic: The extent is the execution of a specified syntactic construct (usually a procedure or block).
- Unrestricted: The extent begins at a programmer-specified point and ends (at least theoretically) at the end of the program's execution.
- Controlled: The programmer specifies both the beginning and end of the extent by explicit construction and destruction of objects.

Objects in COBOL and the blank common block of FORTRAN are examples of static extent. Local variables in ALGOL 60 or Pascal, as well as local variables in FORTRAN subprograms, are examples of automatic extent. (Labeled common blocks in FORTRAN 66 also have automatic extent, see Section 10.2.5 of the standard.) List elements in LISP and objects created by the heap generator of ALGOL 68 have unrestricted extent, and the anonymous variables of Pascal are controlled (created by *new* and discarded by *dispose*).

The possibility of a dangling reference arises whenever a reference can be created to an object of restricted extent. To avoid errors, we must guarantee that the referenced object exists at the times when references to it are actually attempted. A sufficient condition to make this guarantee is the ALGOL 68 rule (also used in LAX) prohibiting assignment of references or procedures in which the extent of the right-hand side is smaller than the reference to which it is assigned. It has the advantage that it can be checked by the compiler in many cases, and a dynamic run-time check can always be made in the absence of objects with controlled extent. When a language provides objects with controlled extent, as do PL/1 and Pascal, then the burden of avoiding dangling references falls exclusively upon the programmer.

LAX constants are the only objects having static extent. Variables are generally automatic, although it is possible to generate unrestricted variables. The language has no objects with controlled extent, because such objects do not result in any new problems for the compiler. Static variables were omitted because the techniques used to deal with automatic variables apply to them essentially without change.

By the *scope* of an identifier definition we understand the region of the program within which we can use the identifier with the defined meaning. The scope of an identifier definition is generally determined statically by the syntactic construct of the program in which it is directly contained. A *range* is a syntactic construct that may have identifier definitions associated with it. In a block-structured language, inner ranges are not part of outer ranges. Usually any range may contain at most one definition of an identifier. Exceptions to this rule may occur when a single identifier may be used for distinct purposes, for example as an object and as the target of a jump. In ALGOL-like languages the scope of a definition includes the range in which it occurs and all enclosed ranges not containing definitions of the same identifier.

Consider the field selection *p.f.* The position immediately following the dot belongs to the scope of the declaration of *p*'s record type. In fact, *only* the field selectors of that record type are permitted in this position. On the other hand, although the statement *s* of the Pascal (or SIMULA) inspection **with** *p* **do** *s* also belongs to the scope of *p*'s record type declaration, the definitions from the inspection's environment remain valid in *s* unless overridden by field selector definitions. In COBOL and PL/1, *f* can be written in place of *p.f* (*partial qualification*) if there is no other definition of *f* in the surrounding range.

The concept of static block structure has the consequence that items not declared in a procedure are taken from the static surrounding of the procedure. A second possibility is that used in APL and LISP: Nonlocal items of functions are taken from the dynamic environment of the procedure call.

In the case of recursive procedure calls, identically-declared objects with nested extents may exist at the same time. Difficulties may arise if an object is introduced (say, by parameter transmission) into a program fragment where its original declaration is hidden by another declaration of the same identifier. Figure 2.3 illustrates the problem. This program makes two nested calls of *p*, so that two incarnations, q_1 and q_2, of the procedure *q* and two variables i_1 and i_2 exist at the same time. The program should print the values 1, 4 and 1 of i_2, i_1 and *k*. This behavior can be explained by using the *contour model*.

The contour model captures the state of the program execution as a combination of the (invariant) program text and the structured set of objects (state) existing at respective points in time. Further, two pointers, *ip* and *ep* belong to the state. *Ip* is the *instruction pointer*, which indicates the position in the program text. For block-structured languages the state consists of a collection of nested local environments called *contours*. Each contour corresponds to a range and contains the objects defined in that range. If the environment pointer *ep* addresses a contour *c*, then all of the objects declared in *c* and enclosing contours are accessible. The contour addressed by *ep* is called the *local contour*. The object identified by a given identifier is found by scanning the contours from inner to outer, beginning at the local contour, until a definition for the specified identifier is found.

The structure of the state is changed by the following actions:

- Construction or removal of an object.
- Procedure call or range entry.
- Procedure return or range exit.
- Jump out of a range.

When an object with automatic extent is created, it lies in a contour corresponding to the program construct in which it was declared; static objects behave exactly like objects declared in the main program with

```
procedure outer;
  var n, k: integer;
  procedure p (procedure f; var j: integer);
    label 1;
    var i: integer;
    procedure q;
      label 2;
      begin (* q *)
      n := n + 1; if n = 4 then q;
      n := n + 1; if n = 7 then 2: j := j + 1;
      i := i + 1;
      end; (* q *)
    begin (* p *)
    i := 0;
    n := n + 1; if n = 2 then p (q, i) else j := j + 1;
    if n = 3 then 1: f;
    i := i + 1;
    writeln ('i =', i : 1);
    end; (* p *)
  procedure empty; begin end;
  begin (* outer *)
  n := 1; k := 0;
  p (empty, k);
  writeln ('k =', k : 1);
  end; (* outer *)
```

Figure 2.3.   Complex Procedure Interactions in Pascal

automatic extent. Objects with unrestricted extent and controlled objects lie in their own contours, which do not correspond to program constructs.

Upon entry into a range, a new contour is established within the local contour and the environment pointer *ep* is set to point to it. Upon range exit this procedure is reversed: the local contour is removed and *ep* set to point to the immediately surrounding contour.

Upon procedure call, a new contour c is established and *ep* set to point to it. In contrast to range entry, however, c is established within the contour c' addressed by *ep* at the time of procedure declaration. We term c' the *static predecessor* of c to distinguish it from c', the *dynamic predecessor*, to which *ep* pointed immediately before the procedure call. The pointer to c' must be stored in c as a local object. Upon return from a procedure the local contour of the procedure is discarded and the environment pointer reset to its dynamic predecessor.

To execute a jump into an enclosing range b, blocks and procedures are exited and the corresponding contours discarded until a contour c corresponding to b is reached such that c contained the contour of the jump. C becomes the new local contour, to which *ep* will point, and *ip* is set to the jump target. If the jump target is determined dynamically as a parameter or the content of a label variable, as is possible in ALGOL 60, then that parameter or variable must specify both the target address and the contour that will become the new local contour.

Figures 2.4 and 2.5 show the contour model for the state existing at two points during the execution of the program of Figure 2.3. Notice that several contours correspond to the same range when a procedure is called recursively. Further, the values of actual parameters of a procedure call should be computed before the environment pointer is altered. If this is not done, the pointer for parameter computation must be restored (as is necessary for name parameters in ALGOL 60).

In order to unify the state manipulation, procedures and blocks are often processed identically. A block is then a parameterless procedure called 'on the spot'. The contour of a block thus has a dynamic predecessor identical with its static predecessor. The lifetimes of local objects in blocks can be determined by the compiler, and a static overlay structure for them can be set up within the contour of the enclosing procedure. The main program is counted as a procedure for this purpose. The scope rules are not altered by this transformation. Contours for blocks can be dispensed with, and all objects placed in the contour of the enclosing procedure. Arrays with dynamic bounds lead to difficulties with this optimization, since the bounds can be determined only at the time of actual block entry.

The rules discussed so far do not permit description of either LISP or SIMULA. In LISP a function f may have as its result a function g that

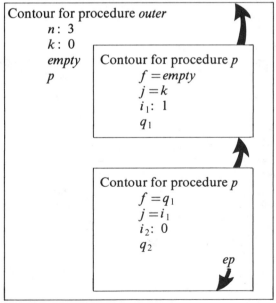

Note: Arrows show dynamic predecessor

Figure 2.4. Contours Existing When Control Reaches Label 1 in Figure 2.3

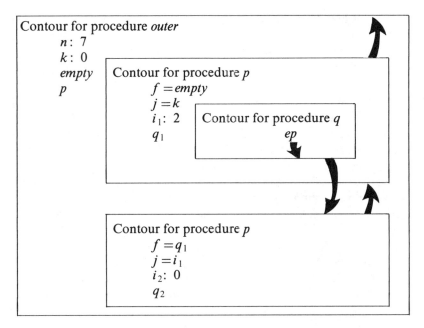

Figure 2.5. Contours Existing When Control Reaches Label 2 in Figure 2.3

accesses the local storage of f. Since this storage must also exist during the call of g, the contour of f must be retained at least until g becomes inaccessible. Analogously, a SIMULA class k (an object of unrestricted extent) may have name parameters from the contour in which it was instantiated. This contour must therefore be retained at least until k becomes inaccessible.

We solve these problems by adopting a *uniform retention strategy* that discards an object only when that object becomes inaccessible. Accessibility is defined relative to the current contour. Whenever an object in a contour c references another object in a different contour, c', we implement that reference by an explicit pointer from c to c'. (Such references include the dynamic predecessors of the contour, all reference parameters, and any explicit pointers established by the user.) A contour is accessible if it can be reached from the current contour by following any sequence of pointers or by a downhill walk. The dangling reference problem vanishes when this retention strategy is used.

2.5.3. Binding   An identifier b is termed *bound* (or *local*) in a range if this range contains a definition for b; otherwise b is *free* (or *global*) in this range. As definitions we have:
- Declarations of object identifiers (including procedure identifiers).
- Definitions: Label definitions, type definitions, FORTRAN labeled common blocks, etc.
- Formal parameter definitions.

In the first and second cases the defined value along with all of its attributes is obvious from the definition. In the third case only the identifier and type of the defined value are available via the program text. The actual parameter, the *argument*, will be associated with the identifier by parameter transmission at the time of the procedure call. We distinguish five essentially different forms of parameter transmission:

1. Value (as in ALGOL 60, SIMULA, Pascal, Ada, for example): The formal parameter identifies a local variable of the procedure, which will be initialized with the argument value at the procedure call. Assignment to the parameter does not affect the caller.

2. Result (Ada): The formal parameter identifies a local variable of the procedure with undefined initial value. Upon return from the procedure the content of this local variable is assigned to the argument, which must be a variable.

3. Value/Result (FORTRAN, Ada): The formal parameter identifies a local variable of the procedure, which will be initialized with the argument value at the procedure call. Upon return from the procedure the content of this local variable is assigned to the argument if the argument is a variable. The argument variable may be fixed prior to the call or redetermined upon return.

4. Reference (FORTRAN, Pascal, Ada): A reference to the argument is transmitted to the procedure. All operations on the formal parameter within the procedure are carried out via this reference. (If the argument is an expression but not a variable, then the result is placed in a temporary variable for which the reference is constructed. Some languages, such as Pascal, do not permit use of an expression as an argument in this case.)

5. Name (ALGOL 60): A parameterless procedure p, which computes a reference to the argument, is transmitted to the procedure. (If the argument is an expression but not a variable then p computes the value of the expression, stores it in a temporary variable h, and yields a reference to h.) All operations on the formal parameter first invoke p and then operate via the reference yielded by p.

Call by value is occasionally restricted to a strict value transmission in which the formal parameter identifies not a local variable, but rather a local constant. Call by name is explained in many language definitions by textual substitution of the argument for the parameter. ALGOL 60 provides for argument evaluation in the environment of the caller through a consistent renaming.

The different parameter mechanisms can all be implemented in terms of (strict) call by value, if the necessary kinds of data are available. For cases (2)-(4), the language must provide the concept of arbitrary references as values. Call by name also requires the concept of procedures as values (of procedure variables). Only when these concepts are unavailable are the transmission mechanisms (2)-(5) important. This is clear in the language

SIMULA, which (in addition to the value and name calls inherited from ALGOL 60) provides call by reference for classes and strings. A more careful study shows that in truth this could be handled by an ordinary value call for references. In ALGOL 68 the call by reference is stated in terms of the strict call by value, by using an identity declaration to make the formal parameter fp an alias of the argument ap:

ref int $fp = ap$

Expressions that do not yield references are not permitted as arguments if this explanation of call by reference is used, since the right hand side of the identity declaration must yield a reference.

LAX follows the style of ALGOL 68, explaining its argument bindings in terms of identity declarations. This provides a uniform treatment of all parameter mechanisms, and also eliminates the parameter mechanism as a distinct means of creating new access paths. Finally, the identity declaration gives a simple implementation model.

Many language definitions do not specify parameter transmission mechanisms explicitly. The compiler writer must therefore attempt to delineate the possibilities by a careful consideration of their effects. For example, both case (3) and case (4) satisfy the conditions of the FORTRAN 66 Standard, but none of the others do. Ada generally requires case (1), (2) or (3). For composite objects, however, case (4) is permitted as an alternative. Use of this alternative is at the discretion of the implementor, and the programmer is warned that any assumptions about the particular transmission mechanism invalidates the program.

Programs whose results depend upon the parameter transmission mechanism are generally difficult to understand. The dependencies arise when an object has two access paths, say via two formal parameters or via a global variable and a formal parameter. This can be seen in the program of Figure 2.6a, which yields the results of Figure 2.6b for the indicated parameter mechanisms.

In addition to knowing what value an identifier is bound to, it is important to know *when* the binding takes place. The parameter transmission differences discussed above can, to a large extent, be explained in terms of binding times. In general, we can distinguish the following binding times (explained in terms of the identity declaration **ref real** $x = a[i, j + 3]$):

1. Binding at each access (corresponding to call by name): Upon each access to x the identity of $a[i, j + 3]$ is re-determined.
2. Binding at first access: Upon the first access to x the identity of $a[i, j + 3]$ will be determined. All assignments to i and j up to that point will have an effect.
3. Binding upon declaration (corresponding to call by reference): After elaboration of the identity declaration the identity of $a[i, j + 3]$ is fixed. In several languages the identifiers on the right-hand side must not be declared in the same range, to avoid circular definitions.

```
begin
int m := 1, n ;
proc p = (??? int j , ??? int k ) int:
   begin j := j + 1; m := m + k ; j + k end;
n := p (m , m + 3)
end
```

Note: '???' depends upon the parameter mechanism.

a) An ALGOL 68 program

Mechanism	m	n	j	k	Comment
Value	5	6	2	4	Strict value is not possible due to the assignment to j.
Value/Result	2	6	2	4	Pure result is unreasonable in this example.
Reference	6	10	6	4	Only j is a reference parameter because an expression is illegal as a reference parameter in ALGOL 68. Hence k is a value parameter.
Name	7	17	7	10	

Note: m and n were evaluated at the end of the main program, j and k at the end of p.

b) The effect of different parameter mechanisms

Figure 2.6. Parameter Transmission

4. Static binding: The identity of $a[i, j + 3]$ is fixed throughout the entire program. In this case a must have static extent and statically-determined size. The values of i and j must be defined prior to program execution and be independent of it (hence they must be constants).

In this spectrum, call by result would be classified as binding after access. Call by value is a binding of the value, not of the reference.

Determination of identity is least costly at run time for static binding and most costly for binding at access. During the analysis of the program, the compiler writer is most concerned with gathering as much information as possible, to bind as early as he can. For this reason static binding breaks into two subcases, which in general depend not upon the language but upon other considerations:

4a. Binding at compilation time. The identity of the bound values is determined during compilation.

4b. Binding at program initialization: The identity of files or of external procedures will be determined during a pre-process to program execution.

In case 4a the knowledge of the bound values can be used in optimization.

Case 4b permits repeated execution of the program with different bindings without re-compilation.

Free identifiers, which are not defined in a procedure, must be explained in the context of the procedure so that their meaning can be determined. The definitions of standard identifiers, which may be used in any program without further declaration, are fitted into this scheme by assuming that the program is embedded in a standard environment containing definitions for them.

By an *external entity* we mean an entity identified by a free identifier with no definition in either the program or the standard environment. A program with external entities cannot be compiled and then directly executed. Another step, which obtains the objects associated with external entities from a program library, must be introduced. We shall discuss this step, the binding of programs, in Chapter 11. In the simplest case the binding can be separated from the compilation as an independent terminal step. This separation is normally chosen for FORTRAN implementations. One consequence is that the compiler has no complete overview of the properties of external entities and hence cannot verify that they are used consistently. Thus in FORTRAN it is not usually possible for the compiler to determine whether external subprograms and functions are called with the correct number and type of parameters. For such checking, but also to develop the correct accesses, the compiler must have specifications like those for formal parameters for every external entity. Many implementations of ALGOL 60, Pascal, etc. provide that such specifications precede or be included in independently compiled procedures. Since in these languages, as in many others, separate compilation of language units is not specified by the language definition, the compiler writer himself must design the handling of external values in conjunction with introduction of these possibilities. Ada contains a far-reaching specification scheme for external entities.

2.6. Notes and References

We draw our examples from a number of languages. In order to avoid the necessity for referencing the proper definition each time a language property is discussed, we give an exhaustive list of the languages we use and their defining documents at the beginning of the Bibliography.

Descriptions of languages in the ALGOL family are interpretive, as are those of FORTRAN and COBOL. The description of PL/1 with the help of the Vienna definition method (VDL [Lucas 1969, Wegner 1972]) is likewise interpretive. Other definition methods are the *axiomatic* [Hoare 1973] and the *denotational* [Gordon 1979, Tennent 1981].

Many languages are described by a given implementation. We have nothing against this, provided that the implementation is stated in an abstract form such as that of EVALQUOTE, the function that implements the kernel of LISP interpretively. Often, however, it is never defined in a high-level manner and a new implementation of the same language is very difficult. The macro implementation of SNOBOL4 [Griswold 1972], although highly successful, exhibits this problem.

We have associated the concept of *type* with the set of operations possible on a value. This led us to conclude that *size* was a distinct property. Both ALGOL 68 and Pascal, however, treat values of distinct sizes as having distinct types. Habermann [1973] gives a critical assessment of this philosophy and its effect in Pascal.

We have only skimmed the properties of numeric types. Knuth [1969] presents the general view of floating point numbers and shows how floating point operations relate to the corresponding mathematical operations on real numbers. A machine-oriented model that relates the parameters of the number system to specific characteristics of the target machine is given by Brown [1977, 1981].

The contour model was originally described by Dijkstra [1960, 1963] as an implementation technique for ALGOL 60. Johnston [1971] coined the name and introduced the graphical representation used here. A formal proof that the contour model is equivalent to consistent renaming and the copy rule as used in the definition of ALGOL 60 was given by Jones and Lucas [1971].

Parallel processing, exception handling and some other features of modern languages have been intentionally omitted from the overview given in this chapter.

EXERCISES

2.1. [Housden 1975, Morrison 1982] Consider the manipulation of character string data in a general purpose programming language.
   a. What set of operations should be available on strings?
   b. Should strings be regarded as elementary or composite objects? Why?
   c. Should strings be regarded as objects of a separate type (or types), or as arrays of characters? Support your position.

2.2. Suppose that Pascal were changed so that the structural equivalence rule (Section 2.2.5) held for types and so that '↑' could precede any type constructor. Show that the types m and p given in the text are equivalent, and that they are also equivalent to the type q defined as follows:

type q = **record** x: *real*; y: ↑ **record** x: *real*; y: ↑ q **end end**;

2.3. Why is the Boolean expression $(x \geqslant -1)$ **and** $(sqrt(1+x) > y)$ meaningless in Pascal, FORTRAN or ALGOL 60? Consider only *structurally equivalent* expressions in the various languages, making any necessary syntactic changes. Give a similar expression in Ada that is meaningful.

2.4. Give the rules for contour creation and destruction necessary to support the module concept in Ada.

2.5. Consider a block-structured language such as SIMULA, in which coroutines are allowed. Generalize the contour model with a retention strategy to handle the following situation: If n coroutines are started in block b, all have contour c as dynamic predecessor. By means of call-by-name parameters, a coroutine can obtain access to an object o belonging to c; on the other hand, contour c can disappear (because execution of b has terminated) long before termination of the coroutine. o is then nonexistent, but the access path via the name parameter remains. What possible solutions do you see for this problem?

2.6. The retention strategy discussed in connection with SIMULA in Exercise 2.5 could be used to support parallel processing in ALGOL 68. Quote sections of the ALGOL 68 Report to show that a simpler strategy can be used.

2.7. What problems arise from result parameters in a language that permits jumps out of procedures?

2.8. Consider a program in which several procedures execute on different processors in a network. Each processor has its own memory. What parameter mechanisms are appropriate in such a program?

CHAPTER 3
Properties of Real and Abstract Machines

In this chapter we shall discuss the target machine properties relevant for code generation, and the mapping of the language-oriented objects and operations onto objects and operations of the target machine. Systematic code generation must, of course, take account of the peculiarities and weaknesses of the target computer's instruction set. It cannot, however, become bogged down in exploitation of these special idiosyncrasies; the payoff in code efficiency will not cover the implementation cost. Thus the compiler writer endeavors to derive a model of the target machine that is not distorted by exceptions, but is as uniform as possible, to serve as a base for code generator construction. To this end some properties of the hardware may be ignored, or gaps in the instruction set may be filled by subroutine invocations or inline sequences treated as elementary operations. In particular, the instruction set is extended by the operations of a run-time system that interfaces input/output and similar actions to the operating system, and attends to storage management.

Further extension of this idea leads to construction of abstract target machines implemented on a real machine either interpretively or by means of a further translation. (Interpretive abstract machines are common targets of code generation for microprocessors due to the need for space efficiency.) We shall not attempt a systematic treatment of the goals, methods and criteria for the design of abstract target machines here; see the Notes and References for further guidance.

46

3.1. Basic Characteristics

Most computers have machine languages that are typeless in the sense of Section 2.2: The interpretation of an object is determined by the operations applied to it. Exceptions are computers like the Burroughs 5000 and its descendants that associate 'tag bits' with each word. The extra bits reduce the number of possible interpretations of the word, or even make that interpretation unique.

Objects reside in storage of various *classes*. *Access paths*, characteristic of the particular storage class, are used to access these objects as operands or results of *operations*. Storage classes, access paths and operations together constitute a model defining the computer for code generation purposes.

In this section we shall survey typical storage classes, access paths and operations, and indicate how instructions may be encoded. The remainder of the chapter will show how these facilities can be used to implement the source language concepts presented in Chapter 2.

3.1.1. Storage Classes
Computer storage can usually be classified as follows for code generation purposes:

- Main Storage: Randomly-accessible array of identically-sized locations.
- Stack: Storage accessed in a last-in, first-out manner.
- Integer Accumulator: Storage on which integer arithmetic instructions operate.
- Floating point Accumulator: Storage on which floating point arithmetic instructions operate.
- Base Register: Storage used in operand access functions to hold addresses.
- Index Register: Storage used in operand access functions to hold integer offsets.
- Program Counter: Storage used to hold the address of the next instruction to be executed.
- Condition Code: Storage used to hold the result of a comparison or test instruction.
- Other Special Register (e.g. Stack Pointer, Programmable Boolean Flag).

Examples of this classification applied to typical machines are given in Figure 3.1.

Every computer provides at least the main storage and program counter classes. (Whether main storage is virtual or real is of no concern.) A particular storage component may belong to more than one class. For example, the base register and index register classes are identical on most computers. On the IBM 370 these are the 'general-purpose registers', which also serve as integer accumulators. Storage classes may also overlap without being identical, as in the case of the Univac 1100 series. These computers have sixteen 'index registers' belonging to the index and base register classes and sixteen 'general-purpose registers' belonging to the integer accumulator and floating

Main storage.

General registers R0,...,R15 serving as integer accumulators, base
registers or index registers.

Register pairs (R0,R1),(R2,R3),...,(R14,R15) serving as integer accumulators.

Floating point registers F0,F2,F4,F6 serving as floating point accumulators.

Program counter

Condition code

a) IBM 370

Main storage

Data registers D0,...,D7 serving as integer accumulators or index
registers.

Address registers A0,...,A7 serving as base or index registers.

Program counter PC

Condition code

Stack pointer A7

b) Motorola 68000

Figure 3.1. Storage Classes

point accumulator classes. However, the two storage classes overlap, with
four registers belonging to both. These four registers may be accessed as
index registers or as general-purpose registers, and their properties depend
upon the access path used.

Whether a particular storage class exists, and if so what its properties are,
is partially a decision of the compiler writer. If, for example, he chooses to
access a specific portion of the main memory of the Motorola 68000 only via
stack operations relative to register A7 then this portion of the memory
belongs to the storage class 'stack' and not the class 'main storage'. (Such a
decision can be made differently for the generated code and the run-time
system, implying that the memory belongs to one class as far as the generated code is concerned and another for the run-time system.) Also, since
the properties of a storage class depend to a certain extent upon the available access paths, a Motorola 68000 stack will differ from that of a Burroughs 6700/7700.

Most storage classes consist of a sequence of numbered elements, the
storage cells. (The numbering may have gaps.) The number of a storage cell
is called its *address*. Every access path yields an algorithm, the *effective
address* of the access path, for computing the address of the storage cell
being accessed. We speak of *byte-oriented* computers if the cells in the main
storage class have a size of 8 bits, otherwise (e.g. 16, 24, 32, 48 or 60 bits per
cell) we term the computer *word-oriented.* For a word-oriented computer the
cell sizes in the main storage and register classes are usually identical,
whereas the registers of a byte-oriented computer (except for some

microprocessors) are 2, 4 or possibly 8 bytes long. In this case the storage cell of the integer accumulator class is usually termed a word.

All storage is ultimately composed of bits. Some early computers (such as the IBM 1400 series) used decimal arithmetic and addressing, and many current computers provide a packed decimal (4 bits per digit) encoding. None of these architectures, however, consider decimal digits to be atoms of storage that cannot be further decomposed; all have facilities for accessing the individual bits of the digit in some manner.

Single bits and bit sequences such as the decimal digits discussed above cannot be accessed directly on most machines. Instead, the bit sequence is characterized by a *partial-word access path* specifying the address of a storage cell containing the sequence, the position of the sequence from the left or right boundary of this unit, and the size of the sequence. Often this partial word access path must be simulated by means of shifts and logical operations.

Aggregates hold objects too large for a single storage cell. An aggregate will usually be specified by the address of its first storage cell, and the cells making up the aggregate by their addresses relative to that point. Often the address of the aggregate must be divisible by a given integer, called the *alignment*. Figure 3.2 lists main storage operand sizes and alignments for typical machines.

Aggregates also appear in classes other than main storage. For example, the 16 general purpose registers of the IBM 370 form a storage class of 4-byte cells addressed by the numbers 0 through 15. Every register whose address is even forms the first element of a larger entity (a register pair) used in multiplication, division and shift operations. When a single-length

Operand	Size (bits)	Alignment
Byte	8	1
Halfword	16	2
Word	32	4
Doubleword	64	8
String	up to 256x8	1

a) IBM 370 - Storage cell is an 8-bit byte

Operand	Size (bits)	Alignment
Bit	1	-
Digit	4	-
Byte	8	1
Word	16	2
Longword	32	2

b) Motorola 68000 - Storage cell is an 8-bit byte

Figure 3.2. Operand Sizes

operand for such an operation is supplied, it should be placed in the proper register of a pair rather than in an arbitrary register. The other register of the pair is then automatically reserved for the operation, and cannot be used for other purposes.

The entities of a particular level in a hierarchy of aggregates may overlap. This occurs, for example, for the *segments* in the main storage class of the Intel 8086 (65536-byte blocks whose addresses are divisible by 16) or the 4096-byte blocks addressable via a base or index register in the IBM 370.

Operations on registers usually involve the full register contents. When an object whose size is smaller than that of a register is moved between a register and storage of some other class, a change of representation may occur. The *value* of the object must, however, remain invariant. Depending upon the type of the object, it may be lengthened by inserting leading or trailing zeros, or by inserting leading or trailing copies of the sign. When it is shortened, we must guarantee that no significant information is lost. Thus the *working length* of an object must be distinguished from the *storage length*.

3.1.2. Access Paths

An access path describes the value or location of an operand, result or jump target. We classify an instruction as a 0-, 1-, 2-, or 3-address instruction according to the number of access paths it specifies. Very seldom are there more than three access paths per instruction, and if more do exist then they are usually implicit. (For example, in the MVCL instruction of the IBM 370 the two register specifications R1 and R2 actually define four operands in registers R1, R1 + 1, R2 and R2 + 1 respectively.)

Each access path specifies the initial element of an operand or result in a storage class. Access paths to some of the storage classes (such as the stack, program counter, condition code and special registers) are not normally explicit in the instruction. They will appear only when there is some degree of freedom associated with their use, as in the PDP11 where any register can be used as a stack pointer.

The most common explicit access paths involve one of the following computations:
- Constant. The value appears explicitly in the instruction.
- Register. The content of the register is taken as the value.
- Register + constant. The sum of the content of the register and a constant appearing explicitly in the instruction is taken as the value.
- Register + register. The sum of the contents of two registers is taken as the value.
- Register + register + constant. The sum of the contents of two registers and a constant appearing in the instruction is taken as the value.

The computed value may itself be used as the operand (*immediate*), it may be used as the effective address of the operand in main storage (*direct*), or it may be used as the address of an address (*indirect*). On some machines the object fetched from main storage in the third case may specify another computation and further indirection, but this feature is rarely used in practice.

i: Operand is the byte i from the instruction.

d(m,n): Operand is the 24-bit value obtained by $(Rm)+(Rn)+d$. Only the low-order 24 bits of each register are used, and the value is interpreted as positive. Overflow in the addition is ignored. If m or n is 0 then the content of the register is assumed to be 0; the actual content of general register 0 is not used.

m: Operand is the content of general register Rm.

m: Operand is the content of general register pair $(Rm,Rm+1)$.

m: Operand is the content of floating point register Fm.

d(m,n): Operand is the content of a memory area whose address is the value computed as discussed above.

Implicit access to the condition code and program counter.

Note: $0\leqslant i<2^8, 0\leqslant d<2^{12}, 0\leqslant m,n<2^4$

a) IBM 370

$=$i16: Operand is the word following the instruction.

$=$i32: Operand is the doubleword following the instruction.

i16: Operand is the value $(PC)+i16$.

i8(Am): Operand is the value $(PC)+(Am)+i8$.

i8(Dn): Operand is the value $(PC)+(Dn)+i8$.

Am: Operand is the content of address register Am.

Dn: Operand is the content of data register Dn.

(Am): Operand is the content of a memory area whose address is the content of address register Am.

i16(Am): Operand is the content of a memory area whose address is the value of $(Am)+i16$.

i8(Am,Dn): Operand is the content of a memory area whose address is the value of $(Am)+(Dn)+i8$.

(Am)$+$: Operand is the content of a memory area whose address is the content of Am. Am is then incremented by the operand length. The increment is never less than 2 for A7.

-(Am): Am is decremented by the operand length. Operand is then the content of a memory area whose address is the content of Am. The decrement is never less than 2 for A7.

Implicit access to the condition code and program counter.

b) Motorola 68000

Figure 3.3. Access Paths

Figure 3.3 illustrates these concepts for typical machines.

The addresses of registers must almost always appear explicitly as constants in the instruction. In special cases they may be supplied implicitly, as when the content of the (unspecified) program counter is added to a constant given in the instruction (*relative addressing*). If the computed value is used as an address then the registers must belong to the base register or index register class; the sum of the (unsigned) base address and (signed) index is often interpreted modulo the address size. The values of constants in instructions are frequently restricted to nonnegative values, and often their maximum values are far less than the maximum address. (An example is the restriction to the range [0,4095] of the IBM 370.)

Not all computers allow every one of the access paths discussed above; restrictions in the combination (operation, access path) can also occur. Many of these restrictions arise from the properties of the machine's registers. We distinguish five architectural categories based upon register structure:

- Storage-to-storage. All operands of a computational operation are taken from main storage, and the result is placed into main storage (IBM 1400 series, IBM 1620). Storage-to-storage operations appear as a supplementary concept in many processors.
- Stack. All operands of a computational operator are removed from the top of the stack, and the result is placed onto the top of the stack (Burroughs 5000, 6000 and 7000 series, ICL 2900 family). The stack appears as a supplementary concept in many processors.
- Single Accumulator. One operand of a computational operator is taken from the accumulator, and the result is placed into the accumulator; all other registers, including any accumulator extension, have special tasks or cannot participate in all operations (IBM 7040/7090, Control Data 3000 series, many process-control computers, Intel 8080 and microprocessors derived from it).
- Multiple Accumulator. One operand of a computational operator is taken from one of the accumulators, and the result is returned to that accumulator; long operands and results are accommodated by pairing the accumulators (DEC PDP11, Motorola 68000, IBM 370, Univac 1100)
- Storage Hierarchy. All operands of a computational operator are taken from accumulators, and the result is returned to an accumulator (Control Data 6000, 7000 and Cyber series). This architecture is identical to the storage-to-storage architecture if we view the accumulators as primary storage and the main storage as auxiliary storage.

3.1.3. Operations   Usually the instruction set of a computer provides four general classes of operation:

- Computation: Implements a function from n-tuples of values to m-tuples of values. The function may affect the state. Example: A divide instruction whose arguments are a single-length integer divisor and a double-length integer dividend, whose results are a single-length integer quotient and a single-length integer remainder, and which may produce a divide check interrupt.
- Data transfer: Copies information, either within one storage class or from one storage class to another. Examples: A move instruction that copies the contents of one register to another; a read instruction that copies information from a disc to main storage.

- Sequencing: Alters the normal execution sequence, either conditionally or unconditionally. Examples: A halt instruction that causes execution to terminate; a conditional jump instruction that causes the next instruction to be taken from a given address if a given register contains zero.
- Environment control: Alters the environment in which execution is carried out. The alteration may involve a transfer of control. Examples: An interrupt disable instruction that prohibits certain interrupts from occurring; a procedure call instruction that updates addressing registers, thus changing the program's addressing environment.

It is not useful to attempt to assign each instruction unambiguously to one of these classes. Rather the classes should be used as templates to evaluate the properties of an instruction when deciding how to implement language operations (Section 3.2.3)

It must be possible for the control unit of a computer to determine the operation and all of the access paths from the encoding of an instruction. Older computer designs usually had a single instruction size of, say, 24 or 36 bits. Fixed subfields were used to specify the operation and the various access paths. Since not all instructions require the same access paths, some of these subfields were unused in some cases. In an information-theoretic sense, this approach led to an inefficient encoding.

Coding efficiency is increased in more modern computers by using several different instruction sizes. Thus the IBM 370 has 16, 32 and 48 bit (2, 4 and 6 byte) instructions. The first byte is the operation code, which determines the length and layout of the instruction as well as the operation to be carried out. Nearly all microprocessors have variable-size operation codes as well. In this case the encoding process carried out by the assembly task may require larger tables, but otherwise the compiler is not affected. Variable-length instructions may also lead to more complex criteria of optimality.

On some machines one or more operation codes remain unallocated to hardware functions. Execution of an instruction specifying one of these operation codes results in an interrupt, which can be used to activate a subprogram. Thus these undefined operations can be given meaning by software, allowing the compiler writer to extend the instruction set of the target machine. Such programmable extension of the instruction set is sometimes systematically supported by the hardware, in that the access paths to operands at specific positions are placed at the disposal of the subprogram as parameters. The XOP instruction of the Texas Instruments 990 has this property. (TRAP allows programmable instruction set extension on the PDP11, but does not make special access path provisions.)

3.2. Representation of Language Elements

In this and following sections we shall discuss the mapping of the language elements of Chapter 2 onto the machine elements of Section 3.1. This mapping is really the specification of the tasks of the code generator and the run-time system, and must be performed for each language/machine pair.

3.2.1. Elementary Objects   A combination of space and instruction questions must be answered in order to determine the mapping of elementary types such as integer, real, character, Boolean and other enumerations. Implementation of the relevant basic operations is particularly important for Boolean values.

For integers, the first decision is whether to use a decimal (4 bits/digit) or binary encoding. Decimal encoding implies that decimal operations exist (as on the IBM 370), or at least that there is a facility to detect a carry (result digit > 9) and to increment the next higher position (as on many microprocessors). The values of variables have varying size with this encoding, which complicates assignment operations. Decimal encoding is worth considering if very few operations take place on each value (the cost of the translation from decimal to binary on input and the reverse translation on output is greater than the expected gain from using binary operations internally), or if the numeric incompatibility of binary and decimal arithmetic is a significant problem (as with some financial applications).

Binary encodings are normally fixed-length, and hence when a binary encoding is chosen we must fix the length of the representation in terms of the maximum source language integer. Since most programming languages leave the range of integer values unspecified, we fall back upon the rule of thumb that all addresses be representable as integers. This causes us to consider integer representations of 16, 24 or 32 bits. The representation must at least include all conceivable indexes; 16 bits will suffice for this purpose on small machines. We must also consider available instructions. For example, on the IBM 370 we would rule out 16 bits because no divide instruction is included for 16 bit operands and because the test to determine whether intermediate 32-bit results could be represented in 16 bits would slow execution considerably. The extra instructions would, in many cases, wipe out the savings resulting from the 16-bit representation. Similar reasoning would eliminate the 24-bit representation on most computers.

A binary encoding with n bits can represent 2^n distinct values, an even number. Any range of integers symmetric about 0, however, contains an *odd* number of values. This basic mismatch leads to anomalous behavior of machine arithmetic. The exact nature of the anomaly depends upon the representation chosen for negative numbers. A sign-magnitude or diminished-radix complement (e.g. 1's-complement) representation results in two zero values, one positive and the other negative; a radix complement (e.g. 2's-complement) representation results in a 'most negative' number that has no positive counterpart. The extra-zero anomaly is usually the more difficult of the two for the compiler writer. It may involve additional instructions to ensure that comparisons yield the correct result, or complicated analysis to prove that these instructions need not be generated.

Comparisons may prove difficult if they are not provided as machine instructions. Arithmetic instructions must then be used, and precautions taken against erroneous results due to over- and underflow. For example, consider a machine with integers in the range [-32767,32767]. If $a > b$ is implemented as $(a - b) > 0$ then an overflow will occur when comparing values $a = 16384$ and $b = -16384$. The comparison code must either anticipate and avoid this case, or handle the overflow and interpret the result properly. In either case, a long instruction sequence may be required. Underflow may occur in floating point comparisons implemented by a subtraction when the operand difference is small. Since many machines deliver 0 as a result, without indicating that an underflow has occurred, anticipation and avoidance are required.

Actually, the symptom of the floating point underflow problem is that a comparison asserts the equality of two numbers when they are really different. We could argue that the inherent inaccuracy of floating point operations makes equality testing a risky business anyway. The programmer must thoroughly understand the algorithm and its interaction with the machine representation before using equality tests, and hence we can inform him of the problem and then forget about it. This position is defensible provided that we can guarantee that a comparison will never yield an incorrect relative magnitude (i.e. it will never report $a > b$ when a is less than b, or vice-versa).

If, as in Pascal, subranges $m..n$ of integers can be specified as types, the compiler writer must decide what use to make of this information. When the usual integer range can be exceeded (not possible in Pascal) this forces the introduction of higher-precision arithmetic (in the extreme case, of variable-length arithmetic). For small subranges the size of the range can be used to reduce the number of bits required in the representation, if necessary by replacing the integer i by ($i - lower\_bound$), although this last is not recommended. The important question is whether arithmetic operations exist for the shorter operands, or at least whether the conversion between working length and storage length can easily be carried out. (Recall that no significant bits may be discarded when shortening the representation.)

The possibilities for mapping real numbers are constrained by the floating point operations of the hardware or the given subroutine package. (If neither is available on the target machine then implementation should follow the IEEE standard.) The only real choice to be made involves the precision of the significand. This decision must be based upon the milieu in which the compiler will be used and upon numeric problems whose discussion is beyond the scope of this book.

For characters and character strings the choice of mapping is restricted to the specification of the character code. Assuming that this is not fixed by the source language, there are two choices: either a standard code such as the ISO 7-bit code (ASCII), or the code accepted by the target computer's operating system for input/output of character strings (EBCDIC or other 6-

1 Bit The bit position is specified by two masks, $M0 = B'\ 0...010...0'$ and $M1 = B'\ 1...101...1'$.

1 Byte Let 0 represent *false*, K represent *true*.

a) Possible representations for Boolean values

Construct	Code, depending on representation			
	Byte		Bit	
q:=p	MVC	q,p		TM	M0,p
				BO	L1
				NI	M1,q
				B	L2
			L1	OI	M0,q
			L2	continuation	
p := **not** *p*	XI	K,p		XI	M0,p
q := *q* **or** *p*	OC	q,p		TM	M0,p
				BZ	L1
				OI	M0,q
			L1	continuation	
q := *q* **and** *p*	NC	q,p		TM	M0,p
				BO	L1
				NI	M0,q
			L1	continuation	

(The masks M0 and M1 are those appropriate to the second operand of the instruction in which they appear.)

b) Code using the masks from (a)

Figure 3.4. Boolean Operations on the IBM 370

or 8-bit code; note that EBCDIC varies from one manufacturer to another). Since most computers provide quite efficient instructions for character translation, use of the standard code is often preferable.

The representation of other finite types reduces to the question of suitably representing the integers $0..n-1$, which we have already discussed. One exception is the Boolean values *false* and *true*. Only a few machines are provided with instructions that access single bits. If these instructions are absent, bit operations must be implemented by long sequences of code (Figure 3.4). In such cases it is appropriate to implement Boolean variables and values as bytes or words. Provided that the source language has not constrained their coding, the choice of representation depends upon the realization of operations with Boolean operands or Boolean results. In making this decision, note that comparison and relational operations occur an order of magnitude more frequently than all other Boolean operations. Also, the operands of **and** and **or** are much more frequently relations than Boolean variables. In particular, the implementation of **and** and **or** by jump cascades (Section 3.2.3) introduces the possibilities (*false* = 0, *true* $\neq$ 0) and (*false* $\geqslant$ 0, *true* < 0) or their inverses in addition to the classical (*false* $=0$, *true* $=1$). These possibilities underscore the use of more than one bit to represent a Boolean value.

3.2.2. Composite Objects   For composite objects, we are interested in the properties of the standard representation and the possibilities for reducing storage requirements.

An object a: **array** $[m..n]$ **of** M will be represented by a sequence of $(n-m+1)$ components of type M. The address of element $a[i]$ becomes:

$$address\,(a[m])+(i-m)*\,|\,M\,|\ =\ address\,(a[0])+i*\,|\,M\,|$$

Here $|\,M\,|$ is the size of an element in address units and $address\,(a[0])$ is the 'fictitious starting address' of the array. The address of $a[0]$ is computed from the location of the array in storage; such an element need not actually exist. In fact, $address\,(a[0])$ could be an invalid address lying outside of the address space.

The usual representation of an object b: **array** $[m_1..n_1, \ldots, m_r..n_r]$ **of** M occupies $k_1 * k_2 * \cdots * k_r * |\,M\,|$ contiguous memory cells, where $k_j = n_j - m_j + 1$, $j = 1, \ldots, r$. The address of element $b[i_1, \ldots, i_r]$ is given by the following storage mapping function when the array is stored in *row-major order*:

$$address\,(b[m_1, \ldots, m_r])+(i_1-m_1)*k_2* \cdots *k_r*\,|\,M\,|$$
$$+ \cdots +(i_r-m_r)*\,|\,M\,|$$
$$=address\,(b[0, \ldots, 0])+i_1*k_2*...*k_r*\,|\,M\,|+ \cdots +i_r*\,|\,M\,|$$

By appropriate factoring, this last expression can be rewritten as:

$$address\,(b[0, \ldots, 0])+((\cdots (i_1*k_2+i_2)*k_3+ \cdots +i_r)*\,|\,M\,|$$

If the array is stored in *column-major order* then the order of the indices in the polynomial is reversed:

$$address\,(b[0, \ldots, 0])+((\cdots (i_r*k_{r-1}+i_{r-1})*k_{r-2}+ \cdots +i_1)*\,|\,M\,|$$

The choice of row-major or column-major order is a significant one. ALGOL 60 does not specify any particular choice, but many ALGOL 60 compilers have used row-major order. Pascal implicitly requires row-major order, and FORTRAN explicitly specifies column-major order. This means that Pascal arrays must be transposed in order to be used as parameters to FORTRAN library routines. In the absence of language constraints, make the choice that corresponds to the most extensive library software on the target machine.

Access to $b[i_1, \ldots, i_r]$ is undefined if the relationship $m_j \leqslant i_j \leqslant n_j$ is not satisfied for some $j = 1, \ldots, r$. To increase reliability, this relationship should be checked at run time if the compiler cannot verify it in other ways (for example, that i_j is the controlled variable of a loop and the starting and ending values satisfy the condition). To make the check, we need to evaluate a storage mapping function with the following fixed parameters (or its product with the size of the single element):

$$r, address(b[0, \ldots, 0]), m_1, \ldots, m_r, n_1, \ldots, n_r$$

Together, these parameters constitute the *array descriptor*. The array descriptor must be stored explicitly for dynamic and flexible arrays, even in the trivial case $r = 1$. For static arrays the parameters may appear directly as immediate operands in the instructions for computing the mapping function. Several array descriptors may correspond to a single array, so that in addition to questions of equality of array components we have questions of equality or identity of array descriptors.

An r dimensional array b can also be thought of as an array of $r - 1$ dimensional arrays. We might apply this perception to an object c: **array** $[1..m, 1..n]$ **of** *integer*, representing it as m one-dimensional arrays of type $t = $**array** $[1..n]$ **of** *integer*. The fictitious starting addresses of these arrays are then stored in an object a: **array** $[1..m]$ **of** $\uparrow t$. To be sure, this *descriptor technique* raises the storage requirements of c from $m*n$ to $m*n + m$ locations for integers or addresses; in return it speeds up access on many machines by replacing the multiplication by n in the mapping function $address(c[0,0]) + (i*n + j)* \mid integer \mid$ by an indexed memory reference. The saving may be particularly significant on computers that have no hardware multiply instruction, but even then there are contraindications: Multiplications occurring in array accesses are particularly amenable to elimination via simple optimizations.

The descriptor technique is supported by hardware on Burroughs 6700/7700 machines. There, the rows of a two-dimensional array are stored in segments addressed by special *segment descriptors*. The segment descriptors, which the hardware can identify, are used to access these rows. Actual allocation of storage to the rows is handled by the operating system and occurs at the first reference rather than at the declaration. The allocation process, which is identical to the technique for handling page faults, is also applied to one-dimensional arrays. Each array or array row is divided into pages of up to 256 words. Huge arrays can be declared if the actual storage requirements are unknown, and only that portion actually referenced is ever allocated.

Character strings and sets are usually implemented as arrays of character and Boolean values respectively. In both cases it pays to pack the arrays. In principle, character string variables have variable length. Linked lists provide an appropriate implementation; each list element contains a segment of the string. List elements can be introduced or removed at will. Character strings with fixed maximum length can be represented by arrays of this length. When an array of Boolean values is packed, each component is represented by a single bit, even when simple Boolean variables are represented by larger storage units as discussed above.

A record is represented by a succession of fields. If the fields of a record have alignment constraints, the alignment of the entire record must be constrained also in order to guarantee that the alignment constraints of the fields are met. An appropriate choice for the alignment constraint of the record is the most stringent of the alignment constraints of its fields. Thus a record containing fields with alignments of 2, 4 and 8 bytes would itself have an alignment of 8 bytes. Whenever storage for an object with this record type is allocated, its starting address must satisfy the alignment constraint. Note that this applies to anonymous objects as well as objects declared explicitly.

The amount of storage occupied by the record may depend strongly upon the order of the fields, due to their sizes and alignment constraints. For example, consider a byte-oriented machine on which a character variable is represented by one byte with no alignment constraint and an integer variable occupies four bytes and is constrained to begin at an address divisible by 4. If a record contained an integer field followed by a character field followed by a second integer field then it would occupy 12 bytes: There would be a 3-byte gap following the character field, due to the alignment constraint on integer variables. By reordering the fields, this gap could be eliminated. Most programming languages permit the compiler to do such reordering.

Records with variants can be implemented with the variants sharing storage. If it is known from the beginning that only one variant will be used and that the value of the variant selector will never change, then the storage requirement may be reduced to exactly that for the specified variant. This requirement is often satisfied by anonymous records; Pascal distinguishes the calls *new(p)* and *new(p,variant_selector)* as constructors for anonymous records. In the latter case the value of the variant selector may not change, whereas in the former all variants are permitted.

The gaps arising from the alignment constraints on the fields of a record can be eliminated by simply ignoring those constraints and placing the fields one after another in memory. This *packing* of the components generally increases the cost in time and instructions for field access considerably. The cost almost always outweighs the savings gained from packing a single record; packing pays only when many identical records are allocated simultaneously. Packing is often restricted to partial words, leaving objects of word length (register length) or longer aligned. On byte-oriented machines it may pay to pack only the representation of sets to the bit level.

Packing alters the access function of the components of a composite object: The selector must now specify not only the relative address of the component, but also its position within the storage cell. On some computers extraction of a partial word can be specified as part of an operand address, but usually extra instructions are required. This has the result that packed components of arrays, record and sets may not be accessible via normal machine addresses. They cannot, therefore, appear as reference parameters.

Machine-dependent programs sometimes use records as templates for hardware objects. For example, the assembly phase of a compiler might use a record to describe the encoding of a machine instruction. The need for a fixed layout in such cases violates the abstract nature of the record, and some additional mechanism (such as the *representation specification* of Ada) is necessary to specify this. If the language does not provide any special mechanism, the compiler writer can overload the concept of packing by guaranteeing that the fields of a packed record will be allocated in the order given by the programmer.

Addresses are normally used to represent pointer values. Addresses relative to the beginning of the storage area containing the objects are often sufficient, and may require less storage than full addresses. If, as in ALGOL 68, pointers have bounded lifetime, and the correctness of assignments to reference variables must be checked at run time, we must add information to the pointer from which its lifetime may be determined. In general the starting address of the activation record (Section 3.3) containing the reference object serves this purpose; reference objects of unbounded extent are denoted by the starting address of the stack. A comparison of these addresses for relative magnitude then represents inclusion of lifetimes.

3.2.3. Expressions   Because of the diversity of machine instruction sets, we can only give the general principles behind the mapping of expressions here. An important point to remember throughout the discussion, both here and in Section 3.2.4, is that the quality of the generated code is determined by the way it treats cases normally occurring in practice rather than by its handling of the general case. Moreover, local code characteristics have a greater impact than any optimizations on the overall quality. Table 3.5 shows the static frequencies of operations in a large body of Pascal text. Note the preponderance of memory accesses over computation, but remember that indexing generally involves both multiplication and addition. Remember also that these are *static* frequencies; dynamic frequencies might be quite different because a program usually spends about 90% of its time in heavily-used regions accounting for less than 10% of the overall code.

Single target machine instructions directly implement operations appearing in the structure tree only in the simplest cases (such as integer arithmetic). A node of the structure tree generally corresponds to a sequence of machine instructions, which may appear either directly in the generated code or as a subroutine call. If subroutines are used then they may be gathered together into an interpreter consisting of a control loop containing a large case statement. The operations are then simply selectors used to choose the proper case, and may be regarded as instructions of a new (abstract) machine. This approach does not really answer the question of realizing language elements on a target machine; it merely changes the target machine, hopefully simplifying the problem.

A closed sequence is invariably slower than the corresponding open sequence because of the cost of the transfers in and out. It would therefore

Table 3.5. Static Frequencies of Pascal Operators [Carter 1982]

Structure Tree Operator	Percent of All Operators
Access a variable	27
Assign	13
Select a field of a record	9.7
Access a value parameter	8.1
Call a procedure	7.8
Index an array (each subscript)	6.4
Access an array	6.1
Compare for equality (any operands)	2.7
Access a variable parameter	2.6
Add integers	2.3
Write a text line	1.9
Dereference a pointer variable	1.9
Compare for inequality (any operands)	1.3
Write a single value	1.2
Construct a set	1.0
not	0.7
and	0.7
Compare for greater (any operands)	0.5
Test for an element in a set	0.5
or	0.4
All other operators	3.8

be used only if commensurate savings in space were possible. Some care must be taken in evaluating the tradeoffs, because both open and closed sequences usually involve setup code for the operands. It is easy to overlook this code, making erroneous assumptions about the operand locations, and thereby arrive at the wrong decision. Recall from Section 3.1.3 that it is sometimes possible to take advantage of unused operation codes to access closed instruction sequences. Depending upon the details of the hardware, the time overhead for this method may be either higher or lower than that of a conventional call. It is probably most useful for implementing facilities that might be provided by hardware. The typical example is floating point arithmetic on a microprocessor with integer operations only. A floating point operation usually involves a long sequence of instructions on such a machine (which may not even be capable of integer multiplication or division), and thus the entry/exit overhead is negligible. If the user later adds a floating-point chip, and controls it with the previously unused operation codes, no changes to the code generator are required. Even when different operation codes are used the changes are minimal.

An object, label or procedure is *addressable* if its effective address can be expressed by the relevant access path of an instruction. For entities that are not addressable, additional operations and temporary storage are required to compute the effective address. The allowable combinations of operation

```
L      R1,I
A      R1,J       Result in R1
M      R0,K       Multiplicand from R1, product to (R0,R1)
D      R0,L       Dividend from (R0,R1)
```
           a) Code for the expression $((i + j)*k /l)$

```
L         R0,I
A         R0,J
A         R0,K       Result in R0
SRDA      R0,32      Extend to double, result in (R0,R1)
D         R0,L       Dividend from (R0,R1)
```
           b) Code for the expression $((i + j + k)/l)$

Figure 3.6. Optimum Instruction Sequences for the IBM 370

and access function exert a very strong influence upon the code generation process because of this. On the Motorola 68000, for example, specification of the operation can be largely separated from selection of the access path, and operand addressability is almost independent of the operator. Many IBM 370 instructions, on the other hand, work only when the second operand is in a register. In other cases memory access is possible, but only via a base register without indexing. This leads to the problem that an operand may be addressable in the context of one operation but not in the context of another.

When an instruction set contains such asymmetries, the simplest solution is to define the abstract machine for the source-to-target mapping with a uniform access function, reserving the resources (usually one or two registers) needed to implement the uniform access function for *any* instruction. Many code sequences require additional resources internally in any event. These can often be standardized across the code sequences and used to provide the uniform access function in addition. The only constraint on resources reserved for the uniform access function is that they have no inter-sequence meaning; they can be used arbitrarily within a sequence.

Consider the tree for an expression. The addressability of entities described by leaves is determined by the way in which the environment is encoded in the machine state. (We shall discuss possibilities for environment encoding in Section 3.3.) For entities described by interior nodes, however, the addressability depends upon the code sequence that implements the node. It is often possible to vary a code sequence, without changing its cost, to meet the addressability requirements of another node. Figure 3.6 shows a typical example. Here the constraints of the IBM 370 instruction set require that a multiplicand be in the odd-numbered register of a pair, and that the even-numbered register of that pair be free. Similarly, the optimum mechanism for converting a single-length value to double-length requires its argument to be in the even register of the pair used to hold its result. An important part of the source-to-target mapping design is the determination of the information made available by a node to its neighbors in the tree, and how this information affects the individual code sequences.

Interior nodes whose operations yield addresses, such as indexing and field selection nodes, may or may not result in code sequences. Addressability is the key factor in this decision: No code is required if an access function describing the node's result can be built, and if that access function is acceptable to the instruction using the result. The richer the set of access functions, the more nodes can be implemented simply by access function restructuring. In fact, it is often possible to absorb nodes describing normal value operations into access functions that use their result. Figure 3.7 is a tree for $b[i + 12]$. As we shall see in Section 3.3, the local byte array b might have access function 36(13) on an IBM 370 (here register 13 gives the base address of the local contour, and 36 is the relative byte location of b within that contour). After loading the value of i into register 1, the effects of the index and addition nodes can be combined into the access function 48(13,1). This access function (Figure 3.3a) can be used to obtain the second argument in any RX-format instruction on the IBM 370.

Some machines incorporate automatic incrementing or decrementing of a register content into certain access functions. These facilities are easy to use in source-to-target mappings for special purposes such as stack manipulation. Their general use, for example in combining the increment of a loop control variable with the last use of that variable as an index, is much more difficult because it leads to 'combinatorial explosion' in the number of cases that the code generator must examine. Such optimizations should be provided by a separate process (peephole optimization), rather than being incorporated into the source-to-target mapping.

Many Boolean expressions occur in contexts such as conditional statements and loops, where the result is used only to determine the flow of control. Moreover, most of these expressions either are relations themselves or are composed of relations. On the majority of computers a relation is

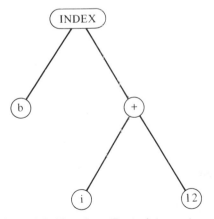

Figure 3.7. Tree for a Typical Array Access

if $(a < b)$ **and** $(c = d)$ **or** $(e > f)$ **then** *statement* ;

a) A conditional

	L	R1,a	
	C	R1,b	
	BNL	L10	Note condition reversal here
	L	R1,c	
	C	R1,d	
	BEQ	L1	Condition is not reversed here
L10	L	R1,e	
	C	R1,f	
	BNH	L2	Reversed
L1	...		Code for *statement*
L2	...		Code following the conditional

b) IBM 370 code corresponding to (a)

Figure 3.8. Jump Cascades

evaluated by performing a comparison or arithmetic operation and then executing a transfer of control based upon the result. The upshot is that such expressions can be implemented most conveniently by omitting Boolean computations completely! Figure 3.8 illustrates the concept, which is called a *jump cascade*.

The concept of a jump cascade is completely independent of the concept of short-circuit evaluation discussed in Section 2.3. It appears that Figure 3.8 is performing short-circuit evaluation because, for example, c is not fetched unless the value of a is less than that of b. But fetching a simple variable has no side effect, and hence the short-circuit evaluation is not detectable. If c were a parameterless function with a side effect then it should be invoked prior to the start of the code sequence of Figure 3.8b, and the c in that code sequence would represent temporary storage holding the function result. Thus we see that questions of short-circuit evaluation affect only the relative placement of code belonging to the jump cascade and code for evaluating the operands of the relations.

3.2.4. Control Structures   A node representing a control structure generally results in several disjoint code sequences rather than a single code sequence. The meanings of and relationships among the sequences depend primarily upon the source language, and hence general schemata can be used to specify them. Each of the disjoint sequences then can be thought of as an abstract machine operation with certain defined properties and implemented individually.

The **goto** statement is implemented by an unconditional jump instruction. If the jump leaves a block or procedure then additional operations, discussed in Section 3.3, are needed to adjust the state. In expression-oriented languages, a jump out of an expression may require adjustment of a

```
            condition(e,L1,L2)
L1:         clause
L2:
```

a) **if** e **then** clause ;

```
            condition(e,L1,L2)
L1:         clause₁
            GOTO L
L2:         clause₂
L:
```

b) **if** e **then** $clause_1$ **else** $clause_2$;

```
            select(e, k₁,L1, . . . , kₙ ,Ln,L0)
L1:         clause₁
            GOTO L

            ...

Ln:         clauseₙ
            GOTO L
L0:         clause₀
L:
```

c) **case** e **of** k_1 :$clause_1$; $\cdots$; k_n :$clause_n$ **else** $clause_0$;

```
            GOTO L
L1:         clause
L:          condition(e,L1,L2)
L2:
```

d) **while** e **do** clause ;

```
L1:         clause
            condition(e,L2,L1)
L2:
```

e) **repeat** clause **until** e

```
            forbegin(i ,e₁,e₂,e₃)
            clause
            forend(i ,e₂,e₃)
```

f) **for** i :$=e_1$ **by** e_2 **to** e_3 **do** clause ;

Figure 3.9. Implementation Schemata for Common Control Structures

hardware stack used for temporary storage of intermediate values. This adjustment is not necessary when the stack is simply an area of memory that the compiler manages as a stack, computing the necessary offsets at compile time. (Unless use of a hardware stack permits cheaper access functions, it should be avoided for this reason.)

Schemata for common control structures are given in Figure 3.9. The operation 'condition(expression,true_label,false_label)' embodies the jump

target : **array** [*kmin..kmax*] **of** *address* ;
k : *integer* ;
k := *e* ;
if $k \geqslant kmin$ **and** $k \leqslant kmax$ **then goto** *target* [*k*] **else goto** *L* 0;

a) General schema for 'select' (Figure 3.9c)

	LA	$1, e_1$	$e_1 = \text{constant} < 2^{12}$
LOOP	ST	$1, i$	
	...		Body of the clause
	L	$1, i$	
	LA	$2, e_2$	$e_2 = \text{constant} < 2^{12}$
	LA	$3, e_3$	$e_3 = \text{constant} < 2^{12}$
	BXLE	1,2,LOOP	

b) IBM 370 code for special-case forbegin ... forend

$i := e_1; t := e_3$;
if $i > t$ **then goto** *l* 3 **else goto** *l* 2;
l 1: $i := i + 1$;
l 2: $\cdots$ (* Body of the clause *)
if $i < t$ **then goto** *l* 1;
l 3:

c) Schema for forbegin...forend when the step is 1

Figure 3.10. Implementing Abstract Operations for Control Structures

cascade discussed in Section 3.2.3. The precise mechanism used to implement the analogous 'select' operation depends upon the set $\{k_1 \cdots k_m\}$. Let k_{min} be the smallest and k_{max} the largest values in this set. If 'most' of the values in the range $[k_{min}, k_{max}]$ are members of the set then 'select' is implemented as shown in Figure 3.10a. Each element of *target* that does not correspond to an element of $\{k_1 \cdots k_m\}$ is set to 'L0'. When the selector set is sparse and its span is large (for example, the set 0, 5000, 10000), a decision tree or perfect hash function should be used instead of an array. The choice of representation is strictly a space/time tradeoff, and must be made by the code generator for each case clause. The source-to-target mapping must specify the parameters to be used in making this choice.

By moving the test to the end of the loop in Figure 3.9d, we reduce by one the number of jumps executed each time around the loop without changing the total number of instructions required. Further, if the target machine can execute independent instructions in parallel, this schema provides more opportunity for such parallelism than one in which the test is at the beginning.

'Forbegin' and 'forend' can be quite complex, depending upon what the compiler can deduce about the bounds and step, and how the language definition treats the controlled variable. As an example, suppose that the step and bounds are constants less than 2^{12}, the step is positive, and the language definition states that the value of the controlled variable is undefined on exit from the loop. Figure 3.10b shows the best IBM 370 implementation for this case, which is probably one of the most common. (We assume that the body of the loop is too complex to permit retention of values in registers.) Note that the label LOOP is defined *within* the 'forbegin' operation, unlike the labels used by the other iterations in Figure 3.9. If we permit the bounds to be general expressions, but specify the step to be 1, the general schema of Figure 3.10c holds. This schema works even if the value of the upper bound is the largest representable integer, since it does not attempt to increment the controlled variable after reaching the upper bound. More complex cases are certainly possible, but they occur only infrequently. It is probably best to implement the abstract operations by subroutine calls in those cases (Exercise 3.9).

Procedure and function invocations are control structures that also manipulate the state. Development of the instruction sequences making up these invocations involves decisions about the form of parameter transmission, and the construction of the *activation record* — the area of memory containing the parameters and local variables.

A normal procedure invocation, in its most general form, involves three abstract operations:

- Callbegin: Obtain access to the an activation record of the procedure.
- Transfer: Transfer control to the procedure.
- Callend: Relinquish access to the activation record of the procedure.

Argument computation and transmission instructions are placed between 'callbegin' and 'transfer'; instructions that retrieve and store the values of result parameters lie between 'transfer' and 'callend'. The activation record of the procedure is accessible to the caller between 'callbegin' and 'callend'.

In simple cases, when the procedure calls no other procedures and does not require complex parameters, the activation record can be deleted entirely and the parameters treated as local variables of the environment statically surrounding the procedure declaration. The invocation then reduces to a sequence of assignments to these variables and a simple subroutine jump. If, as in the case of elementary functions, only one or two parameters are involved then they can be passed in registers. Note that such special treatment leads to difficulties if the functions are invoked as formal parameters. The identity of the procedure is not fixed under those circumstances, and hence special handling of the call or parameter transmission is impossible.

Invocations of formal procedures also cause problems if, as in ALGOL 60, the number and types of the parameters is not statically specified and must be verified at execution time. These dynamic checks require additional instructions not only at the call site, but also at the procedure entry. The latter instructions must be avoided by a normal call, and therefore it is useful for the procedure to have two distinct entry points — one with and one without the tests.

Declarations of local variables produce executable code only when some initialization is required. For dynamic arrays, initialization includes bounds computation, storage allocation, and construction of the array descriptor. Normally only the bounds computation would be realized as in-line code; a library subroutine would be invoked to perform the remaining tasks.

At least for test purposes, every variable that is not explicitly initialized should be implicitly assigned an initial value. The value should be chosen so that its use is likely to lead to an error report; values recognized as illegal by the target machine hardware are thus best. Under no circumstances should 0 be used for implicit initialization. If it is, the programmer will too easily overlook missing explicit initialization or assume that the implicit initialization is a defined property of the language and hence write incorrect programs.

Procedure and type declarations do not usually lead to code that is executed at the site of the declaration. Type declarations only result in machine instructions if array descriptors or other variables must be initialized. As with procedures, these instructions constitute a subprogram that is not called at the point of declaration.

ALGOL 68 identity declarations of the form m id $=expression$ are consistently replaced by initialized variable declarations m $id' := expression$. Here id' is a new internal name, and every applied occurrence of id is consistently replaced by $id' \uparrow$. The initialization remains the only assignment to id'. Simplification of this schema is possible when the expression can be evaluated at compile time and all occurrences of id replaced by this value.

The same schema describes argument transmission for the reference and strict value mechanisms, in particular in ALGOL 68. Transmission of a reference parameter is implemented by initialization of an internal reference variable: **ref** m $parameter = argument$ becomes **ref** m $variable := argument$.

We have already met the internal transformation used by the value and name mechanisms in Section 2.5.3. In the result and value/result mechanisms, the result is conveniently assigned to the argument after return. In this way, transmission of the argument address to the procedure is avoided. When implementing value/result transmission for FORTRAN, one should generate the result assignment only in the case that the argument was a variable. (Note that if the argument address is transmitted to the procedure then the caller must always treat the argument as a variable. If the programmer uses a constant, the compiler must either flag it as an error or move the constant value to a temporary storage location and transmit the address of that temporary.)

For function results, the compiler generally produces temporaries of suitable type at the call site and in the function. Within the function, the result is assigned to the local temporary. Upon return, as in the case of a result parameter, the local temporary is copied into the global temporary. The global temporary is only needed if the result cannot be used immediately. (An example of this case is the value of $\cos(x)$ in $\cos(x) + \sin(y)$.)

Results delivered by function procedures can, in simple cases, be returned in registers. (For compatibility with jump cascades, it may be useful for a Boolean function to encode its result by returning to two different points.) Transmission of composite values as function results can be difficult, especially when these are arrays whose sizes are not known to the caller. This means that the caller cannot reserve storage for the result in his own environment a priori; as a last resort such objects may be left on the heap (Section 3.3.3).

3.3. Storage Management

Until now we have dealt with the representation of single objects in memory; in this section we shall discuss management of storage for collections of objects, including temporary variables, during their lifetimes. The important goals are the most economical use of memory and the simplicity of access functions to individual objects. Source language properties govern the possible approaches, as indicated by the following questions (see also Section 2.5.2):

- Is the exact number and size of all objects known at compilation time?
- Is the extent of an object restricted, and what relationships hold between the extents of distinct objects (e.g. are they nested)?
- Does the static nesting of the program text control a procedure's access to global objects, or is access dependent upon the dynamic nesting of calls?

3.3.1. Static Storage Management   We speak of static storage management if the compiler can provide fixed addresses for all objects at the time the program is translated (here we assume that translation includes binding), i.e. we can answer the first question above with 'yes'. Arrays with dynamic bounds, recursive procedures and the use of anonymous objects are prohibited. The condition is fulfilled for languages like FORTRAN and BASIC, and for the objects lying on the outermost contour of an ALGOL 60 or Pascal program. (In contrast, arrays with dynamic bounds can occur even in the outer block of an ALGOL 68 program.)

If the storage for the elements of an array with dynamic bounds is managed separately, the condition can be forced to hold in this case also. That is particularly interesting when we have additional information that certain procedures are not recursive, for example because recursivity must be noted specially (as in PL/1) or because we have determined it from analysis of the procedure calls. We can then allocate storage statically for contours other than the outermost.

Static storage allocation is particularly valuable on computers that allow access to any location in main memory via an absolute address in the instruction. Here, static storage corresponds exactly to the class of objects with direct access paths in the sense of Section 3.2.2. If, however, it is unknown during code generation whether or not an object is directly address-able (as on the IBM 370) because this depends upon the final addressing carried out during binding, then we must also access statically-allocated objects via a base register. The only advantage of static allocation then consists of the fact that no operations for storage reservation or release need be generated at block or procedure entry and exit.

3.3.2. Dynamic Storage Management Using a Stack   As we have already noted in Section 2.5.2, all declared values in languages such as Pascal and SIMULA have restricted lifetimes. Further, the environments in these languages are nested: The extent of all objects belonging to the contour of a block or procedure ends before that of objects from the dynamically enclosing contour. Thus we can use a stack discipline to manage these objects: Upon procedure call or block entry, the activation record containing storage for the local objects of the procedure or block is pushed onto the stack. At block end, procedure return or a jump out of these constructs the activation record is popped off of the stack. (The entire activation record is stacked, we do not deal with single objects individually!)

An object of automatic extent occupies storage in the activation record of the syntactic construct with which it is associated. The position of the object is characterized by the base address, b, of the activation record and the relative location (*offset*), R, of its storage within the activation record. R must be known at compile time but b cannot be known (otherwise we would have static storage allocation). To access the object, b must be determined at run time and placed in a register. R is then either added to the register and the result used as an indirect address, or R appears as the constant in a direct access function of the form 'register + constant'.

Every object of automatic extent must be decomposable into two parts, one of which has a size that can be determined statically. (The second part may be empty.) Storage for the static parts is allocated by the compiler, and makes up the static portion of the activation record. (This part is often called the *first order storage* of the activation record.) When a block or procedure is activated, the static part of its activation record is pushed onto the stack. If the activation record contains objects whose sizes must be determined at run time, this determination is carried out and the activation record extended. The extension, which may vary in size from activation to activation, is often called the *second order storage* of the activation record. Storage within the extension is always accessed indirectly via information held in the static part; in fact, the static part of an object may consist solely of a pointer to the dynamic part.

An array with dynamic bounds is an example of an object that has both static and dynamic parts. In most languages, the number of dimensions of an array is fixed, so the size of the array descriptor is known at compile time. Storage for the descriptor is allocated by the compiler in the static part of the activation record. On encountering the declaration during execution, the bounds are evaluated and the amount of storage needed for the array elements is determined. The activation record is extended by this amount and the array descriptor is initialized appropriately. All accesses to elements of the array are carried out via the array descriptor.

We have already noted that at compile time we do not know the base address of an activation record; we know only the range to which it belongs. From this we must determine the base address, even in the case where recursion leads to a number of activation records belonging to the same range. The range itself can be specified by its *block nesting depth*, *bnd*, defined according to the following rules based on the static structure of the program:

- The main program has $bnd = 1$.
- A range is given $bnd = t + 1$ if and only if the immediately enclosing range has $bnd = t$.

Bnd = t indicates that during execution of the range the state consists of a total of t nested contours.

If, as in all ALGOL-like languages, the scopes of identifiers are statically nested then at every point in the execution history of a program there is at most one activation record accessible at a given nesting depth. The base address of a particular activation record can then be found by noting the corresponding nesting depth at compile time and setting up a mapping *s* : *nesting depth* → *base address* during execution. The position of an object in the fixed part of the activation record is fully specified by the pair (*bnd*, *R*); we shall therefore speak of 'the object (*bnd, R*)'.

The mapping *s* changes upon range entry and exit, procedure call and return, and jumps out of blocks or procedures. Updating *s* is thus one of the tasks (along with stack pointer updating and parameter or result transmission) of the state-altering operations that we met in Section 2.5.2. We shall describe them semi-formally below, assuming that the stack is described by:

k : **array** [0..*upper_limit*] **of** *storage_cell*; k_top : 0..*upper_limit*;

We assume further that a storage cell can hold exactly one address, and we shall treat address variables as integer variables with which we can index k.

The contour nesting and pointer to dynamic predecessor required by the contour model are represented by address values stored in each activation record. Together with the return address, and possibly additional information depending upon the implementation, they constitute the 'administrative overhead' of the activation record. A typical activation record layout is shown in Figure 3.11; the corresponding state change operations are given in Figure 3.12. We have omitted range entry/exit operations. As noted in Section 2.5.2, procedures and blocks can be treated identically by regarding a block as a parameterless procedure called 'on the spot', or contours corresponding to blocks can be eliminated and objects lying upon them can be placed on the contour of the enclosing procedure. If blocks are to be given separate activation records, the block entry/exit operations are identical to those for procedures except that no return address is saved on entry

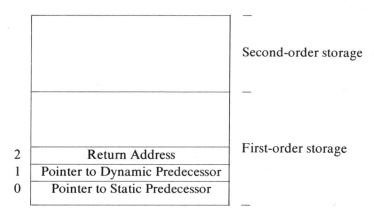

Figure 3.11. Typical Activation Record Layout

$k[k\_top] := (*$ static predecessor of the procedure $*)$;
$k[k\_top + 1] := ep$; $(*$ dynamic predecessor $*)$
$k[k\_top + 2] := ip$; $(*$ return address $*)$
$ep := k\_top$; $(*$ current environment $*)$
$k\_top := k\_top + size$; $(*$ first free location $*)$
$ip := (*$ procedure code address $*)$

a) Procedure entry

$k\_top := ep$;
$ep := k[k\_top + 1]$; $(*$ back to the dynamic predecessor $*)$
$ip := k[k\_top + 2]$;

b) Procedure exit

$k\_top := ep$;
$ep := (*$ target environment of the jump $*)$;
while $k[k\_top + 1] \neq ep$ **do**
  $k\_top := k[k\_top + 1]$; $(*$ leave all intermediate environments $*)$
$ip := (*$ target address of the jump $*)$;

c) Jump out of a procedure

Figure 3.12. Environment Change Operations

and ip is not set on exit. Jumps out of blocks are treated exactly as shown in Figure 3.12c in any case.

The procedure and jump addresses indicated by the comments in Figures 3.12a and c are supplied by the compiler; the environment pointers must be determined at run time. If a procedure is invoked directly, by stating its identifier, then it must lie within the current environment and its environment pointer can be obtained from the stack by following the chain of static predecessors until the proper block nesting depth is reached:

$environment := ep$;
for $i := bndcaller$ **downto** $bndprocedure$ **do**
  $environment := k[environment]$;

The value $(bndcaller - bndprocedure)$ is known at compile time and is usually small, so the loop is sometimes 'unrolled' to a fixed sequence of $environment := k[environment]$ operations.

When a procedure is passed as a parameter and then the parameter is called, the static predecessor cannot be obtained from the stack because the called procedure may not be in the environment of the caller. (Figures 2.3 and 2.5 illustrate this problem.) Thus a procedure parameter must be represented by a *pair* of addresses: the procedure entry point and the activation record address for the environment statically enclosing the procedure declaration. This pair is called a *closure*. When a procedure parameter is invoked, the address of the static predecessor is obtained from the closure that represents the parameter. Figure 3.13 shows the stack representing the contours of Figure 2.5; note the closures appearing in the activation records for procedure p.

Jumps out of a procedure also involve changing the state (Figure 3.12c). The mechanism is essentially the same as that discussed above: If the label is referenced directly then it lies in the current environment and its environment pointer can be obtained from the stack. A label variable or label parameter, however, must be represented by a closure and the environment pointer obtained from that closure.

Access to any object in the environment potentially involves a search down the chain of static predecessors for the pointer to the activation record containing that object. In order to avoid the multiple memory accesses required, a copy of the addresses can be kept in an array, called a *display*, indexed by the block nesting depth. Access to the object (bnd, R) is therefore provided by $display[bnd] + R$; we need only a single memory access, loading $display[bnd]$ into a base register, to set up the access function.

The Burroughs 6000/7000 series computers have a 32-register display built into the hardware. This limits the maximum block nesting depth to 32, which is no limitation in practice. Even a restriction to 16 is usually no problem, but 8 is annoying. Thus the implementation of a display within the register set of a multiple-register machine is generally not possible, because it leads to unnatural restrictions on the block nesting depth. The display can be allocated to a fixed memory location, or we might keep only a partial display (made up of the addresses of the most-frequently accessed activation records) in registers. Which activation record addresses should be kept is, of course, program-dependent. The current activation record address and that of the outermost activation record are good choices in Pascal; the latter should probably be replaced with that of the current module in an implementation of any language providing modules.

22	
	location after 1:f
	12
19	5
	$i = 0$
	11 (reference to i)
	5 (q's environment)
	entry point address for q
	location after $p(q, i)$
	5
12	0
	$i = 2$
	4 (reference to k)
	0 (*empty*'s environment)
	entry point address for *empty*
	location after $p(empty, k)$
	0
5	0
	$k = 0$
	$n = 7$
	0
	0
0	0

Activation record for procedure q

Activation record for procedure p

Activation record for procedure p

Activation record for procedure *outer*

Note:

$k\_top = 22$
$ep = 19$
ip = address of label 2

Figure 3.13. Stack Configuration Corresponding to Figure 2.5

If any sort of display, partial or complete, is used then it must be kept up to date as the state changes. Figure 3.14 shows a general procedure for bringing the display into synchronism with the static chain. It will alter only those elements that need alteration, halting when the remainder is guaranteed to be correct. In many cases the test for termination takes more

procedure *update_display* (*bndnew, bndold* : *integer* ; *a* : *address*):
  (* Make the display consistent with the static chain
    On entry -
      bndnew = nesting depth of the new activation record
      a = address of the new activation record
      bndold = nesting depth of the current activation record
    On exit -
      The display specifies the environment of the new contour
  *)
var
  i : *integer* ;
  h : *address* ;
begin (* *update_display* *)
i := *bndnew* ;
h := *a* ;
while *display*[*i*] $\neq$ *h* **or** *i* > *bndold* **do**
  begin
  display[*i*] := *h* ;
  i := *i* − 1; *h* := *k*[*h*]
  end
end; (* *update_display* *)

Figure 3.14. Setting the Display

time than it saves, however, and a more appropriate strategy may be simply to reload the entire display from the static chain.

Note that the full generality of *update_display* is needed only when returning from a procedure or invoking a procedure whose identity is unknown. If a procedure at level *bndnew* in the current addressing environment is invoked, the single assignment *display*[*bndnew*] := *a* suffices. (Here *a* is the address of the new activation record.) Display manipulation can become a significant overhead for short procedures operating at large nesting depths. Recognition of special cases in which this manipulation can be avoided or reduced is therefore an important part of the optimization of such procedures.

In SIMULA and Ada, as in all languages that contain coroutines and concurrently-executing tasks, activation record creation and destruction need not follow a strict stack discipline. Each coroutine or task corresponds to a set of activation records, and these sets are growing and shrinking independently. Thus each coroutine or task requires an independent stack, and these stacks themselves follow a stack discipline. The result is called a *tree* or *cactus* stack and is most easily implemented in a segmented virtual memory. Implementation in a linear memory is possible by fixing the sizes of the component stacks, but this can only be done when limitations can be placed upon recursion depth and spawning of further tasks.

3.3.3. Dynamic Storage Management Using a Heap

If none of the questions stated at the beginning of Section 3.3 lead to sufficient reduction in the lifetime and visibility of objects, the last resort is to allocate storage on a *heap*: The objects are allocated storage arbitrarily within an area of memory. Their addresses are determined at the time of allocation, and they can only be accessed indirectly. Examples of objects requiring heap storage are anonymous objects such as those created by the Pascal *new* function and objects whose size changes unpredictably during their lifetime. (Linked lists and the flexible arrays of ALGOL 68 belong to the latter class.)

Notice that the static and dynamic chain pointers were the only interconnections among the activation records discussed in Section 3.3.2. The use of a stack storage discipline is not required, but simply provides a convenient mechanism for reclaiming storage when a contour is no longer relevant. By storing the activation records on a heap, we broaden the possibilities for specifying the lifetimes of objects. This is the way in which the uniform retention strategy mentioned at the end of Section 2.5.2 is implemented. Storage for an activation record is released only if the program fragment (block, procedure, class) to which it belongs has been left *and* no pointers to objects within this activation record exist.

Heap allocation is particularly simple if all objects required during execution can fit into the designated area at the same time. In most cases, however, this is not possible. Either the area is not large enough or, in the case of virtual storage, the working set becomes too large. A detailed discussion of heap storage management policies is beyond the scope of this book (see Section 3.5 for references to the relevant literature). We shall only sketch three possible recycling strategies for storage and indicate the support requirements placed upon the compiler by these strategies.

If a language provides an explicit 'release' operation, such as Pascal's *dispose* or PL/1's *free*, then heap storage may be recycled by the user. This strategy is simple for the compiler and the run-time system, but it is unsafe because access paths to the released storage may still exist and be used eventually to access recycled storage with its earlier interpretation. The release operation, like the allocation operation, is almost invariably implemented as a call on a support routine. Arguments that describe the size and alignment of the storage area must be supplied to these calls by the compiler on the basis of the source type of the object.

Automatic reclamation of heap storage is possible only if the designers of a language have considered this and made appropriate decisions. The key is that it must be possible to determine whether or not a variable contains an address. For example, only a variable of pointer type may contain an address in a Pascal program. A special value, *nil*, indicates the absence of a pointer. When a pointer variable is created, it could be initialized to *nil*. Unfortunately, Pascal also provides variant records and does not require such records to have a tag field indicating which variant is in force. If one variant contains a pointer and another does not, it is impossible to determine whether or not the corresponding variable contains a pointer. Detailed discussion of the tradeoffs involved in such a decision by a language designer is beyond the scope of this text.

Storage can be recycled automatically by a process known as *garbage collection*, which operates in two steps:

- Mark. All accessible objects on the heap are marked as being accessible.
- Collect. All heap storage is scanned. The storage for unmarked objects is recycled, and all marks are erased.

This has the advantage that no access paths can exist to recycled storage, but it requires considerable support from the compiler and leads to periodic pauses in program execution. In order to carry out the mark and collect steps, it must be possible for the run-time system to find all pointers into the heap from outside, find all heap pointers held within a given object on the heap, mark an object without destroying information, and find all heap objects on a linear sweep through the heap. Only the questions of finding pointers affect the compiler; there are three principal possibilities for doing this:

1. The locations of all pointers are known beforehand and coded into the marking algorithm.
2. Pointers are discovered by a dynamic type check. (In other words, by examining a storage location we can discover whether or not it contains a pointer.)
3. The compiler creates a template for each activation record and for the type of every object that can appear on the heap. Pointer locations and (if necessary) the object length can be determined from the template.

Pointers in the stack can also be indicated by linking them together into a chain, but this would certainly take too much storage on the heap.

Most LISP systems use a combination of (1) and (2). For (3) we must know the target type of every pointer in order to be able to select the proper template for the object referenced. This could be indicated in the object itself, but storage would be saved if the template carried the number or address of the proper template as well as the location of the pointer. In this manner we also solve the problem of distinguishing a pointer to a record from the pointer to its first component. Thus the template for an ALGOL 68 structure could have the following structure:

- Length of the structure (in storage units)
- For each storage unit, a Boolean value 'reference'
- For each reference, the address of the template of the referenced type.

If dynamic arrays or variants are allowed in records then single Boolean values indicating the presence of pointers are no longer adequate. In the first case, the size and number of components are no longer known statically. The template must therefore indicate the location of descriptors, so that they can be interpreted by the run-time system. In the second case the position of the variant selector and the different interpretations based upon its value must be known. If, as in Pascal, variant records without explicit tag fields are allowed, then garbage collection is no longer possible.

Garbage collection also requires that all internal temporaries and registers that can contain references must be identified. Because this is very difficult in general it is best to arrange the generated code so that, whenever a garbage collection might occur, no references remain in temporaries or registers.

The third recycling strategy requires us to attach a counter to every object in the heap. This counter is incremented whenever a reference to the object is created, and decremented whenever a reference is destroyed. When the counter is decremented to its initial value of 0, storage for the object can be recycled because the object is obviously inaccessible. Maintenance of the counters results in higher administrative and storage costs, but the overheads are distributed. The program simply runs slower overall; it does not periodically cease normal operation to reclaim storage. Unfortunately, the reference counter method does not solve all problems:

- Reference counts in a cyclic structure will not become 0 even after the structure as a whole becomes inaccessible.
- If a counter overflows, the number of references to the object is lost.

A complete solution requires that the reference counters be backed up by a garbage collector.

To support storage management by reference counting, the compiler must be able to identify all assignments that create or destroy references to heap objects. The code generated for such assignments must include appropriate updating of the reference counts. Difficulties arise when variant records may contain references, and assignments to the tag field identifying the variant are allowed: When such an assignment alters the variant, it destroys the reference even though no direct manipulation of the reference has taken place. Similar hidden destruction occurs when there is a jump out of a procedure that leads to deletion of a number of activation records containing references to heap objects. Creation of references is generally easier to keep track of, the most difficult situation probably being assignment of a composite value containing references as minor components.

3.4. Mapping Specifications

The results of the analysis discussed in the earlier sections of this chapter should be embodied in a document called a *mapping specification* (Figure 3.15) for the particular source language/target machine pair. It should not only give the final results, but also the reasoning that led to them. Even when a particular choice was obvious, a brief statement of its basis should be made. For example, one normally chooses the representation of integer values to be that assumed by the hardware 'add integer' instruction; a single sentence stating this fact should appear in the specification.

L TO *M* MAPPING SPECIFICATION

1. The Abstract *M*
   - 1.1. Storage Classes
     One subsection per storage class (see Section 3.1.1).
   - 1.2. Access Paths
     One subsection per access path (see Section 3.1.2).
   - 1.3. Instructions
     One subsection per operation class (see Section 3.1.3).

2. Storage Mapping
   - 2.1. Primitive Data Types
     One subsection per primitive data type of *L* (see Section 3.2.1).
   - 2.2. Composite Data Types
     One subsection per composite data type of *L* (see Section 3.2.2).
   - 2.3. Computation State
     One subsection describing register usage, one describing the use of space for code and constants, and one per storage area type (e.g. static, stack, heap - see Section 3.3) required by *L* .

3. Operation Mapping
   - 3.1. Routine Invocation
     One subsection per operation (e.g. procedure call, procedure entry, formal call, jump out of a procedure) required by *L* . Block entry/exit should also be covered when *L* requires that these operations manipulate the computation state.
   - 3.2. Control Structures
     One subsection per control structure of *L* (see Section 3.2.4).
   - 3.3. Expressions
     - 3.3.1. Attributes
       Information to be exchanged among the nodes of an expression (see Section 3.2.3).
     - 3.3.2. Encodings
       Encoding of each *L* operation as a sequence of instructions and access paths from the abstract *M*, as a function of the information exchanged among expression nodes.

Figure 3.15. Outline of a Mapping Specification

Section 1 of the mapping specification relies heavily on the manufacturer's manual for the target machine. It describes the machine as it will be seen by the code generator, with anomalies smoothed out and omitted operations (to be implemented by code sequences or subroutines) in place. The actual details of realizing the abstraction might be included, or this information might be the subject of a separate specification. We favor the latter approach, because the abstraction *should* be almost entirely language-independent. It is clear that the designer must decide which facilities to include in the abstract machine and which to implement as part of the operation mapping. We cannot give precise criteria for making this choice. (The problem is one of modular decomposition, with the abstraction constituting a module and the operation encoding using the facilities of that module.)

The most difficult part of Section 2 of the mapping specification is Section 2.3, which is tightly coupled to Section 3.1. Procedure mechanisms advocated by the manufacturer are often ill-suited to the requirements of a given language. Several alternative mechanisms should be explored, and detailed cost estimates prepared on the basis of some assumptions about the relative numbers of calls at various static nesting depths and accesses to variables. It is imperative that these assumptions be carefully stated, even though there is only tenuous justification for them; unstated assumptions lead to conflicting judgements and usually to a suboptimal design. Also, if measurements later indicate that the assumptions should be changed, the dependence of the design upon them is clearly stated.

Control structure implementation can be described adequately using notation similar to that of Figure 3.9. When a variety of information is exchanged among nodes of an expression, however, description of the encoding for each node is complicated. The best notation available seems to be the extended-entry decision table, which we discuss in this context in Section 10.3.2.

A mapping specification is arrived at by an iterative process, one that should be allotted sufficient time in scheduling a compiler development project. The cost is dependent upon the complexities of both the source language and the target machine. In one specific case, involving a Pascal implementation for the Motorola 68000, two man-months of effort was required over a six-month period. One person should be responsible for the specification, but at least one other (and preferably several) should be involved in frequent critical reviews. The objective of these reviews should be to test the reasoning based upon the stated assumptions, making certain that it has no flaws. Challenging the assumptions is less important unless specific evidence against them is available.

Sections 2.1 and 2.2 of the mapping specification should probably be written first. They are usually straightforward, and give a basis on which to build. Sections 2.3 and 3.1 should be next. As indicated earlier, these sections interact strongly and involve difficult decisions. The remainder of Section 3 is tedious, but should be carried out in full detail. It is only by being very explicit here that one learns the quirks and problems of the machine, and discovers the flaws in earlier reasoning about storage mapping. Section 1 should be done last, not because it is the least important, but because it is basically a modification of the machine manual in the light of the needs generated by Section 3.

3.5. Notes and References

The question of mapping programming language constructs onto hardware has been considered piecemeal by a number of authors. Tanenbaum [1976] gives a good overview of the issues involved, and further information can be gleaned from specific abstract machine designs [Richards 1971, Tanenbaum 1978, Waite 1977]. Floating point abstractions are discussed by Brown [1977, 1981] and Cody [1980], and a standard has been defined by a committee of IEEE [IEEE 1981]. McLaren [1970] provides a comprehensive discussion of data structure packing and alignment. Randell and Russell [1964] detail the implementation of activation record stacks and displays in the context of ALGOL 60; Hill [1976] updates this treatment to handle the problems of ALGOL 68.

Static storage management is not the only possible strategy for FORTRAN implementations. Both the 1966 and 1978 FORTRAN standards restrict the extent of objects, and thus permit dynamic storage management via a stack. We have not pursued the special storage allocation problems of COMMON blocks and EQUIVALENCE statements here; the interested reader is referred to Chapter 10 of the book by Aho and Ullman [1977a] and the original literature cited there.

Our statements about the probability of access to objects at various nesting depths are debatable because no really good statistics exist. These probabilities are dependent upon the hierarchical organization of the program, and may vary considerably between applications and system programs.

The fact that a procedure used as a parameter must carry its environment with it appears in the original treatment of LISP [McCarthy 1960]. Landin [1964] introduced the term 'closure' in connection with his mechanization of Lambda expressions. More detailed discussions are given by Moses [1970] and Waite [1973a]. Hill [1976] applied the same mechanism to the problem of dynamic scope checking in ALGOL 68.

An overall treatment of storage management is beyond the scope of this book. Knuth [1968b] provides an analysis of the various general strategies, and a full discussion of most algorithms known at the time. A general storage management package that permits a wide range of adaptation was presented by Ross [1967]. The most important aspect of this package is the interface conventions, which are suitable for most storage management modules.

Both general principles of and algorithms for garbage collection and compaction (the process of moving blocks under the user's control to consolidate the free space into a single block) are covered by Waite [1973a]. Wegbreit [1972] discusses a specific algorithm with an improved worst-case running time.

Several authors [Deutsch 1976, Barth 1977, Morris 1978] have shown how to reduce the cost of reference count systems by taking special cases into account. Clark and Green [1977] demonstrated empirically that over 90% of the objects in typical LISP programs never have reference counts greater than 1, a situation in which the technique operates quite efficiently.

EXERCISES

3.1. List the storage classes and access paths available on some machine with which you are familiar. Did you have difficulty in classifying any of the machine's resources? Why?

3.2. Consider access to data occupying a part of a word on some machine with which you are familiar. Does the best code depend upon the bit position within the word? Upon the size of the accessed field? Try to characterize the set of 'best' code sequences. What information would you need to choose the proper sequence?

3.3. [Steele 1977] Consider the best code for implementing multiplication and division of an integer by a power of 2 on some machine with which you are familiar.
   a. Would multiplication by 2 best be implemented by an add, a multiply or a shift? Give a detailed analysis, taking into account the location and possible values of the multiplicand.
   b. If you chose to use a shift for division, would the proper result be obtained when the dividend was negative? Explain.
   c. If your machine has a condition code that is set as a side effect of arithmetic operations, would it be set correctly in all of the cases discussed above?

3.4. For some computer with which you are familiar, design encodings for the elementary types *boolean, integer, real* of Pascal. Carefully defend your choice.

3.5. Consider the representation of a multi-dimensional array.
   a. In what manner can a user of ALGOL, FORTRAN or Pascal determine whether the elements are stored in row- or column-major order?
   b. Write optimum code for some computer with which you are familiar that implements the following doubly-nested loop over an object of type **array** $[1..m, 1..n]$ **of** *integer* stored in row-major order. Do not alter the sequence of assignments to array elements. Compare the result with the same code for an array stored in column-major order.
      for $i := 1$ **to** m **do**
         for $j := 1$ **to** n **do**
            $a[i,j] := 0;$
   c. Explain why a test that the affective address of an array element falls within the storage allocated to the array is not sufficient to guarantee that the access is defined.

3.6. Carefully describe the implementation of the access function for an array element (Section 3.2.2) in each of the following cases:
   a. The fictitious starting address lies outside of the address space of the computer.
   b. The computer provides only base registers (i.e. the registers involved in the access computation of Section 3.1.3 cannot hold signed values).

3.7. Consider a computer requiring certain data items to be stored with alignment 2, while others have no alignment constraints. Give an algorithm that will rearrange any arbitrary record to occupy minimum storage. Can this algorithm be extended to a machine whose alignment constraints require addresses divisible by 2, 4 and 8?

3.8. Give a mapping of a Pascal **while** statement that places the condition at the beginning and has the same number of instructions as Figure 3.9d. Explain why there is less opportunity for parallel execution in your mapping than in Figure 3.9d. Under what circumstances would you expect your expansion to execute in *less* time than Figure 3.9d? What information would the compiler need in order to decide between these schemata on the basis of execution time?

3.9. Consider the mapping of a BASIC FOR statement with the general form:

FOR $I = e_1$ TO e_2 STEP e_3

. . .

NEXT I

Give implementations of forbegin and forend under each of the following conditions:

a. $e_1 = 1, e_2 = 10, e_3 = 1$

b. $e_1 = 1, e_2 = 10, e_3 = 7$

c. $e_1 = 10, e_2 = 1, e_3 = -3$

d. $e_1 = 10, e_2 = 1, e_3 = 1$

e. $e_1 = A, e_2 = B, e_3 = C$

Does your answer to (e) work when A is the largest negative integer representable on the target machine? When B is the largest positive representable integer? If not, what is the cost of repairing this defect? Would you consider this cost acceptable in the light of the probability of such bounds?

3.10. For some machine with which you are familiar, compare the cost of access to statically-allocated objects, objects allocated at fixed locations in an activation record, elements of dynamic arrays and objects allocated on the heap. Be sure to account for any necessary base register loads.

3.11. The state change operations summarized in Figure 3.2 are actually implemented by a combination of code at the call site, code in the procedure or block, and common code in system subprograms. Consider their realization on some machine with which you are familiar.
   a. Operations at the call site should be minimized, at least when the procedure is called directly. What is the minimum code you can use? (You may change the activation record layout of Figure 3.11 arbitrarily to suit your implementation.)
   b. How do you handle the fact that a given procedure may be called either directly or as a parameter? Show that the environment is properly initialized in both cases.

     c. Compare the cost of using a display with that of using simply static and dynamic pointers. On the basis of your answer to Exercise 3.8, determine the break-even point for a display in terms of number of variable accesses.

3.12. Code the display update routine of Figure 3.4 for some machine with which you are familiar. What average nesting depth constitutes the break-even point for the early termination test? On the basis of your own experience, should the test be included or not?

3.13. Under what circumstances is it impossible to compare the extents of two objects by comparing their addresses?

3.14. For some machine with which you are familiar, design a schema for representing type templates. Be sure to handle variant records and dynamic arrays.

3.15. Suppose that a machine provides no 'undefined' value. What values would you propose to use as implicit initializations for Pascal boolean, integer and real variables? Explain your choices.

3.16. Under what circumstances would you consider transmitting arguments and results in registers? Illustrate your answer with several real machines.

3.17. Consider the following LAX fragment:

       declare
       procedure $p(a : $ **array** [] **of** *integer*); ...;
       procedure $q : $ **array** [] **of** *integer* ; ...
       begin $p(q)$ **end**;

     a. Explain why this fragment is illegal.
     b. Suppose that the fragment were legal, and had the obvious effect: Procedure q creates an array, which is then passed to procedure p. Discuss a storage management strategy for the array elements. Where should the storage be allocated? Can we avoid copying the array? What tradeoffs are involved?

CHAPTER 4
Abstract Program Representations

Decomposition of the compilation process leads to interfaces specified by abstract data types, and the basic purposes of these interfaces are largely independent of the source language and target machine. Information crossing an interface between major compilation tasks constitutes a representation of the program in an intermediate language. This representation may or may not be embodied in a concrete data structure, depending upon the structure and goals of a particular compiler. Similarly, the characteristics of a particular compiler may make it useful to summarize the properties of objects in tables stored separately from the program text.

The general characteristics of each interface stem from the modular decomposition of the compiler discussed in Chapter 1. In this chapter we consider several important intermediate languages and tables in detail. By determining the content and possible realization of these interfaces, we place more concrete requirements upon the major compilation tasks.

4.1. Intermediate Languages

Our decomposition leads to four intermediate languages: the token sequence, the structure tree, the computation graph and the target tree. A program is transformed from one to the other in the order given, and they will be presented here in that order.

4.1.1. Token Sequence Chapter 2 pointed out that a source program is composed of a sequence of basic symbols. These basic symbols, rather than the characters from which they are formed, are the relevant units of the source text. We shall use the term *symbol* to denote the external representation of a basic symbol (or an encoding thereof); a *token* is the internal representation.

LAX symbols are described in Section A.1. Production A.1.0.1 classifies them as identifiers, denotations and delimiters respectively. Comments are not basic symbols, and therefore do not appear in the token sequence.

We can characterize the information carried by one token in terms of the type declarations shown in Figure 4.1. *Location* encodes the information required to relate an error message to the source language listing. Section 12.1.3 discusses error reporting mechanisms in detail, and hence we leave the specification of the type *coordinates* open until then.

Most syntactic classes (encoded by members of the enumerated type *tokens*) contain only a single symbol. Tokens representing such symbols need specify only the syntactic class. Only identifiers and denotations require additional information.

A LAX identifier has no intrinsic meaning that can be determined from the character string constituting that identifier. As a basic symbol, therefore, the only property distinguishing one identifier from another is its external representation. This property is embodied in the *sym* field of the token. Section 4.2.1 will consider the type *symbol*, and explain how the external representation is encoded.

The field *intv* or *fptv* is a representation of the value denoted by the source language denotation that the token abstracts. There are several possibilities, depending upon the goals of the particular compiler; Section 4.2.2 considers them in detail.

4.1.2. Structure Tree   A structure tree is a representation of a compilation unit in terms of source concepts. It is an ordered tree (in the sense of Section B.1) whose structure is that of an abstract syntax of the source

```
type
    tokens =(                        (* classification of LAX tokens *)
        identifier,                  (* A.1.0.2 *)
        integer_denotation,          (* A.1.0.6 *)
        floating_point_denotation,   (* A.1.0.7 *)
        plus, . . . , equivalent,    (* specials: A.1.0.10 *)
        and_kw, . . . , while_kw);   (* keywords: A.1.0.11 *)

    abstract_token = record
        location : coordinates ;     (* for error reports *)
        case classification: tokens of
            identifier: (sym : symbol );
            integer_denotation : (intv : integer_value );
            floating_point_denotation: (fptv: real_value);
        end;
```

Figure 4.1. LAX Abstract Token

language. Additional information is attached to the nodes during semantic analysis and the beginning of code generation. We call this information *attributes*, and, to emphasize the attribution, the augmented tree is sometimes termed an *attributed* structure tree. Important attributes are the identity of the internal object corresponding to an identifier, the types of the operands and result of an expression, or the operation corresponding to an operator indication (e.g. the distinction between integer and real addition, both originally specified by '+').

Each node of the structure tree corresponds to a rule of the language definition. Because the structure tree follows the abstract rather than the concrete syntax, some rules will never have corresponding nodes in any structure tree. Furthermore, the concrete syntax may use several names for a single construct of the abstract syntax. Figure 4.2 illustrates these concepts with an example from LAX. The nodes of the tree have been labelled in Figure 4.2a with the corresponding rules from Appendix A. A single rule in Appendix A may incorporate many definitions for the same construct, and we have appended lower-case letters to the rule number in order to distin-

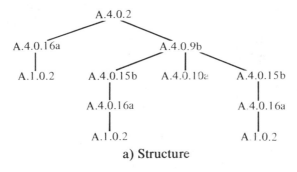

a) Structure

expression, assignment, disjunction, conjunction, comparison, relation, sum, term, factor, primary:
primode, postmode: entity

name:
mode: entity

eqop, relop, addop, mulop, unop:
rator: operation

identifier:
sym: symbol
ent: entity

b) Attributes

Figure 4.2. Structure Tree for $x := y + z$

guish these definitions. Thus 'A.4.0.9b' is the second alternative for rule A.4.0.9 — *sum* :: = *sum addop term*. *Expression, assignment, disjunction,* and so forth are different names appearing in the concrete syntax for the expression construct of the abstract syntax. This means that any node corresponding to a rule defining any of these will have the attributes of an expression attached to it. Figure 4.2b indicates which of the names defined by rules used in Figure 4.2a are associated with the same abstract syntax construct.

The *sym* attribute of an identifier is just the value of the *sym* field of the corresponding token (Figure 4.1). This attribute is known as soon as the node to which it is attached is created. We call such attributes *intrinsic*. All of the other attributes in the tree must be computed. The details of the computations will be covered in Chapters 8 and 9; here we merely sketch the process.

Ent characterizes the object (for example, a particular integer variable) corresponding to the identifier *sym*. It is determined by the declarations valid at the point where the identifier is used, and gives access to all of the declarative information. Section 4.2.3 discusses possible representations for an *entity*.

The *mode* attribute of a name is the type of the object named. In our example it can be obtained directly from the declarative information made accessible by the *ent* attribute of the descendant node. In any case, it is computed on the basis of attributes appearing in the 'A.4.0.16a' node and its descendants. The term *synthesized* is used to describe such attributes.

Two types are associated with each expression node in the tree. The first, *primode,* is the type determined without regard to the context in which the expression is embedded. This is a synthesized attribute, and in our example the *primode* of an expression defined by an 'A.4.0.15b' node is simply the *mode* of the name below it. The second type, *postmode,* is the type demanded by the context in which the expression is embedded. It is computed on the basis of attributes of the expression node, its siblings, and its ancestors. Such attributes are called *inherited*.

If *primode* $\neq$ *postmode* then either a semantic error has occurred or a coercion is necessary. For example, if *y* and *z* in Figure 4.2 were declared to be of types *boolean* and *real* respectively then there is an error, whereas if they were declared to be *integer* and *real* then a coercion would be necessary.

Three classes of operation, *creation, access* and *assignment* are necessary to manipulate the structure tree. A creation operation establishes a new node of a specified type. Assignment operations are used to interconnect nodes and to set attribute values, while access operations are used to extract this information. With these operations we can build trees, traverse them computing attribute values, and alter their structure. Structure tree operations are invoked as the source program is parsed, constructing the tree and setting intrinsic attribute values. One or more additional traversals of the completed tree may be necessary to establish all attribute values. In some cases the structure of the tree may be altered during attribute computation.

process node A;
if node A is not a leaf **then**
    process all subtrees of A from left to right;

a) Prefix traversal

if node A is not a leaf **then**
    process all subtrees of A from left to right;
process node A;

b) Postfix Traversal

process node A;
while subtrees of A remain **do**
    begin
    process next (to the right) subtree of A;
    process node A;
    end;

c) Hybrid traversal

Figure 4.3. Traversal Strategies

Chapter 8 explains how the necessary traversals of the structure tree can be derived from the dependence relations among the attributes. (Figure 4.3 shows some basic traversal strategies.)

The result of processing a structure tree is a collection of related information. It may be possible to produce this result without ever actually constructing the tree. In that case, the structure and attributes of the tree were effectively embedded in the processing code. Another possibility is to have an explicit data structure representing the tree. Implementation constraints often prevent the compiler from retaining the entire data structure in primary memory, and secondary storage must be used. If the secondary storage device is randomly-addressable, only the implementation of the structure tree operations need be changed. If it is sequential, however, constraints must be placed upon the sequences of invocations that are permitted. An appropriate set of constraints can usually be derived rather easily from a consideration of the structure tree traversals required to compute the attributes.

Any of the traversal strategies described by Figure 4.3 could be used with a sequential storage device: In each case, the operation 'process node A' implies that A is the currently-accessible element of the device. It may be read, altered, and written to another device. The remaining operations advance the device's 'window', making another element accessible. Figure 4.4 illustrates the correspondence between the tree and the sequential file. The letters in the nodes of Figure 4.4a stand for the attribute information. In Figures 4.4b and 4.4c, the letters show the position of this information on the file. Figure 4.4d differs from the others in that each interior node is associated with *several* elements of the file. These elements correspond to the

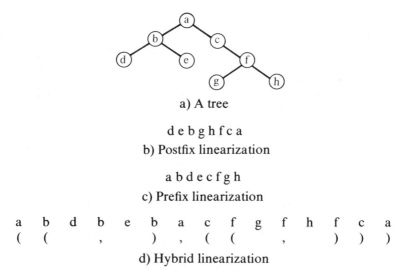

a) A tree

d e b g h f c a

b) Postfix linearization

a b d e c f g h

c) Prefix linearization

a	b	d	b	e	b	a	c	f	g	f	h	f	c	a
(	(		,		)	,	(	(		,		)	)	)

d) Hybrid linearization

Figure 4.4. Linearization by Tree Traversal

prefix encounter of the node during the traversal (flagged with '('), some number of *infix encounters* (flagged with ','), and the *postfix encounter* (flagged with ')'). Information from the node could be duplicated in several of these elements, or divided among them.

The most appropriate linearization of the tree on the basis of tree traversals and tree transformations is heavily dependent upon the semantic analysis, optimization and code generation tasks. We shall return to these questions in Chapter 14. Until then, however, we shall assume that the structure tree may be expressed as a linked data structure.

4.1.3. Computation Graph   A computation graph is an abstract representation of a compilation unit in terms of target concepts. It is a directed graph whose nodes correspond to target operations and whose edges describe control and data flow. The access to identified variables and intermediate results is not represented.

Each node of the computation graph specifies a single abstract target machine operation. In addition to the operation, the node specifies its successor(s) and an appropriate set of operands. An operand may be another computation graph node (indicating the result of that node's computation), an identified variable (indicating the address of that variable) or a constant (indicating the value of that constant). Figure 4.5 is a computation graph describing the algorithm of Figure 1.1a in terms of an abstract target machine based on Exercise 1.3.

Note that the accumulator is never mentioned in Figure 4.5. This is indicative of the abstract nature of the computation graph: It uses target *operations*, but not target *instructions*, separating operations from access paths. Moreover, the concept of a value has been separated from that of a variable.

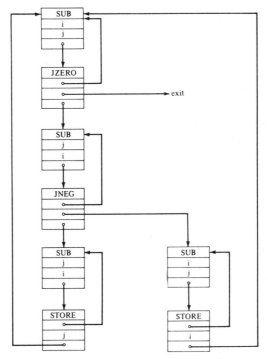

Figure 4.5. A Computation Graph

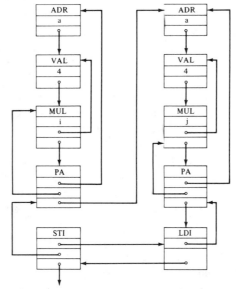

Note: PA adds an integer to an address, yielding an address

Figure 4.6. Constant Operations and Array Access

Triple	Operation	Operands	
1	VAL	i	
2	VAL	j	
3	SUB	(1)	(2)
4	JZERO	(3)	(19)
5	VAL	j	
6	VAL	i	
7	SUB	(5)	(6)
8	JNEG	(7)	(14)
9	VAL	j	
10	VAL	i	
11	SUB	(9)	(10)
12	STORE	j	(11)
13	JMP	(1)	
14	VAL	i	
15	VAL	j	
16	SUB	(14)	(15)
17	STORE		(16)
18	JMP	(1)	

Note: (t) is a reference to triple t

Figure 4.7. Triple Representation of Figure 4.5

As we shall see in Chapter 13, this is a crucial point for common subexpression recognition.

Figure 4.6 describes the array assignment $a[i]:=a[j]$, assuming a byte-addressed target machine and an array with 4-byte elements. The address computation described at the beginning of Section 3.2.2 appears explicitly. *Address*$(a[0])$ is represented by the identifier a and the PA operation adds an integer to an address, yielding an address.

Computation graphs are often linearized as sequences of tuples. The tuples are implicitly linked in the order of the sequence, and hence the last field of the nodes in Figures 4.5 and 4.6 can be dropped. An explicit JMP operation is introduced to allow arbitrary linkage. 'Triples' (Figure 4.7) and 'quadruples' are examples of this technique. The only difference between them is that in the latter the node identification is given explicitly while in the former it is assumed to be the index of the node in the sequence. Figure 4.8 shows a more convenient notation for human consumption.

4.1.4. Target Tree   The target tree forms the interface between code generation and assembly. Its structure and most of the attribute values for its nodes are established during code generation; some attribute values may be added during assembly. The structure of the tree embodies code sequence information, while the attributes specify particular machine instructions and address computations. These characteristics are largely

$$t_1:i \uparrow \qquad t_4:j \uparrow$$
$$t_2:t_1*4 \qquad t_5:t_4*4$$
$$t_3:a+t_2 \qquad t_5:a+t_5$$
$$t_7:t_3:=t_6$$

Figure 4.8. Human-Readable Representation of Figure 4.6

independent of both the source language and the target computer.

The operations necessary to manipulate the target tree fall into the same classes as those necessary to manipulate the structure tree. As with the structure tree, memory constraints may require that the target tree be placed in secondary memory. The most reasonable linearization to use in this case is one corresponding closely to the structure of a normal symbolic assembly language.

Figure 4.9 gives a typical layout for a target tree node. *Machine_op* would be a variant record that could completely describe any target computer instruction. This record might have fields specifying the operation, one or more registers, addresses and addressing modes. Similarly, *constant_specification* must be capable of describing any constant representable on the target computer. For example, the specification of a literal constant would be similar to that appearing in a token (Figure 4.1 and Section 4.2.2); an address constant would be specified by a pointer to an expression node defining the address. In general, the amount of space to be occupied by the constant must also be given.

```
type
  instructions =(      (* Classification of target abstractions *)
    operation,          (* machine instruction *)
    constant,           (* constant value *)
    label,              (* address definition *)
    sequence,           (* code sequence *)
    expression );       (* address expression *)

  target_node = ↑ t_node_block ;
  t_node_block = record
    link : target_node ;
    case classification: instructions of
      operation : (instr : machine_op );
      constant : (value : constant_specification);
      label : (addr : address );
      sequence: (seq, origin: target_node);
      expression : (rator : expr_op ; rand_2: target_node );
    end;
```

Figure 4.9. Target Code Node

A label is an address constant. The label node is placed in a code sequence at some arbitrary point, and represents the address at that point. When this address is used as an operand in an address expression, one of the operands of the expression node is a pointer to the label node. The *addr* field is an example of an attribute whose value is established during assembly: It specifies the actual machine address, in a form that can be used as an expression operand. It is important to stress that this attribute is *not* set by the code generator; the code generator is responsible only for establishing the label node and any linkages to it.

A target program may consist of an arbitrary number of code sequences, each of which consists of instructions and/or data placed contiguously in the target computer memory. Each sequence appears in the target tree as a list of operation, constant and label nodes rooted in a sequence node. If the *origin* field of the sequence node specifies an address expression then the sequence begins at the address which is the value of that expression. Thus the placement of a sequence can be specified relative to another sequence or absolutely in the target computer memory. In the absence of an origin expression, a sequence will be placed in an arbitrary position that guarantees no overlap between it and any other sequence not based upon it. (A sequence s_1 is based upon a sequence s_2 when the origin expression of s_1 depends upon a label node in s_2 or in some sequence based upon s_2.) Related code sequences whose origin expressions result in gaps between them serve to reserve uninitialized storage, while overlapping sequences indicate run-time overlays.

Address expressions may contain integers and machine addresses, combined by the four basic integer operations with the normal restrictions for subexpressions having machine addresses as operands. The code generator must guarantee that the result of an address expression will actually fit into the field in which it is being used. For some machines, this guarantee cannot be made in general. As a result, either restrictions must be placed upon the expressions used by the code generator or the assembler must take over some aspects of the code generation task. Examples of the latter are the final selection of an instruction from a set whose members differ only in address field size (e.g. short vs. long jumps), and selection of a base register from a set used to access a block of memory. Chapter 11 will consider such problems in detail.

4.2. Global Tables

We extract specific information from the token sequence, structure tree, computation graph or target tree and represent it in special tables to simplify the program representation, to speed up search processes, or to avoid many repetitions of the same data. In particular, we often replace variable-length data by fixed-length keys and thereby simplify storage management.

4.2.1. Symbol Table   The purpose of the symbol table is to provide a unique, fixed-length encoding for the identifiers (and possibly the keywords) occurring in a program. In most programming languages the number of possible identifiers, and hence the length of the encoding, is very large. Since only a tiny fraction of the possible identifiers occur in any particular program, a much shorter encoding suffices and the symbol table must uniquely map the identifiers into this encoding. If the entire set of identifiers is not known a priori then such a mapping can be achieved only by comparing each input character string against those already encountered.

A symbol table module provides three basic operations:

- *initialize*: Enter the standard identifiers.
- *give_symbol (identifier_string) symbol*: Obtain the encoding of a specified identifier.
- *give_string(symbol)identifier_string*: Obtain the identifier having a specified encoding.

Additional operations for delivering identifiers in alphabetical order are necessary if cross-reference tables are to be produced.

Although the symbol table is used primarily for identifiers, we advocate inclusion of keywords as well. No separate recognition procedure is then required for them. With this understanding, we shall continue to speak of the symbol table as though its only contents were identifiers.

The symbol is used later as a key to access the identifier's attributes, so it is often encoded as a pointer to a table containing those attributes. A pointer is satisfactory when only one such table exists and remains in main storage. Positive integers provide a better encoding when several tables must be combined (as for separate compilation in Ada) or moved to secondary storage. In the simplest case the integers chosen would be 1,2,...

Identifiers may be character strings of any length. Since it may be awkward to store a table of strings of various lengths, many compilers either fix the maximum length of an identifier or check only a part of the identifier when computing the mapping. We regard either of these strategies as unacceptable. Clearly the finite size of computer memory will result in limitations, but these should be placed on the *total* number of characters rather than the length of an individual identifier. Failure to check the entire identifier may result in incorrect analysis of the source program with no indication to the programmer.

The solution is to implement the symbol table as two distinct components: a *string table* and a *lookup mechanism*. The string table is simply a very large, packed array of characters, capable of holding all of the distinct identifiers appearing in a program. It is implemented using a conventional virtual storage scheme (Exercise 4.4), which provides for allocation of storage only as it is needed. The string forms of the identifiers are stored contiguously in this array, and are specified by initial index and length.

In view of the large number of entries in the symbol table (often resulting mainly from standard identifiers), hash techniques are preferable to search trees for implementing the lookup mechanism. The length of the hash table must be specified statically, before the number of identifiers is known, so we choose the scheme known as 'open hashing' or 'hash with chaining': A computation is performed on the string to select one of M lists, which is then searched sequentially. If the computation distributes the strings uniformly over the lists, then the length of each will be approximately (number of distinct identifiers)$/M$. By making M large enough the lengths of the lists can be reduced to one or two items.

The first decision to be made is the choice of hash function. It should yield a relatively smooth distribution of the strings across the M lists, evaluation should be rapid, and it must be expressible in the implementation language. One computation that gives good results is to express the string as an integer and take the residue modulo M. M should be a prime number not close to a power of the number of characters in the character set. For example, $M = 127$ would not be a good choice if we were dealing with a 128-character set; $M = 401$, on the other hand, should prove quite satisfactory.

There are two problems with the division method: It is time-consuming for strings whose integer representations exceed the single-length integer range of the implementation language, and it cannot be expressed at all if the implementation language is strongly typed. To solve the former, we generally select some substring for the hash computation. Heads or tails of the string are poor choices because they tend to show regularities (SUM1, SUM2, SUM3 or REDBALL, BLUEBALL, BLACKBALL) that cause the computation to map too many strings into the same list. A better selection is the *center* substring:

if $\mid s \mid \leqslant n$ **then** s **else** *substr*$(s, (\mid s \mid -n)$ **div** $2, n)$;

(Here s is the string, $\mid s \mid$ is the length of s and n is the length of the longest string representable as a single-length integer. The function *substr*(s, f, l) yields the l-character substring of s beginning at the fth character.)

The constraints of a strongly-typed implementation language could be avoided by providing a primitive transfer function to convert a sufficiently short string into an integer for type checking purposes. It is important that this transfer function not involve computation. For example, if the language provides a transfer function from characters to integers, a transfer function from strings to integers could be synthesized by a loop. This approach defeats the whole purpose of the hashing function, however, by introducing a time-consuming computation. It would probably be preferable to use a single character to select the list in this case and accept a longer search!

Comparison of the input identifier with the symbols already present in the table can be speeded up by a variety of quick checks, the simplest of which is comparison of string lengths. Whether or not such checks are useful depends upon the precise costs of string comparison and string table access.

In a multi-pass compiler, the lookup mechanism may be discarded after the lexical analysis has converted identifiers to symbols. The string table must, however, be retained for later tasks such as module linking.

4.2.2. Constant Table

Literal constant values appearing in the program must be retained and possibly manipulated during compilation. Compile-time computation involving numeric operations must be carried out using the semantics of the target machine. In other words, integer operations must conform to the range of the target machine's integer arithmetic, and floating point operations must conform to its radix, range, precision and rounding characteristics. Because of this, we regard the constant table as an abstract data type: It defines a set of values, and any computations involving these values must be carried out by operations that the constant table provides.

We distinguish three conceptually distinct representations of a constant: the character representation appearing in the source program, the internal representation defined by the constant table, and the representation required by the target machine. The constant table module provides conversion operations to accept source representations and return internal representations, and to accept internal representations and return target representations. Source-to-internal conversions are invoked during lexical analysis, while internal-to-target conversions are invoked during assembly. Although the three representations are conceptually distinct, two or more of them may be physically identical in a particular compiler. For example, a LAX floating point constant might have identical internal and target representations.

The constant table module could use a string table of the form introduced in the previous section to store string constants. Since identical string constants occur rarely in a program, no search is needed to enter strings into the table; each is simply inserted as it is encountered. A fixed-length encoding then consists of a string table index and length, which the constant table module delivers as the internal value of the constant. In a multi-pass compiler the string table could reside in secondary storage except during lexical analysis and assembly.

In addition to conversions, the constant table module must provide computational and comparison operations for the internal representations. These operations are used not only for manipulating denotations that appear in the source program, but also for carrying out all computations and comparisons of program-defined values during semantic analysis and code generation. For example, consider the Pascal type constructor **array** [*l..u*] **of** *m*. During semantic analysis, constant table operations are used to verify that the lower bound does not exceed the upper; during code generation they are used to compute the size and alignment of the array.

The requirements of semantic analysis and code generation determine the set of operations that must be provided. In general, these operations should duplicate the behavior of the equivalent operations on the target machine. For example, a character comparison should follow the target machine collating sequence. The range of integer values, however, must normally be larger than that of the target machine. Suppose that we compile a program containing the type constructor of the previous paragraph for the PDP11 (*maxint* $=32767$). Suppose further that $l = -5000$, $u = 5000$ and m is *real*. This is a perfectly legal declaration of an array that will easily fit into the 65536-byte memory of the PDP11, but computation of its size in bytes (40004) overflows the PDP11's integer range.

If the compiler is being executed on the target machine, this requirement for increased range implies that the computational and comparison operations of the constant table must use a multiple-precision representation. Knuth [1969] describes in detail how to implement such a package.

Although, as shown above, overflow of the target machine's arithmetic range is legitimate in some cases, it is often forbidden. When the user writes an expression consisting only of constants, and that expression overflows the range of the target machine, the overflow must be detected if the expression is evaluated by the compiler. This leads to a requirement that the constant table module provide an overflow indicator that is set appropriately by each computational operator to indicate whether or not the computation would overflow on the target machine. Regardless of the state of the overflow indicator, however, the constant table should yield the (mathematically) correct result.

In most programming languages, a particular numeric value can be expressed in many different ways. For example, each of the following LAX floating point numbers expresses the value 'one thousand':

$$1000000E\text{-}3 \quad 1.0E3 \quad .001E6 \quad 1000.0$$

The source-to-internal conversion operators of the constant module should accept only a standardized input format. Nonzero integers are normally represented by a sequence of digits, the first of which is nonzero. A suitable representation for nonzero floating point numbers is the pair (significand, exponent), in which the significand is a sequence of digits without leading or trailing zeros and the exponent is suitably adjusted. The significand can be interpreted either as an integer or a normalized decimal fraction. 'One thousand' would then be represented either as ('1',3) or as ('1',4) respectively. A fractional significand is preferable because it can be truncated or rounded without changing the exponent. Zero is represented by ('0',0). In Section 6.2 we shall show how the standardized format is obtained by the lexical analyzer.

If no floating point arithmetic is provided by the constant table then the significand can be stored in a string table. The internal representation is the triple (string table index, significand length, adjusted exponent). When compile-time floating point operations *are* available, floating point numbers are converted to an internal representation of appropriate accuracy for which the arithmetic of the target machine can be simulated exactly. (Note that decimal arithmetic is satisfactory only if the target machine also uses decimal arithmetic.)

4.2.3. Definition Table   Types, variables, procedures and parameters are examples of *entities*: components of the program whose attributes are established by declaration. Most of the leaves of the structure tree represent uses of entities, at which the entity's attributes must be made available. A definition table abstracts the entities, avoiding the need to explicitly reproduce all of the attributes of an entity at each of the leaves representing its uses. There is one definition table entry for each declared entity, and this entry holds all attributes of that entity. A leaf representing the use of an entity contains a reference to the definition table.

We must emphasize that a definition table merely restates structure tree information in a more compact and accessible form. (Section 8.3.2 will show how to partially automate the choice of information to be included in a definition table.) Thus each form of the structure tree has, at least conceptually, an associated definition table. Transformations of the structure tree imply corresponding transformations of the definition table. Whether the definition table is actually transformed, or a new definition table is built from the transformed tree, is an implementation decision that depends upon two factors:

- The relative costs of transformation and reconstruction.
- The relationship between the traversal needed to reconstruct the information and the traversal using that information.

When assessing the relative costs, we must be certain to consider the extra storage required during the transformation as well as the code involved.

The second factor mentioned above may require some elaboration: Consider the definition table used during semantic analysis and that used during code generation. Although the structure tree may be almost the same for these two processes, the interesting attributes of defined objects are usually quite different. During semantic analysis we are concerned with source properties; during code generation with target properties. Thus the definition tables for the two processes will differ. Suppose further that our code generation strategy requires a single depth-first, left-to-right traversal of the structure tree *given that the definition table is available*.

If the definition table can be rebuilt during a single depth-first, left-to-right traversal of the structure tree, and every attribute becomes available before it is needed for code generation, then rebuilding can be combined with code generation and the second factor noted above does not lead to increased costs. When this condition is *not* satisfied, the second factor *does* increase the rebuilding cost and this must be taken into account. It may then be cheaper to transform the definition table between the last semantic analysis traversal and the first code generation traversal. (The attribute dependency analysis presented in Section 8.2 is used to decide whether the condition is satisfied.)

A definition table is generally an unstructured collection of entries. Any arbitrary entry can be accessed via a pointer in order to read an attribute or assign a new value. In a one-pass compiler, a stack strategy could also be used: At every definition a new entry is pushed onto the top of the stack, and at the end of a range all definitions found in the range are popped. This organization has the advantage that only relevant entries must be held in storage.

Copies of some of the more-frequently accessed attributes of an entity may be included in each leaf representing a use of that entity. The choice of such attributes depends upon the particular compiler design; we shall return to this question several times, in Chapters 9, 10 and 14. It may be that these considerations lead to including *all* attributes in the leaf. The definition table then ceases to exist as a separate data structure.

4.3. Notes and References

Postfix, triples, and quadruples are often discussed in isolation as 'internal forms' of the program, without reference to the structures they represent (see Gries [1971] for example). Such discussions tend to bog down in a morass of special cases and extensions once they move beyond the treatment of arithmetic expressions. We believe that thinking in terms of a tree helps the compiler designer to concentrate on the important relationships present in the text and to arrive at a more coherent representation. Once this has been derived, a variety of linearizations may be used depending upon the particular compiler design.

Most authors lump the various tables discussed in Section 4.2 into a single dictionary, which they often call 'the symbol table' [Gries 1971, Bauer 1976, Aho 1977a]. The concept of separate tables seems to be restricted to descriptions of multi-pass compilers, as a mechanism for reducing main storage requirements [Naur 1964]. This is not invariably true, however, especially when one considers the literature on ALGOL 68 [Peck 1971]. In his description of a multi-pass Pascal compiler, Hartmann [1977] uses separate tables both to reduce core requirements and to provide better compiler structure.

Lookup mechanisms have concerned a large number of authors; the most comprehensive treatment is that of Knuth [1973]. He gives details of a variety of mechanisms, including hashing, and shows how they compare for different applications. It appears that hashing is the method of choice for symbol table implementation, but there may be some circumstances in which binary trees are superior [Palmer 1974]. For symbol tables with a fixed number of known entries (e.g. keywords) Cichelli [1980] and Cercone [1982] describe a way of obtaining a hash function that does not have any collisions and hence requires no collision resolution.

Exercises

4.1. [Sale 1971, McIlroy 1974] Specify abstract tokens for FORTRAN 66.

4.2. Specify a *target_node* (Figure 4.6) suitable for some machine with which you are familiar.

4.3. Is a symbol table needed to map identifiers in a compiler for Minimal Standard BASIC? Explain.

4.4. Implement a string table module, using a software paging scheme: Statically allocate an array of pointers (a 'page table') to blocks of fixed size ('pages'). Initially no additional blocks are allocated. When a string must be stored, try to fit it into a currently-allocated page. If this cannot be done, dynamically allocate a new page and place a pointer to it in the page table. Carefully define the interface to your module.

4.5. Implement a symbol table module that provides a lookup mechanism, and uses the module of Exercise 4.4 to store the identifier string.

4.6. Identifier strings are specified in the module of Exercise 4.5 by the pair (string table index, length). On a computer like the DEC PDP11, this specification occupies 8 bytes. Comment on the relative merits of this scheme versus one in which identifier strings are stored directly if they are no longer than k bytes, and a string table is used for those whose length exceeds k. What should the value of k be for the PDP11? Would this scheme be appropriate for a multipass compiler?

4.7. Consider the FORTRAN expression 'X * 3.14159265358979932385 * Y'. Assume that no explicit type has been given for X, and that Y has been declared DOUBLE PRECISION.
   a. Should the constant be interpreted as a single or double precision value? Explain.
   b. For some machine with which you are familiar, estimate the relative errors in the single and double precision representations of the constant.
   c. Explain the relevance of this example to the problem of selecting the internal representation to be provided by the constant table for floating point numbers.

CHAPTER 5
Elements of Formal Systems

Formal grammars, in particular context-free grammars, are the tools most frequently used to describe the structure of programs. They permit a lucid representation of that structure in the form of parse trees, and one can (for the most part mechanically) specify automata that will accept all correctly-structured programs (and only these). The automata are easy to modify so that they output any convenient encoding of the parse tree.

We limit our discussion to the definitions and theorems necessary to understand and use techniques explained in Chapters 6 and 7, and many theorems are cited without proof. In the cases where we do sketch proofs, we restrict ourselves to the constructive portions upon which practical algorithms are based. (We reference such constructions by giving the number of the associated theorem.) A formally complete treatment would exceed both the objectives of and size constraints on this book. Readers who wish to delve more deeply into the theoretical aspects of the subject should consult the notes and references at the end of this chapter.

5.1. Descriptive Tools

In this section we first review the standard mathematical notation used to describe sets of strings. We then introduce some formal systems for the production of such sets and with these define certain classes of languages. Finally, we discuss the representation of the structure of strings by means of trees and give a complete example.

5.1.1. Strings and Rewriting Systems We begin with a *vocabulary* (or *alphabet*), V: A finite, nonempty set of *symbols* having no discernible structure. (At least we take no notice of further structure on the level of abstraction we are considering.) One example of a vocabulary is the set of characters available on a particular computer, others are the set of basic symbols defined by a particular language (e.g. identifier, integer, +, **begin**) and the set of syntactic terms we use to describe the structure of a program. We may attach semantic significance to some of the symbols in the vocabulary, without explaining them further by means of the formal systems introduced in this chapter.

The set of all finite strings $x_1 \cdots x_n$, $n \geqslant 1$, formed by concatenating elements of V is denoted by V^+. V^* denotes V^+ augmented by adding the *empty string* (which contains no symbols). We shall denote the empty string by ϵ; it is both a left and right identity for concatenation: $\epsilon\chi = \chi\epsilon = \chi$, $\chi \in V^*$. The count, n, of symbols in a string $\chi = x_1 \cdots x_n$ is called the *length* of χ, and is denoted by $|\chi|$. Thus $|\epsilon| = 0$.

Definition 5.1. Let $\chi = \alpha\omega$, $\alpha, \omega \in V^*$. The string α is called a *head*, and the string ω a *tail*, of χ. If $\alpha \neq \epsilon$ ($\omega \neq \epsilon$) then it is a *proper* head (tail) of χ.

Each subset of V^* is called a *language* over vocabulary V. The elements of a language are called *sentences*. Interesting languages generally contain infinitely many sentences, and hence cannot be defined by enumeration. We therefore define each such language, L, by specifying a process that generates all of its sentences, and no other elements of V^*. This process may be characterized by a binary, transitive relation $\Rightarrow^+$ over V^*, such that $L = \{\chi \mid \zeta \Rightarrow^+ \chi\}$ for a distinguished string ζ in V^*. We term the relation $\Rightarrow^+$ a *derivative relation*.

Definition 5.2. A pair $(V, \Rightarrow^+)$ consisting of a vocabulary V and a derivative relation $\Rightarrow^+$, is called a *formal system*.

A derivative relation usually cannot be defined by enumeration either. We shall concern ourselves only with relations that can be described by a finite set of pairs (σ, τ) of strings from V^*. We call such pairs *productions*, and write them as $\sigma \rightarrow \tau$. The transitive closure of the finite relation described by these productions yields a derivative relation. More precisely:

Definition 5.3. A pair (V, P), consisting of a vocabulary V and a finite set, P, of productions $\sigma \rightarrow \tau$ ($\sigma, \tau \in V^*$) is called a *general rewriting* (or *Semi-Thue*) system.

Definition 5.4. A string χ is *directly derivable* from a string π (symbolically $\pi \Rightarrow \chi$) by a general rewriting system (V, P) if there exist strings σ, τ, μ, ν in V^* such that $\pi = \mu\sigma\nu$, $\chi = \mu\tau\nu$ and $\sigma \rightarrow \tau$ is an element of P.

Definition 5.5. A string χ is *derivable* from a string π (symbolically $\pi \Rightarrow^+ \chi$)

by a general rewriting system (V, P) if there exist strings $\rho_0, \ldots, \rho_n$ in V^* $(n \geqslant 1)$ such that $\pi = \rho_0$, $\rho_n = \chi$ and $\rho_{i-1} \Rightarrow \rho_i$, $i = 1, \ldots, n$. The sequence $\rho_0, \ldots, \rho_n$ is called a *derivation of length n.*

We write $\pi \Rightarrow^* \chi$ to indicate that either $\pi = \chi$ or $\pi \Rightarrow^+ \chi$. If χ is (directly) derivable from π, we also say that χ is *(directly) reducible to* π. Without loss of generality, we shall assume that derivations $\pi \Rightarrow^+ \pi$ of a string from itself are impossible.

5.1.2. Grammars   Using the general rewriting system defined by Figure 5.1, it is possible to derive from E every correct algebraic expression consisting of the operators $+$ and $*$, the variable i, and the parentheses ( ). Many other strings can be derived also, as shown in Figure 5.2. In the remainder of this chapter we shall concentrate on rewriting systems in which the vocabulary is made up of two disjoint subsets: T, a set of *terminals*, and N, a set of *nonterminals (syntactic variables)*. We will ultimately be interested only in those strings derivable from a distinguished nonterminal (the *axiom* or *start symbol*) and consisting entirely of terminals. (Thus we speak of *generative* systems. One could instead consider *analytic* systems in which the axiom is derived from a string of terminals. We shall return to this concept with Definitions 5.12 and 5.20.)

$$\{E, T, F, +, *, (,), i\}$$
a) The vocabulary V

$$\{\, E \rightarrow T, \quad E \rightarrow E + T,$$
$$T \rightarrow F, \quad T \rightarrow T * F,$$
$$F \rightarrow i, \quad F \rightarrow (E) \,\}$$
b) The productions P

Figure 5.1. A General Rewriting System (V, P)

$$E \Rightarrow T$$
$$T \Rightarrow T * F$$
$$T * F \Rightarrow T * i$$

a) Some immediate derivations

$$E \Rightarrow^* T * i \qquad \text{(length 3)}$$
$$E \Rightarrow^* i + i * i \qquad \text{(length 8)}$$
$$TiE \Rightarrow^* iii \qquad \text{(length 5)}$$
$$TiE \Rightarrow^* TiE \qquad \text{(length 0)}$$
$$E \Rightarrow^* T \qquad \text{(length 1)}$$

b) Additional derivations

Figure 5.2. Derivations

Definition 5.6. A quadruple $G = (T,N,P,Z)$ is called a *grammar* for the language $L(G) = \{\chi \in T^* \mid Z \Rightarrow^* \chi\}$ *if T and N are disjoint,* $(T \cup N,P)$ *is is a general rewriting system, and Z is an element of N.* We say that two grammars G and G' are *equivalent* if $L(G) = L(G')$.

Figure 5.3 illustrates these concepts with two grammars that generate algebraic expressions in the variable i. These grammars are equivalent

$$T = \{+,^*,(,),i\}$$

$$N = \{E,T,F\}$$

$$P = \{\begin{array}{ll} E \rightarrow T, & E \rightarrow E+T, \\ T \rightarrow F, & T \rightarrow T^*F, \\ F \rightarrow i, & F \rightarrow (E) \} \end{array}$$

$$Z = E$$

a) A grammar incorporating (V,P) from Figure 5.1

$$T = \{+,\ ^*,(,),i\}$$

$$N = \{E,E',T,T',F\}$$

$$P = \{\begin{array}{ll} E \rightarrow T, & E \rightarrow TE', \\ E' \rightarrow +T, & E' \rightarrow +TE', \\ T \rightarrow F, & T \rightarrow FT', \\ T' \rightarrow ^*F, & T' \rightarrow ^*FT, \\ F \rightarrow i, & F \rightarrow (E) \} \end{array}$$

$$Z = E$$

b) A grammar incorporating another general rewriting system

Figure 5.3. Equivalent Grammars

according to Definition 5.6.

Grammars may be classified by the complexity of their productions:

Definition 5.7. (Chomsky Hierarchy). The grammar $G = (T,N,P,Z)$ is a

- *type 0* grammar if each production has the form $\sigma \rightarrow \tau$, $\sigma \in V^+$ and $\tau \in V^*$.
- *type 1* (*context-sensitive*) grammar if each production has the form $\mu A \nu \rightarrow \mu \chi \nu$, $\mu, \nu \in V^*$, $A \in N$ and $\chi \in V^+$.
- *type 2* (*context-free*) grammar if each production has the form $A \rightarrow \chi$, $A \in N$ and $\chi \in V^*$.
- *type 3* (*regular*) grammar if each production has either the form $A \rightarrow a$, $A \in N$ and $a \in T \cup \{\epsilon\}$ or the form $A \rightarrow aB$, $A,B \in N$ and $a \in T$.

If a grammar that generates a language is context-sensitive (context-free, regular), then we also term the language itself context-sensitive (context-free, regular). Regular and context-free grammars are the most interesting to compiler writers. The former are usually used to describe the basic symbols (e.g. identifiers, constants) of a language, while the latter describe the structure of a program. From now on, we restrict our attention to these two grammar classes.

Although we admit *ε-productions* (productions whose right-hand side consists of the empty string) in context-free grammars, we are interested only in languages that do not include the empty string. Such languages can always be described by *ε-free grammars* — grammars without ε-productions. Therefore ε-productions will only be used when they result in more convenient descriptions.

We assume further that every symbol in the vocabulary will appear in the derivation of at least one sentence. Thus the grammar will not contain any *useless* symbols. (This is not always true for actual descriptions of programming languages, as illustrated by the LAX definition of Appendix A.)

5.1.3. Derivations and Parse Trees   Each production in a regular grammar can have at most one nonterminal on the right-hand side. This property guarantees—in contrast to the context-free grammars—that each sentence of

$$T = \{n, ., +, -, E\}$$

$$N = \{C, F, I, X, S, U\}$$

$$P = \{C \to n, C \to nF, C \to .I,$$
$$F \to .I, F \to ES,$$
$$I \to n, I \to nX,$$
$$X \to ES,$$
$$S \to n, S \to +U, S \to -U,$$
$$U \to n \}$$

$$Z = C$$

a) A grammar for real constants

C	C	C
n	.I	nF
	.n	n.I
		n.nX
		n.nES
		n.nE + U
		n.nE + n

b) Three derivations according to the grammar of (a)

Figure 5.4. Derivations According to a Regular Grammar

$$
\begin{array}{lll}
E & E & E \\
E+T & E+T & E+T \\
T+T & E+T*F & E+T*F \\
F+T & T+T*F & E+T*i \\
i+T & T+F*F & E+F*i \\
i+T*F & T+F*i & E+i*i \\
i+F*F & F+F*i & T+i*i \\
i+i*F & i+F*i & F+i*i \\
i+i*i & i+i*i & i+i*i
\end{array}
$$

Figure 5.5. Derivations According to a Context-Free Grammar

the language has exactly one derivation when the grammar is unambiguous (Definition 5.11).

Figure 5.4a is a regular grammar that generates the integers and real numbers if n represents an arbitrary sequence of digits. Three derivations according to this grammar are shown in Figure 5.4b. Each string except the last in a derivation contains exactly one nonterminal, from which a new string must be derived in the next step. The last string consists only of terminals. The sequence of steps in each derivation of this example is determined by the derived sentence.

The situation is different for context-free grammars, which may have any number of nonterminals on the right-hand side of each production. Figure 5.5 shows that several derivations, differing only in the sequence of application of the productions, are possible for a given sentence. (These derivations are constructed according to the grammar of Figure 5.3a.)

In the left-hand column, a *leftmost derivation* was used: At each step a new string was derived from the leftmost nonterminal. Similarly, a *rightmost derivation* was used in the right-hand column. A nonterminal was chosen arbitrarily at each step to produce the center derivation.

A grammar ascribes structure to a string not by giving a particular sequence of derivation steps but by showing that a particular substring is derived from a particular nonterminal. For example, in Figure 5.5 the substring $i*i$ is derived from the single nonterminal T. We interpret this property of the derivation to mean that $i*i$ forms a single *semantic* unit: an instance of the operator $*$ applied to the i's as operands. It is important to realize that the grammar was constructed in a particular way specifically to ascribe a semantically relevant structure to each sentence in the language. We cannot be satisfied with *any* grammar that defines a particular language; we must choose one reflecting the semantic structure of each sentence. For example, suppose that the rules $E \rightarrow E+T$ and $T \rightarrow T*F$ of Figure 5.3a had been replaced by $E \rightarrow E*T$ and $T \rightarrow T+F$ respectively. The modified grammar would describe the same language, but would ascribe a different structure to its sentences: It would imply that additions should take precedence over multiplications.

Substrings derived from single nonterminals are called *phrases*:

Definition 5.8. Consider a grammar $G = (T,N,P,Z)$. The string $\chi \in V^+$ is a *phrase* (for X) of $\mu\chi\nu$ if and only if $Z \Rightarrow^* \mu X\nu \Rightarrow^+ \mu\chi\nu$ $(\mu,\nu \in V^*, X \in N)$. It is a *simple phrase* of $\mu\chi\nu$ if and only if $Z \Rightarrow^* \mu X\nu \Rightarrow \mu\chi\nu$.

Notice that a phrase need not consist solely of terminals.

Each of the three derivations of Figure 5.5 identifies the same set of simple phrases. They are therefore equivalent in the sense that they ascribe identical *phrase structure* to the string $i+i*i$. In order to have a single representation for the entire set of equivalent derivations, one that makes the structure of the sentence obvious, we introduce the notion of a parse tree (see Appendix B for the definition of an ordered tree):

Definition 5.9. Consider an ordered tree (K, D) with root k_0 and label function $f : K \rightarrow M$. Let $k_1, \ldots, k_n$, $(n > 0)$ be the immediate successors of k_0. (K, D) is a *parse tree according to the grammar* (T, N, P, Z) if the following conditions hold:

(a) $M \subseteq V \cup \{\epsilon\}$
(b) $f(k_0) = Z$
(c) $Z \rightarrow f(k_1) \cdots f(k_n) \in P$
(d) if $f(k_i) \in T$, or if $n = 1$ and $f(k_i) = \epsilon$, then k_i is a leaf
(e) if $f(k_i) \in N$ then k_i is the root of a parse tree according to the grammar $(T,N,P,f(k_i))$

Figure 5.6 is a tree for $i+i*i$ according to the grammar of Figure 5.3a, as can be shown by recursive application of Definition 5.9.

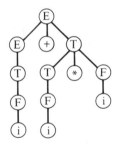

Figure 5.6. The Parse Tree for $i+i*i$

We can obtain any string in any derivation of a sentence from the parse tree of that sentence by selecting a minimum set of nodes, removal of which will break all root-to-leaf paths. (Such a set of nodes is called a *cut* — see Definition B.8.) For example, in Figure 5.6 the set $\{T, +, T, *, F\}$ (the third row of nodes, plus '$+$' from the second row) has this property and $T+T*F$ is the fourth step in the center derivation of Figure 5.5.

Theorem 5.10. *In a parse tree according to a grammar* $G = (T,N,P,Z)$, *a set of nodes* $(k_1, \ldots, k_n)$ *is a cut if and only if* $Z \Rightarrow^* f(k_1) \cdots f(k_n)$.

A parse tree specifies the phrase structure of a sentence. With the grammars given so far, only one parse tree corresponds to each sentence. This may not always be true, however, as illustrated by Figure 5.7. The grammar of Figure 5.7a describes the same language as that of Figure 5.3a, but many sentences have several parse trees.

Definition 5.11. A sentence is *ambiguous* if its derivations may be described by at least two distinct parse trees (or leftmost derivations or rightmost derivations). A grammar is ambiguous if there is at least one ambiguous sentence in the language it defines; otherwise the grammar is *unambiguous*.

Figure 5.7b shows two parse trees for $i + i*i$ that are essentially different for our purposes because we associate two distinct sequences of operations with them. If we use an ambiguous grammar to describe the language (and this may be a useful thing to do), then either the ambiguity must involve only phrases with no semantic relevance or we must provide additional rules for removing the ambiguity.

$$T = \{+, *, i\}$$

$$N = \{E\}$$

$$P = \{E \rightarrow E + E, E \rightarrow E * E, E \rightarrow i\}$$

$$Z = E$$

a) An ambiguous grammar

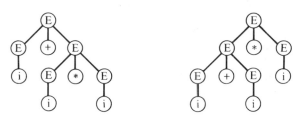

b) Two parse trees for $i + i*i$

Figure 5.7. Ambiguity

5.1.4. Extended Backus-Naur Form

Appendix A uses a notation known as *extended Backus-Naur form* (EBNF) to describe LAX. This notation allows us to describe a grammar in a more compact form. Moreover, as we shall see in Chapter 7, a parser can be derived easily from the specification of a language written in EBNF. In this section we illustrate the techniques we have been discussing by giving a formal definition of EBNF; an informal description appears at the beginning of Appendix A.

Figure 5.8a is the grammar for EBNF. When a specification is written in EBNF, character strings are used to represent the elements of T as indicated in Figure 5.8b. A complete specification for EBNF itself appears in Figure 5.8c. Given a specification such as that of Figure 5.8c, we can derive one or more grammars that define the same language. In this manner we establish the 'meaning' of the specification.

The derivation proceeds from a parse tree (K,D) of the given specification according to the grammar of Figure 5.8a. In addition to the label function f from Definition 5.9, we define $h:K \rightarrow L \cup I$, where L is the set of identifiers and literals appearing in the specification and I is a set of unique identifiers. L and I are disjoint; h associates an element of L with every leaf of K and an element of I with every non-leaf node. An ele-

$T = \{identifier,literal,is,or,lpn,rpn,lbk,rbk,plus,star,period,separator\}$

$N = \{specification,rule,expression,tertiary,secondary,primary,unit,atom\}$

$P = \{specification \rightarrow rule,\ specification \rightarrow specification\ rule,$
$\quad\quad rule \rightarrow identifier\ is\ expression\ period$
$\quad\quad expression \rightarrow tertiary,\ expression \rightarrow expression\ separator\ atom,$
$\quad\quad tertiary \rightarrow secondary,\ tertiary \rightarrow tertiary\ or\ secondary,$
$\quad\quad secondary \rightarrow primary,\ secondary \rightarrow secondary\ primary,$
$\quad\quad primary \rightarrow unit,\ primary \rightarrow unit\ star,\ primary \rightarrow unit\ plus,$
$\quad\quad primary \rightarrow lbk\ expression\ rbk,$
$\quad\quad unit \rightarrow atom,\ unit \rightarrow lpn\ expression\ rpn,$
$\quad\quad atom \rightarrow identifier,\ atom \rightarrow literal\}$

$Z = \quad specification$

a) Grammar for EBNF

identifier: Sequence of letters, digits and underscores.
literal: String delimited by apostrophes.

lpn : (	*rpn* :)	*lbk* : [	*rbk* :]	*is* : ::=
or : |	*star* : *	*plus* : +	*period* : .	*separator* : ||

b) Representation used in this book for EBNF terminals

$specification ::= rule + .$
$rule ::= identifier\ '::='\ expression\ '.'.$
$expression ::= (primary + \ |\ \ '|'\ |\ expression\ '|'\ |\ '\ atom\ .$
$primary ::= unit\ ['*'\ |\ '+']\ |\ '['\ expression\ ']'.$
$unit ::= atom\ |\ '('\ expression\ ')'.$
$atom ::= identifier\ |\ literal\ .$

c) A possible EBNF specification for EBNF

Figure 5.8. Extended Backus-Naur Form

ment of L may be associated with any number of leaves, but there is a 1-1 correspondence between non-leaf nodes and elements of I.

$L \cup I$ is the vocabulary of the grammar that we shall derive from the EBNF specification. All elements of I are nonterminals of the grammar, as are identifiers appearing on the left of ':: =' in an EBNF rule. All literals and identifiers not appearing on the left of ':: =' are terminals. Formally:

$$R = \{h(k) \mid (k', k) \in D, f(k') = rule, f(k) = identifier\}$$

$$T = L - R$$

$$N = R \cup I$$

Here R is the set of *rule identifiers*. If the EBNF specification is well-formed then there will be exactly one element of R that does not appear on the right of ':: =' in any rule. This element is the axiom of the derived grammar:

$$Z = r \in (R - \{h(k) \mid (k', k) \in D, f(k') = atom\})$$

A set of productions can be derived from every non-leaf node of the parse tree, and P is the union of those sets. Consider each subtree formed from a non-leaf node k_0 and its ordered immediate successors $k_1, k_2, \ldots, k_n$. The derived productions depend upon the structure of the subtree (given by a production of Figure 5.8a) and the labels of the nodes in the subtree as follows:

For subtree	derive the production set
rule → identifier is expression period	$\{h(k_1) \rightarrow h(k_3)\}$
expression → expression separator atom	$\{h(k_0) \rightarrow h(k_1), h(k_0) \rightarrow$ $h(k_0) \, h(k_3) \, h(k_1)\}$
tertiary → tertiary or secondary	$\{h(k_0) \rightarrow h(k_1), h(k_0) \rightarrow h(k_3)\}$
secondary → secondary primary	$\{h(k_0) \rightarrow h(k_1) \, h(k_2)\}$
primary → unit star	$\{h(k_0) \rightarrow \epsilon, h(k_0) \rightarrow h(k_0) \, h(k_1)\}$
primary → unit plus	$\{h(k_0) \rightarrow h(k_1), h(k_0) \rightarrow h(k_0) \, h(k_1)\}$
primary → lbk expression rbk	$\{h(k_0) \rightarrow \epsilon, h(k_0) \rightarrow h(k_2)\}$
unit → lpn expression rpn	$\{h(k_0) \rightarrow h(k_2)\}$

Derive the empty set of productions for any subtree with $h(k_0) = specification$, and derive $\{h(k_0) \rightarrow h(k_1)\}$ for any subtree not yet mentioned.

The grammar derived from Figure 5.8c by this process will have more productions than Figure 5.8a. The extra productions can be removed by a simple substitution: If $B \in N$ occurs exactly twice in a grammar, once in a production of the form $A \rightarrow \mu B \nu$ and once in a production of the form $B \rightarrow \beta$ ($\mu, \beta, \nu \in V^*$), then B can be eliminated and the two productions replaced by $A \rightarrow \mu \beta \nu$. After all such substitutions have been made, the resulting grammar will differ from Figure 5.8a only in the representation of vocabulary symbols.

5.2. Regular Grammars and Finite Automata

A grammar specifies a process for generating sentences, and thus allows us to give a finite description of an infinite language. The analysis phase of the compiler, however, must recognize the phrase structure of a given sentence: It must *parse* the sentence. Assuming that the language has been described by a grammar, we are interested in techniques for automatically generating a recognizer from that grammar. There are two reasons for this requirement:

- It provides a guarantee that the language recognized by the compiler is identical to that defined by the grammar.
- It simplifies the task of the compiler writer.

We shall use automata, which we introduce as special cases of general rewriting systems, as models for the parsing process. In this section we develop a theoretical basis for regular languages and finite automata, and then extend the concepts and algorithms to context-free languages and pushdown automata in Section 5.3. The implementation of the automata is covered in Chapters 6 and 7.

5.2.1. Finite Automata

Definition 5.12. A *finite automaton (finite state acceptor)* is a quintuple $A = (T,Q,R,q_0,F)$, where Q is a nonempty set, $(T \cup Q,R)$ is a general rewriting system, q_0 is an element of Q and F is a subset of Q. The sets T and Q are disjoint. Each element of R has the form $qt \rightarrow q'$, where q and q' are elements of Q and t is an element of T. We say that A *accepts* a set of strings $L(A) = \{\tau \in T^* \mid q_0\tau \Rightarrow^* q, q \in F\}$. Two automata, A and A' are *equivalent* if and only if $L(A) = L(A')$.

We can conceive of the finite automaton as a machine that reads a given input string out of a buffer one symbol at a time and changes its internal state upon absorbing each symbol. Q is the set of internal states, with q_0 being the *initial state* and F the set of *final states*. We say that a finite automaton is *in state q* when the current string in the derivation has the form $q\tau$. It *makes a transition* from state q to state q' if $\tau = t\chi$ and $qt \rightarrow q'$ is an element of R. Each state transition removes one symbol from the input string.

Theorem 5.13. *For every regular grammar, G, there exists a finite automaton, A, such that $L(A) = L(G)$.*

The proof of this theorem is an algorithm to construct A, given $G = (T,N,P,Z)$. Let $A = (T,N \cup \{f\},R,Z,F)$, $f \notin N$. R is constructed from P by the following rules:

1. If $X \to t$ $(X \in N, t \in T)$ is a production of P then let $Xt \to f$ be a production of R.
2. If $X \to tY$ $(X, Y \in N, t \in T)$ is a production of P then let $Xt \to Y$ be a production of R.

Further, $F = \{f\} \cup \{X \mid X \to \epsilon \in P\}$. Figure 5.9 is an automaton constructed by this process from the grammar of Figure 5.4a.

$$T = \{n, ., +, -, E\}$$

$$Q = \{C, F, I, X, S, U, q\}$$

$$R = \{ \; Cn \to q, \; Cn \to F, \; C. \to I,$$
$$F. \to I, \; FE \to S,$$
$$In \to q, \; In \to X,$$
$$XE \to S,$$
$$Sn \to q, \; S + \to U, \; S - \to U,$$
$$Un \to q \; \}$$

$$q_0 = C$$

$$F = \{q\}$$

Figure 5.9. An Automaton Corresponding to Figure 5.4a

One can show by induction that the automaton constructed in this manner has the following characteristic: For any derivation $Z\tau\chi \Rightarrow^* X\chi \Rightarrow^* q$ $(\tau, \chi \in T^*, X \in N, \tau\chi \in L(A), q \in F)$, the state X specifies the nonterminal symbol of G that must have been used to derive the string χ. Clearly this statement is true for the initial state Z if $\tau\chi$ belongs to $L(G)$. It remains true until the final state q, which does not generate any further symbols, is reached. With the help of this interpretation it is easy to prove that each sentence of $L(G)$ also belongs to $L(A)$ and vice-versa.

Figure 5.9 is an unsatisfactory automaton in practice because at certain steps — for example in state I with input symbol n — several transitions are possible. This is not a theoretical problem since the automaton is *capable* of producing a derivation for any string in the language. When implementing this automaton in a compiler, however, we must make some arbitrary decision at each step where more than one production might apply. An incorrect decision requires *backtracking* in order to seek another possibility. There are three reasons why backtracking should be avoided if possible:

● The time required to parse a string with backtracking may increase exponentially with the length of the string.

● If the automaton does not accept the string then it will be recognized as incorrect. A parse with backtrack makes pinpointing the error almost impossible. (This is illustrated by attempting to parse the string

$n.nE++n$ with the automaton of Figure 5.9 trying the rules in the sequence in which they are written.)

- Other compiler actions are often associated with state transitions. Backtracking then requires unraveling of actions already completed, generally a very difficult task.

In order to avoid backtracking, additional constraints must be placed upon the automata that we are prepared to accept as models for our recognition algorithms.

Definition 5.14. An automaton is *deterministic* if every derivation can be continued by at most one move.

A finite automaton is therefore deterministic if the left-hand sides of all rules are distinct. It can be completely described by a *state table* that has one row for each element of Q and one column for each element of T. Entry (q,t) contains q' if and only if the production $qt \to q'$ is an element of R. The rows corresponding to q_0 and to the elements of F are suitably marked.

Backtracking can always be avoided when recognizing strings in a regular language:

Theorem 5.15. *For every regular grammar, G, there exists a deterministic finite automaton, A, such that $L(A)=L(G)$.*

Following construction 5.13, we can derive an automaton from a regular grammar $G=(T,N,P,Z)$ such that, during acceptance of a sentence in $L(G)$, the state at each point specifies the element of N used to derive the remainder of the string. Suppose that the productions $X \to tU$ and $X \to tV$ belong to P. When t is the next input symbol, the remainder of the string could have been derived either from U or from V. If A is to be deterministic, however, R must contain exactly one production of the form $Xt \to q'$. Thus the state q' must specify a *set* of nonterminals, any one of which could have been used to derive the remainder of the string. This interpretation of the states leads to the following inductive algorithm for determining Q, R and F of a deterministic automaton $A = (T,Q,R,q_0,F)$. (In this algorithm, q represents a subset N_q of $N \cup \{f\}$, $f \notin N$):

1. Initially let $Q = \{q_0\}$ and $R = \varnothing$, with $N_{q_0} = \{Z\}$.

2. Let q be an element of Q that has not yet been considered. Perform steps (3)-(5) for each $t \in T$.

3. Let $next(q,t) = \{U \mid \exists\ X \in N_q$ such that $X \to tU \in P\}$.

4. If there is an $X \in N_q$ such that $X \to t \in P$ or $X \to \epsilon \in P$ then add f to $next(q,t)$ if it is not already present.

5. If $next(q,t) \neq \varnothing$ then let q' be the state representing $N_{q'} = next(q,t)$.

Add q' to Q and $qt \rightarrow q'$ to R if they are not already present.

6. If all states of Q have been considered then let $F = \{q \mid f \in N_q\}$ and stop. Otherwise return to step (2).

You can easily convince yourself that this construction leads to a deterministic finite automaton A such that $L(A)=L(G)$. In particular, the algorithm terminates: All states represent subsets of $N \cup \{f\}$, of which there are only a finite number.

To illustrate this procedure, consider the construction of a deterministic finite automaton that recognizes strings generated by the grammar of Figure 5.4a. The state table for this grammar, showing the correspondence between states and sets of nonterminals, is given in Figure 5.10a. You should derive

	n	$.$	$+$	$-$	E	
q_0	q_1	q_2				$\{C\}$
q_1		q_2			q_3	$\{f,F\}$
q_2	q_4					$\{I\}$
q_3	q_5		q_6	q_6		$\{S\}$
q_4					q_3	$\{f,X\}$
q_5						$\{f\}$
q_6	q_5					$\{U\}$

a) The state table

$$T = \{n,.,+,-,E\}$$

$$Q = \{q_0,q_1,q_2,q_3,q_4,q_5,q_6\}$$

$$\begin{aligned} P = \{ \ & q_0 n \rightarrow q_1, q_0. \rightarrow q_2, \\ & q_1. \rightarrow q_2, q_1 E \rightarrow q_3, \\ & q_2 n \rightarrow q_4, \\ & q_3 n \rightarrow q_5, q_3 + \rightarrow q_6, q_3 - \rightarrow q_6, \\ & q_4 E \rightarrow q_3, \\ & q_6 n \rightarrow q_5 \ \} \end{aligned}$$

$$F = \{q_1,q_4,q_5\}$$

b) The complete automaton

Figure 5.10. A Deterministic Automaton Corresponding to Figure 5.4a

this state table for yourself, following the steps of the algorithm. Begin with a single empty row for q_0 and work across it, filling in each entry that corresponds to a valid transition. Each time a distinct set of nonterminal symbols is generated, add an empty row to the table. The algorithm terminates when all rows have been processed.

Theorem 5.16. *For every finite automaton, A, there exists a regular grammar, G, such that $L(G) = L(A)$.*

Theorems 5.15 and 5.16 together establish the fact that finite automata and regular grammars are equivalent. To prove Theorem 5.16 we construct the production set P of the grammar $G = (T,Q,P,q_0)$ from the automaton (T,Q,R,q_0,F) as follows:

$$P = \{q \to tq' \mid qt \to q' \in R\} \cup \{q \to \epsilon \mid q \in F\}$$

5.2.2. State Diagrams and Regular Expressions   The phrase structure of the basic symbols of the language is usually not interesting, and in fact may simply make the description harder to understand. Two additional formalisms, both of which avoid the need for irrelevant structuring, are available for regular languages. The first is the representation of a finite automaton by a directed graph:

Definition 5.17.: Let $A = (T,Q,R,q_0,F)$ be a finite automaton, $D = \{(q,q') \mid \exists t, qt \to q' \in R\}$, and $f:(q,q') \to \{t \mid qt \to q' \in R\}$ be a mapping from D into the powerset of T. The directed graph (Q,D) with edge labels $f((q,q'))$ is called the *state diagram* of the automaton A.

Figure 5.11a is the state diagram of the automaton described in Figure 5.10b. The nodes corresponding to elements of F have been represented as squares, while the remaining nodes are represented as circles. Only the state numbers appear in the nodes: 0 stands for q_0, 1 for q_1, and so forth.

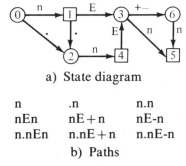

a) State diagram

n	.n	n.n
nEn	nE+n	nE-n
n.nEn	n.nE+n	n.nE-n

b) Paths

Figure 5.11. Another Description of Figure 5.10b

In a state diagram, the sequence of edge labels along a path beginning at q_0 and ending at a state in F is a sentence of $L(A)$. Figure 5.11a has exactly 12 such paths. The corresponding sentences are given in Figure 5.11b.

A state diagram specifies a regular language. Another characterization is the regular expression:

Definition 5.18. Given a vocabulary V, and the symbols E, ϵ, $+$, $*$, (and) not in V. A string ρ over $V \cup \{E, \epsilon, +, *, (,)\}$ is a *regular expression* over V if
1. ρ is a single symbol of V or one of the symbols E or ϵ, or if
2. ρ has the form $(X+Y)$, (XY) or $(X)^*$ where X and Y are regular expressions.

Every regular expression results from a finite number of applications of rules (1) and (2). It describes a language over V: The symbol E describes the empty language, ϵ describes the language consisting only of the empty string, $v \in V$ describes the language $\{v\}$, $(X+Y) = \{\omega \mid \omega \in X \text{ or } \omega \in Y\}$, $(XY) = \{\chi\gamma \mid \chi \in X, \gamma \in Y\}$. The closure operator (*) is defined by the following infinite sum:

$$X^* = \epsilon + X + XX + XXX + \cdots$$

As illustrated in this definition, we shall usually omit parentheses. Star is unary, and takes priority over either binary operator; plus has a lower priority than concatenation. Thus $W + XY^*$ is equivalent to the fully-parenthesized expression $(W + (X(Y^*)))$.

Figure 5.12 summarizes the algebraic properties of regular expressions. The distinct representations for X^* show that several regular expressions can be given for one language.

The main advantage in using a regular expression to describe a set of strings is that it gives a precise specification, closely related to the 'natural language' description, which can be written in text form suitable for input to a computer. For example, let l denote any single letter and d any single digit. The expression $l(l+d)^*$ is then a direct representation of the natural language description 'a letter followed by any sequence of letters and digits'.

The equivalence of regular expressions and finite automata follows from:

Theorem 5.19. *Let R be a regular expression that describes a subset, S, of T^*. There exists a deterministic finite automaton, $A = (T,Q,P,q_0,F)$ such that $L(A) = S$.*

The automaton is constructed in much the same way as that of Theorem 5.15: We create a new expression R' by replacing the elements of T occurring in R by distinct symbols (multiple occurrences of the same element will receive distinct symbols). Further, we prefix another distinct symbol to the altered expression; if $R = E$, then R' consists only of this starting symbol. (As symbols we could use, for example, natural numbers with 0 as the starting symbol.) The states of our automaton correspond to subsets of the sym-

$$X + Y = Y + X \qquad\qquad \text{(commutative)}$$

$$(X + Y) + Z = X + (Y + Z) \qquad \text{(associative)}$$
$$(XY)Z = X(YZ)$$

$$X(Y + Z) = XY + XZ \qquad \text{(distributive)}$$
$$(X + Y)Z = XZ + YZ$$

$$X + E = E + X = X \qquad\qquad \text{(identity)}$$
$$X\epsilon = \epsilon X = X$$

$$XE = EX = E \qquad\qquad \text{(zero)}$$

$$X + X = X \qquad\qquad \text{(idempotent)}$$

$$(X^*)^* = X^*$$
$$X^* = \epsilon + XX^*$$
$$X^* = X + X^*$$

$$\epsilon^* = \epsilon$$

$$E^* = \epsilon$$

Figure 5.12. Algebraic Properties of Regular Expressions

$$R = 1(1 + d)\,*$$
$$R' = 0\,1\,(2 + 3)*$$

a) Modifying the Regular Expression

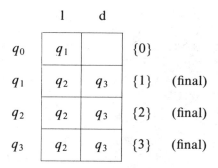

	1	d		
q_0	q_1		$\{0\}$	
q_1	q_2	q_3	$\{1\}$	(final)
q_2	q_2	q_3	$\{2\}$	(final)
q_3	q_2	q_3	$\{3\}$	(final)

b) The resulting state table

Figure 5.13. Regular Expressions to State Tables

bol set. The set corresponding to the initial state q_0 consists solely of the starting symbol. We inspect the states of Q one after another and add new states as required. For each $q \in Q$ and each $t \in T$, let q' correspond to the set of symbols in R' that replace t and follow any of the symbols of the set corresponding to q. If the set corresponding to q' is not empty, then we add

$qt \rightarrow q'$ to P and add $\{q'\}$ to Q if it is not already present. The set F of final states consists of all states that include a possible final symbol of R'.

Figure 5.13 gives an example of this process. Starting with $q_0 = \{0\}$, we obtain the state table of Figure 5.13b, with states q_1, q_1 and q_3 as final states. Obviously this is not the simplest automaton which we could create for the given language; we shall return to this problem in Section 6.2.2.

5.3. Context-Free Grammars and Pushdown Automata

Regular grammars are not sufficiently powerful to describe languages such as algebraic expressions, which have nested structure. Since most programming languages contain such structures, we must change to a sufficiently powerful descriptive method such as context-free grammars. Because regular grammars are a subclass of context-free grammars, one might ask why we bother with regular languages at all. As we shall see in this section, the analysis of phrase structure by means of context-free grammars is so much more costly that one falls back upon the simpler methods for regular grammars whenever possible.

Here, and also in Chapter 7, we assume that all context-free grammars (T,N,P,Z) contain a production $Z \rightarrow S$. This is the only production in which the axiom Z appears. (Any grammar can be put in this form by addition of such a production.) We assume further that the terminator # follows each sentence. This symbol identifies the condition 'input text completely consumed' and does not belong to the vocabulary. Section 5.3.3 assumes further that the productions are consecutively numbered. The above production has the number 1, n is the total number of productions and the ith production has the form $X_i \rightarrow \chi_i$, $\chi_i = x_{i,1} \cdots x_{i,m}$. The length, m, of the right-hand side is also called the length of the production. We shall denote a leftmost derivation $X \Rightarrow^* Y$ by $X \Rightarrow^L Y$ and a rightmost derivation by $X \Rightarrow^R Y$.

We find the following notation convenient for describing the properties of strings: The k-head $k{:}\omega$ of ω gives the first $\min(k, |\omega|+1)$ symbols of ω#. $FIRST_k(\omega)$ is the set of all terminal k-heads of strings derivable from ω. The set $EFF_k(\omega)$ ('ϵ-free first') contains all strings from $FIRST_k(\omega)$ for which no ϵ-production $A \rightarrow \epsilon$ was applied at the last step in the rightmost derivation. The set $FOLLOW_k(\omega)$ comprises all terminal k-heads that could follow ω. By definition $FOLLOW_k(Z) = \{\#\}$ for any k. Formally:

$$k{:}\omega = \begin{cases} \omega\# & \text{when } |\omega| < k \\ \alpha & \text{when } \omega = \alpha\gamma \text{ and } |\alpha| = k \end{cases}$$

$$FIRST_k(\omega) = \{\tau \mid \exists\, \nu \in T^* \text{ such that } \omega \Rightarrow^* \nu,\ \tau = k{:}\nu\}$$

$$EFF_k(\omega) = \{\tau \in FIRST_k(\omega) \mid \exists A \in N, \nu \in T^* \text{ such that } \omega \Rightarrow^R A\tau\nu \Rightarrow \tau\nu\}$$

$$FOLLOW_k(\omega) = \{\tau \mid \exists \ \nu \in V^* \text{ such that } Z \Rightarrow^* \mu\omega\nu, \ \tau = k : \nu\}$$

We omit the index k when it is 1. These functions may be applied to sets of strings, in which case the result is the union of the results of applying the function to the elements of its argument. Finally, if α is a string and Ω is a set of strings, we shall define $\alpha\Omega = \{\alpha\omega \mid \omega \in \Omega\}$.

5.3.1. Pushdown Automata   For finite automata, we saw that the state specifies the set of nonterminal symbols of G that could have been used to derive the remainder of the input string. Suppose that a finite automaton has reached the first right parenthesis of the following expression (which can be derived using a context-free grammar):

$$(a_1 + (a_2 + (\cdots + (a_m) \cdots)))$$

It must then be in a state specifying some set of nonterminal symbols that can derive *exactly m* right parentheses. Clearly there must be a distinct state for each m. But if m is larger than the number of states of the automaton (and this could be arranged for *any* given number of states) then there cannot be a distinct state for each m. Thus we need a more powerful automaton, which can be obtained by providing a finite automaton with a *stack* as an additional storage structure.

Definition 5.20. A *pushdown automaton* is a septuple $A = (T,Q,R,q_0,F,S,s_0)$, where $(T \cup Q \cup S, R)$ is a general rewriting system, q_0 is an element of Q, F is a subset of Q, and s_0 is an element of S or $s_0 = \epsilon$. The sets T and Q are disjoint. Each element of R has the form $\sigma q a \tau \rightarrow \sigma' q' \tau$, where σ and σ' are elements of S^*, q and q' are elements of Q, a is an element of T or $a = \epsilon$, and τ is an element of T^*.

Q, q_0 and F have the same meaning as the corresponding components of a finite automaton. S is the set of *stack symbols*, and s_0 is the initial content of the stack. The pushdown automaton accepts a string $\tau \in T^*$ if $s_0 q_0 \tau \Rightarrow^* q$ for some q in F. If each sentence is followed by #, the pushdown automaton A defines the language $L(A) = \{\tau \mid s_0 q_0 \tau \# \Rightarrow^* q \#, q \in F, \tau \in T^*\}$. (In the literature one often finds the requirement that σ be an element of S rather than S^*; our automaton would then be termed a *generalized* pushdown automaton. Further, the definition of 'accept' could be based upon either the relation $s_0 q_0 \tau \Rightarrow^* \sigma q$, $\sigma \in S^*, q \in F$, or the relation $s_0 q_0 \tau \Rightarrow^* q$, q arbitrary. Under the given assumptions these definitions prove to be equivalent in power.)

   We can picture the automaton as a machine with a finite set Q of internal states and a stack of arbitrary length. If we have reached the *configuration* $s_1 \cdots s_n q \tau$ in a derivation, then the automaton is in state q, τ is the unread part of the input text being analyzed, and $s_1 \cdots s_n$ is the content of the stack (s_1 is the bottom item and s_n the top). The transitions of the automaton either read the next symbol of the input text (*symbol-controlled*) or are *spon-*

taneous and do not shorten the input text. Further, each transition may alter the topmost item of the stack; it is termed a *stacking, unstacking* or *replacing* transition, respectively, if it only adds items, deletes items, or changes them without altering their total number.

The pushdown automaton can easily handle the problem of nested parentheses: When it reads a left parenthesis from the input text, it pushes a corresponding symbol onto the stack; when it reads the matching right parenthesis, that symbol is deleted from the stack. The number of states of the automaton plays no role in this process, and is independent of the parenthesis nesting depth.

Theorem 5.21. *For every context-free grammar, G, there exists a pushdown automaton, A, such that $L(A) = L(G)$.*

As with finite automata, one proves this theorem by construction of A. There are two construction procedures, which lead to distinct automata; we shall go into the details of these procedures in Sections 5.3.2 and 5.3.3 respectively. The automata constructed by the two procedures serve as the basic models for two fundamentally different parsing algorithms.

A pushdown automaton is not necessarily deterministic even if the left sides of all productions are distinct. For example, suppose that $\sigma_1 q \tau \to \sigma' q' \tau'$ and $\sigma_2 q \tau \to \sigma'' q'' \tau''$ are two distinct productions and σ_2 is a proper tail of σ_1. Thus $\sigma_1 = \sigma\sigma_2$ and both productions are applicable to the configuration $\sigma\sigma_2 q \tau \chi$. If we wish to test formally whether the productions unambiguously specify the next transition, we must make the left-hand sides the same length. Determinism can then be tested, as in the case of finite automata, by checking that the left-hand sides of the productions are distinct. We shall only consider cases in which the state q and k lookahead symbols of the input string are used to determine the applicable production.

Unfortunately, it is not possible to sharpen Theorem 5.21 so that the pushdown automaton is always deterministic; Theorem 5.15 for regular grammars cannot be generalized to context-free grammars. Only by additional restrictions to the grammar can one guarantee a deterministic automaton. Most programming languages can be analyzed deterministically, since they have grammars that satisfy these restrictions. (This has an obvious psychological basis: Humans also find it easier to read a deterministically-analyzable program.) The restrictions imposed upon a grammar to obtain a deterministic automaton depend upon the construction procedure. We shall discuss the details at the appropriate place.

5.3.2. Top-Down Analysis and LL(k) Grammars Let $G = (T, N, P, Z)$ be a context-free grammar, and consider the pushdown automaton $A = (T, \{q\}, R, q, \{q\}, V, Z)$ with $V = T \cup N$ and R defined as follows:

$$R = \{tqt \to q \mid t \in T\} \cup \{Bq \to b_n \cdots b_1 q \mid$$
$$B \to b_1 \cdots b_n \in P, n \geqslant 0, B \in N, b_i \in V\}$$

This automaton accepts a string in $L(G)$ by constructing a leftmost derivation of that string and comparing the symbols generated (from left to right) with the symbols actually appearing in the string.

Figure 5.14 is a pushdown automaton constructed in this manner from the grammar of Figure 5.3a. In the left-hand column of Figure 5.15 we show the derivation by which this automaton accepts the string $i + i * i$. The right-hand column is the leftmost derivation of this string, copied from Figure 5.5. Note that the automaton's derivation has more steps due to the rules that compare a terminal symbol on the stack with the head of the input

$$T = \{ +, *, (,), i \}$$

$$Q = \{ q \}$$

$$R = \{ \ Eq \rightarrow Tq, Eq \rightarrow T + Eq,$$
$$Tq \rightarrow Fq, Tq \rightarrow F * Tq,$$
$$Fq \rightarrow iq, Fq \rightarrow)E(q,$$
$$+q+ \rightarrow q, *q* \rightarrow q, (q(\rightarrow q, \ )q) \rightarrow q, iqi \rightarrow q \ \}$$

$$q_0 = q$$

$$F = \{ q \}$$

$$S = \{ +, *, (,), i, E, T, F \}$$

$$s_0 = E$$

Figure 5.14. A Pushdown Automaton Constructed from Figure 5.3a

Stack	Input	Leftmost derivation
$E \quad q$	$i + i * i$	E
$T + E \quad q$	$i + i * i$	$E + T$
$T + T \quad q$	$i + i * i$	$T + T$
$T + F \quad q$	$i + i * i$	$F + T$
$T + i \quad q$	$i + i * i$	$i + T$
$T + \quad q$	$+ i * i$	
$T \quad q$	$i * i$	
$F * T \quad q$	$i * i$	$i + T * F$
$F * F \quad q$	$i * i$	$i + F * F$
$F * i \quad q$	$i * i$	$i + i * F$
$F * \quad q$	$* i$	
$F \quad q$	i	
$i \quad q$	i	$i + i * i$
q		

Figure 5.15. Top-Down Analysis

string and delete both. Figure 5.16 shows a reduced set of productions combining some of these steps with those that precede them.

$$R' = \{ \; Eq \to Tq, Eq \to T + Eq,$$
$$Tq \to Fq, Tq \to F*Tq,$$
$$Fqi \to q, Fq(\to)Eq,$$
$$+q+\to q, *q*\to q,)q)\to q \; \}$$

Figure 5.16. Reduced Productions for Figure 5.14

The analysis performed by this automaton is called a *top-down* (or *predictive*) analysis because it traces the derivation from the axiom (top) to the sentence (bottom), predicting the symbols that should be present. For each configuration of the automaton, the stack specifies a string from V^* used to derive the remainder of the input string. This corresponds to construction 5.13 for finite automata, with the stack content playing the role of the state and the state merely serving to mark the point reached in the input scan.

We now specify the construction of deterministic, top-down pushdown automata by means of the LL(k) grammars introduced by Lewis and Stearns [1969]:

Definition 5.22. A context-free grammar $G = (T,N,P,Z)$ is $LL(k)$ for given $k \geqslant 0$ if, for arbitrary derivations

$$Z \Rightarrow^L \mu A \chi \Rightarrow \mu \nu \chi \Rightarrow^* \mu \gamma \quad \mu, \gamma \in T^*, \nu, \chi \in V^*, A \in N$$

$$Z \Rightarrow^L \mu A \chi \Rightarrow \mu \omega \chi \Rightarrow^* \mu \gamma' \quad \gamma' \in T^*, \omega \in V^*$$

$(k{:}\gamma = k{:}\gamma')$ implies $\nu = \omega$.

Theorem 5.23. *For every LL(k) grammar, G, there exists a deterministic pushdown automaton, A, such that $L(A) = L(G)$.*

A reads each sentence of the language $L(G)$ from *left* to right, tracing a *left*most derivation and examining no more than k input symbols at each step. (Hence the term 'LL(k) prime .')

In our discussion of Theorem 5.13, we noted that each state of the finite automaton corresponding to a given grammar specified the nonterminal of the grammar that must have been used to derive the string being analyzed. Thus the state of the automaton characterized a step in the grammar's derivation of a sentence. We can provide an analogous characterization of a step in a context-free derivation by giving information about the production being applied and the possible right context: Each state of a pushdown automaton could specify a triple (p, j, Ω), where $0 \leqslant j \leqslant n_p$ gives the number of symbols from the right-hand side of production $X_p \to x_{p,1} \cdots x_{p,n_p}$ already analyzed and Ω is the set of k-heads of strings that could follow the string derived from X_p. This triple is called a *situation*, and is written in the following descriptive form:

$$[X_p \to \mu \cdot \nu; \Omega] \quad \mu = x_{p,1} \cdots x_{p,j}, \quad \nu = x_{p,j+1} \cdots x_{p,n_p}$$

The dot (which is assumed to be outside of the vocabulary) marks the position of the analysis within the right-hand side. (In most cases Ω contains a single string. We shall then write it without set brackets.)

Given a grammar (T,N,P,Z), we specify the states Q and transitions R of the automaton inductively as follows:

1. Initially let $Q = \{q_0\}$ and $R = \varnothing$, with $q_0 = [Z \to \cdot S; \#]$. (Note that $FOLLOW_k(Z) = \{\#\}$.) The initial state is q_0, which is also the initial stack content of A. (We could have chosen an arbitrary state as the initial stack content.) The automaton halts if this state is reached again, the stack is empty, and the next input symbol is the terminator $\#$.
2. Let $q = [X \to \mu \cdot \nu; \Omega]$ be an element of Q that has not yet been considered.
3. If $\nu = \epsilon$ then add $q\epsilon \to \epsilon$ to R if it is not already present. (The notation $q\tau \to \tau$ is shorthand for the set of spontaneous unstacking transitions $q'q\tau \to q'\tau$ with arbitrary q'.)
4. If $\nu = t\gamma$ for some $t \in T$ and $\gamma \in V^*$, let $q' = [X \to \mu t \cdot \gamma; \Omega]$. Add q' to Q and $qt \to q'$ to R if they are not already present.
5. If $\nu = B\gamma$ for some $B \in N$ and $\gamma \in V^*$, let $q' = [X \to \mu B \cdot \gamma; \Omega]$ and $H = \{[B \to \cdot \beta_i; FIRST_k(\gamma\Omega)] \mid B \to \beta_i \in P\}$. Set $Q := Q \cup \{q'\} \cup H$ and $R := R \cup \{q\tau_i \to q'h_i\tau_i \mid h_i \in H, \tau_i \in FIRST_k(\beta_i\gamma\Omega)\}$.
6. If all states in Q have been examined, stop. Otherwise, return to step (2).

The construction terminates in all cases, since the set of situations is finite. One can show that the resulting automaton is deterministic if and only if G is an LL(k) grammar, and therefore the construction provides a test for the LL(k) property.

Consider the grammar of Figure 5.17a. We can apply Construction 5.23 with $k = 3$ to show that this grammar is LL(3), obtaining the states of Figure 5.17b and the transitions of Figure 5.17c.

With $k = 2$ the construction leads to identical states. In state q_7, however, we obtain the following transitions:

$$q_7ca \to q_{10}q_{11}ca, \quad q_7ca \to q_{10}q_{12}ca$$

The automaton is therefore nondeterministic and hence the grammar is LL(3), but not LL(2). The example also shows that the lookahead symbols are examined only at spontaneous, stacking transitions that correspond to entry into a new production. As soon as such a transition is executed, the reading of terminal symbols and the decision to terminate the production with an unstacking transition proceeds without further lookahead.

There exist grammars that do not have the LL(k) property for any k. Among the possible reasons is the occurrence of *left recursive* nonterminals – nonterminals A for which a derivation $A \Rightarrow A\omega$, $\omega \neq \epsilon$, is possible. In a

$$P = \{ \ Z \to X,$$
$$X \to Y, X \to bYa,$$
$$Y \to c, Y \to ca \ \}$$

a) An LL(3) grammar

$q_0 = [Z \to \cdot X; \#]$	$q_9 = [Y \to c \cdot a; \#]$
$q_1 = [Z \to X \cdot; \#]$	$q_{10} = [X \to bY \cdot a; \#]$
$q_2 = [X \to \cdot Y; \#]$	$q_{11} = [Y \to \cdot c; a\#]$
$q_3 = [X \to \cdot bYa; \#]$	$q_{12} = [Y \to \cdot ca; a\#]$
$q_4 = [X \to Y \cdot; \#]$	$q_{13} = [Y \to ca \cdot; \#]$
$q_5 = [Y \to \cdot c; \#]$	$q_{14} = [X \to bYa \cdot; \#]$
$q_6 = [Y \to \cdot ca; \#]$	$q_{15} = [Y \to c \cdot; a\#]$
$q_7 = [X \to b \cdot Ya; \#]$	$q_{16} = [Y \to c \cdot a; a\#]$
$q_8 = [Y \to c \cdot; \#]$	$q_{17} = [Y \to ca \cdot; a\#]$

b) States of the automaton, with the situations they represent

$$R = \{ \quad q_0 c \, \# \to q_1 q_2 c \, \#, \qquad q_7 ca \, \# \to q_{10} q_{11} ca \, \#,$$
$$q_0 ca \, \# \to q_1 q_2 ca \, \#, \qquad q_7 caa \to q_{10} q_{12} caa,$$
$$q_0 bca \to q_1 q_3 bca, \qquad q_8 \to \epsilon,$$
$$q_1 \to \epsilon, \qquad q_9 a \to q_{13},$$
$$q_2 c \, \# \to q_4 q_5 c \, \#, \qquad q_{10} a \to q_{14},$$
$$q_2 ca \, \# \to q_4 q_6 ca \, \#, \qquad q_{11} c \to q_{15},$$
$$q_3 b \to q_7, \qquad q_{12} c \to q_{16},$$
$$\qquad q_{13} \to \epsilon,$$
$$q_4 \to \epsilon, \qquad q_{14} \to \epsilon,$$
$$q_5 c \to q_8, \qquad q_{15} \to \epsilon,$$
$$q_6 c \to q_9, \qquad q_{16} a \to q_{17},$$
$$q_{17} \to \epsilon \}$$

c) Production set of the Automaton

Figure 5.17. Constructing a Deterministic Top-Down Automaton

predictive automaton, left recursive nonterminals lead to cycles that can be broken only by examining a right context of arbitrary length. They can, however, be eliminated through a transformation of the grammar.

Theorem 5.24. *An LL(k) grammar can have no left recursive nonterminal symbols.*

Theorem 5.25. *For every context-free grammar $G = (T,N,P,Z)$ with left recursive nonterminals, there exists an equivalent grammar $G' = (T,N',P',Z)$ with no left recursive nonterminals.*

Let the elements of N be numbered consecutively: $N = \{X_1, \ldots, X_n\}$. If we choose the indices such that the condition $i < j$ holds for all productions $X_i \to X_j \omega$ then G has no left recursive nonterminals. If such a numbering is not possible for G, we can guarantee it for G' through the following construction:

1. Let $N'=N$, $P'=P$. Perform steps (2) and (3) for $i=1,\ldots,n$.

2. For $j=1,\ldots,i-1$ replace all productions $X_i \to X_j\omega\in P'$ by $\{X_i \to \chi_j\omega \mid X_j \to \chi_j \in P'\}$. (After this step, $X_i \Rightarrow^+ X_j\gamma$ implies $i\leqslant j$.)

3. Replace the entire set of productions of the form $X_i \to X_i\omega\in P'$ (if any exist) by the productions $\{B_i \to \omega B_i \mid X_i \to X_i\omega\in P'\}\cup\{B_i \to \epsilon\}$, adding a new symbol B_i to N'. At the same time, replace the entire set of productions $X_i \to \chi$, $\chi\neq X_i\gamma$, by $X_i \to \chi B_i$. The symbols added during this step will be given numbers $n+1, n+2, \ldots,$

If the string ω in the production $X_i \to X_i\omega$ does not begin with X_j, $j\leqslant i$ then we can replace $X_i \to X_i\omega$ by $\{B_i \to \omega, B_i \to \omega B_i\}$ and $X_i \to \chi$ by $\{X_i \to \chi, X_i \to \chi B_i\}$ in step (3). This approach avoids the introduction of ϵ-productions; it was used to obtain the grammar of Figure 5.3b from that of Figure 5.3a.

Note that left recursion such as $E \to T$, $E \to E+T$ is used in the syntax of arithmetic expressions to reflect the left-association of the operators. This semantic property can also be seen in the transformed productions $E \to TE'$, $E' \to +TE'$, $E' \to \epsilon$, but not in $E \to T$, $E \to T+E$. In EBNF the left associativity of an expression can be conveniently represented by $E ::= T\ ('+'T)^*$.

One of the constructions discussed above results in ϵ-productions, while the other does not. We can always eliminate ϵ-productions from an LL(k) grammar, but by doing this we may increase the value of k:

Theorem 5.26. *Given an LL(k) grammar G with ϵ-productions. There exists an LL($k+1$) grammar without ϵ-productions that generates the language $L(G)-\{\epsilon\}$.*

Conversely, k can be reduced by introducing ϵ-productions:

Theorem 5.27. *For every ϵ-free LL($k+1$) grammar G, $k>0$, there exists an equivalent LL(k) grammar with ϵ-productions.*

The proof of Theorem 5.27 rests upon a grammar transformation known as *left-factoring*, illustrated in Figure 5.18. In Figure 5.18a, we cannot distinguish the productions $X \to Yc$ and $X \to Yd$ by examining any fixed number of symbols from the input text: No matter what number of symbols we choose, it is possible for Y to derive a string of that length in either production.

We avoid the problem by deferring the decision. Since both productions begin with Y, it is really not necessary to distinguish them until *after* the string derived from Y has been scanned. The productions can be combined

$$P = \{ \ Z \to X,$$
$$X \to Yc, X \to Yd,$$
$$Y \to a, Y \to bY \ \}$$

a) A grammar that is not LL(k) for any k

$$P = \{ \ Z \to X,$$
$$X \to YX',$$
$$X' \to c, X' \to d,$$
$$Y \to a, Y \to bY \ \}$$

b) An equivalent LL(1) grammar

Figure 5.18. Left Factoring

by 'factoring out' the common portion, as shown in Figure 5.18b. Now the decision is made at exactly the position where the productions begin to differ, and consequently it is only necessary to examine a single symbol of the input string.

In general, by deferring a decision we obtain more information about the input text we are analyzing. The top-down analysis technique requires us to decide which production to apply *before* analyzing the string derived from that production. In the next section we shall present the opposite technique, which does not require a decision until *after* analyzing the string derived from a production. Intuitively, this technique should handle a larger class of grammars because more information is available on which to base a decision; this intuition can be proven correct. The price is an increase in the complexity of both the analysis procedure and the resulting automaton, but in practice the technique remains competitive.

5.3.3. Bottom-Up Analysis and LR(k) Grammars
Again let $G = (T,N,P,Z)$ be a context-free grammar, and consider the pushdown automaton $A = (T,\{q\},R,q,\{q\},V,\epsilon)$ with $V = T \cup N$, and R defined as follows:

$$R = \{x_1 \cdots x_n q \to Xq \ | \ X \to x_1 \cdots x_n \in P\} \cup \{qt \to tq \ | \ t \in T\} \cup \{Zq \to q\}$$

This automaton accepts a string in $L(G)$ by working backward through a rightmost derivation of the string.

Figure 5.19 is a pushdown automaton constructed in this manner from

$$T = \{+,*,(,),i\}$$

$$R = \{ \ Tq \to Eq, E+Tq \to Eq,$$
$$Fq \to Tq, T*Fq \to Tq,$$
$$iq \to Fq, (E)q \to Fq,$$
$$q+ \to +q, q* \to *q, q(\to (q, \ q) \to)q, qi \to iq,$$
$$Eq \to q \ \}$$

$$S = \{+,*,(,),i,E,T,F\}$$

Figure 5.19. A Pushdown Automaton Constructed from Figure 5.3a

Stack	Input	Reverse rightmost derivation
q	$i+i*i$	$i+i*i$
$i\ q$	$+i*i$	
$F\ q$	$+i*i$	$F+i*i$
$T\ q$	$+i*i$	$T+i*i$
$E\ q$	$+i*i$	$E+i*i$
$E+\ q$	$i*i$	
$E+i\ q$	$*i$	
$E+F\ q$	$*i$	$E+F*i$
$E+T\ q$	$*i$	$E+T*i$
$E+T*\ q$	i	
$E+T*i\ q$		
$E+T*F\ q$		$E+T*F$
$E+T\ q$		$E+T$
$E\ q$		E
q		

Figure 5.20. Bottom-Up Analysis

$$R' = \{\ \ Tq \to Eq, E+Tq \to Eq,$$
$$Fq \to Tq, T*Fq \to Tq,$$
$$qi \to Fq, (Eq) \to Fq,$$
$$q+ \to +q, q* \to *q, q(\to(q,$$
$$Eq \to q\ \}$$

Figure 5.21. Reduced Productions for Figure 5.17

the grammar of Figure 5.3a. In the left-hand column of Figure 5.20, we show the derivation by which this automaton accepts the string $i+i*i$. The right-hand column is the reverse of the rightmost derivation of this string, copied from Figure 5.5. The number of steps required for the automaton's derivation can be decreased by combining productions as shown in Figure 5.21. (This reduction is analogous to that of Figure 5.16.)

The analysis performed by this automaton is called a *bottom-up* analysis because of the fact that it traces the derivation from the sentence (bottom) to the axiom (top). In each configuration of the automaton the stack contains a string from S^*, from which the portion of the input text already read can be derived. The state merely serves to mark the point reached in the input scan. The meaningful information is therefore the pair (ρ, σ), where $\rho \in S^*$ denotes the stack contents and $\sigma \in T^*$ denotes the remainder of the input text.

The pairs (ρ, σ) that describe the configurations of an automaton tracing such a derivation may be partitioned into equivalence classes as follows:

Definition 5.28. For $p = 1, \ldots, n$ let $X_p \to \chi_p$ be the pth production of a context-free grammar $G = (T, N, P, Z)$. The *reduction classes*, R_j, $j = 0, \ldots, n$ are defined by:

$$R_0 = \{(\rho, \sigma) \mid \rho = \mu\gamma, \ \sigma = \nu\omega \text{ such that } Z \Rightarrow^R \mu A \omega, \ A \Rightarrow^{R'} \gamma\nu, \ \nu \neq \epsilon\}$$

$$R_p = \{(\rho, \sigma) \mid \rho = \mu\chi_p, \ Z \Rightarrow^R \mu X_p \sigma\}$$

'$A \Rightarrow^{R'} \alpha$' denotes the relation '$A \Rightarrow^R \alpha$ and the last step in the derivation does not take the form $B\alpha \Rightarrow \alpha$'.

The reduction classes contain all pairs of strings that could appear during the bottom-up parse of a sentence in $L(G)$ by the automaton described above. Further, the reduction class to which a pair belongs characterizes the transition carried out by the automaton when that pair appears as a configuration. There are three possibilities:

1. $(\rho, \sigma) \in R_0$. The simple phrase χ is not yet completely in the stack; the transition $qt \to tq$ with $t = 1{:}\sigma$ is applied (*shift transition*).

2. $(\rho, \sigma) \in R_p$, $1 \leqslant p \leqslant n$. The simple phrase χ is complete in the stack and the *reduce transition* $\chi_p q \to X_p q$ is applied. (For $p = 1$ the transition $Zq \to q$ occurs and the automaton halts.)

3. $(\rho, \sigma) \notin R_j$, $0 \leqslant j \leqslant n$. No further transitions are possible; the input text does not belong to $L(G)$.

A pushdown automaton that bases its decisions upon the reduction classes is obviously deterministic if and only if the grammar is unambiguous.

Unfortunately the definition of the sets R_j uses the entire remainder of the input string in order to determine the reduction class to which a pair (ρ, σ) belongs. That means that our bottom-up automaton must inspect an arbitrarily long lookahead string to make a decision about the next transition, if it is to be deterministic. If we restrict the number of lookahead symbols to k, we arrive at the following definition:

Definition 5.29. For some $k \geqslant 0$, the sets $R_{j,k}$, $j = 0, \ldots, n$, are called *k-stack classes* of a grammar G if:

$$R_{j,k} = \{(\rho, \tau) \mid \exists \ (\rho, \sigma) \in R_j \text{ such that } \tau = k{:}\sigma\}$$

If the k-stack classes are pairwise-disjoint, then the pushdown automaton is deterministic even when the lookahead is restricted to k symbols. This property characterizes a class of grammars introduced by D. E. Knuth [1965]:

Definition 5.30. A context-free grammar $G = (T,N,P,Z)$ is $LR(k)$ for given $k \geqslant 0$ if, for arbitrary derivations

$$Z \Rightarrow^R \mu A \omega \Rightarrow \mu\chi\omega \quad \mu \in V^*, \omega \in T^*, A \to \chi \in P$$

$$Z \Rightarrow^R \mu' B \omega' \Rightarrow \mu'\gamma\omega' \quad \mu' \in V^*, \omega' \in T^*, B \to \gamma \in P$$

$$(\mid \mu\chi \mid + k){:}\mu\chi\omega = (\mid \mu'\gamma \mid + k){:}\mu'\gamma\omega' \text{ implies } \mu = \mu', A = B \text{ and } \chi = \gamma.$$

The automaton given at the beginning of this section scans the input text from left to right, tracing the reverse of a rightmost derivation and examining no more than k input symbols at each step. (Hence the term "LR(k)".)

Theorem 5.31. *A context-free grammar is LR(k) if and only if its k-stack classes are pairwise-disjoint.*

On the basis of this theorem, we can test the LR(k) property by determining the intersection of the k-stack classes. Unfortunately the k-stack classes can contain infinitely many pairs (ρ, τ): The length restriction permits only a finite number of strings τ, but the lengths of the stack contents are unrestricted. However, we can give a regular grammar G_j for each k-stack class $R_{j,k}$ such that $L(G_j) = \{(\rho \& \tau) \mid (\rho, \tau) \in R_{j,k}\}$. Since algorithms exist for determining whether two regular languages are disjoint, this construction leads to a procedure for testing the LR(k) property.

Theorem 5.32. *Let $G = (T,N,P,Z)$ be a context-free grammar, and let $k \geqslant 0$. Assume that $\&$ is not an element of the vocabulary $V = T \cup N$. There exists a set of regular grammars G_j, $j = 0, \ldots, n$ such that $L(G_j) = \{\rho \& \tau \mid (\rho,\tau) \in R_{j,k}\}$.*

The regular grammars that generate the k-stack classes are based upon the situations introduced in connection with Theorem 5.23:

$$W = \{[X \rightarrow \mu \cdot \nu; \omega] \mid X \rightarrow \mu\nu \in P, \ \omega \in FOLLOW_k(X)\}$$

These situations are the nonterminal symbols of the regular grammars. To define the grammars themselves, we first specify a set of grammars that generate the k-stack classes, but are not regular:

$$G'_j = (V \cup \{\&, \#\}, W, P' \cup P'' \cup P_j, [Z \rightarrow \cdot S; \#])$$

The productions in $P' \cup P''$ build the ρ components of the k-stack class. They provide the finite description of the infinite strings. Productions in P_j attach the τ component, terminating the k-stack class:

$$P' = \{[X \rightarrow \mu \cdot \nu \gamma; \omega] \rightarrow \nu[X \rightarrow \mu\nu \cdot \gamma; \omega] \mid \nu \in V\}$$

$$P'' = \{[X \rightarrow \mu \cdot B \gamma; \omega] \rightarrow [B \rightarrow \cdot \beta; \tau] \mid B \rightarrow \beta \in P, \ \tau \in EFF_k(\gamma\omega)\}$$

$$P_0 = \{[X \rightarrow \mu \cdot \nu; \omega] \rightarrow \& \tau \mid \nu \neq \epsilon, \ \tau \in EFF_k(\nu\omega)\}$$

$$P_p = \{[x_p \rightarrow \chi_p \cdot; \omega] \rightarrow \& \omega\} \ p = 1, \ldots, n$$

Remember that the lengths of τ and ω are limited to k symbols, so the number of possible strings $\& \tau$ and $\& \omega$ is finite. If we regard these strings as single terminal symbols, productions in P' and P_j, $j = 0, \ldots, n$, are allowable in a regular grammar. Productions in P'' are not allowable, however, since they are of the form $A \rightarrow B, A, B \in N$. Thus G'_j is not regular.

It is always possible to rewrite a grammar so that it contains no productions such as those in P''. The key is the *closure* of a nonterminal:

$$H(A) = \{A\} \cup \{B \mid C \to B \in P, C \in H(A)\}$$

The procedure for rewriting the grammar is:

1. Select an $A \in N$ for which $H(A) \neq \{A\}$.
2. Set $P = P - \{A \to B \mid B \in N\}$.
3. Set $P = P \cup \{A \to \beta \mid B \to \beta \in P, B \in H(A), \beta \notin N\}$.

The algorithm terminates when no selection can be made in step (1).

We obtain G_j from G'_j by applying this algorithm. The strings β are all of the form $v[\cdots]$, & τ or & ω, and therefore all introduced productions satisfy the conditions for a regular grammar.

Theorem 5.33. *For every LR(k) grammar G there exists a deterministic push-down automaton A such that* $L(A) = L(G)$.

Let $G = (T, N, P, Z)$. We base construction of the automaton on the grammars G_j, effectively building a machine that simultaneously generates the k-stack classes and checks them against the reverse of a rightmost derivation of the string. Depending upon the particular k-stack class, the automaton pushes the input symbol onto the stack or reduces some number of stacked symbols to a nonterminal. The construction algorithm generates the necessary situations as it goes, and uses the closure operation discussed above 'on the fly' to avoid considering productions from P''. As in the construction associated with Theorem 5.15, a state of the automaton must specify a *set* of situations, any one of which might have been used in deriving the current k-stack class. It is convenient to restate the definition of a closure directly in terms of a set of situations M:

$$H(M) = M \cup \{[B \to \cdot \beta; \tau] \mid \exists \, [X \to \mu \cdot B \gamma; \omega] \in H(M),$$
$$B \to \beta \in P, \tau \in FIRST_k(\gamma \omega)\}$$

The elements of Q and R are determined inductively as follows:

1. Initially let $Q = \{q_0\}$ and $R = \varnothing$, with $q_0 = H(\{[Z \to \cdot S; \#]\})$.

2. Let q be an element of Q that has not yet been considered. Perform steps (3)-(5) for each $v \in V$.

3. Let $basis(q, v) = \{[X \to \mu v \cdot \gamma; \omega] \mid [X \to \mu \cdot v \gamma; \omega] \in q\}$.

4. If $basis(q, v) \neq \varnothing$, then let $next(q, v) = H(basis(q, v))$. Add $q' = next(q, v)$ to Q if it is not already present.

5. If $basis(q, v) \neq \varnothing$ and $v \in T$ then set

$$R := R \cup \begin{cases} \{qv \to qq'\} & \text{if } k \leqslant 1 \\ \{qv\tau \to qq'\tau \mid [X \to \mu \cdot v \gamma; \omega] \in q, \, \tau \in FIRST_{k-1}(\gamma\omega)\} & \text{otherwise} \end{cases}$$

q_0: $[Z \to \cdot X ; \#]$ q_4: $[Y \to c \cdot ; \#]$
         $[X \to \cdot Y ; \#]$ $[Y \to c \cdot a ; \#]$
         $[X \to \cdot bYa ; \#]$
         $[Y \to \cdot c ; \#]$ q_5: $[X \to bY \cdot a ; \#]$
         $[Y \to \cdot ca ; \#]$ q_6: $[Y \to c \cdot ; a\#]$
q_1: $[Z \to X \cdot ; \#]$ $[Y \to c \cdot a ; a\#]$
q_2: $[X \to Y \cdot ; \#]$ q_7: $[Y \to ca \cdot ; \#]$
q_3: $[X \to b \cdot Ya ; \#]$ q_8: $[X \to bYa \cdot ; \#]$
         $[Y \to \cdot c ; a\#]$ q_9: $[Y \to ca \cdot ; a\#]$
         $[Y \to \cdot ca ; a\#]$

a) States

$$R = \{ \quad q_0 bc \to q_0 q_3 c,$$
$$q_0 c \# \to q_0 q_4 \#,$$

$$q_3 ca \to q_3 q_6 a,$$
$$q_4 a \# \to q_4 q_7 \#,$$
$$q_5 a \# \to q_5 q_8 \#,$$
$$q_6 aa \to q_6 q_9 a,$$
$$q_0 q_2 \# \to q_0 q_1 \#,$$
$$q_0 q_4 \# \to q_0 q_2 \#,$$
$$q_3 q_6 a \# \to q_3 q_5 a \#,$$
$$q_0 q_4 q_7 \# \to q_0 q_2 \#,$$
$$q_0 q_3 q_5 q_8 \# \to q_0 q_1 \#,$$
$$q_3 q_6 q_9 a \# \to q_3 q_5 a \# \}$$

b) Transitions

Figure 5.22. A Deterministic Bottom-Up Automaton for Figure 5.17a

6. If all elements of Q have been considered, perform step (7) for each $q \in Q$ and then stop. Otherwise return to step (2).

7. For each $[X \to \chi \cdot ; \omega] \in q$, where $\chi = x_1 \cdots x_n$, set $R := R \cup \{q_1 \cdots q_n q \omega \to q_1 q' \omega \mid [X \to \cdot \chi ; \omega] \in q_1, q_{i+1} = next(q_i, x_i) (i = 1, \ldots, n-1), q = next(q_n, x_n), q' = next(q_1, X)\}$

The construction terminates in all cases, since only a finite number of situations $[X \to \chi \cdot \gamma ; \omega]$ exist.

Figure 5.22 illustrates the algorithm by applying it to the grammar of Figure 5.17a with $k = 2$. In this example $k = 1$ would yield the same set of states. (For $k = 0$, q_4 and q_7 would be coalesced, as would q_7 and q_9.) Nevertheless, a single lookahead symbol is not sufficient to distinguish between the shift and reduce transitions in state 6. The grammar is thus LR(2), but not LR(1).

We shall conclude this section by quoting the following theoretical results:

Theorem 5.34. *For every LR(k) grammar with k > 1 there exists an equivalent LR(1) grammar.*

Theorem 5.35. *Every LL(k) grammar is also an LR(k) grammar.*

Theorem 5.36. *There exist LR(k) grammars that are not LL(k') for any k'.*

Theorem 5.37. *There exists an algorithm that, when given an LR(k) grammar G, will decide in a finite number of steps whether there exists a k' such that G is LL(k').*

As a result of Theorem 5.34 we see that it might possibly be sufficient to concern ourselves only with LR(1) grammars. (As a matter of fact, the transformation underlying the proof of this theorem is unsuitable for practical purposes.) The remaining theorems support our intuitive thoughts at the end of Section 5.3.2.

5.4. Notes and References

The basic symbols of a programming language are often described by arbitrary context-free productions, as illustrated by the LAX definition of Appendix A.1. This description does not provide a suitable starting point for mechanical construction of a lexical analyzer, and must therefore be recast by hand in terms of a regular set or regular grammar.

Our interpretation of finite automata and pushdown automata as special cases of general rewriting systems follows Salomaa [1973]. By this means we avoid a special definition of concepts such as configurations or transitions of an automaton.

BNF notation was first used to describe ALGOL 60 [Naur 1963]. Many authors have proposed extensions similar to our EBNF, using quoted terminals rather than bracketed nonterminals and having a regular expression capability. EBNF definitions are usually shorter than their BNF equivalents, but the important point is that they are textual representations of syntax charts [Jensen 1974, ANSI 1978]. This means that the context-free grammar can actually be developed and described to the user by means of pictures.

Pushdown automata were first examined by Samelson and Bauer [1960] and applied to the compilation of a forerunner of ALGOL 60. Theoretical mastery of the concepts and the proofs of equivalence to general context-free grammars followed later. Our introduction of LR(k) grammars via reduction classes follows the work of Langmaack [1971].

Aho and Ullman [1972] (and many other books dealing with formal languages) cover essentially the same material as this chapter, but in much greater detail. The proofs that are either outlined here or omitted entirely can be found in those texts.

EXERCISES

5.1. Prove that there is no loss of generality by prohibiting formal systems in which a derivation $\pi \Rightarrow^+ \pi$ of a string from itself is possible.

5.2. Choose some useless nonterminal from the LAX definition and briefly justify its inclusion in Appendix A.

5.3. Give an intuitive justification of Theorem 5.10.

5.4. Write a program to examine a finite automaton A and return the accepted language $L(A)$ in closed form as a regular expression.

5.5. Regular expressions $X_1, \ldots, X_n$ can also be defined implicitly via systems of regular equations of the form:

$$X_i = a_{i,0} + a_{i,1}X_i + \cdots + a_{i,n}X_n, \quad i = 1,\ldots,n$$

Here the $a_{i,j}$ are known regular expressions. State the conditions under which such a system has a unique solution, and give an algorithm to compute this solution. (Hint: For $b \neq \epsilon$, the equation $X = aX + b$ has the solution b^*a.)

5.6. Give an explanation of the need for '$\Rightarrow^{R'}$' in Definition 5.28.

5.7. Prove that the algorithm for rewriting G to remove productions of the form $A \rightarrow B, A, B \in N$ results in a grammar G such that $L(G) = L(G)$.

CHAPTER 6
Lexical Analysis

Lexical analysis converts the source program from a character string to a sequence of semantically-relevant symbols. The symbols and their encoding form the intermediate language output from the lexical analyzer.

In principle, lexical analysis is a subtask of parsing that could be carried out by the normal parser mechanisms. To separate these functions, the source language grammar G must be partitioned into subgrammars $G_0, G_1, G_2, \ldots$ such that $G_1, G_2, \ldots$ describe the structure of the basic symbols and G_0 describes the structure of the language in terms of the basic symbols. $L(G)$ is then obtained by replacing the terminal symbols of G_0 by strings from $L(G_1), L(G_2), \ldots$

The separation of lexical analysis from parsing gives rise to higher organizational costs that can be justified only by realizing greater savings in other areas. Such savings are possible in table-driven parsers through reduction in table size. Further, basic symbols usually have such a simple structure that faster procedures can be used for the lexical analysis than for the general parsing.

We shall first discuss the partitioning of the grammar and the desired results of lexical analysis, and then consider implementation with the help of finite automata.

6.1. Modules and Interfaces

In this section we devote ourselves to the 'black box' aspects of lexical analysis: Decomposition of the grammar and with it the definition of the tasks of lexical analysis, arriving at the interface between the lexical analyzer and the remainder of the compiler.

135

6.1.1. Decomposition of the Grammar   Delimiters (keywords, meaningful special characters and combinations of special characters), identifiers and constants together are termed *basic symbols*. In sharp contrast to other language elements, their structure and representation may be arbitrarily changed (say by introducing French or German keywords or by representing '$<$' by '.LT.') without altering the power of the language. Further, the structure of the basic symbols can generally be described with regular grammars or regular expressions.

The productions of Section A.1 describe the basic symbols of LAX. (Conversion to a regular grammar is left to the reader.) The productions A.1.0.1, A.1.0.9-12 are superfluous because only the nonterminals *identifier* and *constant*, single keywords, special characters and special character combinations (other than '(*') occur in the remainder of the grammar.

In many languages the grammar for basic symbols (*symbol grammar*) is not so easily determined from the language definition, or it results in additional difficulties. For example, the ALGOL 60 Report defines keywords, letters, digits, special characters and special character combinations as basic symbols; it does not include identifiers, numbers and strings in this category. This description must be transformed to meet the requirements of compiler construction. In PL/1, as in other languages in which keywords are lexically indistinguishable from identifiers, context determines whether an identifier (e.g. IF) is to be treated as a keyword or a freely-chosen identifier. Two symbol grammars must therefore be distinguished on the basis of context; one accepts identifiers and not keywords, the other does the converse. An example of similar context-dependence in FORTRAN is the first identifier of a statement: In an assignment it is interpreted as the identifier of a data object, while in most other cases it is interpreted as a keyword. (Statement classification in FORTRAN is not an easy task — see the discussion by Sale [1971] for details.)

Even if it is necessary to consult context in order to determine which symbols are possible at the given point in the input text, a finite automaton often suffices. The automaton in this case has several starting states corresponding to the distinct symbol grammars. We shall not pursue this point further.

6.1.2. Lexical Analyzer Interface   The lexical analyzer is organized as a module with several local state variables and implements the following elementary operations:

- *initialize_lexical_analysis*

- *next_token*

- *wrapup_lexical_analysis*

The central operation *next_token* is used by the parser to obtain the next token in the token sequence (Section 4.1.1). (A coroutine, activated for each token, might be used instead of a procedure.) If the parser does not interact directly with the lexical analyzer, then a file of tokens must be constructed by calls to *next_token*. The parser obtains the tokens by reading this file. Even if direct calls are possible, such a file is necessary when the parsing is done in several passes (as for ALGOL 68).

The lexical analyzer itself uses the following elementary operations:

- *next_character*   (Source program input module)
- *report_lexical_error*   (Error module)
- *identify_symbol*   (Symbol table module)
- *enter_constant*   (Constant table module)

The information flow involving the lexical analyzer module is shown in Figure 6.1.

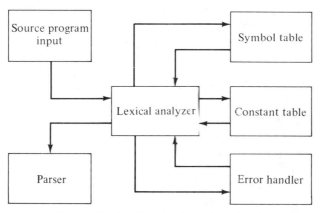

Figure 6.1. Lexical Analyzer Interfaces

The lexical analyzer reads the input text one character at a time by executing the *next_character* operation. Both the transition to a new line (if it is significant) and the encounter with the end of the input text are represented by characters in order to preserve the uniformity of the interface. (If *next_character* is executed again after the end of the input text has been encountered then it continues to deliver the termination character.) Usually *next_character* is the most frequently executed operation in the entire compiler, and thus strongly influences the speed of compilation. We shall consider the implementation of this operation in detail in Section 6.2.3.

The error reporting module is invoked when *lexical errors* (unrecognized input characters and violations of the basic symbol grammar) are encountered. This module will then determine the continuation of lexical analysis (Section 12.2.3).

When a sequence of characters has been identified as a basic symbol, the lexical analyzer will either create a token describing it or will restart in a new state. Different representations of the same basic symbol are resolved at this point. For example, if we were to allow the symbol '<' to be written

'LESS' or 'LT' also, all three would lead to creation of the same token. The operation *identify_symbol* is used during token creation to perform the mapping discussed in Section 4.2.1. If the basic symbol is a literal constant, rather than an identifier, the *enter_constant* operation is used instead of *identify_symbol* (Section 4.2.2).

6.2. Construction

We assume that the basic symbols are described by some set of regular grammars or regular expressions as discussed in Section 6.1.1. According to Theorem 5.15 or Theorem 5.19 we can construct a set of finite automata that accept the basic symbols. Unfortunately, these automata assume the end of the string to be *known a priori*; the task of the lexical analyzer is to extract the next basic symbol from the input text, *determining* the end of the symbol in the process. Thus the automaton only partially solves the lexical analysis problem. To enhance the efficiency of the lexical analyzer we should use the automaton with the fewest states from the set of automata that accept the given language. Finally, we consider implementation questions.

In order to obtain the classification for the basic symbol (Figure 4.1) we partition the final states of the automaton into classes. Each class either provides the classification directly or indicates that it must be found by using the operation *identify_symbol*. The textual representation of constants, and the strings used to interrogate the symbol table, are obtained from the input stream. The automaton is extended for this purpose to a *finite-state transducer* that emits a character on each state transition. (In the terminology of switching theory, this transducer is a special case of a Mealy machine.) The output characters are collected together into a character string, which is then used to derive the necessary information.

6.2.1. Extraction and Representation   A semicolon is an ALGOL 60 basic symbol, and is not a head of any other basic symbol. When an ALGOL 60 lexical analysis automaton reaches the final state corresponding to semicolon, it can halt and accept the semicolon. The end of the accepted string has been determined, and the input pointer is positioned for the next symbol. A colon is also an ALGOL 60 basic symbol, but it is a head of $:=$. Therefore the automaton must look ahead when it reaches the final state corresponding to colon. A more complex lookahead is required in the case of FORTRAN, where a digit sequence d is a basic symbol and also a head of the basic symbol d.E1. Since .EQ. is also a basic symbol, the automaton must look ahead three characters (in certain cases) before it can determine the end of the symbol string.

By applying the tests of Section 5.3.3 to the original grammar G, we could determine (for fixed k) whether a k-character lookahead is sufficient to resolve ambiguity. Because of the effort involved, this is usually not done.

Instead, we apply the *principle of the longest match*: The automaton continues to read until it reaches a state with no transition corresponding to the current input character. If that state is a final state, then it accepts the symbol scanned to that point; otherwise it signals a lexical error. The feasibility of the principle of the longest match is determined by the representation of the symbols (the grammars G_1, G_2,...) and by the sequences of symbols permitted (the grammar G_0).

The principle of the longest match in its basic form as stated above is unsuitable for a large number of grammars. For example, an attempt to extract the next token from '3.EQ.4' using the rules of FORTRAN would result in a lexical error when 'Q' was encountered. The solution is to retain information about the most-recently encountered final state, thus providing a 'fall-back' position. If the automaton halts in a final state, then it accepts the symbol; otherwise it restores the input stream pointer to that at the most-recently encountered final state. A lexical error is signaled only if no final state had been encountered during the scan.

We have tacitly assumed that the initial state of the automaton is independent of the final state reached by the previous invocation of *next_token*. If this assumption is relaxed, permitting the state to be retained from the last invocation, then it is sometimes possible to avoid even the limited backtracking discussed above (Exercise 6.3). Whether this technique solves all problems is still an open question.

The choice of a representation for the keywords of a language plays a central role in determining the representations of other basic symbols. This choice is largely a question of language design: The definitions of COBOL, FORTRAN and PL/1 (for example) prescribe the representations and their relationship to freely-chosen identifiers. In the case of ALGOL 60 and its descendants, however, these characteristics are not discussed in the language definitions. Here we shall briefly review the possibilities and their consequences.

The simplest possibility is the representation of keywords by *reserved words* — ordinary identifiers that the programmer is not permitted to use for any other purpose. This approach requires that identifiers be written without gaps, so that spaces and newlines can serve as separators between identifiers and between an identifier and a number. Letters may appear within numbers, and hence they must not be separated from the preceding part of the number by spaces. The main advantage of this representation is its lucidity and low susceptibility to typographical errors. Its main disadvantage is that the programmer often does not remember all of the reserved words and hence incorrectly uses one as a freely-chosen identifier. Further, it is virtually impossible to modify the language by adding a new keyword because too many existing programs might have used this keyword as a freely-chosen identifier.

If keywords are distinguished lexically then it is possible to relax the restrictions on placement of spaces and newlines. There is no need for the programmer to remember all of the keywords, and new ones may be introduced without affecting existing programs. The rules for distinguishing keywords are known as *stropping conventions*; the most common ones are:

- Underlining the keyword.

- Bracketing the keyword by special delimiters (such as the apostrophes used in the DIN 66006 standard for ALGOL 60).
- Prefixing the keyword with a special character and terminating it at the first space, newline or character other than a letter or digit.

- Using upper case letters for keywords and lower case for identifiers (or vice-versa).

All of these conventions increase the susceptibility of the input text to typo-graphical errors. Some also require larger character sets than others or rela-tively complex line-imaging routines.

6.2.2. State Minimization   Consider a completely-specified finite auto-maton $A = (T,Q,R,q_0,F)$ in which a production $qt \rightarrow q'$ exists for every pair (q,t), $q \in Q$, $t \in T$. Such an automaton is termed *reduced* when there exists no equivalent automaton with fewer states.

Theorem. *For every completely-specified finite automaton $A = (T,Q,R,q_0,F)$ there exists a reduced finite automaton $A' = (T,Q',R',q_0',F')$ with $L(A') = L(A)$.*

To construct A' we first delete all states q for which there exists no string ω such that $q_0\omega \Rightarrow^* q$. (These states are termed *unreachable*.) We then apply the refinement algorithm of Section B.3.2 to the state diagram of A, with the initial partition $\{q \mid q \in F\}$, $\{q \mid q \notin F\}$. Let Q' be the set of all blocks in the resulting partition, and let $[q]$ denote the block to which $q \in Q$ belongs. The definition of A' can now be completed as follows:

$$R' = \{[q]t \rightarrow [q'] \mid qt \rightarrow q' \notin R\}$$

$$q_0' = [q_0]$$

$$F' = \{[q] \mid q \in F\}$$

As an example, consider the automaton of Figure 5.13, which recognized the regular expression $l(l+d)^*$. The initial partition consists of two blocks $\{q_0\}$ and $\{q_1, q_2, q_3\}$ and is not refined, leading to the automaton of Figure 6.2. We would have achieved the same result if we had begun with the regu-lar expression $(A +B + \cdots +Z)(A +B + \cdots +Z +0+ \cdots +9)^*$.

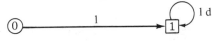

Figure 6.2. Reduced Automaton Accepting $l(l +d)^*$

In order to apply the algorithm of Section B.3.2 to this example we must complete the original automaton, which permits only l as an input character in state q_0. To do this we introduce an 'error state', q_e, and transitions $qt \to q_e$ for all pairs $(q, t), q \in Q, t \in T$, not corresponding to transitions of the given automaton. (In the example, $q_0 d \to q_e$ suffices.) In practice, however, it is easier to modify the algorithm so that it does not require explicit error transitions.

If c denotes any character other than the quote, then the regular expression $"" + "(c + "")(c + "")*"$ describes the characters and strings of Pascal. Figure 6.3a shows the automaton constructed from this expression according to the procedure of Theorem 5.19, and the reduced automaton is shown in Figure 6.3b.

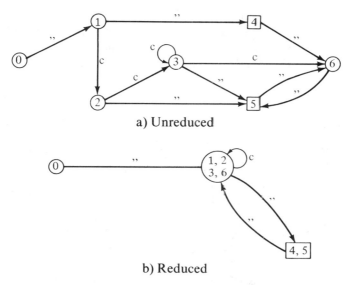

a) Unreduced

b) Reduced

Figure 6.3. Finite Automata Accepting '$"" + "(c + ")(c + ")*$'

In our application we must modify the equivalence relation still further, and only treat final states as equivalent when they lead to identical subsequent processing. For an automaton recognizing the symbol grammar of LAX, we divide the final states into the following classes:

• Identifiers or keywords

• Special characters

• Combinations of special characters

• Integers

• Floating point numbers

• Floating point numbers with exponents

This results in the reduced automaton of Figure 6.4. Letters denote the following character classes:

- a = all characters other than '*'
- a' = all characters other than '*' or ')'
- c = all characters other than quote
- d = digits
- l = letters
- s = '+' '-' '*' '<' '>' '↑' ';' ',' ')' '[' ']'

Figure 6.4 illustrates several methods of obtaining the code corresponding to a basic symbol. States, 1, 6, 7, 9, and 12-18 all provide the code directly. *Identify_symbol* must be used in state 4 to distinguish identifiers from keywords. In state 19 we might also use *identify_symbol,* or we might use some other direct computation based on the character codes.

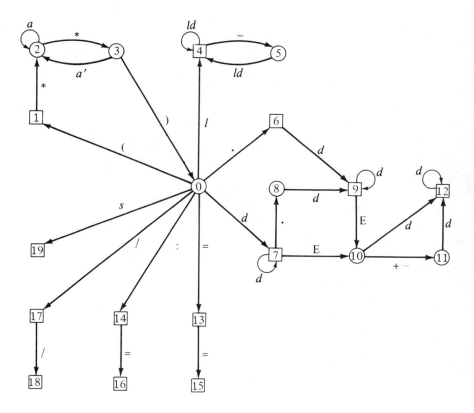

Figure 6.4. Finite Automaton Accepting LAX Basic Symbols

The state reduction in these examples could be performed by hand with no display of theory, but the theory is required if we wish to mechanically implement a lexical analyzer based upon regular expressions.

6.2.3. Programming the Lexical Analyzer

In order to extract the basic symbol that follows a given position p in the input stream we must recognize and delete irrelevant characters such as spaces and newlines, use the automaton to read the symbol, and fix the terminal position p'.

Superfluous spaces can be deleted by adding transitions $q'' \to q$ to all states q in which such spaces are permitted. Since newlines (card boundaries or carriage returns) are input characters if they are significant, we can handle them in the same way as superfluous spaces in many languages.

There are two possibilities from which to choose when programming the automaton:

- Representing the transition table as a matrix, so that the program for the automaton has the general form:

  > **while** *basic_symbol_not_yet_complete* **do**
  > *state*: = *table* [*state,next_character*];

- Programming the transition table as a case clause for each state.

The first method is generally expensive in terms of memory. For LAX we need a 20×57 matrix, even without considering characters that may occur only in comments. We can reduce the size of this matrix by grouping together all characters that are treated uniformly by the lexical analyzer and provide one column for each such *character class*. The class to which a character belongs is then obtained from an array indexed by the character. This array makes the remainder of the compiler relatively independent of changing character sets and their encoding, thus increasing its machine-independence. For LAX the classes are: {letters other than E}, {E}, {digits}, {_}, {(),)}, {*}, {+ −}, {;}, {=}, {/}, {"}, {.}, {:}, {< > ↑, [ ]}, {space tab newline}, {terminator (#)}, {characters allowed only in comments}; the matrix size is then 20×18. The storage requirements can often be reduced still further, possibly by means of techniques introduced in the next chapter.

In contrast to the matrix representation, mechanical implementation of the transition table by case clauses can be carried out only at great cost. Hand coding is rather simple, however, and one usually obtains a much smaller lexical analyzer. Steps can also be taken to speed up execution of the most-frequently performed transitions.

The simplest way to provide output from the automaton is to add the input character to a string — empty at the start of the basic symbol — during each state transition. This strategy is generally inadequate. For example, the quotes bounding a Pascal character or string denotation should be omitted and any doubled internal quote should be replaced by a single quote.

Thus more general actions may need to be taken at each state transition. It usually suffices, however, to provide the following four options:

- Add (some mapping of) the input character to the output string.

- Add a given character to the output string.

- Set a pointer or index to the output string.

- Do nothing.

Figure 6.5 illustrates three of these actions applied to produce output from the automaton of Figure 6.3b. A slash separates the output action from the input character; the absence of a slash indicates the 'do nothing' action.

In order to produce the standard representation of floating point numbers (see Section 4.2.2), we require three indices to the characters of the significand:

beg: Initially indexes the first character of the significand, finally indexes the first nonzero digit.

pnt: Indexes the first position to the right of the decimal point.

lim: Initially indexes the first position to the right of the significand, finally indexes the first position to the right of the last nonzero digit.

By moving the indices *beg* and *lim*, the leading and trailing zeros are removed so that the significand is left over in standard form. If e is the value of the explicit exponent, then the adjusted exponent e' is given by:

$$e' := e + (beg - pnt) \quad \text{significand interpreted as a fraction}$$
$$e' := e + (pnt - lim) \quad \text{significand interpreted as an integer}$$

The standard representation of a floating point zero is the pair $('0', 0)$. This representation is obtained by taking a special exit from the standardization algorithm if *beg* becomes equal to *lim* during the zero-removal process.

Many authors suggest that the *next_character* operation be implemented by a procedure. We have already pointed out that the implementation of *next_character* strongly influences the overall speed of the compiler; in many cases simple use of a procedure leads to significant inefficiency. For

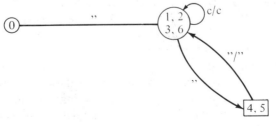

Figure 6.5. Finite Transducer for Pascal Strings

Table 6.6. Lexical Analysis on a Control Data 6400 [Dunn 1974]

| Translator | Program | Lexical Analysis Time | |
		Microseconds per character	Fraction of total compile time
	Page Formatter	3.56	14%
	without comments	3.44	9%
	Flowchart Generator	3.3	11.5%
COMPASS 2.0	I/O Package	5.1	21%
Pascal 3.4	Pascal Compiler	35.6	39.6%

example, Table 6.6 shows the results of measuring lexical analysis times for three translators running on a Control Data 6400 under KRONOS 2.0. RUN 2.3 is a FORTRAN compiler that reads one line at a time, storing it in an array; the *next_character* operation is implemented as a fetch and index increment in-line. The COMPASS 2.0 assembler implements some instances of *next_character* by procedure calls and others by in-line references, while the Pascal compiler uses a procedure call to fetch each character. The two test programs for the FORTRAN compiler had similar characteristics: Each was about 5000 lines long, composed of 30-40 heavily-commented subprograms. The test program for COMPASS contained 900 lines, about one-third of which were comments, and that for Pascal (the compiler itself) had 5000 lines with very few comments.

Further measurements on existing compilers for a number of languages indicate that the major subtasks of lexical analysis can be rank-ordered by amount of time spent as follows:

1. Skipping spaces and comments.
2. Collecting identifiers and keywords.
3. Collecting digits.
4. All other tasks.

In many cases there are large (factor of at least 2) differences in the amount of time spent between adjacent elements in this hierarchy. Of course the precise breakdown depends upon the language, compiler, operating system and coding technique of the user. For example, skipping a comment is trivial in FORTRAN; on the other hand, an average non-comment card in FORTRAN has 48 blank columns out of the 66 allocated to code [Knuth 1971].

Taken together, the measurements discussed in the two paragraphs above lead to the conclusion that the lexical analyzer should be partitioned further: Tasks 1-3 should be incorporated into a *scanner* module that implements the *next_character* operation, and the finite automaton and its underlying regular grammar (or regular expression) should be defined in terms of the characters *digit_string*, *identifier*, *keyword*, etc. This decomposition drastically reduces the number of invocations of *next_character*, and also the influence of the automaton implementation upon the speed of the lexical analyzer.

Tasks 1-3 are trivial, and can be implemented 'by hand' using all of the coding tricks and special instructions available on the target computer. They can be carefully integrated with the I/O facilities provided by the operating system to minimize overhead. In this way, serious inefficiencies in the lexical analyzer can be avoided while retaining systematic construction techniques for most of the implementation.

6.3. Notes and References

The fact that the basic symbols are regular was first exploited to generate a lexical analyzer mechanically in the RWORD System [Johnson 1968, Gries 1971]. More recently, DeRemer [1974] has proposed the use of a modified LR technique (Section 5.3.3) for this generation. Lesk [1975] describes how such a system can be linked to the remainder of a compiler.

Lexical analyzer generators are still the exception rather than the rule. The analyzers used in practice are simple, and hand coding is not prohibitively expensive. There are also many indications that the hand-coded product provides significant savings in execution time over the products of existing generators. Many of the coding details (table formats, output actions, limited backtrack and character class tradeoffs) are discussed by Waite [1973a] in his treatment of string-directed pattern matching.

Two additional features, macros and compiler control commands (compiler options, compile-time facilities) complicate the lexical analyzer and its interface to the parser. Macro processing can usually be done in a separate pre-pass. If, however, it is integrated into the language (as in PL/M or Burroughs Extended ALGOL) then it is a task of the lexical analyzer. This requires additional information from the parser regarding the scope of macro definitions.

We recommend that control commands always be written on a separate line, and be easily recognizable by the lexical analyzer. They should *also* be syntactically valid, so that the parser can process them if they are not relevant to lexical analysis. Finally, it is important that there be only *one* form of control command, since the user should not be forced to learn several conventions because the compiler writer decides to process commands in several places.

EXERCISES

6.1. Derive a regular grammar from the LAX symbol grammar of Appendix A.1. Derive a regular expression.

6.2. [Sale 1971, McIlroy 1974] Consider the definition of FORTRAN 66.
   a. Partition the grammar as discussed in Section 6.1.1. Explain why you distinguished each of the symbol subgrammars G_i.
   b. Carefully specify the lexical analyzer interface. How do you invoke different symbol subgrammars?

6.3. Consider the following set of tokens, which are possible in a FORTRAN assignment statement [McIlroy 1974] (*identifier* is constructed as usual, *d* denotes a nonempty sequence of digits, and *s* denotes either '+' or '−'):

   $+ - * / ** ( ) , =$
   .TRUE. .FALSE.
   .AND. .OR. .NOT.
   .LT. .LE. .EQ. .NE. .GE. .GT.
   identifier
   d   d.   d.d   .d
   d Ed   d.Ed   d.d Ed   .d Ed
   d Esd   d.Esd   d.d Esd   .d Esd

Assume that any token sequence is permissible, and that the ambiguity of '***' may be resolved in any convenient manner.
   a. Derive an analysis automaton using the methods of Section 5.2, and minimize the number of states by the method of Section B.3.3.
   b. Derive an analysis automaton using the methods given by Aho and Corasick [1975], and minimize the number of states.
   c. Describe in detail the interaction between the parser and the automaton derived in (b). What information must be retained? What form should that information take?
   d. Can you generalize the construction algorithms of Aho and Corasick to arbitrary regular expression inputs?

6.4. Write a line-imaging routine to accept an arbitrary sequence of printable characters, spaces and backspace characters and create an image of the input line. You should recognize an extended character set which includes arbitrary underlining, plus the following overstruck characters:

   c overstruck by / interpreted as 'cents'
   = overstruck by / interpreted as 'not equal'

(Note: Overstrikes may occur in any order.) Your image should be an integer array, with one element per character *position*. This integer should encode the character (e.g. 'cents') resulting in that position from the arbitrary input sequence.

6.5. Write a program to implement the automaton of Figure 6.4 as a collection of case clauses. Compile the program and compare its size to the requirements for the transition table.

6.6. Attach output specifications to the transitions of Figure 6.4. How will the inclusion of these specifications affect the program you wrote for Exercise 6.5? Will their inclusion change the relationship between the program size and transition table size significantly?

6.7. Consider the partition of a lexical analyzer for LAX into scanner and an automaton.

    a. Restate the symbol grammar in terms of *identifier*, *digit_string*, etc. to reflect the partition. Show how this change affects Figure 6.4.

    b. Carefully specify the interface between scanner and automaton.

    c. Rewrite the routine of Exercise 6.5, using the interface defined in (b). Has the overall size of the lexical analyzer changed? (Don't forget to include the scanner size!) Has the relationship between the two possible implementations of the automaton (case clauses or transition tables) changed?

    d. Measure the time required for lexical analysis, comparing the implementation of (c) with that of Exercise 6.5. If they differ, can you attribute the difference to any specific feature of your environment (e.g. an expensive procedure mechanism)? If they do not differ, can you explain why?

6.8. Suppose that LAX is being implemented on a machine that supports both upper and lower case letters. How would your lexical analyzer change under each of the following assumptions:

    a. Upper and lower case letters are indistinguishable.

    b. Upper and lower case may be mixed arbitrarily in identifiers, but all occurrences of a given identifier must use the same characters. (In other words, if an identifier is introduced as *ArraySize* then no identifier such as *arraysize* can be introduced in the same range.) Keywords must always be lower case.

    c. As (b), except that upper and lower case may be mixed arbitrarily in keywords, and need not always be the same.

    d. Choose one of the schemes (a)-(c) and argue in favor of it on grounds of program portability, ease of use, documentation value, etc.

CHAPTER 7
Parsing

The parsing of a source program determines the semantically-relevant phrases and, at the same time, verifies syntactic correctness. As a result we obtain the parse tree of the program, at first represented implicitly by the sequence of productions employed during the derivation from (or reduction to) the axiom according to the underlying grammar.

In this chapter we concern ourselves with the practical implementation of parsers. We begin with the parser interface and the appropriate choice of parsing technique, and then go into the construction of deterministic parsers from a given grammar. We shall consider both the top-down and bottom-up parsing techniques introduced in Section 5.3.2 and 5.3.3. Methods for coding parsers by hand and for generating them mechanically will be discussed.

7.1. Design

To design a parser we must define the grammar to be processed, augment it with *connection points* (points at which information will be extracted) and choose the parsing algorithm. Finally, the augmented grammar must be converted into a form suited to the chosen parsing technique. After this preparation the actual construction of the parser can be carried out mechanically. Thus the process of parser design is really one of grammar design, in which we derive a grammar satisfying the restrictions of a particular parsing algorithm and containing the connection points necessary to determine the semantics of the source program.

Even if we are given a grammar for the language, modifications may be necessary to obtain a useful parser. We must, of course, guarantee that the modified grammar actually describes the same language as the original, and

149

that the semantic structure is unchanged. Structural syntactic ambiguity leading to different semantic interpretations can only be corrected by altering the language. Other ambiguities can frequently be removed by deleting productions or restricting their applicability depending upon the parser state.

7.1.1. The Parser Interface

A parser accepts a sequence of basic symbols, recognizes the extant syntactic structure, and outputs that structure along with the identity of the relevant symbols. If the syntactic structure is not error-free, the parser invokes the error handler to report errors and to aid in recovery so that processing can continue. (The details of the recovery mechanism will be discussed in Section 12.2.2.) Figure 7.1 shows the information flow involved in the parsing process.

Three possible interface specifications are suggested by Figure 7.1, depending upon the overall organization of the compiler. The most common is for the parser module to provide the operation *parse_program*. It invokes the lexical analyzer's *next_symbol* operation for each basic symbol, and reports each connection point by invoking an appropriate operation of some other module. (We term this invocation a *parser action.*) Control of the entire transduction process resides within the parser in this design. By moving the control out of the parser module, we obtain the two alternative designs: The parser module provides either an operation *parse_symbol* that is invoked with a token as an argument, or an operation *next_connection* that is invoked to obtain a connection point specification.

It is also possible to divide the parsing over more than one pass. Properties of the language and demands of the parsing algorithm can lead to a situation where we need to know the semantics of certain symbols before we can parse the context of the definitions of these symbols. ALGOL 68, for example, permits constructs whose syntactic structure can be recognized by deterministic left-to-right analysis only if the complete set of type identifiers

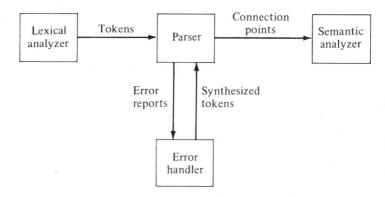

Figure 7.1. Parser Information Flow

is known beforehand. When the parsing is carried out in several passes, the sequence of symbols produced by the lexical analyzer will be augmented by other information collected by parser actions during previous passes. The details depend upon the source language.

We have already considered the interface between the parser and the lexical analyzer, and the representation of symbols. The parser looks ahead some number of symbols in order to control the parsing. As soon as it has accepted one of the lookahead symbols as a component of the sentence being analyzed, it reads the next symbol to maintain the supply of lookahead symbols. Through the use of LL or LR techniques, we can be certain that the program is syntactically correct up to and including the accepted symbol. The parser thus need not retain accepted symbols. If the code for these symbols, or their values, must be passed on to other compiler modules via parser actions, these actions must be connected directly to the acceptance of the symbol. We shall term connection points serving this purpose *symbol connections.*

We can distinguish a second class of connection point, the *structure connection.* It is used to connect parser actions to the attainment of certain sets of situations (in the sense of Section 5.3.2) and permits us to trace the phrases recognized by the parser in the source program. Note carefully that symbol and structure connections provide the *only* information that a compiler extracts from the input text.

In order to produce the parse tree as an explicit data structure, it suffices to provide one structure connection at each reduction of a simple phrase and one symbol connection at acceptance of each symbol having a symbol value; at the structure connections we must know which production was applied. We can fix the connection points for this process mechanically from the grammar. This process has proved useful, particularly with bottom-up parsing.

Parser actions that enter declarations into tables or generate code directly cannot be fixed mechanically, but must be introduced by the programmer. Moreover, we often know which production is to be applied well before the reduction actually takes place, and we can make good use of this knowledge. In these cases we must explicitly mark the connection points and parser actions in the grammar from which the parser is produced. We add the symbol encoding (code and value) taken from the lexical analyzer as a parameter to the symbol connections, whereas parser actions at structure connections extract all of their information from the state of the parser.

Figure 7.2a illustrates a grammar with connection points. The character % marks structure connections, the character & symbol connections. Following these characters, the parser action at that point is specified. Definitions of the parser actions are given in Figure 7.2b. The result of these specifications is a translation of arithmetic expressions from infix to postfix form.

Expression ::= *Term* (*'+' Term %Addop*)* .
Term ::= *Factor* (*'*' Factor %Mulop*)* .
Factor ::= *'Identifier' &Ident* | *'(' Expression ')'* .

a) A grammar for expressions

Addop :   Output "+"
Mulop :   Output "*"
Ident :   Output the identifier returned by the lexical analyzer

b) Parser actions to produce postfix

Figure 7.2. Connection Points

The processes for parser generation to be described in Sections 7.2 and
7.3 can interpret symbol and structure connections introduced explicitly into
the grammar as additional nonterminals generating the null string. Thus the
connection points do not require special treatment; only the generated parsing algorithm must distinguish them from symbols of the grammar. In addition, none of the transformations used during the generation process alters
the invocation sequence of the associated parser actions.

The introduction of connection points can alter the properties of the
grammar. For example, the grammar whose productions are $\{Z \to S,$
$S \to abc, S \to abd\}$ is LR(0). The modified grammar $\{Z \to S, S \to a\&Abc,$
$S \to a\&Bbd\}$ no longer possesses this property: After reading a it is not yet
clear which of the parser actions should be carried out.

If a grammar does not have a desired property before connection points
are introduced, then their inclusion will not provide that property. This does
not, however, prohibit a parser action from altering the state of the parser
and thus simulating some desirable property. For example, one can occasionally distinguish among several possible state transitions through the use
of semantic information and in this manner establish an LL property not
previously present. More problems are generally created than avoided by
such ad hoc measures, however.

7.1.2. Selection of the Parsing Algorithm   The choice of which parsing
technique to use in a compiler depends more upon the economic and implementation viewpoint than upon the source language and its technical properties. Experience with a particular technique and availability of a program to construct the parser (or the cost of developing such a program) are
usually stronger criteria than the suitability of the technique for the given
source language. The reason is that, in many cases, the grammar for a
language can be modified to satisfy the restrictions of several parsing techniques.

As we have previously stressed, the parser should work deterministically
under all circumstances. Only in this way can we parse correct programs in

a time linearly dependent upon program length, avoiding backtrack and the need to unravel parser actions. We have already pointed out the LL and LR algorithms as special cases of deterministic techniques that recognize a syntactic error at the first symbol, t, that cannot be the continuation of a correct program; other algorithms may not discover the error until attempting to reduce the simple phrase in which t occurs. Moreover, LR(k) grammars comprise the largest class whose sentences can be parsed using deterministic pushdown automata. In view of these properties we restrict ourselves to the discussion of LL and LR parsing algorithms. Other techniques can be found in the literature cited in Section 7.4.

Usually the availability of a parser generator is the strongest motive for the choice between LL and LR algorithms: If one has such a generator at one's disposal, then the technique it implements is given preference. If no parser generator is available, then an LL algorithm should be selected because the LL conditions are substantially easier to verify by hand. Also a transparent method for obtaining the parser from the grammar exists for LL but not for LR algorithms. By using this approach, recognizers for large grammars can be programmed relatively easily by hand.

LR algorithms apply to a larger class of grammars than LL algorithms, because they postpone the decision about the applicable production until the reduction takes place. The main advantage of LR algorithms is that they permit more latitude in the representation of the grammar. As the example at the end of Section 7.1.1 shows, however, this advantage may be neutralized if distinct structure connections that frustrate deferment of a parsing decision must be introduced. (Note that LL and LR algorithms behave identically for all language constructs that begin with a special keyword.)

We restrict our discussion to parsers with only one-symbol lookahead, and thus to LL(1) and LR(1) grammars. Experience shows that this is not a substantial restriction; programming languages are usually so simply constructed that it is easy to satisfy the necessary conditions. In fact, to a large extent one can manage with no lookahead at all. The main reason for the restriction is the considerable increase in cost (both time and space) that must be invested to obtain more lookahead symbols in the parser generator and in the generated parser.

When dealing with LR grammars, not even the restriction to the LR(1) case is sufficient to obtain practical tables. Thus we use an LR(1) parse algorithm, but control it with tables obtained through a modification of the LR(0) analyzer.

7.1.3. Parser Construction

LL and LR parsers are pushdown automata. Given a grammar $G = (T,N,P,Z)$, we can use either construction 5.23 (LL) or construction 5.33 (LR) to derive a parsing automaton $A = (T,Q,R,q_0,\{q_0\},Q,q_0)$. To implement this automaton, we must represent the transitions of R in a convenient form so that we can determine the next transition quickly and at the same time keep the total storage requirement reasonable.

For this purpose we derive a *transition function*, $f(q, v)$, from the production set R. It specifies which of the possible actions (e.g. read a symbol, reduce according to a production from P, report an error) should be taken in state q when the input string begins with the element $v \in T$. In the LR case we also define $f(q, v)$ for $v \in N$; it then specifies the action to be taken in state q after a reduction to v. The transition function may be represented by a (transition) matrix.

Some of the entries of $f(q, v)$ may be unreachable, regardless of the terminal string input to the parser. (We shall give examples in Section 7.3.1.) Because these entries can never be reached, the actions they specify are irrelevant. In the terminology of sequential machines, these entries are *don't-cares* and the transition function is *incompletely specified*. The presence of don't-cares leads to possible reduction in table size by combining rows or columns that differ only in those elements.

The transition function may be stored as program fragments rather than as a matrix. This is especially useful in an LL parser, where there are simple rules relating the program fragments to the original grammar.

Parser generation is actually compilation: The source program is a grammar with embedded connection points, and the target program is some representation of the transition function. Like all compilers, the parser generator must first analyze its input text. This analysis phase tests the grammar to ensure that it satisfies the conditions (LL(1), LR(1), etc.) assumed by the parser. Some generators, like 'error correcting' compilers, will attempt to transform a grammar that does not meet the required conditions. Other transformations designed to optimize the generated parser may also be undertaken. In Sections 7.2 and 7.3 we shall consider some aspects of the 'semantic analysis' (condition testing) and optimization phases of parser generators.

Table 7.3 summarizes the computational complexity of the parser generation algorithms presented in the remainder of this chapter. (The parameter n is the sum of the lengths of the right-hand sides of all productions.) It should be emphasized that the expressions of Table 7.3 represent asymptotic

Table 7.3. Computational Complexity of
Parser Generation [Hunt 1975]

Grammar Type	Test	Parser generation
LL(1)	n^2	n^2
Strong LL(k)	n^{k+1}	n^{k+1}
LL(k)	n^{2k}	$2^{n^k + (k+1)\log n}$
SLR(1)	n^2	$2^{n + \log n}$
SLR(k)	n^{k+2}	$2^{n + k\log n}$
LR(k)	$n^{2(k+1)}$	$2^{n^{k+1} + k\log n}$

bounds on execution time. All of the bounds given are sharp, since in every case grammars exist whose parsers require an amount of table space proportional to the time bound specified for parser construction.

7.2. LL(1) Parsers

LL(1) parsers are top-down pushdown automata that can be obtained by construction 5.23. We shall first sharpen the definition of an LL grammar and thereby simplify the construction of the automaton. Next we explain the relationship between a given LL(1) grammar and the implementation of the pushdown automaton. Finally we develop the algorithms for an LL(1) parser generator. We defer the problem of error handling until Section 12.2.2.

7.2.1. Strong LL(k) Grammars   Consider an LL(k) grammar $G = (T,N,P,Z)$ and a left derivation:

$$Z \Rightarrow^L \mu A \nu \Rightarrow \mu \gamma \qquad \mu,\gamma \in T^*, A \in N, \nu \in V^*$$

According to Definition 5.22, we can predict the next applicable production $A \to \chi$ if μ and $k:\gamma$ are given. The dependence upon μ is responsible for the fact that, in construction 5.23, we must carry along the right context ω in the situation $[A \to \alpha \cdot \beta; \omega]$. Without this dependence we could use the following in place of step 5 of the construction algorithm:

5′ If $\nu = B\gamma$ for some $B \in N$ and $\gamma \in V^*$, let $q' = [X \to \mu B \cdot \gamma; \Omega]$ and $H = \{[B \to \cdot \beta_i; FOLLOW_k(B)] \mid B \to \beta_i \in P\}$. Set $Q := Q \cup \{q'\} \cup H$, and $R := R \cup \{q\tau \to q'h_i\tau \mid h_i \in H, \tau \in FIRST_k(\beta_i FOLLOW_k(B))\}$.

In this way, situations distinct only in the right context always belong to the same state. This simplification is made possible by the strong LL(k) grammars introduced by Rosenkrantz and Stearns [1970]:

Definition 7.1. A context free grammar $G = (T,N,P,Z)$ is called a *strong* $LL(k)$ grammar for given $k > 0$ if, for arbitrary derivations

$$Z \Rightarrow^L \mu A \chi \Rightarrow \mu \nu \chi \Rightarrow^* \mu \gamma \qquad \mu,\gamma \in T^*, \nu,\chi \in V^*, A \in N$$
$$Z \Rightarrow^L \mu' A \chi' \Rightarrow \mu' \omega \chi' \Rightarrow^* \mu' \gamma' \quad \mu',\gamma' \in T^*, \omega,\chi' \in V^*$$

$(k:\gamma = k:\gamma')$ implies $\nu = \omega$.

The grammar with $P = \{Z \to aAab, Z \to bAbb, A \to a, A \to \epsilon\}$ is LL(2), as can be seen by writing down all derivations. On the other hand, the derivations $Z \Rightarrow aAab \Rightarrow aab$ and $Z \Rightarrow bAbb \Rightarrow babb$ violate the conditions for strong LL(2) grammars.

The dependence upon μ, the stack contents of the automaton, is reflected in the fact that two distinct states $q = [X \to \mu \cdot \nu; \omega]$ and $q' = [X \to \mu \cdot \nu; \omega']$, identical except for the right context, can occur in construction 5.23 and lead to distinct sequences of transitions. Without this dependence the further course of the parse is determined solely by $X \to \mu \cdot \nu$, and $FOLLOW_k(X)$ cannot distinguish the right contexts ω, ω'.

Theorem 7.2. ($LL(1)$ *condition*) *A context free grammar* G *is* $LL(1)$ *if for two productions* $X \to \chi$, $X \to \chi'$, $\chi \neq \chi'$ *implies that* $FIRST(\chi\ FOLLOW(X))$ *and* $FIRST(\chi'\ FOLLOW(X))$ *are disjoint.*

To prove Theorem 7.2 we assume a $t \in T$ that is an element of both $FIRST(\chi\ FOLLOW(X))$ and $FIRST(\chi'\ FOLLOW(X))$.
Then one of the following cases must hold:

1. $t \in FIRST(\chi), t \in FIRST(\chi')$
2. $\epsilon \in FIRST(\chi), t \in FIRST(\chi'), t \in FOLLOW(X)$
3. $\epsilon \in FIRST(\chi'), t \in FIRST(\chi), t \in FOLLOW(X)$
4. $\epsilon \in FIRST(\chi), \epsilon \in FIRST(\chi'), t \in FOLLOW(X)$

With the aid of the definition of $FOLLOW$ we can easily see that each of these cases contradicts Definition 5.22 for $k = 1$. Thus G is not an LL(1) grammar; in fact, in case (4) the grammar is ambiguous. If, on the other hand, the grammar does not fulfill the specifications of Definition 5.22, then one of the above cases holds and the grammar does not satisfy the LL(1) condition. (Note that Theorem 5.24 may be derived directly from the LL(1) condition.)

If the grammar is ϵ-free, the LL(1) condition can be simplified by omitting $FOLLOW(X)$. Obviously it is fulfilled if and only if G is a strong LL(k) grammar. Thus Theorem 7.3 follows from Theorem 7.2:

Theorem 7.3. *Every LL(1) grammar is a strong LL(1) grammar.*

Theorem 7.3 cannot be generalized to $k > 1$, as illustrated by the LL(2) grammar with $P = \{Z \to aAab, Z \to bAbb, A \to a, A \to \epsilon\}$ cited above. The simplification of pushdown automata mentioned at the beginning of the section thus applies only to the LL(1) case; it is not applicable to LL(k) grammars with $k > 1$.

7.2.2. The Parse Algorithm   A matrix representation of the transition function for the LL(1) case does not provide as much insight into the parsing process as does the conversion of the productions of the grammar to recursive procedures. We shall thus begin our treatment by discussing the technique known as *recursive descent*.

In a recursive descent parser we use a position in the parser to reflect the state of the automaton. The stack therefore contains locations at which exe-

Transition set	Program schema
$q \to \epsilon$	q: **end**
$qt \to q'$	q: **if** $symbol = t$ **then** $next\_symbol$ **else** $error$; q': $\cdots$

$qt_1 \to q'q_1t_1$
 $\cdots$
 $qt_m \to q'q_m t_m$
	q: X; q': $\cdots$
	 $\cdots$
	 proc X:
	   begin
	   case $symbol$ **of**
	     t_1: **begin** q_1: $\cdots$ **end**;
	     $\cdots$
	     t_m: **begin** q_m: $\cdots$ **end**
	     otherwise $error$
	   end
	   end;

Figure 7.4. Program Schemata for an LL(1) Parser

cution of the parser may resume. When a state represents a situation $[X \to \mu \cdot B \nu; \omega]$, $B \in N$, we must enter information into the stack about the following state $[X \to \mu B \cdot \nu; \omega]$ before proceeding to the consideration of the production $B \to \beta$. If we are using a programming language that permits recursive procedures, we may associate a procedure with each nonterminal B and use the standard recursion mechanism of the language to implement the automaton's stack.

With this approach, the individual steps in construction 5.23 lead to the program schemata shown in Figure 7.4. These schemata assume the existence of a global variable $symbol$ containing the value of the last symbol returned by the lexical analyzer, which is reset by a call to $next\_symbol$.

Consider the grammar of Figure 7.5a, which, like the grammar of Figure 5.3b, satisfies the LL(1) condition. By construction 5.23, with the simplification discussed in Section 7.2.1, we obtain the pushdown automaton whose states are shown in Figure 7.5b and whose transitions appear in Figure 7.5c. Figure 7.6 shows a parser for this grammar implemented by recursive descent. As suggested, the procedures correspond to the nonterminals of the grammar. We have placed the code to parse the axiom on the end as the main program. The test of the lookahead symbol in state q_1 guarantees that the input has been completely processed.

This systematically-constructed program can be simplified, also systematically, as shown in Figure 7.7a. The correspondence between the productions of Figure 7.5a and the code of Figure 7.7a results from the following transformation rules:

1. Every nonterminal X corresponds to a procedure X; the axiom of the grammar corresponds to the main program.

$$Z \rightarrow E$$
$$E \rightarrow FE_1$$
$$E_1 \rightarrow \epsilon \mid +FE_1$$
$$F \rightarrow i \mid (E)$$

a) The grammar

q_0: $[Z \rightarrow \cdot E]$	q_8: $[E_1 \rightarrow \cdot +FE_1]$
q_1: $[Z \rightarrow E\cdot]$	q_9: $[F \rightarrow i\cdot]$
q_2: $[E \rightarrow \cdot FE_1]$	q_{10}: $[F \rightarrow (\cdot E)]$
q_3: $[E \rightarrow F\cdot E_1]$	q_{11}: $[E_1 \rightarrow +\cdot FE_1]$
q_4: $[F \rightarrow \cdot i]$	q_{12}: $[F \rightarrow (E\cdot)]$
q_5: $[F \rightarrow \cdot(E)]$	q_{13}: $[E_1 \rightarrow +F\cdot E_1]$
q_6: $[E \rightarrow FE_1\cdot]$	q_{14}: $[F \rightarrow (E)\cdot]$
q_7: $[E_1 \rightarrow \cdot e]$	q_{15}: $[E_1 \rightarrow +FE_1\cdot]$

b) The states of the parsing automaton

$q_0 i \rightarrow q_1 q_2 i, q_0 \rightarrow q_1 q_2 ($,
$q_1 \rightarrow \epsilon$,
$q_2 i \rightarrow q_3 q_4 i, q_2 \rightarrow q_3 q_5 ($,
$q_3 \# \rightarrow q_6 q_7 \#, q_3 \rightarrow q_6 q_7, q_3 + \rightarrow q_6 q_8 +$,
$q_4 i \rightarrow q_9$,
$q_5 \rightarrow q_{10}$,
$q_6 \rightarrow \epsilon$,
$q_7 \rightarrow \epsilon$,
$q_8 + \rightarrow q_{11}$,
$q_9 \rightarrow \epsilon$,
$q_{10} i \rightarrow q_{12} q_2 i, q_{10} \rightarrow q_{12} q_2 ($,
$q_{11} i \rightarrow q_{13} q_4 i, q_{11} (\rightarrow q_{13} q_5 ($,
$q_{12} \rightarrow q_{14}$,
$q_{13} \# \rightarrow q_{15} q_7 \#, q_{13}) \rightarrow q_{15} q_7), q_{13} + \rightarrow q_{15} q_8 +$,
$q_{14} \rightarrow \epsilon$,
$q_{15} \rightarrow \epsilon$

c) The transitions of the parsing automaton

Figure 7.5. A Sample Grammar and its Parsing Automaton

2. The body of procedure X consists of a case clause that distinguishes the productions with X as left-hand side. Every nonterminal on the right-hand side of a production is converted to a call of the corresponding procedure. Every terminal leads to a call of *next_symbol*, after the presence of the terminal has been verified.

```
    procedure parser;

        procedure E; forward;

      procedure F;
        begin (* F *)
        case symbol of
          'i':
            begin
            (* q₄: *) if symbol = 'i' then next_symbol else error;
            (* q₉: *) end;
          '(':
            begin
            (* q₅: *) if symbol = '(' then next_symbol else error;
            (* q₁₀: *) E;
            (* q₁₂: *) if symbol = ')' then next_symbol else error;
            (* q₁₄: *) end
          otherwise error
          end;
        end; (* F *)

      procedure E1;
        begin (* E1 *)
        case symbol of
          '#', ')':
            (* q₇: *);
          '+':
            begin
            (* q₈:*) if symbol = '+' then next_symbol else error;
            (* q₁₁:*) F;
            (* q₁₃:*) E1;
            (* q₁₅:*) end
          otherwise error
          end;
        end; (* E1 *)

      procedure E;
        begin (* E *)
        (* q₂: *) F;
        (* q₃: *) E1;
        (* q₆: *) end; (* E *)

  begin (* parser *)
  (* q₀: *) E;
  (* q₁: *) if symbol <> '#' then error;
  end; (* parser *)
```

Figure 7.6. A Recursive Descent Parser for the Grammar of Figure 7.5

```
    procedure parser ;

     procedure E ; forward;

    procedure F ;
      begin (* F *)
      case symbol of
        'i':
          next _symbol ;
        '(':
          begin
          next _symbol ;
          E ;
          if symbol = ')' then next _symbol else error ;
          end
        otherwise error
        end;
      end; (* F *)

    procedure E 1;
      begin (* E 1 *)
      case symbol of
        '#',  ')':
          ;
        '+':
          begin next _symbol ; F ; E 1 end
        otherwise error
        end;
      end; (* E 1 *)

    procedure E ;
      begin F ; E 1 end;

  begin (* parser *)
  E ;
  if symbol < > '#' then error ;
  end; (* parser *)
              a) Errors detected within E 1

  procedure E 1;
    begin (* E 1 *)
    if symbol = '+' then begin next _symbol ; F ; E end;
    end; (* E 1 *)
              b) Errors detected after exit from E 1
```

Figure 7.7. Figure 7.6 Simplified

3. In case none of the expected terminals is present, the error handler is invoked.

If an empty production occurs for a nonterminal, this alternative can, in principle, be deleted. Thus the procedure corresponding to E_1 could also be written as shown in Figure 7.7b. Any errors would then be detected only after return to the calling procedure. In Section 12.2.2 we shall see that the quality of error recovery is degraded by this strategy.

If we already know that a grammar satisfies the LL(1) condition, we can easily use these transformations to write a parser (either by mechanical means or by hand). With additional transformation rules we can generalize the technique sufficiently to convert our extended BNF (Section 5.1.3) and connection points. Some of the additional rules appear in Figure 7.8. Figure 7.9 illustrates the use of these rules.

Element		Program schema
Option	$[x]$	**if** *symbol* **in** $FIRST(x)$ **then** x ;
Closure	$x+$	**repeat** x **until not**(*symbol* **in** $FIRST(x)$)
	$x*$	**while** *symbol* **in** $FIRST(x)$ **do** x ;
List	$x \ \|\| \ d$	x ; **while** *symbol* **in** $FIRST(d)$ **do** **begin** d ; x **end**;
Connection	$t\&Y$	**if** *Symbol* $=t$ **then** **begin** Y; *next_symbol* **end** **else** *error* ;
	$\%Z$	Z

Figure 7.8. Extension of Figure 7.4

Recursive descent parsers are easy to construct, but are not usually very efficient in either time or storage. Most grammars have many nonterminals, and each of these leads to the dynamic cost associated with the call of and return from a recursive procedure. The procedures that recognize nonterminals could be implemented substantially more efficiently than arbitrary recursive procedures because they have no parameters or local variables, and there is only a single global variable. Thus the alteration of the environment pointer on procedure entry and exit can be omitted.

An interpretive implementation of a recursive descent parser is also possible: The control program interprets tables generated from the grammar.

expression ::= *term* ('+' *term* %*addop*)*.
term ::= 'i' &*ident* | '(' *expression* ')'.

a) Grammar (compare Figure 7.2a)

procedure *parser* ;

　procedure *term* ; *forward*;

　procedure *expression* ;
　　begin (* *expression* *)
　　term ;
　　while *symbol* = '+' **do**
　　　begin *next_symbol* ; *term* ; *addop* **end**;
　　end; (* *expression* *)

　procedure *term* ;
　　begin (* *term* *)
　　case *symbol* **of**
　　　'i':
　　　　begin *ident* ; *next_symbol* **end**;
　　　'(':
　　　　begin
　　　　next_symbol ;
　　　　expression ;
　　　　if *symbol* = ')' **then** *next_symbol* **else** *error* ;
　　　　end
　　　otherwise *error*
　　　end;
　　end; (* *term* *)

begin (* *parser* *)
expression ;
if *symbol* < > '#' **then** *error* ;
end (* *parser* *)

b) Parser

Figure 7.9. Parser for an Extended BNF Grammar

Every table entry specifies a basic operation of the parser and the associated data. For example, a table entry might be described as follows:

type *parse_table_entry* = **record**
　operation : *integer* ;　　　　　　　(* Transition *)
　lookahead : **set of** *symbol_code* ;　(* Input or lookahead symbol *)
　next : *integer*　　　　　　　　　　(* Parse table index *)
　end;

States corresponding to situations that follow one another in a single production follow one another in the table. Figure 7.10 specifies a recursive

```
procedure parser ;
  var
    current : integer ;
    stack : array [1..max_stack ] of integer ;
    stack_pointer : 0..max_stack ;
  begin (* parser *)
  current : = 1; stack_pointer : = 0;
  repeat
    with parse_table [current ] do
      case operation of
        1: (* X →μ·t ν*)
            if symbol in lookahead then
              begin next_symbol ; current : = current + 1 end
            else error ;
        2: (* X →χ·*)
            begin
            current : = stack [stack_pointer ];
            stack_pointer : = stack_pointer − 1;
            end;
        3: (* X →μ·B ν *)
            begin
            if stack_pointer = max_stack then abort ;
            stack_pointer : = stack_pointer + 1;
            stack [stack_pointer ]: = current + 1;
            current : = next ;
            end;
        4: (* X →·χᵢ ( not the last alternative ) *)
            if symbol in lookahead then
              current : = current + 1
            else current : = next ;
        5: (* X →·χₘ ( last alternative ) *)
            if symbol in lookahead then
              current : = current + 1
            else error ;
        6: (* X →·t νᵢ ( not the last alternative ) *)
            if symbol in lookahead then
              begin next_symbol ; current : = current + 1 end
            else current : = next
      end;
  until current = 1;
  if symbol < > '#' then error ;
  end; (* Parser *)
```

Figure 7.10. An Interpretive LL(1) Parser

descent interpreter assuming that *parse_table* is an array of *parse_table_entry*.

Alternatives (1)-(5) of the case clause in Figure 7.10 supply the program schemata for $qt \to q'$, $q \to \epsilon$ and $qt_i \to q'q_i t_i$ introduced in Figure 7.4. As before, the transition $qt_i \to q'q_i t_i$ is accomplished in two steps (alternative 3 followed by either 4 or 5). The situations represented by the alternatives are given as comments. Alternative 6 shows one of the possible optimizations, namely the combination of selecting a production $X \to \chi_i$ (alternative 4) with acceptance of the first symbol of χ_i (alternative 1). Further optimization is possible (Exercise 7.6).

7.2.3. Computation of FIRST and FOLLOW Sets

The first step in the generation of an LL(1) parser is to ensure that the grammar $G = (T,N,P,Z)$ satisfies the LL(1) condition. To do this we compute the *FIRST* and *FOLLOW* sets for all $X \in N$. For each production $X \to \chi \in P$ we can then determine the *director set* $W = FIRST(\chi\ FOLLOW(X))$. The director sets are used to verify the LL(1) condition, and also become the lookahead sets used by the parser. With the computation of these sets, the task of generating the parser is essentially complete. If the grammar does not satisfy the LL(1) condition, the generator may attempt transformations automatically (for example, left recursion removal and simple left factoring) or it may report the cause of failure to the user for correction.

The following algorithm can be used to compute *FIRST(X)* and initial values for the director set W of each production $X \to \chi$.

1. Set $FIRST(X)$ empty and repeat steps (2)-(5) for each production $X \to \chi$.
2. Let $\chi = x_1 \cdots x_n$, $i = 0$ and $W = \{\#\}$. If $n = 0$, go to step 5.
3. Set $i := i + 1$ and $W := W \cup FIRST(x_i)$. (If x_i is an element of T, $FIRST(x_i) = \{x_i\}$; if $FIRST(x_i)$ is not available, invoke this algorithm recursively to compute it.) Repeat step 3 until either $i = n$ or $\#$ is not an element of $FIRST(x_i)$.
4. If $\#$ is not an element of $FIRST(x_i)$, set $W := W - \{\#\}$.
5. Set $FIRST(X) := FIRST(X) \cup W$.

Note that if the grammar is left recursive, step (3) will lead to an endless recursion and the algorithm will fail. This failure can be avoided by marking each X when the computation of $FIRST(X)$ begins, and clearing the mark when that computation is complete. If step (3) attempts to invoke the algorithm with a marked nonterminal, then a left recursion has been detected.

This algorithm is executed exactly once for each $X \in N$. If $\#$ is not in W at the beginning of step 5 then W is the complete director set for the production $X \to \chi$. Otherwise the complete director set for $X \to \chi$ is $(W - \{\#\}) \cup FOLLOW(X)$.

Efficient computation of *FOLLOW(X)* is somewhat trickier. The problem is that some elements can be deduced from single rules, while others reflect interactions among rules. For example, consider the grammar of Figure 7.5a. We can immediately deduce that $FOLLOW(F)$ includes $FIRST(E_1)$, because of the production $E_1 \rightarrow +FE_1$ Since $E_1 \Rightarrow^* \epsilon$, $FOLLOW(F)$ also contains $FOLLOW(E_1)$, which includes $FOLLOW(E)$ because of the production $E \rightarrow FE_1$.

Interaction among the rules can be represented by the relation $LAST$:

Definition 7.4. Given a context free grammar $G = (T,N,P,Z)$. For any two nonterminals A, B, A $LAST$ B if $B \rightarrow \mu A \nu \in P$ and $\nu \Rightarrow^* \epsilon$.

This relation can be described by a directed graph $F = (N, D)$, with $D = \{(A,B) \mid A \ LAST \ B\}$. If there is a path from node A to node B in F, then $FOLLOW(A)$ is a subset of $FOLLOW(B)$; all nodes in a strongly connected region of F have identical follow sets. The general strategy for computing follow sets is thus to compute provisional sets $FOL(X) = \{t \mid A \rightarrow \mu X \nu \in P, t \in FIRST(\nu)\}$ - $\{\#\}$ based only upon the relationships among symbols *within* productions, and then use F to combine these sets.

We can easily compute the graph F and the set $FOL(X)$ by scanning the production backward and recalling that $A \Rightarrow^* \epsilon$ if $\#$ is in $FIRST(A)$. Since F is sparse ($\mid D \mid \ll \mid N \times N \mid$), it must be represented by an edge list rather than an adjacency matrix if the efficiency of the remaining computation is to be maintained.

The next step is to form the strongly connected regions of F and derive the directed acyclic graph $F' = (N',D')$ of these regions:

$D' = \{(A',B') \mid (A,B) \in D$ such that A is in the strongly connected region A' and B is in the region $B' \}$

F' can be constructed efficiently by using the algorithm of Section B.3.2 to form the regions and then constructing the edges in one pass over F. At the same time, we can compute the initial follow sets $FOL(A')$ of the strongly connected regions $A' \in N'$ by taking the union of all $FOL(A)$ such that A is a nonterminal in the region A'.

The final computation of $FOLLOW(A')$ is similar to our original computation of $FIRST(A)$:

1. Initially, $FOLLOW(A') = FOL(A')$ for $A' \neq Z'$,   and $FOLLOW(Z') = \{\#\}$.
2. For each immediate successor, B', of A' add $FOLLOW(B')$ to $FOLLOW(A')$. If $FOLLOW(B')$ is not already available, then invoke this algorithm recursively to compute it.

This algorithm also operates upon each element of N' exactly once. For each production $X \rightarrow \chi$ with $\#$ in W, we now obtain the final director sets by setting $W := (W - \{\#\}) \cup FOLLOW(X')$ (X' is the strongly connected region containing X).

7.3. LR Parsers

Using construction 5.33, we can both test whether a grammar is LR(1) and construct a parser for it. Unfortunately, the number of states of such a parser is too large for practical use. Exactly as in the case of strong LL(k) grammars, many of the transitions in an LR(1) parser are independent of the lookahead symbol. We can utilize this fact to arrive at a parser with fewer states, which implements the LR(1) analysis algorithm but in which reduce transitions depend upon the lookahead symbol only if it is absolutely necessary.

We begin the construction with an LR(0) parser, which does not examine lookahead symbols at all, and introduce lookahead symbols only as required. The grammars that we can process with these techniques are the *simple LR(1)* (SLR(1)) grammars of DeRemer [1969]. (This class can also be defined for arbitrary $k > 1$.) Not all LR(1) grammars are also SLR(1) (there is no equivalence similar to that between ordinary and strong LL(1) grammars), but the distinction is unimportant in practice except for one class of problems. This class of problems will be solved by sharpening the definition of SLR(1) to obtain *lookahead LR(1)* (LALR(1)) grammars.

The verifications of the LR(1), SLR(1) and LALR(1) conditions are more laborious than verification of the LL(1) condition. Also, there exists no simple relationship between the grammar and the corresponding LR pushdown automaton. LR parsers are therefore employed only if one has a parser generator. We shall first discuss the workings of the parser and in that way derive the SLR(1) and LALR(1) grammars from the LR(0) grammars. Next we shall show how parse tables are constructed. Since these tables are still too large in practice, we investigate the question of compressing them and show examples in which the final tables are of feasible size. The treatment of error handling will be deferred to Section 12.2.2.

7.3.1. The Parse Algorithm   Consider an LR(k) grammar $G = (T,N,P,Z)$ and the pushdown automaton $A = (T,Q,R,q_0,\{q_0\},Q,q_0)$ of construction 5.33. The operation of the automaton is most easily explained using the matrix form of the transition function:

$$f(q,v) = \begin{cases} q' & \begin{array}{l} \text{if } v = v\gamma \in T^* \text{ and } qv\gamma \rightarrow qq'\gamma \in R \text{ or} \\ \text{if } v \in N \text{ and } q' = next(q,v) \text{ (shift transition)} \end{array} \\ X \rightarrow \chi & \text{if } [X \rightarrow \chi\cdot;v] \in q \text{ (reduce transition)} \\ HALT & \text{if } v = \# \text{ and } [Z \rightarrow S\cdot;\#] \in q \\ ERROR & \text{otherwise} \end{cases}$$

This transition function is easily obtained from construction 5.33: All of the transitions defined in step (2) deliver shift transitions with one terminal symbol, which will be accepted; the remaining transitions result from step

(3) of the construction. We divide the transition $p_1 \cdots p_m q \omega \rightarrow p_1 q' \omega$ referred to in step (3) into two steps: Because $[X \rightarrow \chi \cdot; v]$ is in q we know that we must reduce according to the production $X \rightarrow \chi$ and remove $m = |\chi|$ states from the stack. Further we define $f(p_1, X)$ $= next(p_1, X) = q'$ to be the new state. If $w = \#$ and $[Z \rightarrow S \cdot; \#] \in q$ then the pushdown automaton halts.

Figure 7.11 gives an example of the construction of a transition function for $k = 0$. We have numbered the states and rules consecutively. '+2' indicates that a reduction will be made according to rule 2; '*' marks the halting of the pushdown automaton. Because $k = 0$, the reductions are independent of the following symbols.

Figure 7.11c shows the transition function as the transition diagram of a finite automaton for the grammars of Theorem 5.32. The distinct grammars correspond to distinct final states. As an LR parser, the automaton operates as follows: Beginning at the start state 0, we make a transition to the successor state corresponding to the symbol read. The states through which we pass are stored on the stack; this continues until a final state is reached. In the final state we reduce by means of the given production $X \rightarrow \chi$, delete $|\chi|$ states from the stack and proceed as though X had been 'read'.

$$(1)\ Z \rightarrow E$$
$$(2)\ E \rightarrow E + F \qquad (3)\ E \rightarrow F$$
$$(4)\ F \rightarrow i \qquad\quad\ (5)\ F \rightarrow (E)$$

a) The grammar

	i	$($	$)$	$+$	$\#$	E	F
0	3	4	.	.	.	1	2
1	.	.	.	5	*		
2	+3	+3	+3	+3	+3		
3	+4	+4	+4	+4	+4		
4	3	4	.	.	.	6	2
5	3	4	.	.	.		7
6	.	.	8	5	.		
7	+2	+2	+2	+2	+2		
8	+5	+5	+5	+5	+5		

b) The transition table

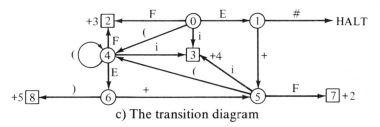

c) The transition diagram

Figure 7.11. An Example of an LR(0) Grammar

The only distinction between the mode of operation of an LR(k) parser for $k > 0$ and the LR(0) parser of the example is that the reductions may depend upon lookahead symbols. In the final states of the automaton, reductions will take place only if the context allows them.

Don't-care entries with $f(q, v) = ERROR$, i.e. entries such that there exists no word χ with $q_0 q_0 \chi \# \Rightarrow^* \omega q v \gamma \#$ with suitable stack contents ω, may occur in the matrix representation of the transition function. Note that all entries (q, X), $X \in N$, with $f(q, X) = ERROR$ are don't-cares. By the considerations in step (3) of construction 5.33, no error can occur in a transition on a nonterminal; it would have been recognized at the latest at the preceding reduction. (The true error entries are denoted by '.', while don't-cares are empty entries in the matrix representation of $f(q, v)$.)

7.3.2. SLR(1) and LALR(1) Grammars

Figure 7.12a is a slight extension of that of Figure 7.11a. It is not an LR(0) grammar, as Figure 7.13 shows. (A star before a situation means that this situation belongs to the basis of the state; the lookahead string is omitted.) In states 2 and 9 we must inspect the lookahead symbols to decide whether to reduce or not. Figure 7.12b gives a transition matrix that performs this inspection.

The operation of the parser can be seen from the example of the reduction of $i + i *(i + i)\#$ (Figure 7.14). The 'Next Symbol' column is left blank when the parser does not actually examine the lookahead symbol. This example shows how, by occasional consideration of a lookahead symbol, we

$$(1)\ Z \rightarrow E$$
$$(2)\ E \rightarrow E + T \qquad (3)\ E \rightarrow T$$
$$(4)\ T \rightarrow T*F \qquad (5)\ T \rightarrow F$$
$$(6)\ F \rightarrow i \qquad\quad (7)\ F \rightarrow (E)$$

a) The grammar

	i	(	)	+	*	#	E	T	F
0	4	5	.	.	.	.	1	2	3
1	.	.	.	6	.	*			
2	.	.	+3	+3	7	+3			
3	+5	+5	+5	+5	+5	+5			
4	+6	+6	+6	+6	+6	+6			
5	4	5	.	.	.	.	8	2	3
6	4	5	.	.	.	.		9	3
7	4	5	.	.	.	.			10
8	.	.	11	6	.	.			
9	.	.	+2	+2	7	+2			
10	+4	+4	+4	+4	+4	+4			
11	+7	+7	+7	+7	+7	+7			

b) The transition table

Figure 7.12. A Non-LR(0) Grammar

State		Situation	v	$f(q,v)$
0	*	$[Z \to \cdot E]$	E	1
		$[E \to \cdot E + T]$		
		$[E \to \cdot T]$	T	2
		$[T \to \cdot T*F]$		
		$[T \to \cdot F]$	F	3
		$[F \to \cdot i]$	i	4
		$[F \to \cdot(E)]$	(	5
1	*	$[Z \to E\cdot]$	#	HALT
	*	$[E \to E\cdot + T]$	+	6
2	*	$[E \to T\cdot]$	#,), +	reduce 3
	*	$[T \to T\cdot *F]$	*	7
3	*	$[T \to F\cdot]$		reduce 5
4	*	$[F \to i\cdot]$		reduce 6
5	*	$[F \to (\cdot E)]$	E	8
		$[E \to \cdot E + T]$		
		$[E \to \cdot T]$	T	2
		$[T \to \cdot T*F]$		
		$[T \to \cdot F]$	F	3
		$[F \to \cdot i]$	i	4
		$[F \to \cdot(E)]$	(	5
6	*	$[E \to E + \cdot T]$	T	9
		$[T \to \cdot T*F]$		
		$[T \to \cdot F]$	F	3
		$[F \to \cdot i]$	i	4
		$[F \to \cdot(E)]$	(	5
7	*	$[T \to T* \cdot F]$	F	10
		$[F \to \cdot i]$	i	4
		$[F \to \cdot(E)]$	(	5
8	*	$[F \to (E\cdot)]$	)	11
	*	$[E \to E\cdot + T]$	+	6
9	*	$[E \to E + T\cdot]$	#,), +	reduce 2
	*	$[T \to T\cdot *F]$	*	7
10	*	$[T \to T*F\cdot]$		reduce 4
11	*	$[F \to (E)\cdot]$		reduce 7

Figure 7.13. Derivation of the Automaton of Figure 7.12b

can also employ an LR(0) parser for a grammar that does not satisfy the LR(0) condition. States in which a lookahead symbol must be considered are called *inadequate*. They are characterized by having a situation $[X \to \chi\cdot]$ that leads to a reduction, and also a second situation. This second situation leads either to a reduction with another production or to a shift transition.

DeRemer [1971] investigated the class of grammars for which these modifications lead to a parser:

Definition 7.5. A context free grammar $G = (T,N,P,Z)$ is SLR(1) if the following algorithm leads to a deterministic pushdown automaton.

The pushdown automaton $A = (T, Q, R, q_0, \{q_0\}, Q, q_0)$ will be defined by its transition function $f(q, v)$ rather than the production set R. The construction follows that of construction 5.33. We use the following as the closure of a set of situations:

$$H(M) = M \cup \{[Y \to \cdot \mu] \mid \exists [X \to \chi \cdot Y \gamma] \in H(M)\}$$

1. Initially let $Q = \{q_0\}$, with $q_0 = H(\{[Z \to \cdot S]\})$.
2. Let q be an element of Q that has not yet been considered. Perform steps (3)-(4) for each $v \in V$.
3. Let $basis(q,v) = \{[X \to \mu v \cdot \gamma] \mid [X \to \mu \cdot v \gamma] \in q\}$.
4. If $basis(q,v) \neq \emptyset$, then let $next(q,v) = H(basis(q,v))$. Add $q' = next(q,v)$ to Q if it is not already present.
5. If all elements of Q have been considered, perform step (6) for each $q \in Q$ and then stop. Otherwise return to step (2).

Right derivation before transition	Stack	Next Symbol	Reduce by Production	Next State
$.i + i*(i + i)\#$	0	i		4
$i. + i*(i + i)\#$	0,4		6	3
$F. + i*(i + i)\#$	0,3		5	2
$T. + i*(i + i)\#$	0,2	$+$	3	1
$E. + i*(i + i)\#$	0,1	$+$		6
$E + .i*(i + i)\#$	0,1,6	i		4
$E + i.*(i + i)\#$	0,1,6,4		6	3
$E + F.*(i + i)\#$	0,1,6,3		5	2
$E + T.*(i + i)\#$	0,1,6,9	$*$		7
$E + T*.(i + i)\#$	0,1,6,9,7	$($		5
$E + T*(.i + i)\#$	0,1,6,9,7,5	i		4
$E + T*(i. + i)\#$	0,1,6,9,7,5,4		6	3
$E + T*(F. + i)\#$	0,1,6,9,7,5,3		5	2
$E + T*(T. + i)\#$	0,1,6,9,7,5,2	$+$	3	8
$E + T*(E. + i)\#$	0,1,6,9,7,5,8	$+$		6
$E + T*(E + .i)\#$	0,1,6,9,7,5,8,6	i		4
$E + T*(E + i.)\#$	0,1,6,9,7,5,8,6,4		6	3
$E + T*(E + F.)\#$	0,1,6,9,7,5,8,6,3		5	9
$E + T*(E + T.)\#$	0,1,6,9,7,5,8,6,9	$)$	2	8
$E + T*(E.)\#$	0,1,6,9,7,5,8	$)$		11
$E + T*(E).\#$	0,1,6,9,7,5,8,11		7	10
$E + T*F.\#$	0,1,6,9,7,10		4	9
$E + T.\#$	0,1,6,9	$\#$	2	1
$E.\#$	0,1	$\#$		HALT
$Z.\#$				

Figure 7.14. A Sample Parse by the Automaton of Figure 7.12b

(1) $Z \rightarrow A$
(2) $A \rightarrow aBb$ (3) $A \rightarrow adc$ (4) $A \rightarrow bBc$ (5) $A \rightarrow bdd$
(6) $B \rightarrow d$

a) The grammar

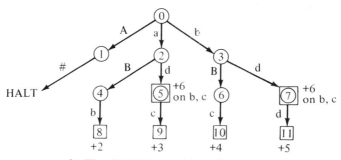

b) The SLR(1) transition diagram

	a	b	c	d	#	A	B
0	2	3	.	.	.	1	
1	.	.	.	.	*		
2	.	.	.	5	.		4
3	.	.	.	7	.		6
4		8	.				
5	.	+6	9	.	.		
6		.	10				
7	.	.	+6	11	.		
8	+2	+2	+2	+2	+2		
9	+3	+3	+3	+3	+3		
10	+4	+4	+4	+4	+4		
11	+5	+5	+5	+5	+5		

c) The LALR(1) transition table

Figure 7.15. A Non-SLR(1) Grammar

6. For all $v \in V$, define $f(q,v)$ by:

$$f(q,v) = \begin{cases} next(q,v) & \text{if } [X \rightarrow \mu \cdot v \gamma] \in q \\ X \rightarrow \chi & \text{if } [X \rightarrow \chi \cdot] \in q \text{ and } v \in FOLLOW(X) \\ HALT & \text{if } v = \# \text{ and } [Z \rightarrow S \cdot] \in q \\ ERROR & \text{otherwise} \end{cases}$$

This construction is almost identical to construction 5.33 with $k = 0$. The only difference is the additional restriction $v \in FOLLOW(X)$ for the reduction (second case).

SLR(1) grammars cover many practically important language constructs not expressible by LR(0) grammars. Compared to the LR(1) construction, the given algorithm leads to substantially fewer states in the automaton. (For the grammar of Figure 7.12a the ratio is 22:12). Unfortunately, even SLR(1) grammars do not suffice for all practical requirements. The problem arises whenever there is a particular sequence of tokens that plays different roles in different places. In LAX, for example, an identifier followed by a colon may be either a label (A.2.0.6) or a variable serving as a lower bound (A.3.0.4). For this reason the LAX grammar is not SLR(1), because the lookahead symbol ':' does not determine whether *identifier* should be reduced to *name* (A.4.0.16), or a shift transition building a *label_definition* should take place.

If the set of lookahead symbols for a reduction could be partitioned according to the state then we could solve the problem, as can be seen from the example of Figure 7.15. The productions of Figure 7.15a do not fulfill the SLR(1) condition, as we see in the transition diagram of Figure 7.15b. In the critical state 5, however, a reduction with lookahead symbol c need not be considered! If c is to follow B then b must have been read before, and we would therefore have had the state sequence 0, 3, 7 and not 0, 2, 5. The misjudgement arises through states in which all of the symbols that could possibly follow B are examined to determine whether to reduce $B \rightarrow d$, without regard to the symbols preceding B. We thus refine the construction so that we do not admit all lookahead symbols in $FOLLOW(X)$ when deciding upon a reduction $X \rightarrow \chi$, but distinguish on the basis of predecessor states lookahead symbols that can actually appear.

We begin by defining the *kernel* of an LR(1) state to be its LR(0) situations:

$$kernel(q) = \{[X \rightarrow \mu \cdot \nu] \mid [X \rightarrow \mu \cdot \nu; \Omega] \in q\}$$

Construction 7.5 above effectively merges states of the LR(1) parser that have the same kernel, and hence any lookahead symbol that could have appeared in any of the LR(1) states can appear in the LR(0) state. The set of all such symbols forms the *exact right context* upon which we must base our decisions.

Definition 7.6. Let $G = (T, N, P, Z)$ be a context free grammar, Q be the state set of the pushdown automaton formed by construction 7.5, and Q' be the state set of the pushdown automaton formed by construction 5.33 with $k = 1$. The *exact right context* of an LR(0) situation $[X \rightarrow \mu \cdot \nu]$ in a state $q \in Q$ is defined by:

$$ERC(q, [X \rightarrow \mu \cdot \nu]) = \{t \in T \mid \exists q' \in Q'' \text{ such that } q \\ = kernel(q') \text{ and } [X \rightarrow \mu \cdot \nu; t] \in q'\}$$

Theorem 5.31 related the LR(k) property to non-overlapping k-stack classes, so it is not surprising that the definition of LALR(1) grammars involves an analogous condition:

Definition 7.7. Let $G = (T, N, P, Z)$ be a context free grammar and Q be the state set of the pushdown automaton formed by construction 7.5. G is LALR(1) if the following sets are pairwise disjoint for all $q \in Q, p \in P$:

$$S_{q,0} = \{t \mid [X \to \mu \cdot \nu] \in q, \ \nu \neq \epsilon, \ t \in EFF(\nu ERC(q, [X \to \mu \cdot \nu]))\}$$

$$S_{q,p} = ERC(q, [X_p \to \chi_p \cdot])$$

Although Definition 7.6 implies that we need to carry out construction 5.33 to determine the exact right context, this is not the case. The following algorithm generates only the LR(0) states, but may consider each of those states several times in order to build the exact right context. Each time a shift transition into a given state is discovered, we propagate the right context. If the propagation changes the third element of any triple in the state then the entire state is reconsidered, possibly propagating the change further. Formally, we define a merge operation on sets of situations as follows:

$$merge(A,B) = \{[X \to \mu \cdot \nu; \Delta \cup \Omega] \mid [X \to \mu \cdot \nu; \Delta] \in A, [X \to \mu \cdot \nu; \Omega] \in B\}$$

The LALR(1) construction algorithm is then:

1. Initially let $Q = \{q_0\}$, with $q_0 = H(\{[Z \to \cdot S; \{\#\}]\})$.
2. Let q be an element of Q that has not yet been considered. Perform steps (3)-(5) for each $v \in V$.
3. Let $basis(q,v) = \{[X \to \mu v \cdot \gamma; \Omega] \mid [X \to \mu \cdot v \gamma; \Omega] \in q\}$.
4. If $basis(q,v) \neq \emptyset$ and there is a $q' \in Q$ such that $kernel(q') = kernel(H(basis(q,v)))$ then let $next(q,v) = merge(H(basis(q,v)), q')$. If $next(q,v) \neq q'$ then replace q' by $next(q,v)$ and mark q' as not yet considered.
5. If $basis(q,v) \neq \emptyset$ and there is no $q' \in Q$ such that $kernel(q') = kernel(H(basis(q,v)))$ then let $next(q,v) = H(basis(q,v))$. Add $q'' = next(q,v)$ to Q.
6. If all elements of Q have been considered, perform step (7) for each $q \in Q$ and then stop. Otherwise return to step (2).
7. For all $v \in V$ define $f(q,v)$ as follows:

$$f(q,v) = \begin{cases} next(q,v) & \text{if } basis(q,v) \neq \emptyset \\ X \to \chi & \text{if } [X \to \chi \cdot; \Omega] \in q, \ v \in \Omega \\ HALT & \text{if } v = \# \text{ and } [Z \to S \cdot; \{\#\}] \in q \\ ERROR & \text{otherwise} \end{cases}$$

Figure 7.15c shows the LALR(1) automaton derived from Figure 7.15a. Note that we can only recognize a B by reducing production 6, and this can be done only with b or c as the lookahead symbol (see rows 5 and 7 of Figure 7.15c). States 4 and 6 are entered only after recognizing a B, and hence the current symbol *must* be b or c in these states. Thus Figure 7.15c has don't-care entries for all symbols other than b and c in states 4 and 6.

	i	(	)	+	*	#	E	T	F
0	-6	5	.	.	.	.	1	2	-5
1	.	.	.	6	.	*			
2	.	.	+3	+3	7	+3			
5	-6	5	.	.	.	.	8	2	-5
6	-6	5	.	.	.	.		9	-5
7	-6	5	.	.	.	.			-4
8	.	.	-7	6	.	.			
9	.	.	+2	+2	7	+2			

Figure 7.16. The Automaton of Figure 7.12 Recast for Shift-Reduce Transitions

7.3.3. Shift-Reduce Transitions   For most programming languages 30-50% of the states of an LR parser are LR(0) reduce states, in which reduction by a specific production is determined without examining the context. In Figure 7.13 these states are 3, 4, 10 and 11. We can combine these reductions with the stacking of the previous symbol to obtain a new kind of transition — the *shift-reduce* transition — specifying both the stacking of the last symbol of the right-hand side and the production by which the next reduction symbol is to be made. Formally:

If $f(q',v)=X \to \chi$ (or $f(q',v)=HALT$) is the only possible action (other than *ERROR*) in state q' then redefine $f(q,v)$ to be 'shift reduce $X \to \chi$' for all states q with $f(q,v)=q'$ and for all $v \in V$. Then delete state q'.

With this simplification the transition function of Figure 7.12 can be written as shown in Figure 7.16. (The notation remains the same, with the addition of $-p$ to indicate a shift-reduce transition that reduces according to the pth production.)

Introduction of shift-reduce transitions into a parsing automaton for LAX reduces the number of states from 131 to 70.

7.3.4. Chain Production Elimination   A *chain production* $A \to B$ is a semantically meaningless element of P with a right-hand side of length 1. In this section we shall denote chain productions by $A \to^c B$ and derivations using only chain productions by $A \Rightarrow^c B$ (instead of $A \Rightarrow^* B$). Any productions not explicitly marked are not chain productions. Chain productions are most often introduced through the description of expressions by rules like *sum* ::= *term* | *sum addop term*. They also frequently arise from the collection of single concepts into some all-embracing concept (as in A.3.0.1, for example).

Reductions according to chain productions are completely irrelevant, and simply waste time. Thus elimination of all chain productions may speed up the parsing considerably. During the parse of the statement $A := B$ in LAX, for example, we must reduce 11 times by productions of length 1 before reaching the form *name* ':=' *expression*, which can be recognized as an assignment. Of these reductions, only the identification of an *identifier* as a *name* (A.4.0.16) has relevant semantics. All other reductions are semantically meaningless and should not appear in the structure tree.

We could remove chain productions by substitution, a process used in conjunction with Theorem 5.25. The resulting definition of the LR parser would lead to far too many states, which we must then laboriously reduce to a manageable number by further processing. A more satisfactory approach is to try to eliminate the reductions by chain productions from the parser during construction. In many cases this technique will also lower the number of states in the final parser.

The central idea is to simultaneously consider all chain productions that could be introduced in a given parser state. Suppose that a state q contains a situation $[X \rightarrow \mu \cdot Av ; t]$ and $A \Rightarrow^+ B$. We must first reduce to B, then to A. If however, the derivation $A \Rightarrow^+ B$ consists solely of chain productions then upon a reduction to B we can immediately reduce to A without going through any intermediate steps.

Construction 7.7, when applied to Figure 7.17a (a simplified version of Figure 7.12a), yields a parser with the state diagram given in Figure 7.17b. If we reach state 2, we can reduce to E given the lookahead symbol #, but we could also reduce to Z immediately. We may therefore take either the

$$(1)\ Z \rightarrow E$$
$$(2)\ E \rightarrow E + T \quad (3)\ E \rightarrow T$$
$$(4)\ T \rightarrow T*i \quad (5)\ T \rightarrow i$$

a) The grammar

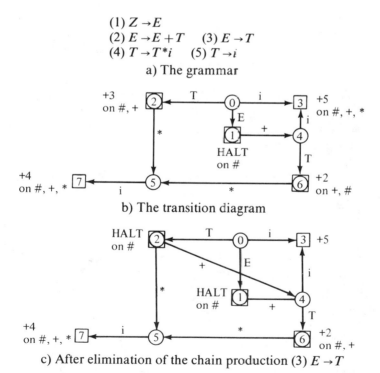

b) The transition diagram

c) After elimination of the chain production (3) $E \rightarrow T$

Figure 7.17. A Simple Case of Chain Production Elimination

actions of state 1 or those of state 2. Figure 7.17c shows the parser that results from merging these two states.

Note that in Figure 7.17b the actions for states 1 and 2 do not conflict (with the exception of the reduction $E \rightarrow T$ being eliminated). This property is crucial to the reduction; fortunately it follows automatically from the LR(1) property of the grammar: Suppose that for $A \neq B$, $A \Rightarrow^c C$ and $B \Rightarrow^c C$. Suppose further that some state q contains situations $[X \rightarrow \mu \cdot A \gamma; \Gamma]$ and $[Y \rightarrow \sigma \cdot B \delta; \Delta]$. The *follower condition* 'FIRST($\gamma\tau$) and FIRST($\delta\Delta$) disjoint' must then hold, since otherwise it would be impossible to decide whether to reduce C to A or B in state $f(q, C)$. Consideration of state 0 in Figure 7.17b with $A = E$, $B = C = T$ illustrates that the follower condition is identical to the absence of conflict required above.

Situations involving chain productions are always introduced by a closure operation. Instead of using these chain production situations when establishing a new state, we use the situations that *introduced* them. This is equivalent to saying that reduction to the right-hand side of the chain production should be interpreted as reduction to the left-hand side. Thus the only change in construction 7.7 comes in computation of $basis(q, v)$:

3'. Let $basis(q, v) = \{[Y \rightarrow \sigma a \cdot \delta; \Delta] \mid [X \rightarrow \mu \cdot v \gamma; \Gamma], [Y \rightarrow \sigma a \delta; \Delta] \in q, a \Rightarrow^c v\}$
$- \{[A \rightarrow B \cdot; \Omega] \mid A \rightarrow^c B\}$.

As an example of the process, assume that the productions $E \rightarrow T$ and $T \rightarrow F$ in the grammar of Figure 7.12a are chain productions. Figure 7.18 shows the derivation of an LALR(1) automaton that does not reduce by these productions. (Compare this derivation with that of Figure 7.13.)

7.3.5. Implementation   In order to carry out the parsing practically, a table of the left sides and lengths of the right sides of all productions (other than chain productions), as well as parser actions to be invoked at connection points, must be known to the transition function. The transition function is partitioned in this way to ease the storage management problems. Because of cost we store the transition function as a packed data structure and employ an access routine that locates the value $f(q, v)$ given (q, v). Some systems work with a list representation of the (sparse) transition matrix; the access may be time consuming if such a scheme is used, because lists must be searched.

The access time is reduced if the matrix form of the transition function is retained, and the storage requirements are comparable to those of the list method if as many rows and columns as possible are combined. In performing this combination we take advantage of the fact that two rows can be combined not only when they agree, but also when they are compatible according to the following definition:

Definition 7.8. Consider a transition matrix $f(q, v)$. Two rows $q, q' \in Q$ are *compatible* if, for each column v, either $f(q, v) = f(q', v)$ or one of the two entries is a don't-care entry.

State		Situation	v	$f(q,v)$
0	*	$[Z \to \cdot E;\{\#\}]$	E	1
		$[E \to \cdot E+T;\{\#\;+\}]$		
		$[E \to \cdot T;\{\#\;+\}]$	T	2
		$[T \to \cdot T*F;\{\#\;+*\}]$		
		$[T \to \cdot F;\{\#\;+*\}]$	F	2
		$[F \to \cdot i;\{\#\;+*\}]$	i	3
		$[F \to \cdot(E);\{\#\;+*\}]$	$($	4
1	*	$[Z \to E\cdot;\{\#\}]$	$\#$	HALT
	*	$[E \to E\cdot+T;\{\#\;+\}]$	$+$	5
2	*	$[Z \to E\cdot;\{\#\}]$	$\#$	HALT
	*	$[E \to E\cdot+T;\{\#\;+\}]$	$+$	5
	*	$[T \to T\cdot*F;\{\#\;+*\}]$	$*$	6
3	*	$[F \to i\cdot;\{\#\;+*)\}]$		reduce 6
4	*	$[F \to (\cdot E);\{\#\;+*)\}]$	E	7
		$[E \to \cdot E+T;\{()+\}]$		
		$[E \to \cdot T;\{()+\}]$	T	8
		$[T \to \cdot T*F;\{()+*\}]$		
		$[T \to \cdot F;\{()+*\}]$	F	8
		$[F \to \cdot i;\{()+*\}]$	i	3
		$[F \to \cdot(E);\{()+*\}]$	$($	4
5	*	$[E \to E+\cdot T;\{\#\;+)\}]$	T	9
		$[T \to \cdot T*F;\{\#\;+*)\}]$		
		$[T \to \cdot F;\{\#\;+*)\}]$	F	9
		$[F \to \cdot i;\{\#\;+*)\}]$	i	3
		$[F \to \cdot(E);\{\#\;+*)\}]$	$($	4
6	*	$[T \to T*\cdot F;\{\#\;+*)\}]$	F	10
		$[F \to \cdot i;\{\#\;+*)\}]$	i	3
		$[F \to \cdot(E);\{\#\;+*)\}]$	$($	4
7	*	$[F \to (E\cdot);\{\#\;+*)\}]$	$)$	11
	*	$[E \to E\cdot+T;\{()+\}]$	$+$	5
8	*	$[F \to (E\cdot);\{\#\;+*\}]$	$)$	11
	*	$[E \to E\cdot+T;\{()+\}]$	$+$	5
	*	$[T \to T\cdot*F;\{()+*\}]$	$*$	6
9	*	$[E \to E+T\cdot;\{\#\;+)\}]$	$\#\;)+$	reduce 2
	*	$[T \to T\cdot*F;\{\#\;+*\}]$	$*$	6
10	*	$[T \to T*F\cdot;\{\#\;+*)\}]$		reduce 4
11	*	$[F \to (E)\cdot;\{\#\;+*)\}]$		reduce 7

Figure 7.18. Chain Production Elimination Applied to Figure 7.12

Compatibility is defined analogously for two columns $v, v' \in V$. We shall only discuss the combination of rows here.

We inspect the terminal transition matrix, the submatrix of $f(q, v)$ with $v \in T$, separately from the nonterminal transition matrix. Often different combinations are possible for the two submatrices, and by exploiting them separately we can achieve a greater storage reduction. This can be seen in the case of Figure 7.19a, which is an implementation of the transition matrix of Figure 7.18. In the terminal transition matrix rows 0, 4, 5 and 6 are compatible, but none of these rows are compatible in the nonterminal transition matrix.

In order to increase the number of compatible rows, we introduce a Boolean *failure* matrix, $F[q, t]$, $q \in Q$, $t \in T$. This matrix is used to filter the access to the terminal transition matrix:

$f(q, t) =$ **if** $F[q, t]$ **then** *error* **else** *entry_in_the_transition_matrix* ;

For this purpose we define $F[q, t]$ as follows:

$$ F[q, t] = \begin{cases} true & \text{if } f(q, t) = ERROR \\ false & \text{otherwise} \end{cases} $$

Figure 7.19b shows the failure matrix derived from the terminal transition matrix of Figure 7.19a. Note that the failure matrix may also contain don't-care entries, derived as discussed at the end of Section 7.3.2. Row and column combinations applied to Figure 7.19b reduce it from 9×6 to 4×4.

With the introduction of the failure matrix, all previous error entries become don't-care entries. Figure 7.19c shows the resulting compression of the terminal transition matrix. The nonterminal transition matrix is not affected by this process; in our example it can be compressed by combining both rows and columns as shown in Figure 7.19d. Each matrix requires an access map consisting of two additional arrays specifying the row (column) of the matrix to be used for a given state (symbol). For grammars of the size of the LAX grammar, the total storage requirements are generally reduced to 5-10% of their original values.

We have a certain freedom in combining the rows of the transition matrix. For example, in the terminal matrix of Figure 7.19a we could also have chosen the grouping $\{(0,4,5,6,9),(1,2,7,8)\}$. In general these groupings differ in the final state count; we must therefore examine a number of possible choices. The task of determining the minimum number of rows reduces to a problem in graph theory: We construct the (undirected) *incompatibility graph* $I = (Q, D)$ for our state set Q, in which two nodes q and q' are connected if the rows are incompatible. Minimization of the number of rows is then equivalent to the task of coloring the nodes with a minimum number of colors such that any pair of nodes connected by a branch are of different colors. (Graph coloring is discussed in Section B.3.3.) Further compression may be possible as indicated in Exercises 7.12 and 7.13.

	i	(	)	+	*	#	E	T	F
0	-6	4	.	.	.	.	1	2	2
1			.	5		*			
2	.	.	.	5	6	*			
4	-6	4	.	.	.	.	7	8	8
5	-6	4	.	.	.	.		9	9
6	-6	4	.	.	:	.			-4
7			-7	5		.			
8	.	.	-7	5	6	.			
9	.	.	+2	+2	6	+2			

a) Transition matrix for Figure 7.18 with shift-reduce transitions

	i	(	)	+	*	#
0	false	false	true	true	true	true
1			true	false		false
2	true	true	true	false	false	false
4	false	false	true	true	true	true
5	false	false	true	true	true	true
6	false	false	true	true	true	true
7			false	false		true
8	true	true	false	false	false	true
9	true	true	false	false	false	false

b) Uncompressed failure matrix for (a)

	i	(	)	+	*	#
0,1,2, 5,6,7,8	-6	4	-7	5	6	*
9			+2	+2	6	+2

c) Compressed terminal transition matrix

	E	T	F
0,1,2	1	2	
4	7	8	
5		9	
6,7,8,9		-4	

d) Compressed nonterminal transition matrix

Figure 7.19. Table Compression

7.4. Notes and References

LL(1) parsing in the form of recursive descent was, according to McClure [1972], the most frequently-used technique in practice. Certainly its flexibility and the fact that it can be hand-coded contribute to this popularity.

LR languages form the largest class of languages that can be processed with deterministic pushdown automata. Other techniques (precedence grammars, (m, n)-bounded context grammars or Floyd-Evans Productions, for example) either apply to smaller language classes or do not attain the same computational efficiency or error recovery properties as the techniques treated here. Operator precedence grammars have also achieved significant usage because one can easily construct parsers by hand for expressions with infix operators. Aho and Ullman [1972] give quite a complete overview of the available parsing techniques and their optimal implementation.

Instead of obtaining the LALR(1) parser from the LR(1) parser by merging states, one could begin with the SLR(1) parser and determine the exact right context only for those states in which the transition function is ambiguous. This technique reduces the computation time, but unfortunately does not generalize to an algorithm that eliminates all chain productions.

Construction 7.7 requires a redundant effort that can be avoided in practice. For example, the closure of a situation $[X \rightarrow \mu \cdot B\gamma; \Omega]$ depends only upon the nonterminal B if the lookahead set is ignored. The closure can thus be computed ahead of time for each $B \in N$, and only the lookahead sets must be supplied during parser construction. Also, the repeated construction of the follower state of an LALR(1) state that develops from the combination of two LR(1) states with distinct lookahead sets can be simplified. This repetition, which results from the marking of states as not yet examined, leaves the follower state (specified as a set of situations) unaltered. It can at most add lookahead symbols to single situations. This addition can also be accomplished without computing the entire state anew.

Our technique for chain production elimination is based upon an idea of Pager [1974].

Use of the failure matrix to increase the number of don't-care entries in the transition matrix was first proposed by Joliat [1973, 1974].

EXERCISES

7.1. Consider a grammar with embedded connection points. Explain why transformations of the grammar can be guaranteed to leave the invocation sequence of the associated parser actions invariant.

7.2. State the LL(1) condition in terms of the extended BNF notation of Section 5.1.3. Prove that your statement is equivalent to Theorem 7.2.

7.3. Give an example of a grammar in which the graph of *LAST* contains a cycle. Prove that $FOLLOW(A) = FOLLOW(B)$ for arbitrary nodes A and B in the same strongly connected subgraph.

7.4. Design a suitable internal representation of a grammar and program the generation algorithm of Section 7.2.3 in terms of it.

7.5. Devise an LL(1) parser generation algorithm that accepts the extended BNF notation of Section 5.1.3. Will you be able to achieve a more efficient parser by operating upon this form directly, or by converting it to productions? Explain.

7.6. Consider the interpretive parser of Figure 7.10.
   a. Define additional operation codes to implement connection points, and add the appropriate alternatives to the case statement. Carefully explain the interface conventions for the parser actions. Would you prefer a different kind of parse table entry? Explain.
   b. Some authors provide special operations for the situations $[X \rightarrow \mu \cdot B]$ and $[X \rightarrow \mu \cdot tB]$. Explain how some recursion can be avoided in this manner, and write appropriate alternatives for the case statement.
   c. Once the special cases of (b) are recognized, it may be advantageous to provide extra operations identical to 4 and 5 of Figure 7.10, except that the conditions are reversed. Why? Explain.
   d. Recognize the situation $[X \rightarrow \mu \cdot t]$ and alter the code of case 4 to absorb the processing of the 2 operation following it.
   e. What is your opinion of the value of these optimizations? Test your predictions on some language with which you are familiar.

7.7. Show that the following grammar is LR(1) but not LALR(1):
$Z \rightarrow A$,
$A \rightarrow aBcB$, $A \rightarrow B$, $A \rightarrow D$,
$B \rightarrow b$, $B \rightarrow Ff$,
$D \rightarrow dE$,
$E \rightarrow FcA$, $E \rightarrow FcE$,
$F \rightarrow b$

7.8. Repeat Exercise 7.5 for the LR case. Use the algorithm of Section 7.3.4.

7.9. Show that $FIRST(A)$ can be computed by any marking algorithm for directed graphs that obtains a 'spanning tree', B, for the graph. B has the same node set as the original graph, G, and its branch set is a subset of that of G.

7.10. Consider the grammar with the following productions:
$Z \rightarrow AXd$, $Z \rightarrow BX$, $Z \rightarrow C$,
$A \rightarrow B$, $A \rightarrow C$,
$B \rightarrow CXb$,
$C \rightarrow c$,
$X \rightarrow \epsilon$
   a. Derive an LALR(1) parser for this grammar.
   b. Delete the reductions by the chain productions $A \rightarrow B$ and $A \rightarrow C$.

7.11. Use the techniques discussed in Section 7.3.5 to compress the transition matrix produced for Exercise 7.8.

7.12. [Anderson 1972] Consider a transition matrix for an LR parser constructed by one of the algorithms of Section 7.3.2.

   a. Show that for every state q there is exactly one symbol $z(q)$ such that
      $f(q',a)$ implies $a = z(q)$.
   b. Show that, in the case of shift-reduce transitions introduced by the algo-
      rithms of Sections 7.3.3 and 7.3.4, an unambiguous symbol $z(A \rightarrow \chi)$ exists
      such that $f(q,a) = $ 'shift and reduce $A \rightarrow \chi$' implies $a = z(A \rightarrow \chi)$.
   c. The states (and shift-reduce transitions) can be numbered in such a way
      that all states in column c have sequential numbers $c_0 + i$, $i = 0, 1, \cdots$
      Thus it suffices to store only the relative number i in the transition matrix;
      the base c_0 is only given once for each column. In exactly the same
      manner, a list of the reductions in a row can be assigned to this row and
      retain only the appropriate index to this list in the transition matrix.
   d. Make these alterations in the transition matrix produced for Exercise 7.8
      before beginning the compression of Exercise 7.11, and compare the result
      with that obtained previously.

7.13. [Bell 1971] Consider an $m \times n$ transition matrix, t, in which all unspecified
      entries are don't-cares. Show that the matrix can be compressed into a $p \times q$
      matrix c, two length-m arrays f and u, and two length-n arrays g and v by
      the following algorithm: Initially $f_i = g_i = \infty$, $1 \leqslant i \leqslant m$, $1 \leqslant j \leqslant n$, and
      $k = 1$. If all occupied columns of the ith row of t uniformly contain the value
      r, then set $f_i := k$, $k := k + 1$, $u_i := r$ and delete the ith row of t. If the jth
      column is uniformly occupied, delete it also and set $g_j := k$, $k := k + 1$, $v_j := r$.
      Repeat this process until no uniformly-occupied row or column remains. The
      remaining matrix is the matrix c. We then enter the row (column) number in
      c of the former i^{th} row (j^{th} column) into u_i (v_j). The following relation then
      holds:

   $t_{i,j} = $ **if** $f_i < g_j$ **then** u_i
                else if $f_i > g_j$ **then** v_j
                else (* $f_i = g_j = \infty$ *) c_{u_i, v_j};

   (Hint: Show that the size of c is independent of the sequence in which the
   rows and columns are deleted.)

CHAPTER 8
Attribute Grammars

Semantic analysis and code generation are based upon the structure tree. Each node of the tree is 'decorated' with attributes describing properties of that node, and hence the tree is often called an *attributed structure tree* for emphasis. The information collected in the attributes of a node is derived from the environment of that node; it is the task of semantic analysis to compute these attributes and check their consistency. Optimization and code generation can be also described in similar terms, using attributes to guide the transformation of the tree and ultimately the selection of machine instructions.

Attribute grammars have proven to be a useful aid in representing the attribution of the structure tree because they constitute a formal definition of all context-free and context-sensitive language properties on the one hand, and a formal specification of the semantic analysis on the other. When deriving the specification, we need not be overly concerned with the sequence in which the attributes are computed because this can (with some restrictions) be derived mechanically. Storage for the attribute values is also not reflected in the specification. We begin by assuming that all attributes belonging to a node are stored within that node in the structure tree; optimization of the attribute storage is considered later.

Most examples in this chapter are included to show constraints and pathological cases; practical examples can be found in Chapter 9.

8.1. Basic Concepts of Attribute Grammars

An attribute grammar is based upon a context-free grammar $G = (N,T,P,Z)$. It associates a set $A(X)$ of *attributes* with each symbol, X, in the vocabulary of G. Each attribute represents a specific (context-sensitive) property of the symbol X, and can take on any of a specified set of values. We write $X.a$ to indicate that attribute a is an element of $A(X)$.

Each node in the structure tree of a sentence in $L(G)$ is associated with a particular set of values for the attributes of some symbol X in the vocabulary of G. These values are established by *attribution rules* $R(p) = \{X_i.a \leftarrow f(X_j.b, \ldots, X_k.c)\}$ for the productions $p:X_0 \rightarrow X_1 \cdots X_n$ used to construct the tree. Each rule defines an attribute $X_i.a$ in terms of attributes $X_j.b, \ldots, X_k.c$ of symbols in the same production. (Note that in this chapter we use upper-case letters to denote vocabulary symbols, rather than using case to distinguish terminals from nonterminals. The reason for this is that *any* symbol of the vocabulary may have attributes, and the distinction between terminals and nonterminals is generally irrelevant for attribute computation.)

rule *assignment* $::=$ *name* $':='$ *expression* .
attribution
   name.environment $\leftarrow$ *assignment.environment* ;
   expression.environment $\leftarrow$ *assignment.environment* ;
   name.postmode $\leftarrow$ *name.primode* ;
   expression.postmode $\leftarrow$
     if *name.primode* $=ref\_int\_type$ **then** *int_type* **else** *real_type* **fi**;

rule *expression* $::=$ *name addop name* .
attribution
   name[1]*.environment* $\leftarrow$ *expression.environment* ;
   name[2]*.environment* $\leftarrow$ *expression.environment* ;
   expression.primode $\leftarrow$
     if *coercible*(*name*[1]*.primode*, *int_type*) **and**
      coercible(*name*[2]*.primode*, *int_type*) **then** *int_type* **else** *real_type* **fi**;
   addop.mode $\leftarrow$ *expression.primode* ;
   name[1]*.postmode* $\leftarrow$ *expression.primode* ;
   name[2]*.postmode* $\leftarrow$ *expression.primode* ;
condition *coercible*(*expression.primode*, *expression.postmode*);

rule *addop* $::=$ $'+'$.
attribution
   addop.operation $\leftarrow$
     if *addop.mode* $=int\_type$ **then** *int_addition* **else** *real_addition* **fi**;

rule *name* $::=$ *identifier* .
attribution
   name.primode $\leftarrow$ *defined_type*(*identifier.symbol* ,*name.environment*);
condition *coercible*(*name.primode*, *name.postmode*);

Figure 8.1. Simplified LAX Assignment

In addition to the attribution rules, a *condition* $B(X_i.a, \ldots, X_j.b)$ involving attributes of symbols occurring in p may be given. B specifies the context condition that must be fulfilled if a syntactically correct sentence is correct according to the static semantics and therefore translatable. We could also regard this condition as the computation of a Boolean attribute *consistent*, which we associate with the left-hand side of the production.

As an example, Figure 8.1 gives a simplified attribute grammar for LAX assignments. Each $p \in P$ is marked by the keyword **rule** and written using EBNF notation (restricted to express only productions). The elements of $R(p)$ follow the keyword **attribution**. We use a conventional expression-oriented programming language notation for the functions f, and terminate each element with a semicolon. Particular instances of an attribute are distinguished by numbering multiple occurrences of symbols in the production (e.g. *name*[1], *name*[2]) from left to right. Any condition is also marked by a keyword and terminated by a semicolon.

In order to check the consistency of the assignment and to further identify the + operator, we must take the operand types into account. For this purpose we define two attributes, *primode* and *postmode,* for the symbols *expression* and *name,* and one attribute, *mode,* for the symbol *addop*. *Primode* describes the type determined directly from the node and its descendants; *postmode* describes the type expected when the result is used as an operand by other nodes. Any difference between *primode* and *postmode*

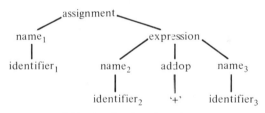

a) Syntactic structure tree

assignment.environment
identifier$_i$.symbol

b) Attribute values given initially $(i = 1, \ldots, 3)$

name$_1$.environment	*expression.environment*	
name$_i$.environment	*name$_1$.primode*	
name$_1$.postmode	*expression.postmode*	*name$_i$.primode*
expression.primode	*name$_1$* condition	
addop.mode	*name$_i$.postmode*	*expression* condition
addop.operation	*name$_i$* condition	

c) Attribute values computed $(i = 2, 3)$

Figure 8.2. Analysis of $x := y + z$

assignment

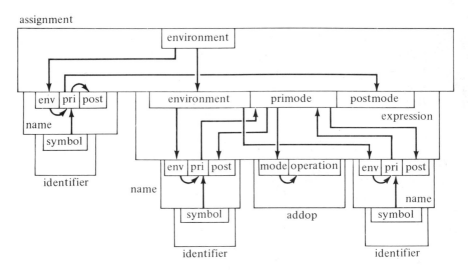

Figure 8.3. Attribute Dependencies in the Tree for $x := y + z$

must be resolved by coercions. The Boolean function *coercible* (t_1, t_2) tests whether type t_1 can be coerced to t_2.

Figure 8.2 shows the analysis of $x := y + z$ according to the grammar of Figure 8.1. (*Assignment.environment* would be computed from the declarations of x, y and z, but here we show it as given in order to make the example self-contained.) Attributes on the same line of Figure 8.2c can be computed collaterally; every attribute is dependent upon at least one attribute from the previous line. These dependency relations can be expressed as a graph (Figure 8.3). Each large box represents the production whose application corresponds to the node of the structure tree contained within it. The small boxes making up the node itself represent the attributes of the symbol on the left-hand side of the production, and the arrows represent the dependency relations arising from the attribution rules of the production. The node set of the dependency graph is just the set of small boxes representing attributes; its edge set is the set of arrows representing dependencies.

We must know all of the values upon which an attribute depends before we can compute the value of that attribute. Clearly this is only possible if the dependency graph is acyclic. Figure 8.3 is acyclic, but consider the following LAX type definition, which we shall discuss in more detail in Sections 9.1.2 and 9.1.3:

type t = **record** x :*real* ; p :**ref** t **end**

We must compute a type attribute for each of the identifiers t, x and p so that the associated type is known at each use of the identifier. The type attribute of t consists of the keyword **record** plus the types and identifiers of the fields.

Now, however, the type of p contains an application of t, implying that the type identified by t depends upon which type a use of t identifies. Thus the type t depends cyclically upon itself. (We shall show how to eliminate the cycle from this example in Section 9.1.3.)

Let us now make the intuition gained from these examples more precise. We begin with the grammar G, a set of attributes $A(X)$ for each X in the vocabulary of G, and a set of attribution rules $R(p)$ (and possibly a condition $B(p)$) for each p in the production set of G.

Definition 8.1. An *attribute grammar* is a 4-tuple, $AG = (G,A,R,B)$. $G = (T,N,P,Z)$ is a reduced context free grammar, $A = \underset{X \in T \cup N}{\cup} A(X)$ is a finite set of attributes, $R = \underset{p \in P}{\cup} R(p)$ is a finite set of attribution rules, and $B = \underset{p \in P}{\cup} B(p)$ is a finite set of conditions. $A(X) \cap A(Y) \neq \emptyset$ implies $X = Y$. For each occurrence of X in the structure tree corresponding to a sentence of $L(G)$, at most one rule is applicable for the computation of each attribute $a \in A(X)$.

Definition 8.2. For each $p : X_0 \to X_1 \cdots X_n \in P$ the set of *defining occurrences* of attributes is $AF(p) = \{X_i.a \mid X_i.a \leftarrow f(\cdots) \in R(p)\}$. An attribute $X.a$ is called *derived* or *synthesized* if there exists a production $p : X \to \chi$ and $X.a$ is in $AF(p)$; it is called *inherited* if there exists a production $q : Y \to \mu X \nu$ and $X.a \in AF(q)$.

Synthesized attributes of a symbol represent properties resulting from consideration of the subtree derived from the symbol in the structure tree. Inherited attributes result from consideration of the environment. In Figure 8.1, the *name.primode* and *addop.operation* attributes were synthesized; *name.environment* and *addop.mode* were inherited.

Attributes such as the value of a constant or the symbol of an identifier, which arise in conjunction with structure tree construction, are called *intrinsic*. Intrinsic attributes reflect our division of the original context-free grammar into a parsing grammar and a symbol grammar. If we were to use the entire grammar of Appendix A as the parsing grammar, we could easily compute the symbol attribute of an *identifier* node from the subtree rooted in that node. No intrinsic attributes would be needed because constant values could be assigned to left-hand side attributes in rules such as *letter* $::=$ 'a'. Thus our omission of intrinsic attributes in Definition 8.2 results in no loss of generality.

Theorem 8.3. *The following sets are disjoint for all X in the vocabulary of G:*

$$AS(X) = \{X.a \mid \exists p : X \to \chi \in P \text{ and } X.a \in AF(p)\}$$
$$AI(X) = \{X.a \mid \exists q : Y \to \mu X \nu \in P \text{ and } X.a \in AF(q)\}$$

Further, there exists at most one rule $X.a \leftarrow f(\cdots)$ in $R(p)$ for each $p \in P$ and $a \in A(X)$.

Suppose that an attribute a belonged to both $AS(X)$ and $AI(X)$. Some derivation $Z \Rightarrow^* \sigma Y\tau \Rightarrow \sigma\mu X\nu\tau \Rightarrow \sigma\mu\chi\nu\tau \Rightarrow^* \omega$ ($\omega \in L(G)$) would then have two different rules for computing the value of attribute a at node X. But this situation is prohibited by the last condition of Definition 8.1. It can be shown that Theorem 8.3 is equivalent to that condition.

Definition 8.1 does not guarantee that a synthesized attribute $a \in A(X)$ will be computable in all cases, because it does not require that $X.a$ be an element of $AF(p)$ for every production $p: X \to \chi$. A similar statement holds for inherited attributes.

Definition 8.4. An attribute grammar is *complete* if the following statements hold for all X in the vocabulary of G:

> For all $p: X \to \chi \in P, AS(X) \subseteq AF(p)$
> For all $q: Y \to \mu X\nu \in P, AI(X) \subseteq AF(q)$
> $AS(X) \cup AI(X) = A(X)$

Further, if Z is the axiom of G then $AI(Z)$ is empty.

As compiler writers, we are only interested in attribute grammars that allow us to compute all of the attribute values in any structure tree.

Definition 8.5. An attribute grammar is *well-defined* if, for each structure tree corresponding to a sentence of $L(G)$, all attributes are effectively computable. A sentence of $L(G)$ is *correctly attributed* if, in addition, all conditions yield *true*.

It is clear that a well-defined attribute grammar must be complete. A complete attribute grammar is well-defined, however, only if no attribute can depend upon itself in any structure tree. We therefore need to formalize the dependency graph introduced in Figure 8.3.

Definition 8.6. For each $p: X_0 \to X_1 \cdots X_n \in P$ the set of *direct attribute dependencies* is given by

$$DDP(p) = \{(X_i.a, X_j.b) \mid X_j.b \leftarrow f(\cdots X_i.a \cdots) \in R(p)\}$$

The grammar is *locally acyclic* if the graph of $DDP(p)$ is acyclic for each $p \in P$.

We often write $(X_i.a, X_j.b) \in DDP(p)$ as $X_i.a \to X_j.b \in DDP(p)$, and follow the same convention for the relations defined below. If no misunderstanding can occur, we omit the specification of the relation. In Figure 8.3 the arrows lying inside each large box are the edges of $DDP(p)$ for a particular p.

We obtain the complete dependency graph for a structure tree by 'pasting together' the direct dependencies according to the syntactic structure of the tree.

Definition 8.7. Let S be the attributed structure tree corresponding to a sentence in $L(G)$, and let $K_0 \cdots K_n$ be the nodes corresponding to application of $p : X_0 \to X_1 \cdots X_n$. We write $K_i.a \to K_j.b$ if $X_i.a \to X_j.b \in DDP(p)$. The set $DT(S) = \{K_i.a \to K_j.b\}$, where we consider all applications of productions in S, is called the *dependency relation over the tree S*.

Theorem 8.8. *An attribute grammar is well-defined if and only if it is complete and the graph of $DT(S)$ is acyclic for each structure tree S corresponding to a sentence of $L(G)$.*

If AG is a well-defined attribute grammar (WAG) then a nondeterministic algorithm can be used to compute all attribute values in the attributed structure tree for a sentence in $L(G)$: We provide a separate process to compute each attribute value, which is started after all operands of the attribution rule defining that value have been computed. Upon completion of this process, the value will be available and hence other processes may be started. Computation begins with intrinsic attributes, which become available as soon as the structure tree has been built. The number of processes depends not upon the grammar, but upon the number of nodes in the structure tree. Well-definedness guarantees that all attributes will be computed by this system without deadlock, independent of the precise construction of the attribute rules.

Before building a compiler along these lines, we should verify that the grammar on which it is based is actually WAG. Unfortunately, exponential time is required to verify the conditions of Theorem 8.8. Thus we must investigate subclasses of WAG for which this cost is reduced.

It is important to note that the choice of subclass is made solely upon practical considerations; all well-defined attribute grammars have the same formal descriptive power. The proof of this assertion involves a 'hoisting' transformation that is sometimes useful in molding a grammar to a pre-specified tree traversal: An inherited attribute of a symbol is removed, along with all synthesized attributes depending upon it, and replaced by a computation in the parent node. We shall see an example of this transformation in Section 8.2.3.

8.2. Traversal Strategies

A straightforward implementation of *any* attribute evaluation scheme will fail in practice because of gigantic storage requirements for attribute values and correspondingly long computation times. Only by selecting an evaluation scheme that permits us to optimize memory usage can the attribute grammar technique be made practical for compiler construction. Section 8.3.2 will discuss optimizations based upon the assumption that we can determine the sequence of visits to a particular node solely from the symbol corresponding to that node. We shall require that each production $p:X_0 \rightarrow X_1 \cdots X_n \in P$ be associated with a fixed *attribution algorithm* made up of the following basic operations:

- Evaluate an element of $R(p)$.
- Move to child node i $(i = 1, \ldots, n)$.
- Move to parent node.

Conceptually, a copy of the algorithm for p is attached to each node corresponding to an application of p. Evaluation begins by moving to the root and ends when the algorithm for the root executes 'move to parent'.

We first discuss algorithms based upon these operations — what they look like and how they interact — and characterize the subclass of WAG for which they can be constructed. We then examine two different construction strategies. The first uses the attribute dependencies to define the tree traversal, while the second specifies a traversal a priori. We only discuss the general properties of each strategy in this section; implementation details will be deferred to Section 8.3.

8.2.1. Partitioned Attribute Grammars

Because of the properties of inherited and synthesized attributes, the algorithms for two productions $p:X \rightarrow \chi$ and $q:Y \rightarrow \mu X \nu$ must cooperate to evaluate the attributes of an interior node of the structure tree. Inherited attributes would be computed by rules in $R(q)$, synthesized attributes by rules in $R(p)$. The attribution of X represents the interface between the algorithms for p and q. In Figure 8.3, for example, the algorithms for *expression* $::=$ *name addop name* and *assignment* $::=$ *name* $':='$ *expression* are both involved in computation of attributes for the *expression* node. Because all computation begins and ends at the root, the general pattern of the (coroutine) interaction would be the following: The algorithm for q computes values for some subset of $AI(X)$ using a sequence of evaluation instructions. It then passes control to the algorithm for p by executing 'move to child i'. After using a sequence of evaluation operations to compute some subset of $AS(X)$, the algorithm for p returns by executing 'move to parent'. (Of course both algorithms could have other attribute evaluations and moves interspersed with these; here we are considering only computation of X's attributes.) This process continues, alternating computation of subsets of $AI(X)$ and $AS(X)$ until all attribute values are available. The last action of each algorithm is 'move to parent'.

Figure 8.4 gives possible algorithms for the grammar of Figure 8.1. Because a symbol like *expression* can appear in several productions on the left or right sides, we always identify the production for the child node by giving only the left-hand-side symbol. We do not answer the question of

Evaluate *name.environment*
Move to *name*
Evaluate *expression.environment*
Move to *expression*
Evaluate *name.postmode*
Move to *name*
Evaluate *expression.postmode*
Move to *expression*
Move to parent

a) Procedure for *assignment* $::=$ *name* $'='$ *expression*

Evaluate *name*[1].*environment*
Move to *name*[1]
Evaluate *name*[2].*environment*
Move to *name*[2]
Evaluate *expression.primode*
Move to parent
Evaluate *name*[1].*postmode*
Move to *name*[1]
Evaluate *addop.mode*
Move to *addop*
Evaluate *name*[2].*postmode*
Move to *name*[2]
Evaluate condition
Move to parent

b) Procedure for *expression* $::=$ *name addop name*

Evaluate *name.primode*
Move to parent
Evaluate condition
Move to parent

c) Procedure for *name* $::=$ *identifier*

Figure 8.4. Attribution Algorithms for Figure 8.1

which production is really used because in general we cannot know. For the same reason we do not specify the parent production more exactly.

The attributes of X constitute the only interface between the algorithms for p and q. When the algorithm for q passes control to the algorithm for p by executing 'move to child i', it expects that a particular subset of $AS(X)$ will be evaluated before control returns. Since the algorithms must work for *all* structure trees, this subset must be evaluated by *every* algorithm corresponding to a production of the form $X \to \chi$. The same reasoning holds for subsets of $AI(X)$ evaluated by algorithms corresponding to productions of the form $Y \to \mu X \nu$.

Definition 8.9. Given a partition of $A(X)$ into disjoint subsets $A_i(X)$,

$i = 1, \ldots, m(X)$ for each X in the vocabulary of G, the resulting partition of the entire attribute set A is *admissible* if, for all X, $A_i(X)$ is a subset of $AS(X)$ for $i = m, m-2, \ldots$ and $A_i(X)$ is a subset of $AI(X)$ for $i = m-1, m-3, \ldots A_i(X)$ may be empty for any i.

Definition 8.10. An attribute grammar is *partitionable* if it is locally acyclic and an admissible partition exists such that for each X in the vocabulary of G the attributes of X can be evaluated in the order $A_1(X), \ldots, A_m(X)$. An attribute grammar together with such a partition is termed *partitioned*.

Since all attributes can be evaluated, a partitionable grammar must be well-defined.

A set of attribution algorithms satisfying our constraints can be constructed if and only if the grammar is partitioned. The admissible partition defines a partial ordering on $A(X)$ that must be observed by every algorithm. Attributes belonging to a subset $A_i(X)$ may be evaluated in any order permitted by $DDP(p)$, and this order may vary from one production to another. No context switch across the X interface occurs while these attributes are being evaluated, although context switches may occur at other interfaces. A move instruction crossing the X interface *follows* evaluation of each subset.

The grammar of Figure 8.1 is partitioned, and the admissible partition used to construct Figure 8.4 was:

$$A_1(expression) = \{environment\} \qquad A_1(name) = \{environment\}$$
$$A_2(expression) = \{primode\} \qquad A_2(name) = \{primode\}$$
$$A_3(expression) = \{postmode\} \qquad A_3(name) = \{postmode\}$$
$$A_4(expression) = \{\} \qquad A_4(name) = \{\}$$

$$A_1(addop) = \{mode\}$$
$$A_2(addop) = \{operation\}$$

A_4 is empty in the cases of both *expression* and *name* because the last nonempty subset in the partition consists of inherited attributes, while Definition 8.9 requires synthesized attributes. At this point the algorithm actually contains a test of the condition, which we have already noted can be regarded as a synthesized attribute of the left-hand-side symbol. With this interpretation, it would constitute the single element of A_4 for each symbol.

8.2.2. Derived Traversals Let us now turn to the questions of how to partition an attribute grammar and how to derive algorithms from an admissible partition that satisfies Definition 8.10, assuming no a priori constraints upon the tree traversal. For this purpose we examine dependency graphs, with which the partitions and algorithms must be compatible.

Suppose that $X.a$ is an element of $A_i(X)$ and $X.b$ is an element of $A_j(X)$

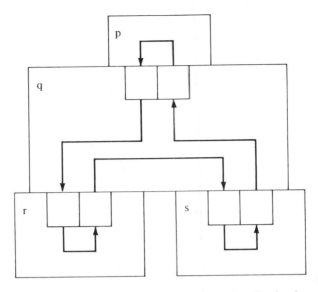

Figure 8.5. A Cycle Involving More Than One Production

in an admissible partition, and $i > j$. Clearly $K_X.a \to K_X.b$ cannot be an element of $DT(S)$ for any structure tree S, because then $X.b$ could not be calculated before $X.a$ as required by the fact that $i > j$. $DDP(p)$ gives direct dependencies for all attributes, but the graph of $DT(S)$ includes indirect dependencies resulting from the interaction of direct dependencies. These indirect dependencies may lead to a cycle in the graph of $DT(S)$ as shown in Figure 8.5. We need a way of characterizing these dependencies that is independent of the structure tree.

In a locally acyclic grammar, dependencies between attributes belonging to $AF(p)$ can be removed by rewriting the attribution rules:

$$
\begin{array}{lcl}
X_i.a \leftarrow f(...,X_j.b,...) & & X_i.a \leftarrow f(...,g(\cdots),...) \\
X_j.b \leftarrow g(\cdots) & \text{becomes} & X_j.b \leftarrow g(\cdots)
\end{array}
$$

In Figure 8.3 this transformation would, among other things, replace the dependency *expression.primode $\to$ addop.mode* by *name*[1].*primode $\to$ addop.mode* and *name*[2].*primode $\to$ addop.mode*. Dependencies that can be removed in this way may require that the attributes *within* a partition element $A_i(X)$ be computed in different orders for different productions, but they have no effect on the usability of the partition itself (Exercise 8.3).

Definition 8.11. For each $p:X_0 \to X_1 \cdots X_n \in P$, the *normalized transitive closure* of $DDP(p)$ is

$$NDDP(p) = DDP(p)^+ - \{(X_i.a,X_j.b) \mid X_i.a,X_j.b \in AF(p)\}$$

The dependencies arising from interaction of nodes in the structure tree are summarized by two collections of sets, IDP and IDS. $IDP(p)$ shows all of the essential dependencies between attributes appearing in production p, while $IDS(X)$ shows those between attributes of symbol X.

Definition 8.12. The *induced attribute dependencies* of an attribute grammar (G,A,R,B) are defined as follows:

1. For all $p \in P$, $IDP(p) := NDDP(p)$.
2. For all X in the vocabulary of G,

$$IDS(X) := \{(X.a, X.b) \mid \exists q \text{ such that } (X.a, X.b) \in IDP(q)^+\}$$

3. For all $p : X_0 \rightarrow X_1 \cdots X_n \in P$,

$$IDP(p) := IDP(p) \cup IDS(X_0) \cup \cdots \cup IDS(X_n)$$

4. Repeat (2) and (3) until there is no change in any IDP or IDS.

$IDP(p)$ and $IDS(X)$ are pessimistic approximations to the desired dependency relations. Any essential dependency that could be present in any structure tree is included in $IDP(p)$ and $IDS(X)$, and *all are assumed to be present simultaneously*. The importance of this point is illustrated by the grammar of Figure 8.6, which is well-defined but not partitioned. Both $c \rightarrow e$ and $d \rightarrow f$ are included in $IDS(Y)$ even though it is clear from Figure 8.7 that only one of these dependencies could occur in any structure tree. A similar situation occurs for $e \rightarrow d$ and $f \rightarrow c$. The result is that $IDS(Y)$ indicates a cycle that will never be present in any DT.

The pessimism of the indirect dependencies is crucial for the existence of a partitioned grammar. Remember that it must *always* be possible to evaluate the attributes of X in the order specified by the admissible partition. Thus the order must satisfy *all* dependency relations simultaneously.

Theorem 8.13. *If an attribute grammar is partitionable then the graph of* $IDP(p)$ *is acyclic for every* $p \in P$ *and the graph of* $IDS(X)$ *is acyclic for every* X *in the vocabulary of* G. *Further, if* $a \rightarrow b$ *is in* $IDS(X)$ *then* $a \in A_i(X)$ *and* $b \in A_j(X)$ *implies* $i \leqslant j$.

Note that Theorem 8.13 gives a necessary, but not sufficient, condition for a partitionable grammar. The grammar of Figure 8.8 illustrates the reason, and provides some further insight into the properties of partitionable grammars.

Given the rules of Figure 8.8, a straightforward computation yields $IDS(X) = \{a \rightarrow b, c \rightarrow d\}$. Three of the five admissible partitions of $\{a, b, c, d\}$ satisfy Theorem 8.13:

$$\{a\}\ \{b\}\ \{c\}\ \{d\}\ \{c\}\ \{d\}\ \{a\}\ \{b\}\ \{a,c\}\ \{b,d\}$$

Figure 8.9 gives the dependency graphs for the two structure trees that can be derived according to this grammar. Simple case analysis shows that none of the three partitions can be used to compute the attributes of X in both

rule $Z ::= X.$ (* Production 1 *)
attribution
   $X.a \leftarrow 1;$

rule $X ::= sY.$ (* Production 2 *)
attribution
   $X.b \leftarrow Y.f;$
   $Y.c \leftarrow X.a;$
   $Y.d \leftarrow Y.e;$

rule $X ::= tY.$ (* Production 3 *)
attribution
   $X.b \leftarrow Y.e;$
   $Y.c \leftarrow Y.f;$
   $Y.d \leftarrow X.a;$

rule $Y ::= u.$ (* Production 4 *)
attribution
   $Y.e \leftarrow 2;$
   $Y.f \leftarrow Y.d;$

rule $Y ::= v.$ (* Production 5 *)
attribution
   $Y.e \leftarrow Y.c;$
   $Y.f \leftarrow 3;$

a) Rules

$IDS(X) = \{a \rightarrow b\}$
$IDS(Y) = \{c \rightarrow e, d \rightarrow f, e \rightarrow d, f \rightarrow c\}$

b) Induced dependencies for symbols

Figure 8.6. A Well-Defined Grammar

trees. For example, consider the first partition. Attribute a must be computed before attribute d. In the first tree $X[1].d$ must be known for the computation of $X[2].a$, so the sequence must be $X[1].a$, $X[1].d$, $X[2].a$, $X[2].d$. This is inadmissible, however, because $X[2].d \rightarrow X[1].a$ is an element of $NDDP(Z \rightarrow sXX)$.

When we choose a partition, this choice fixes the order in which certain attributes may be computed. In this respect the partition acts like a set of dependencies, and its effect may be taken into account by adding these dependencies to the ones arising from the attribution rules.

Definition 8.14. Let $A_1(X), \ldots, A_m(X)$ be an admissible partition of $A(X)$. For each $p : X_0 \rightarrow X_1 \cdots X_n$ in P the set of *dependencies over the production p* is:
$DP(p) = IDP(pP \cup \{(X_i.a, X_i.b) \mid a \in A_j(X_i), b \in A_k(X_i), 0 \leqslant i \leqslant n, j < k\}$

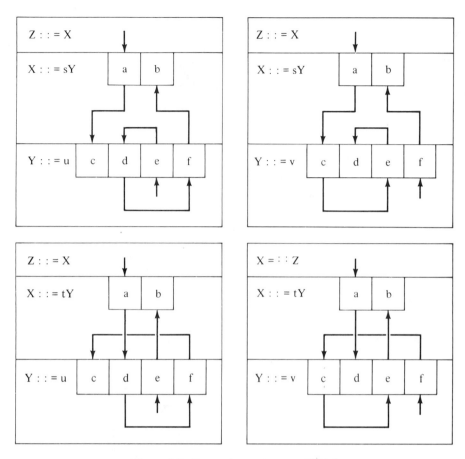

Figure 8.7. Dependency Graphs $DT(s)$

Theorem 8.15. *Given an admissible partition for an attribute grammar, the grammar is partitioned if and only if the graph of $DP(p)$ is acyclic for each $p \in P$.*

Unfortunately, Theorem 8.15 does not lead to an algorithm for partitioning an attribute grammar. Figure 8.10 is a partitioned grammar, but the obvious partition $A_1(X) = \{b\}, A_2(X) = \{a\}$ causes cyclic graphs for both $DP(1)$ and $DP(2)$. In order to avoid the problem we must use $A_1(X) = \{a\}$, $A_2(X) = \{b\}, A_3(X) = \{\}$. A backtracking procedure for constructing the partition begins with the dependency relations of $IDS(X)$ and considers pairs of independent attributes (a, b), one of which is inherited and the other synthesized. It adds $a \to b$ to the dependencies currently assumed and immediately checks all DP graphs for cycles. If a cycle is found then the dependency $b \to a$ is tested. If this also results in a cycle then the procedure backtracks, reversing a previously assumed dependency. Because this procedure involves exponential cost, it is of little practical interest.

rule $Z ::= s\ X\ X$.
attribution
  $X[1].a \leftarrow X[2].d$;
  $X[1].c \leftarrow 1$;
  $X[2].a \leftarrow X[1].d$;
  $X[2].c \leftarrow 2$;

rule $Z ::= t\ X\ X$.
attribution
  $X[1].a \leftarrow 3$;
  $X[1].c \leftarrow X[2].b$;
  $X[2].a \leftarrow 4$:
  $X[2].c \leftarrow X[1].b$;

rule $X ::= u$.
attribution
  $X.b \leftarrow X.a$;
  $X.d \leftarrow X.c$;

Figure 8.8. An Attribute Grammar That Is Not Partitioned

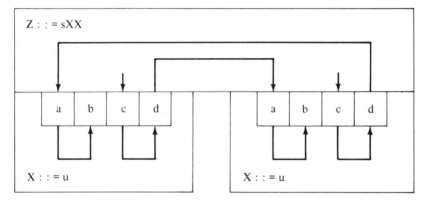

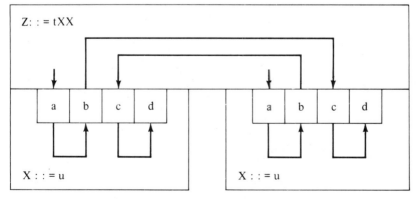

Figure 8.9. Dependency Graphs for Figure 8.8

As in the case of parser construction, where pragmatic considerations forced us to use subclasses of the LL(k) and LR(k) grammars, the cost of obtaining an appropriate partition forces us to consider a subclass of the partitioned grammars. The following definition yields a nonbacktracking procedure for obtaining a partition that evaluates each attribute at the latest point consistent with $IDS(X)$.

Definition 8.16. An attribute grammar is *ordered* if the following partition of A results in a partitioned grammar:

$$A_i(X) = T_{m-i+1}(X) - T_{m-i-1}(X) \quad (i = 1, \ldots, m)$$

Here m is the smallest k such that $T_{k-1}(X) \cup T_k(X) = A(X)$, $T_{-1}(X) = T_0(X) = \varnothing$, and for $k > 0$

$$T_{2k-1}(X) = \{a \in AS(X) \mid a \to b \in IDS(X) \text{ implies } b \in T_j(X), \ j \leqslant (2k-1)\}$$

$$T_{2k}(X) = \{a \in AI(X) \mid a \to b \in IDS(X) \text{ implies } b \in T_j(X), \ j \leqslant 2k\}$$

This definition requires that all $T_j(X)$ actually exist. Some attributes remain unassigned to any $T_j(X)$ if (and only if) the grammar is locally acyclic and some *IDS* contains a cycle.

For the grammar of Figure 8.10, construction 8.16 leads to the 'obvious' partition discussed above, which fails. Thus the grammar is not ordered, and we must conclude that the ordered grammars form a proper subclass of the partitionable grammars.

rule $Z ::= s\ X\ Y$.   (* Production 1 *)
attribution
   $X.b \leftarrow Y.d$;
   $Y.c \leftarrow 1$;
   $Y.e \leftarrow X.a$;

rule $Z ::= t\ X\ Y$.   (* Production 2 *)
attribution
   $X.b \leftarrow Y.f$;
   $Y.c \leftarrow X.a$;
   $Y.e \leftarrow 2$;

rule $X ::= u$.   (* Production 3 *)
attribution
   $X.a \leftarrow 3$;

rule $Y ::= v$.   (* Production 4 *)
attribution
   $Y.d \leftarrow Y.c$;
   $Y.f \leftarrow Y.e$;

Figure 8.10. A Partitioned Grammar

Suppose that a partitioned attribute grammar is given, with partitions $A_1(X), \ldots, A_m(X)$ for each X in the vocabulary. In order to construct an attribution algorithm for a production $p:X_0 \rightarrow X_1 \cdots X_n$, we begin by defining a new attribute $c_{i,j}$ corresponding to each subset $A_i(X_j)$ of attributes not computed in the context of p. (These are the inherited attributes $A_j(X_0)$, $j = m-1, m-3,\ldots$ of the left-hand side and the synthesized attributes $A_i(X_j)$, $i \neq 0$, $j = m, m-2,\ldots$ of the right-hand side symbols.) For example, the grammar of Figure 8.1 is partitioned as shown at the end of Section 8.2.1. In order to construct the attribution algorithm of Figure 8.4b, we must define new attributes as shown in Figure 8.11a.

Every occurrence of an attribute from $A_i(X_j)$ is then replaced by $c_{i,j}$ in $DP(p) \cup DDP(p)$, as illustrated by Figure 8.11b. $DP(p)$ alone does not suffice in this step because it was derived (via $IDP(p)$) from $NDDP(p)$, and thus does not reflect all dependencies of $DDP(p)$. In Figure 8.11b, for example, the dependencies *expression.primode* $\rightarrow$ *name*[i].*postmode* ($i = 1,2$) are in DDP but not DP.

Figure 8.11b has a single node for each $c_{i,j}$ because each partition contains a single attribute. In general, however, partitions will contain more than one attribute. The resulting graph still has only one node for each $c_{i,j}$. This node represents *all* of the attributes in $A_i(X_j)$, and hence any relation involving an attribute in $A_i(X_j)$ is represented by an edge incident upon this node.

The graph of Figure 8.11b describes a partial order. To obtain an attribution algorithm, we augment the partial order with additional dependencies, consistent with each other and with the original partial order, until the nodes are totally ordered. Figure 8.11c shows such additional dependencies for Figure 8.11b. The total order defines the algorithm: Each element that is an attribute in $AF(p)$ corresponds to a computation of that attribute, each element $c_{i,0}$ corresponds to a move to the parent, and each element $c_{i,j}$ ($j > 0$) corresponds to a move to the ith child. Finally, a 'move to parent' operation is added to the end of the algorithm. Figure 8.4b is the algorithm resulting from the analysis of Figure 8.11.

The construction sketched above is correct if we can show that all attribute dependencies from $IDP(p)$ and $DDP(p)$ are accounted for and that the interaction with the moves between nodes is proper. Since $IDP(p)$ is a subset of $DP(p)$, problems can only arise from the merging of attributes that are not elements of $AF(p)$. We distinguish five cases:

$$X_i.a \rightarrow X_i.b \in IDP(p), \qquad a \notin AF(p), b \notin AF(p)$$
$$X_i.a \rightarrow X_i.b \in IDP(p), \qquad a \in AF(p), b \notin AF(p)$$
$$X_i.a \rightarrow X_i.b \in IDP(p), \qquad a \notin AF(p), b \in AF(p)$$
$$X_i.a \rightarrow X_j.b \in IDP(p), \qquad i \neq j, a \notin AF(p)$$
$$X_i.a \rightarrow X_j.b \in IDP(p), \qquad i \neq j, b \notin AF(p)$$

In the first case the dependency is accounted for in all productions q for which a and b are elements of $AF(q)$. In the second and third cases $X_i.a$ and $X_i.b$ must belong to different subsets $A_r(X_i)$ and $A_s(X_i)$. The dependency manifests itself in the ordering condition $r < s$ or $s < r$, and will not be disturbed by collapsing either subset. In the fourth case we compute $X_j.b$ only after all of the attributes in the subset to which $X_i.a$ belongs have been computed; this is simply an additional restriction. The fifth case is excluded by Definition 8.11: $X_i.a \rightarrow X_j.b$ cannot be an element of $DDP(p)$ because $X_j.b$ is not in $AF(p)$; it cannot be an element of any IDS because $i \neq j$.

When an algorithm begins with a visit $c_{j,i}$, this visit may or may not actually be carried out. Suppose that the structure tree has been completed

$$c_{1,0} = \{expression.environment\}$$
$$c_{3,0} = \{expression.postmode\}$$
$$c_{2,1} = \{name[1].primode\}$$
$$c_{4,1} = \{\}$$
$$c_{2,2} = \{addop.operation\}$$
$$c_{2,3} = \{name[2].primode\}$$
$$c_{4,3} = \{\}$$

a) New attributes

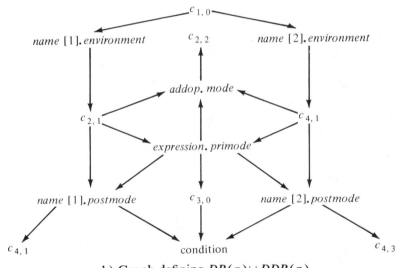

b) Graph defining $DP(p) \cup DDP(p)$

$$c_{2,1} \rightarrow name[2].environment$$
$$c_{3,0} \rightarrow name[1].postmode$$
$$c_{4,1} \rightarrow addop.mode$$
$$c_{2,2} \rightarrow name[2].postmode$$
$$c_{4,3} \rightarrow condition$$

c) Additional dependencies used to establish a total order

Figure 8.11. Deriving the Algorithm of Figure 8.4b

before the attribution is attempted. The traversal then begins at the root, and every algorithm will be initiated by a 'move to child i'. Now if the first action of the algorithm is $c_{1,0}$, i.e. a move to the parent to compute inherited attributes, this move is superfluous because the child is only invoked if these attributes are available. Hence the initial $c_{1,0}$ should be omitted. The situation is reversed if the tree is being processed bottom-up, as when attribution is merged with a bottom-up parse: An initial $c_{i,j}$ that causes a move to the leftmost subtree should be omitted.

Semantic conditions are taken care of in this schema by treating them as synthesized attributes of the left-hand side of the production. They can be introduced into an algorithm at any arbitrary point following computation of the attributes upon which they depend. In practice, conditions should be evaluated as early as possible to enhance semantic error recovery and reduce the lifetime of attributes.

8.2.3. Pre-Specified Traversals   Overall compiler design considerations may indicate use of one or more depth-first, left-to-right and/or right-to-left traversals for attribute evaluation. This allows us to linearize the structure tree as discussed in Section 4.1.2 and make one or more passes over the linearized representation. (For this reason, attribute grammars that specify such traversals are called *multi-pass* attribute grammars.) We shall discuss the left-to-right case in detail here, leaving the analogous right-to-left case to the reader.

Definition 8.17. An attribute grammar is *LAG(1)* if, for every node corresponding to an application of $p:X_0 \rightarrow X_1 \cdots X_n \in P$, the attributes in $AI(X_0)$, $AI(X_1)$, $AS(X_1)$, $AI(X_2)$, ..., $AS(X_n)$, $AS(X_0)$ can be computed in that order.

An LAG(1) grammar is partitioned, with the partition being $A_1(X) = AI(X)$, $A_2(X) = AS(X)$ for all X. Further constraints on the order of evaluation within a production are introduced to force processing of the symbols from left to right.

Theorem 8.18. *An attribute grammar is LAG(1) if and only if it is locally acyclic and, for all $p:X_0 \rightarrow X_1 \cdots X_n \in P$, $X_i.a \rightarrow X_j.b \in DDP(p)$ implies one of the following conditions:*

- $j = 0$
- $i = 0$ *and* $a \in AI(X_0)$
- $1 \leqslant i < j$
- $1 \leqslant i = j$ *and* $a \in AI(X_i)$

Note that Theorem 8.18 makes use only of $DDP(p)$; it does not consider induced attribute dependencies. This is possible because every induced dependency that would affect the computation must act over a path having a 'top' node similar to that in Figure 8.5: An inherited attribute of a symbol depends directly upon a synthesized attribute of the same symbol. This case is prohibited, however, by the conditions of the theorem.

LAG(1) grammars are inadequate even in comparatively simple cases, as can be seen by considering the grammar of Figure 8.1. The production for *assignment* satisfies the conditions of Theorem 8.18, but that for *expression* does not because both *name*[1].*postmode* and *name*[2].*postmode* depend upon *expression.primode*. We can repair the problem in this example by applying the 'hoisting' transformation mentioned at the end of Section 8.1: Delete the inherited attribute *postmode* and move the condition using it upward. A similar change is required to move the operator identification upward (Figure 8.12).

If one tree traversal does not suffice to compute all attributes, a sequence of several traversals might be used. This idea is actually much older and more general than that of attribute grammars. We have already met it in Section 1.3: 'Any language requires at least one pass over the source text, but certain language characteristics require more.' (The procedure

rule *assignment* :: = *name* '*:* =' *expression* .
attribution
   name.environment ← *assignment.environment* ;
   expression.environment ← *assignment.environment* ;
condition
   coercible (
     expression.primode ,
     if *name.primode* = *ref* _*int* _*type* **then** *int* _*type* **else** *real* _*type* **fi**);

rule *expression* :: = *name addop name* .
attribution
   name [1].*environment* ← *expression.environment* ;
   name [2].*environment* ← *expression.environment* ;
   expression.primode ←
     if *coercible* (*name* [1].*primode* , *int* _*type*) **and**
     coercible (*name* [2].*primode* , *int* _*type*) **then** *int* _*type* **else** *real* _*type* **fi**;
   addop.operation ←
     if *expression.primode* = *int* _*type* **then** *int* _*addition* **else** *real* _*addition* **fi**;
condition
   coercible (*name* [1].*primode* , *expression.primode*) **and**
   coercible (*name* [2].*primode* , *expression.primode*);

rule *addop* :: = '+'.

rule *name* :: = *identifier* .
attribution
   name.primode ← *defined_type* (*identifier.symbol* ,*name.environment*);

Figure 8.12. Transformation of Figure 8.1

determine_traversals discussed below describes, in terms of attributes, the fundamental mechanism by which the number of passes of a compiler is determined.) The difference between LAG and RAG appears in the same section as the distinction between forward and backward passes.

All attributes in the structure tree of a sentence derived from any arbitrary well-defined attribute grammar can be evaluated with an unlimited number of traversals, but the cost of determining dynamically whether another traversal is necessary is roughly as high as that of the nondeterministic evaluation procedure in Section 8.1. Here we are interested in cases for which the number of traversals can be determined from the grammar alone, independent of any structure tree.

Definition 8.19. An attribute grammar is LAG(k) if and only if for each X in the vocabulary a partition

$$AI(X) = AI_1(X)\cup \cdots \cup AI_k(X)$$
$$AS(X) = AS_1(X)\cup \cdots \cup AS_k(X)$$

exists such that for all productions $p:X_0\rightarrow X_1 \cdots X_n$, the attributes in $AI_1(X_0)$, $AI_1(X_1)$, ..., $AS_1(X_n)$, $AS_1(X_0)$, $AI_2(X_0)$, ..., $AI_k(X_0)$, ..., $AS_k(X_0)$ can be computed in that order.

Note that this reduces to Definition 8.17 for $k = 1$.

The set of partitions taken together form an admissible partition of the attribute set A with $m(X)=2k$ for every X. We can think of the sets $AI_i(X)$ and $AS_i(X)$ as belonging to an LAG(1) grammar with $AI_j(X)$ and $AS_j(X)(j<i)$ as intrinsic attributes. This reasoning leads to the following LAG(k) condition which closely parallels Theorem 8.18:

Theorem 8.20. *An attribute grammar is LAG(k) if and only if it is locally acyclic and a partition $A =A_1\cup \cdots \cup A_k$ exists such that for all $p:X_0\rightarrow X_1 \cdots X_n \in P$, $X_i.a \rightarrow X_j.b \in DDP(p)$, $a \in A_u(X_i)$, $b \in A_v(X_j)$ implies one of the following conditions:*

- *$u<v$*
- *$u =v$ and $j =0$*
- *$u =v$ and $i =0$ and $a \in AI(X_0)$*
- *$u =v$ and $1\leqslant i <j$*
- *$u =v$ and $1\leqslant i =j$ and $a \in AI(X_i)$*

Theorem 8.20 leads directly to a procedure for determining the partition and the value of k from a locally acyclic grammar (Figure 8.13). For $k =1, 2,...$ this procedure assumes that all remaining attributes belong to A_k and then deletes those for which this assumption violates the theorem. There are two distinct stopping conditions:

- No attribute is deleted. The number of traversals is k and the partition is $A_1, ..., A_k$.

function *determine_traversals* : *integer* ;
 (* Test an attribute grammar for the LAG(k) property
   On entry-
     Attribute grammar (G, A, R, B) is defined as in Section 8.1
     Sets A, $AS(X)$ and $AF(p)$ are defined as in Section 8.1
     Set $DDP(p)$ is defined as in Section 8.2.2
   If the grammar is LAG(k) then on exit-
     determine_traversals $= k$
   Else on exit-
     determine_traversals $= -1$
   *)
 var
   k : *integer* ;   (* current traversal number *)
   candidates,   (* possibly evaluable in the current traversal *)
   later : *attribute_set* ;   (* not evaluable in the first k traversals *)
   candidates_unchanged : *boolean* ;
 begin   (* *determine_traversals* *)
 $k := 0$; *later* $:= A$;   (* no attributes evaluable in 0 traversals *)
 repeat   (* determine the next A_k *)
   $k := k + 1$; *candidates* $:=$ *later*; *later* $:= \varnothing$;
   repeat   (* delete those unevaluable in traversal k *)
     candidates_unchanged $:= true$;
     for all productions $p : X_0 \rightarrow X_1 \cdots X_n$ **do**
       for all $X_j.b \in (AF(p) \cap$ *candidates*) **do**
         for all $X_i.a \in A(p)$ **do**
           if $X_i.a \rightarrow X_j.b \in NDDP(p)$ **then**
             if $X_i.a \in$ *later* **or** $j \neq 0$ **and** $(i > j$ **or** $(i = 0$ **or** $i = j)$
             and $a \in AS(X_i))$ **then**
               begin
               candidates $:=$ *candidates* $- \{X_j.b\}$;
               later $:=$ *later* $\cup \{X_j.b\}$;
               candidates_unchanged $:= false$;
               end;
   until *candidates_unchanged* ;
   $A_k :=$ *candidates* ;
 until *later* $= \varnothing$ **or** *candidates* $= \varnothing$
 if *later* $= \varnothing$ **then** *determine_traversals* $:= k$ **else** *determine_traversals* $:= -1$;
 end; (* *determine_traversals* *)

Figure 8.13. Testing the LAG(k) Property

- All attributes are deleted. The conditions of Theorem 8.20 cannot be met
  and hence the attribute grammar is not LAG(k) for any k.

Analogous constructions are possible for RAG(k) grammars and for the
alternating evaluable attribute grammars ($AAG(k)$). With the latter class,
structure tree attributes are evaluated by traversals that alternate in direction: The first is left-to-right, the second right-to-left, and so forth. We

leave the derivation of these definitions and theorems, plus the necessary processing routines, to the reader.

It is important to note that the algorithm of Figure 8.13 and its analogs for RAG(k) and AAG(k) assign attributes to the *first* traversal in which they might be computed. These algorithms give no indication that it might also be possible to evaluate an attribute in a later traversal without delaying evaluation of other attributes or increasing the total number of traversals.

Figure 8.14 is RAG(1) but not LAG(k) for any k. Each left-to-right traversal can only compute the value of one $X.a$ because of the dependency relation involving the preceding nonterminal W. Hence the number of traversals is not fixed, but is the depth of the recursion. A single right-to-left traversal suffices to compute all $X.a$, however, because traversal of W's subtree follows traversal of $X[2]$'s. If we combine two such attribute relationships with opposite dependencies then we obtain an AAG(2) grammar that is neither LAG(k) nor RAG(k) for any k (Figure 8.15).

It is, of course, possible to construct an appropriate partition for a multipass grammar by hand. The development usually proceeds as follows: On the basis of given properties of the language one determines the minimum number of traversals required, partitions the attributes accordingly, and then constructs the attribute definition rules to make that partition valid. The 'hoisting' transformation referred to earlier is often used implicitly during rule construction.

The disadvantage of this technique is that it is based upon an initial opinion about the number of traversals and the assignment of attributes to traversals that may turn out to be wrong. For example, one may discover when constructing the rules that an attribute can only be computed if additional arguments are available, or even that important attributes are missing

rule $Z ::= X$.
attribution
  $X.b \leftarrow 1;$

rule $X ::= W\ X$.
attribution
  $X[1].a \leftarrow W.c;$
  $X[2].b \leftarrow X[1].b;$
  $W.d \leftarrow X[2].a;$

rule $X ::= 's'$.
attribution
  $X.a \leftarrow X.b;$

rule $W ::= 't'$.
attribution
  $W.c \leftarrow W.d;$

Figure 8.14. An RAG(1) Grammar That Is Not LAG(k)

rule $Z ::= X$.
attribution
$\quad X.b \leftarrow 1;$

rule $X ::= W \; X \; Y$.
attribution
$\quad X[1].a \leftarrow W.d$;
$\quad X[1].e \leftarrow Y.g$;
$\quad X[2].b \leftarrow X[1].b$;
$\quad W.c \leftarrow X[2].a$;
$\quad Y.f \leftarrow X[2].e$;

rule $X ::= 's'$.
attribution
$\quad X.a \leftarrow X.b$;
$\quad X.e \leftarrow X.b$;

rule $W ::= 't'$.
attribution
$\quad W.c \leftarrow W.d$;

rule $Y ::= 'u'$.
attribution
$\quad Y.g \leftarrow Y.f$;

Figure 8.15. An AAG(2) Grammar That Is Neither LAG(k) Nor RAG(k)

entirely. Experience shows that small changes of this kind often have disastrous effects on the basic structure being built. Considering the cost involved in developing a semantic analyzer — an attribute grammar for LAX is barely 30 pages, but specifications for complex languages can easily grow to well over 100 pages — such effects cannot be tolerated. It is more advisable to construct an attribute grammar without regard to the number of traversals. Only when it is certain that all aspects of the language have been covered correctly should substitutions and other alterations to meet a constraint upon the number of traversals be undertaken. The greater part of the grammar will usually be unaffected by such changes.

As soon as a partition of the attribute set satisfying Definition 8.17 or 8.19 is available, it is simple to derive an algorithm via the technique discussed at the end of the last section.

8.3. Implementation Considerations

Section 8.2 showed methods for constructing attribute evaluation algorithms from attribute grammars. Here we concern ourselves with the implementation of these algorithms. First we assume that the structure tree appears as a linked data structure providing storage for the attributes, and later we show how to reduce the storage requirements.

8.3.1. Algorithm Coding Our attribution algorithms are coroutines that transfer control among themselves by executing the basic operations 'move to child i' and 'move to parent'. They might be coded directly, transformed to a collection of recursive procedures, or embodied in a set of tables to be interpreted. We shall discuss each of these possibilities in turn.

The coroutines can be coded directly in SIMULA as classes, one per symbol and one per production. Each symbol class defines the attributes of the symbol and serves as a prefix for classes representing productions with that symbol on the left side. This allows us to obtain access to a subtree having a particular symbol as its root without knowing the production by which it was constructed. Terminal nodes t are represented only by the class t. Each production class contains pointer declarations for all of its descendants $X_1 \cdots X_n$. A structure tree is built using statements of the form $node:-\textbf{new } p$ (or $node:-\textbf{new } t$) to create nodes and assignments of the form $node.x_i:-subnode$ to link them. Since a side effect of **new** is execution of the class body, the first statement of each class body is **detach** (return to caller). (Intrinsic attributes could be initialized by statements preceding this first **detach**.) Figure 8.16 gives the SIMULA coding of the procedure from Figure 8.4b.

Figure 8.17 gives an implementation using recursive procedures. The tree is held in a data structure made up of the nodes defined in Figure 8.17a. When a node corresponding to application of $p:X_0 \rightarrow X_1 \cdots X_n$ is created, its fields are initialized as follows:

$$symb = X_0$$
$$X_0{-}p = p$$
$$x{-}p_i = \text{pointer to node representing } X_i, \ i = 1, \dots, n$$

The body of a coroutine is broken at the **detach** statements, with each segment forming one branch of the case statement in the corresponding procedure. Then **detach** is implemented by simply returning; $resume(X_i)$ is implemented by $sproc\_s(x{-}p_i, k)$, where $sproc\_s$ is the procedure corresponding to symbol X_i and k is the segment of that procedure to be executed. Figure 8.18 shows the result of applying the transformation to Figure 8.16. We have followed the schema closely in constructing this example, but in practice the implementation can be greatly simplified.

A tabular implementation, in which the stack is explicit, can be derived from Figure 8.17. It involves a pushdown automaton that walks the structure tree, invoking *evaluate* in much the same way that the parsing automata of Chapter 7 invoke parser actions to report connection points. In each case the automaton communicates with another processor via a sequence of simple data items. Thus the implementations of the automaton and the communicating processor are quite distinct, and different techniques may be

class *expression* ;
   begin comment Declarations of *primode* , *postmode* and *environment* **end**;
class *name* ;
   begin comment Declarations of *primode* , *postmode* and *environment* **end**;
class *addop* ;
   begin comment Declarations of *mode* and *operation* **end**;

expression **class** $p\,2$;
   begin ref(*name*) $X\,1$; **ref**(*addop*) $X\,2$; **ref**(*name*) $X\,3$;
   comment Initialization of $X\,1$, $X\,2$ and $X\,3$ needed here;
   detach;
   $X\,1.environment := environment$;
   resume $(X\,1)$;
   $X\,3.environment := environment$;
   resume $(X\,3)$;
   $primode := $ **if** $\cdots$;
   detach;
   $X\,1.postmode := primode$;
   resume $(X\,1)$;
   $X\,2.mode := primode$;
   resume $(X\,2)$;
   $X\,3.postmode := primode$;
   resume $(X\,3)$;
   if $\cdots$;   **comment** Evaluate the condition;
   detach;
   end;

Figure 8.16. SIMULA Implementation of Figure 8.4b

used to carry them out. The number of actions is usually very large, and when deciding how to handle them one must take account of any restrictions imposed by the implementation language and its compiler.

Figure 8.19 shows how the pushdown automaton is implemented. Each entry in the table corresponds to an element of some algorithm and there is an auxiliary function, *segment*, such that $segment(k,p)$ is the index of the first entry for the kth segment of the algorithm for production p. If the element corresponds to $X_i.a$ then it specifies the computation in some appropriate manner (perhaps as a case index or procedure address); otherwise it simply contains the pair of integers defining the visit. Because the selectors for a visit must be extracted from the table, rather than being built into the procedure, the tree node must be represented as shown in Figure 8.19b.

Simplifications in the general coding procedure are possible for LAG(k), RAG(k) and AAG(k) grammars. When $k = 1$ the partition for each X is $A_1(X)=AI(X)$, $A_2(X)=AS(X)$, so no intermediate **detach** operations occur in the coroutines. This, in turn, means that no case statement is required in

type
  tree_pointer = ↑ *tree_node* ;
  tree_node = **record**
    case *symbols* **of**
        s :   (* one per symbol in the vocabulary *)
           (· · ·   (* storage for attributes of *S* *)
          case *s_p* : *integer* **of**
            p :   (* one per production *p* :*S* → *X*$_1$ · · · *X*$_n$ *)
              (*x_p* : **array** [1..*n*] *tree_pointer*);
)
    end;

a) General structure of a node

procedure *pproc_p* (*t* : *tree_pointer* ; *k* : *integer*);
  (* one procedure per production *)
  begin (* *pproc_p* *)
  case *k* **of**
    0:
        · · ·   (* actions up to the first *detach* *)
        · · ·   (* successive segments *)
      end;
    end; (* *pproc_p* *)

b) General structure of a production procedure

procedure *sproc_s* (*t* : *tree_pointer* ; *k* : *integer*);
  (* one procedure per symbol *)
  begin (* *sproc_s* *)
  case *t.s_p* **of**
  p : *pproc_p* (*t*, *k*);   (* one case element per production *)
    · · ·
    end;
  end; (* *sproc_s* *)

c) General structure of a symbol procedure

Figure 8.17. Transformation of Coroutines to Procedures

the production procedures or in the interpretive model. For $k > 1$ there are $k + 1$ segments in each procedure *proc_p*, corresponding to the initialization and k traversals. It is best to gather together the procedures for each traversal as though dealing with a grammar for which $k = 1$, and then run them sequentially. When parsing by recursive descent, the tree construction, the calculation of intrinsic attributes and the first tree traversal can be combined with the parsing.

type
  tree_pointer = ↑ *tree_node* ;
  tree_node = **record**
    case *symbols* **of**
      expression :
        (*expression_environment* : *environment* ;
        expression_primode, *expression_postmode* : *type_specification*;
        case *expression_p* : *integer* **of**
          1: (*x_1*:**array** [1..3] **of** *tree_pointer*);
      name :
        (*name_environment* : *environment* ;
        name_primode , *name_postmode* : *type_specification*);
      addop :
        (*addop_mode* : *type_specification*;
        addop_operation : *operations*);
      end;
procedure *sproc_expression* (*t* : *tree_pointer* ; *k* : *integer*);
  begin (* *sproc_expression* *)
  case *t* ↑ .*expression_p* **of**
    1: *pproc_*1(*t*, *k*);
    end;
  end;(* *sproc_expression* *)
procedure *pproc_*1(*t* : *tree_pointer* ; *k* : *integer*);
  begin (* *pproc_*1 *)
  case *k* **of**
    0: (* construction of subtrees *);
    1:
      begin
      t ↑ .*x_*1[1] ↑ .*expression_environment* : = *t* ↑ .*expression_environment* ;
      sproc_name (*t* ↑ .*x_*1[1], 1);
      t ↑ .*x_*1[3] ↑ .*expression_environment* : = *t* ↑ .*expression_environment* ;
      sproc_name (*t* ↑ .*x_*1[3], 1);
      t ↑ .*expression_primode* : = **if** · · · ;
      end;
    2:
      begin
      t ↑ .*x_*1[1].*name_postmode* : = *t* ↑ .*expression_primode* ;
      sproc_name (*t* ↑ .*x_*1[1], 2);
      t ↑ .*x_*1[2].*name_postmode* : = *t* ↑ .*expression_primode* ;
      sproc_addop (*t* ↑ .*x_*1[2], 1);
      t ↑ .*x_*1[3].*addop_postmode* : = *t* ↑ .*expression_primode* ;
      sproc_name (*t* ↑ .*x_*1[3], 2);
      if · · · ;
      end;
    end;
  end; (* *pproc_*1 *)

Figure 8.18. Transformation of Figure 8.16

```
type
  table_entry = record
    case is_computation : boolean of
      true :      (* R_{p, X_i.a} *)
                  (rule : attribute_computation );
      false :     (* C_{segment_number, child} *)
                  (segment_number, child : integer )
    end;
```
a) Structure of a table entry

```
type
  tree_pointer = ↑ tree_node ;
  tree_node = record
    production : integer ;
    X : array [1..max_right_hand_side ] of tree_pointer
  end;
```
b) Structure of a tree node

```
procedure interpret ;
  label 1;
  var
    t : tree_pointer ;
    state, next : integer ;
  begin (* interpret *)
  t := root_of_the_tree ;
  state := segment (0, t ↑ .production );
  repeat
    next := state +1;
    with table [state ] do
      if is_computation then evaluate (t, rule )
      else if segment_number < >0 then
        begin
        stack_push (t, next );
        t := t ↑ .X [child ];
        next := segment (segment_number, t ↑ .production );
        end
      else if stack_empty then goto 1
      else stack_pop (t, next );
    state := next ;
  until false ; (* forever *)
1: end; (* interpret *)
```
c) Table interpreter

Figure 8.19. Tabular Implementation of Attribution Algorithms

8.3.2. Attribute Storage   So far we have assumed that all attributes of a structure tree node were stored within the node itself. Applying this assumption in practice usually leads to a gigantic storage requirement. Several remedies are possible:

- Overlaying of attributes.
- Use of local temporaries of evaluation procedures.
- Storage of specified attributes only at designated nodes.
- Use of global variables and data structures.

Because these optimizations cannot be automated completely (given the present state of the art), the question of attribute storage represents an important part of the development of an attribute grammar implementation.

We classify the attributes of a node as *final* or *intermediate*. Final attributes are necessary in later phases of the compilation and must be available in the structure tree following attribution. Intermediate attributes are used only as aids in computing other attributes or testing conditions; they have a bounded lifetime. The largest intermediate attribute, which we shall discuss in Chapter 9, is the environment used to obtain the meaning of an identifier at a particular point.

Distinct storage must be assigned to final attributes, but this storage can be used earlier to hold one or more intermediate attributes if their lifetimes do not overlap. Minimization of overlap (not minimization of lifetimes for simple attributes) is thus one of the most important uses of our freedom to specify the sequence of attribute evaluations. Usually it is best to begin with the final attributes and work backwards, fixing the sequence so that attributes can take one another's place in storage.

We often discover that two attribute lifetimes overlap, but only briefly. The overlap can be eliminated by defining a new attribute whose lifetime is just this overlap, assigning the first attribute to it, and freeing the first attribute's storage. The second attribute is then computed into that storage. In this manner we reduce the overlap among 'long lived' attributes and increase the number of 'short lived' attributes. The new attributes generally have little overlap among themselves, but even if they had we have gained something: This transformation usually makes other optimizations applicable.

In many cases we can implement short-lived attributes as local variables of the evaluation procedures, thus avoiding the need for space within the node entirely. If the attributes are referenced by other procedures (for the parent or children of the node to which they belong) then their values can be passed as extra parameters. This strategy only works for implementations like that of Figure 8.17, where distinct processing procedures are provided. The tabular implementation discussed at the end of Section 8.2.1 requires stacks instead of procedure parameters or local variables to realize the same strategy.

An attribution rule can only access attributes of the nodes corresponding to the symbols of the associated production. Many of the attributes in a typical grammar are therefore concerned with transmission of information from one part of the tree to another. Since attribute values do not change, they may be transmitted by reference instead of by value. Thus we might store the value of a large attribute at a single node, and replace this attribute in other nodes by a pointer to the stored information. The node at which the value is stored is usually the root of a subtree to which all nodes using this information belong. For example, the environment attribute of a block or procedure node is formed by combining the lists generated by local definitions with the inherited environment. The result is passed to all nodes in the subtree rooted in the block or procedure node. If a pointer to the next enclosing block or procedure node is given during the processing of the nodes in the subtree, then we obtain the same environment: First we reach the local definitions in the innermost enclosing block and, in the same manner, the next outermost, etc. The search of the environment for a suitable definition thus becomes a search of the local definition lists from inner to outer.

Attributes should often be completely removed from the corresponding nodes and represented by global variables or linked structures in global storage. We have already noted that it is usually impossible to retain the entire structure tree in memory. Global storage is used to guarantee that an attribute accessible by a pointer is not moved to secondary storage with the corresponding node. Global storage is also useful if the exact size of an attribute cannot be determined a priori. Finally, global storage has the advantage that it is directly accessible, without the need to pass pointers as parameters to the evaluation procedures.

If the environment is kept as a global attribute then it is represented by a list of local definitions belonging to the nested blocks or procedures. In order to be certain that the 'correct' environment is visible at each node we alter the global attribute during the traversal of the structure tree: When we move to a block or procedure node from its parent, we copy the local definition set to this environment variable; when we return to the parent we delete it.

The description in the previous paragraph shows that in reality we are using a global data structure to describe several related attribute values. This situation usually occurs with recursive language elements such as blocks. The environment attribute shows the typical situation for inherited attributes: Upon descent in the tree we alter the attribute value, for example increasing its size; the corresponding ascent in the tree requires that the previous state be restored. Sometimes, as in the case of the nesting depth attribute of a LAX block, restoration is a simple inverse of the computation done on entry to the substructure. Often there is no inverse, however, and the old value of the attribute must be saved explicitly. (The environment represents an intermediate situation that we shall consider in Section 9.3.) By replacing the global variable with a global stack, we can handle such cases directly.

Global variables and stacks are also useful for synthesized attributes, and the analysis parallels that given above. Here we usually find that attribute values replace each other at successive ascents in the tree. An example is the *primode* computation in a LAX *case _ clause*:

> **rule** *case* :: = *case _ label* ':'*statement _ list* . **attribution**
> *case.primode* ← *statement _ list.primode* ;
> **rule** *cases* :: = *case* .
> **rule** *cases* :: = *cases* ':' *statement _ list* . **attribution**
> *cases* [1].*primode* ← *balance* (*cases* [2].*primode*, *case.primode*);

The value of *cases* [2].*primode* becomes irrelevant as soon as *cases* [1].*primode* has been evaluated. A *case* may, however, contain another *case _ clause*. Hence a stack must be used rather than a variable.

By changing the attribution rules, we can often increase the number of attributes implementable by global variables or stacks. A specific change usually fixes a specific traversal strategy, but any one of several changes (each implying a different traversal strategy) could be used to achieve the desired effect. Thus the designer should avoid such changes until the last possible time, when they can be coordinated with the 'natural' traversal strategies determined by the basic information flow.

8.4. Notes and References

Attribute grammars stem from the 'syntax-directed compilers' introduced by Irons [1961, 1963a]. Irons' grammars had a single, synthesized attribute attached to each nonterminal. This attribute provided the 'meaning' of the subtree rooted in the nonterminal. Knuth [1968a, 1971a] proved that such a scheme was sufficient to define the meaning associated with *any* structure tree, but pointed out that the description could be simplified considerably through the use of inherited attributes in addition. (Sufficiency of synthesized attributes leads immediately to the conclusion that all well-defined attribute grammars have the same descriptive power.) Intrinsic attributes were first characterized by Schulz [1976], although Lewis, Rosenkrantz and Stearns [1974] had previously allowed certain terminal symbols to have 'attributes whose values are not given by rules'. The affix grammars of Koster [1971, 1974] are similar to attribute grammars, the main difference being that affixes are considered to be variables while attributes are constants. Räihä [1980] provides a good overview of the attribute grammar literature as it existed in 1979.

Our treatment of attribute classification differs from that of many authors because we do not begin with disjoint sets of synthesized, inherited and intrinsic attributes. Instead, Definition 8.2 classifies the attributes based upon the placement of the attribution rules. Tienari [1980] has derived results similar to Theorems 8.3 and 8.8 from a definition allowing more than one attribution rule per attribute in a single production. His analog of Theorem 8.8, however, includes the restriction to a single attribution rule as a part of the hypothesis.

Theorem 8.8 assumes 'value semantics' for the attribution rules: The operands of the rule are evaluated before the rule itself, and hence the following represents a circularity:

$$a \leftarrow \text{if } p \text{ then } b \text{ else } 1 \text{ fi}; \quad b \leftarrow \text{if not } p \text{ then } a \text{ else } 2 \text{ fi};$$

'Lazy evaluation', in which an operand is not evaluated until its value is required, would not lead to circularity in this case. The attendant broadening of the acceptable grammars is not interesting for us because we are attempting to define the evaluation sequence statically. Whenever there is a difference between value semantics and lazy evaluation, the evaluation sequence must be determined dynamically.

Dynamic attribute evaluators based on cooperating sequential processes have been reported by Fang [1972] and Banatre [1979]. Borowiec [1977] described a fragment of COBOL in this manner. The process scheduling overhead can be avoided by deriving a dependency graph from the specific tree being processed, and then converting this graph to a partial order. Gallucci [1981] implemented such a system, adding dependency links to the tree and using reference counts to derive the partial order.

One of the major arguments given in support of a dynamic evaluator is that it is simple to implement. The actual evaluation algorithm is simple, but it will fail on certain programs if the grammar is not well-defined. We have already pointed out that WAG testing is exponential [Jazayeri 1975a, 1981], and hence occasional failure of the dynamic evaluator is accepted by most authors advocating this strategy. Acyclicity of $IDP(p)$ and $IDS(X)$, a sufficient condition for WAG, can be tested in polynomial time [Kastens 1980]. This test forms the basis of all systems that employ subclasses of WAG. Such systems are guaranteed never to fail during evaluation.

Kennedy and Warren [1976] termed the subclass of WAG for which $IDP(p)$ and $IDS(X)$ are acyclic for all p and X 'absolutely non-circular attribute grammars' (ANCAG). They developed an algorithm for constructing ANCAG evaluators that grouped attributes together, avoiding individual dependency links for every attribute. The evaluation remains dynamic, but some decisions are shifted to evaluator construction time. In a later paper, Kennedy and Ramanathan [1979] retain the ANCAG subclass but use a pure dynamic evaluator. Their reasoning is that, although this strategy is less efficient at run time, it is easier to understand and simpler to implement.

Ordered attribute grammars were originated by Kastens [1976, 1980], who used the term 'arranged orderly' to denote a partitioned grammar. OAG is a subclass of ANCAG for which no decisions about evaluation order are made dynamically; all have been shifted to evaluator construction time. This means that attribute lifetimes can be determined easily, and the optimizations discussed in Section 8.3.2 can be applied automatically: In a semantic analyzer for Pascal, constructed automatically from an ALADIN description by the GAG [Kastens 1982] system, attributes occupied only about 20% of the total structure tree storage.

Lewis, Rosenkrantz and Stearns [1974] studied the problem of evaluating all attributes during a single depth-first, left-to-right traversal of the structure tree. Making no use of the local acyclicity of $DDP(p)$, they derived the first three conditions we stated in Theorem 8.18. The same conditions were deduced independently by Bochmann [1976], who went on to point out that dependencies satisfying the fourth condition of Theorem 8.18 are allowed if the relationship $NDDP(p)$ is used in place of $DDP(p)$. There is no real need for this substitution, however, because if $DDP(p)$ is locally acyclic then the dependency $X_i.a \rightarrow X_j.b$ immediately rules out $X_j.b \rightarrow X_i.a$. Thus dependencies satisfying the fourth condition of Theorem 8.18 cannot lead to any problem in left-to-right evaluation. Since local acyclicity is a necessary condition for well-definedness, this assumption does not result in any loss of generality.

$LAG(k)$ conditions similar to those of Theorem 8.20 were also stated by Bochmann [1976]. Again, he did not make use of local acyclicity to obtain the last condition of our result. Systems based upon LAG(k) grammars have been developed at the Université de Montreal [Lecarme 1974] and the Technische Universität München [Giegerich 1979]. The theoretical underpinnings of the latter system are described by Ripken [1977], Ganzinger [1978] and Wilhelm [1977]. Wilhelm's work combines tree transformation with attribution.

Alternating-evaluable grammars were introduced by Jazayeri and Walter [1975b] as a generalization of Bochmann's work. Their algorithm for testing the AAG(k) condition does not provide precise criteria analogous to those of Theorem 8.18, but rather uses specifications such as 'occur before [the current candidate] in the present pass' to convey the basic idea. A group at the University of Helsinki developed a compiler generator based upon this form of grammar [Räihä 1977, Räihä 1978].

Asbrock [1979] and Pozefsky [1979] both consider the question of attribute overlap minimization in more detail.

Jazayeri and Pozefsky give a completely different method of representing a structure tree and evaluating a multi-pass attribute grammar [Jazayeri 1977, Pozefsky 1979]. They propose that the parser create k sequential files D_i such that D_i contains the sequence of attribution rules with parameters for pass i of the evaluation. Thus D_i contains, in sequential form, the entire structure of the tree; only the attribute values, arbitrarily arranged and without pointers to subnodes, are retained in memory. Pozefsky also considers the question of whether the evaluation of a multi-pass grammar can be arranged to permit overlaying of the attributes in memory.

EXERCISES

8.1. Write an attribute grammar describing a LAX basic symbol as an *identifier*, *integer* or *floating_point*. (Section A.1 describes these basic symbols.) Your grammar should compute the intrinsic attributes discussed in Section 4.1.1 for

8.1. Write an attribute grammar describing a LAX basic symbol as an *identifier, integer* or *floating_point.* (Section A.1 describes these basic symbols.) Your each basic symbol (with the exception of *location*) as synthesized attributes. Use no intrinsic attributes in your grammar. Be sure to invoke the appropriate symbol and constant table operations during your computation.

8.2. [Banatre 1979] Write a module for a given well-defined attribute grammar (G, A, R, B) that will build the attributed structure tree of a sentence of $L(G)$. The interface for the module must provide creation, access and assignment operations as discussed in Section 4.1.2. The creation and assignment operations will be invoked by parser actions to build the structure tree and set intrinsic attribute values; the access operation will be invoked by other modules to examine the structure of the tree and attribute values of the nodes. Within the module, access and assignment operations are used to implement attribution rules. You may assume that all invocations of creation and assignment operations from outside the module will precede any invocation of an access operation from outside. Invocations from within the module must, of course, be scheduled according to the dependencies of the attribute grammar. You may provide an additional operation to be invoked from outside the module to indicate the end of the sequence of external creation and assignment invocations.

8.3. Consider the following attribute grammar:
rule $Z ::= s \ X$.
attribution
  $X.a \leftarrow X.c$;
  $X.b \leftarrow X.a$;

rule $Z ::= t \ X$.
attribution
  $X.b \leftarrow X.d$;
  $X.a \leftarrow X.b$;

rule $X ::= u$.
attribution
  $X.d \leftarrow 1$;
  $X.c \leftarrow X.d$;

rule $X ::= v$.
attribution
  $X.c \leftarrow 2$;
  $X.d \leftarrow X.c$;
  a. Show that this grammar is partitionable using the admissible partition $A_1(X) = \{c, d\}, A_2(X) = \{a, b\}, A_3(X) = \{\}$.
  b. Compute $IDP(p)$ and $IDS(X)$ replacing $NDDP(p)$ by $DDP(p)$ in Definition 8.12. Explain why the results are cyclic.
  c. Modify the grammar to make $IDP(p)$ and $IDS(X)$ acyclic under the modification of Definition 8.12 postulated in (b).
  d. Justify the use of $NDDP(p)$ in Definition 8.12 in terms of the modification of (c).

8.4. Compute IDP and IDS for all p and X in the grammar of Figure 8.1. Apply construction 8.16, obtaining a partition (different from that given at the end of Section 8.2.1), and verify that Theorem 8.13 is satisfied. Compute *DP* for all *p*, and verify that Theorem 8.15 is satisfied.

8.5. Show that a partitionable grammar that is not ordered can be made into an ordered grammar by adding suitable 'artificial dependencies' $X.a \rightarrow X.b$ to some $IDS(X)$. (In other words, the gap between partitionable and ordered grammars can always be bridged by hand.)

8.6. Define a procedure *EvaluateP* for each production of an LAG(1) grammar such that all attributes of a structure tree can be evaluated by applying *EvaluateZ* (where Z is the production defining the axiom) to the root.

8.7. A right-to-left attribute grammar may have both inherited and synthesized attributes. All of the attribute values can be obtained in some number of depth-first, right-to-left traversals of the structure tree. State a formal definition for RAG(k) analogous to Definition 8.19 and prove a theorem analogous to Theorem 8.20.

8.8. [Jazayeri 1975a] Define the class of alternating evaluable attribute grammars AAG(k) formally, state the condition they must satisfy, and give an analysis procedure for verifying this condition. (Hint: Proceed as for LAG($2k$), but make some of the conditions dependent upon whether the traversal number is odd or even.)

8.9. Extend the basic definitions for multi-pass attribute grammars to follow the hybrid linearization strategy of Figure 4.4d: Synthesized attributes can be evaluated not only at the last visit to a node but also after the visit to the ith subnode, $1 \leqslant i \leqslant n$, or even prior to the first subnode visit ($i = 0$). How does this change the procedure *determine_traversals*?

8.10. Show that the LAG(k), RAG(k) or AAG(k) condition can be violated by a well-defined attribute grammar only when a syntactic rule leads to recursion.

8.11. Complete the class definitions of Figure 8.16 and fill in the remaining details to obtain a complete program that parses an assignment statement by recursive descent and then computes the attributes. If you do not have access to SIMULA, convert the schema into MODULA2, Ada or some other language providing coroutines or processes.

8.12. Under what conditions will the tabular implementation of an evaluator for a partitioned attribute grammar require less space than the coroutine implementation?

8.13. Give detailed schemata similar to Figure 8.17 for LAG(k) and AAG(k) evaluators, along the lines sketched at the end of Section 8.3.1.

8.14. Consider the implementation strategies for attribution algorithms exemplified by Figures 8.17 and 8.19.
   a. Explain why the tree node of Figure 8.19b is less space-efficient than that of Figure 8.17a.
   b. Show that, by coding the interpreter of Figure 8.19c in assembly language and assigning appropriate values to the *child* field of Figure 8.19a, it is possible to use the tree node of Figure 8.17a and also avoid the need for the

sproc__s procedures of Figure 8.17c.

8.15. Modify Figure 8.1 by replacing *name* with *expression* everywhere, and changing the second rule to *expression* $::=$ $'('$ *expression addop expression* $')'$. Consider an interpretive implementation of the attribution algorithms that follows the model of Exercise 8.16.

a. Show the memory layout of every possible node.

b. Define another rule, *addop* $::=$ $'-'$, with a suitable attribution procedure. What nodes are affected by this change, and how?

c. Show that the *addop* node can be incorporated into the *expression* node without changing the attribution procedures for *addop*. What is the minimum change necessary to the interpreter and the attribution procedure for *expression*? (Hint: Introduce a second interpretation for $c_{i,j}$.)

CHAPTER 9
Semantic Analysis

Semantic analysis determines the properties of a program that are classed as static semantics (Section 2.1.1), and verifies the corresponding context conditions — the consistency of these properties.

We have already alluded to all of the tasks of semantic analysis. The first is name analysis, finding the definition valid at each use of an identifier. Based upon this information, operator identification and type checking determine the operand types and verify that they are allowable for the given operator. The terms 'operator' and 'operand' are used here in their broadest sense: Assignment is an operator whether the language definition treats it as such or not; we also speak of procedure parameter transmission and block end (end of extent) as operations.

Section 9.1 is devoted to developing a formal specification of the source language from which analysis algorithms can be mechanically generated by the techniques of Chapters 5-8. Our goal for the specification is clarity, so that we can convince ourselves of its correctness. This is an important point, because the correspondence between the specification and the given source language cannot be checked formally. In the interest of clarity, we often use impractically inefficient descriptions that give the *effect* of auxiliary functions, but do not reflect their actual implementation. Section 9.2 discusses the practical implementation of these auxiliary functions by modules.

9.1. Description of Language Properties via Attribute Grammars

The description of a programming language by an attribute grammar provides a formal definition of both its context-free syntax and its static semantics. (Dynamic semantics, such as expression evaluation, could be included

220

also; we shall not pursue that point, however.) We therefore approach the total problem of analysis via attribute grammars as follows:

- First we develop an attribute grammar and replace the informal language description with it.
- From the attribute grammar we extract the context-free syntax and transform it to a parsing grammar in the light of the chosen parsing technique.
- Finally we implement the attribution rules to obtain the semantic analyzer.

The parsing grammar and implementation of the attribution rules can be derived individually from the informal language definition, as we have done implicitly up to this point. The advantage of using attribute grammars (or some other formal description tool such as denotational semantics) lies in the fact that one has a comprehensive and unified specification. This ensures that the parsing grammar, structure tree and semantic analysis 'fit together' without interface problems.

Development of an attribute grammar consists of the following interdependent steps:

- Development of the context-free syntax.
- Determination of the attributes and specification of their types.
- Development of the attribution rules.
- Formulation of the auxiliary functions.

Three major aspects of semantic analysis described via attribution are scope and name analysis, types and type checking, and operator identification in expressions. With a few exceptions, such as the requirement for distinct case labels in a case clause (Section A.4.5), all of the static semantic rules of LAX fall into these classes. Sections 9.1.1 to 9.1.4 examine the relevant attribution rules in detail.

Many of the attribution rules in a typical attribute grammar are simple assignments. To reduce the number of such assignments that must be written explicitly, we use the following conventions: A simple assignment to a synthesized attribute of the left-hand side of a production may be omitted when there is exactly one symbol on the right-hand side that has a synthesized attribute with the same name. Similarly, simple assignments of inherited attributes of the left-hand side to same-named inherited attributes of any number of right-hand side symbols may be omitted. In important cases we shall write these (semantic) *transfers* for emphasis. (Attribute grammar specification languages such as ALADIN [Kastens 1982] contain even more far-reaching conventions.)

We assume for every record type R used to describe attributes the existence of a function N_R whose parameters correspond to the fields of the record. This function creates a new record of type R and sets its fields to the parameter values. Further, we may define a list of objects by records of the form:

type
   $t\_list = \uparrow t\_list\_element$;
   $t_list_element = $ **record** $first: t$; $rest : t\_list$ **end**;

If e is an object of type t then we shall also regard e as a single element of type t_list wherever the context requires this interpretation. We write $l_1 \& l_2$ to indicate concatenation of two lists, and hence $e \& l$ describes addition of the single element e to the front of the list l. 'Value semantics' are assumed for list assignment: A copy of the entire list is made and this copy becomes the value of the attribute on the left of the arrow.

9.1.1. Scope and Name Analysis   The scope of identifiers is specified in most languages by the hierarchical structure of the program. In block structured languages the scopes are nested. Languages like FORTRAN have only a restricted number of levels in the hierarchy (level 1 contains the subprogram and COMMON names, level 2 the local identifiers of a subprogram including statement numbers). Further considerations are the use of implicit definition (FORTRAN), the admissibility (ALGOL 60) or inadmissibility (LIS) of new definitions in inner blocks for identifiers declared in outer blocks, and the restriction of scope to the portion of the block following the definition (Pascal). We shall consider the special properties of field selectors in Section 9.1.3.

Every definition of an identifier is represented in the compiler by a variant record. The types of Figure 9.1a suffice for LAX; different variants would be required for other languages. For example, the variant *type_definition* would be missing in a language without type identifiers and FORTRAN would require additional variants for subprograms and COMMON blocks because these are not treated as objects. The definition record could also specify further characteristics (such as the parameter passing mechanism for ALGOL 60 parameters or the access rights to Ada objects) that are known at the defining occurrence and used at the applied occurrences.

The definition class *unknown_definition* is important because semantic functions must deliver a value under all circumstances. If no definition is available for an identifier, one must be supplied (with the variant *unknown_definition*).

Records of type *definition* are collected into linear lists referenced as the *environment* attribute by every construct that uses an identifier. The rules for this attribute describe the scope rules of the language. Figure 9.1b gives the type of this attribute, and Figure 9.1c shows a typical example of its use. (Examples such as that of Figure 9.1c will normally contain only the attribution rules necessary for the point that we are trying to make. Do not assume, therefore, that no additional attributes or attribution rules are associated with the given syntax rule.)

type
  definition_class = (
    object _definition,   (* Section A.3.1 *)
    type _definition,   (* Section A.3.1 *)
    label _definition,   (* Section A.2.6 *)
    unknown _definition);   (* Undefined identifier *)
  definition = **record**
    uid : *interger* ;   (* Discussed in Section 9.1.3 *)
    ident : *symbol* ;   (* Identifier being defined *)
    case *k* : *definition_class* **of**
      object _definition: (*object _type* : *mode*); (* *mode* is discussed *)
      type _definition: (*defined_type* : *mode*);   (* in Section 9.1.2 *)
      label _definition,
      unknown _definition: ()
  end;

a) The attributes of an identifier

  definition_table = ↑ *dt _element* ;
  dt _element = **record** *first*: *definition*; *rest* : *definition_table* **end**;

b) Type of the environment attribute

  rule *name* ::= *identifier_use* .
  condition
    identifier_use.corresponding _definition.k = *object _definition*;

  rule *identifier_use* ::= *identifier* .
  attribution
    identifier_use.corresponding _definition ←
      current _definition(*identifier.sym* ,*identifier_use.environment*);

c) Use of an environment

Figure 9.1. Environments

The introduction of an additional nonterminal *identifier_use* in Figure 9.1c is necessary because we cannot attach the attribute *corresponding _ definition* to either the nonterminal *name* or the terminal *identifier*. For the former the attribute would be meaningless in the production *name* ::= *name* ' ↑ ', while for the latter we would have difficulty with defining occurrences of identifiers.

In LAX, the environment attribute is changed only upon entry to ranges (A.2.0.2). Figure 9.2a shows the change associated with a *statement_list* . For language constructs that are not ranges, the environment attribute is simply passed along unchanged as illustrated in Figure 9.2b. (Figure 9.2b is an example of a 'transfer rule', where we would normally not write the attribute assignment.)

The synthesized attribute *statements.definitions* is a *definition_table* that

rule *statement _list* :: = *statements* .
attribution
  statements.environment ←
    statements.definitions & *statement _list.environment* ;
condition
  unambiguous (*statements.definitions*);

  a) Language construct that changes the environment

rule *unlabelled _statement* :: = *expression* .
attribution
  expression.environment ← *unlabelled _statement.environment* ;

  b) Language construct that does not change the environment

Figure 9.2. Environment Manipulation

has one entry for each label definition. It describes the identifiers given new meanings in the *statement _list*. This attribute is constructed as shown in Figure 9.3. (Note that the rule *statements* :: = *statement* is simply a transfer, and hence the attribution rules are omitted.) The function *gennum* is a source of unique integers: Each invocation of *gennum* yields a new integer.

Section A.2.2 gives the visibility rules for LAX. Implementation of these rules in the attribute grammar is illustrated by Figures 9.1c and 9.2a. The function *unambiguous* is used in Figure 9.2a to verify that

rule *statements* :: = *statement* .

rule *statements* :: = *statements* ';' *statement* .
attribution
  statements [1].*definitions* ←
    statements [2].*definitions* & *statement.definitions*;

rule *statement* :: = *label _definition statement* .
attribution
  statement [1].*definitions* ←
    label _definition.def & *statement* [2].*definitions*;

rule *statement* :: = *unlabelled _statement* .
attribution
  statement.definitions ← **nil**;

rule *label _definition* :: = *identifier* ':' .
attribution
  label _definition.def ←
    N _definition(*gennum* ,*identifier.sym* ,*label _definition*);

Figure 9.3. Label Definition

statements.definitions contains no more than one definition of any identifier. *Current _definition* (Figure 9.1c) searches the environment linearly from left to right and selects the first definition for the desired identifier. As shown in Figure 9.2a, the local definitions are placed at the front of the environment list; they therefore 'hide' any definitions of the same identifiers appearing in outer ranges because a linear search will find them first.

We must reiterate that attributes belonging to different symbols in a production or to different nodes in a structure tree are different, even if they are identically named. Thus there is not just one attribute *environment,* but as many as there are nodes in the structure tree. The fact that these many environments will be represented by a single definition table in the implementation discussed in Section 9.2 does not concern us in the specification. In the same way, it does not follow from the informal specification of *current _definition* given above that the implementation must also use an inefficient linear search; this strategy is only a simple specification of the desired effect.

If the scope of a definition begins at that definition, and not at the beginning of the range in which it appears (an important property for one-pass compilers), then the environment must be passed 'along the text' as shown in Figure 9.4. The right-recursive solution of Figure 9.4a requires the parser to accumulate entries for all of the declarations on its stack before it can begin reducing declaration lists. This can lead to excessive storage requirements. A better approach is to use left recursion, as shown in Figure 9.4b. In this case the parser will never have more than one declaration entry on its stack, no matter how many declarations appear in the declaration list. Figure 9.4b is easy to understand, but it has the unpleasant property that for each declaration the original environment is augmented by all of the definitions resulting from earlier declarations in the list. Figure 9.4c, where the environment is extended in a stepwise manner, is the best strategy.

Figure 9.4c makes the passing of the environment 'along the text' explicit. *Declaration_list* has an (inherited) attribute *environment_in* that describes the initial state and a (synthesized) attribute *environment_out* that describes the final state. The latter consists of the former augmented by the current definition. Although this solution appears to be quite costly because of the multiple environments, it is actually the most efficient: Simple analysis shows that all of the environments replace one another and therefore all of them can be represented by a single data structure.

It is clear that all of the definitions of Figure 9.4 are equivalent from the standpoint of the language definition. If, however, we wish to specify the semantic analyzer then we prefer Figure 9.4c. Examining a given attribute grammar for optimizations of this kind often pays dividends.

The implicit declarations of FORTRAN are described in a similar fashion, with each *identifier_use* a potential declaration (Figure 9.5). We pass the environment along the text of the expressions and statements, modi-

rule *declaration_list* ::= *declaration* ';' *declaration_list* .
attribution
  declaration.environment ← *declaration_list*[1].*environment* ;
  declaration_list[2].*environment* ←
    declaration.definitions & *declaration_list*[1].*environment* ;
  declaration_list[1].*definitions* ←
    declaration.definitions & *declaration_list*[2].*definitions*;

a) Right-recursive solution

rule *declaration_list* ::= *declaration_list* ';' *declaration* .
attribution
  declaration_list[2].*environment* ← *declaration_list*[1].*environment*
  declaration.environment ←
    declaration_list[2].*definitions* & *declaration_list*[1].*environment* ;
  declaration_list[1].*definitions* ←
    declaration_list[2].*definitions* & *declaration.definitions*;

b) Left-recursive solution

rule *declaration_list* ::= *declaration_list* ';' *declaration* .
attribution
  declaration_list[2].*environment_*∈ ← *declaration_list*[1].*environment_*∈;
  declaration.environment ← *declaration_list*[2].*environment_out* ;
  declaration_list[1].*environment_out* ←
    declaration_list[2].*environment_out* & *declaration.definitions*;
  declaration_list[1].*definitions* ←
    declaration_list[2].*definitions* & *declaration.definitions*;

c) Stepwise environment construction

Figure 9.4. Scope Beginning at the Declaration

rule *identifier_use* ::= *identifier* .
attribution
  identifier_use.implicit_definitions ←
    if *found* (*identifier.sym* ,*identifier_use.environment*) **then nil**
    else
      N_definition(
      gennum,
      identifier.sym,
      object_definition,
      identifier.implicit_type);
  identifier_use.corresponding_definition ←
    current_definition(
    identifier.sym,
    identifier_use.implicit_definitions & *identifier_use.environment*);

Figure 9.5. Implicit Declarations in FORTRAN

fying it at each operand, by rules analogous to those of Figure 9.4c. This strategy avoids the problem of double implicit declarations in expressions such as $I*I$.

Greater difficulties arise from the fact that the Pascal fragment shown in Figure 9.6 is illegal because i is declared in p but used prior to its declara-

> **const** $i = 17$;
> **type** $t = \cdots$;   (* First declaration of t *)
> **procedure** p ;
>   **const**
> $j = i$;   (* Use of i illegal here *)
> $i = 1$;   (* This makes the previous line illegal *)
>   **type**
> $tt = \uparrow t$;   (* Refers to second declaration of t *)
> $t = \cdots$;   (* Second declaration of t *)

Figure 9.6. Definition Before Use in Pascal

tion. This is not allowed, even though a declaration of i exists outside of p. On the other hand, the use of t in the declaration of tt is correct and identifies the type whose declaration appears on the next line. This problem can be solved by a variant of the standard technique for dealing with declarations in a one-pass ALGOL 60 compiler (Exercise 9.5).

9.1.2. Types A type specifies the possible operations on an entity and the coercions that can be applied to it. During semantic analysis this information is used to identify operators and verify the compatibility of constructs with their environment. We shall concentrate on languages with manifest types. Languages with latent types, in which type checking and operator identification occur during execution, are treated in the same manner except that these tasks are deferred.

In order to perform the tasks outlined in the previous paragraph, every structure tree node that represents a value must have an attribute describing its type. These attributes are usually tree-valued, and are built of linked records. For uniformity, the compiler writer should define a single record format to be used in building all of them. The record format must therefore be capable of representing the type of *any* value that could appear in a source program, regardless of whether the language definition explicitly describes that value as being typed. For example, the record format used in a LAX compiler must be capable of representing the type of *nil* because *nil* can appear as a value. Section A.3.1 does not describe *nil* as having a specific type, but says that it 'denotes a value of type **ref** t, for arbitrary t'.

Figure 9.7 defines a record that can be used to build attributes describing LAX types. Type class *bad_type* is used to indicate that errors have made it impossible to determine the proper type. The type itself must be retained, however, since all attributes *must* be assigned values during semantic

type
  type_class = (
    bad_type, *nil_type*, *void_type*, *bool_type*, *int_type*, *real_type*,
    ref_type,
    arr_type,
    rec_type,
    proc_type,
    unidentified_type,   (* See Section 9.1.3 *)
    identified_type);   (* See Section 9.1.3 *)
  mode = **record**
    case k : *type_class* **of**
      bad_type, *nil_type*, *void_type*, *bool_type*, *int_type*, *real_type* : ();
      ref_type : (*target* : ↑ *mode*);
      arr_type : (*dimensions* : *integer*; *element* : ↑ *mode*);
      rec_type : (*fields*: *definition_table*);
      proc_type : (*parameters* : *definition_table*; *result* : ↑ *mode*);
      unidentified_type : (*identifier*: *symbol*);
      identified_type : (*definition*: *integer*)
    end;

Figure 9.7. Representation of LAX Types

analysis. *Nil_type* is the type of the predefined identifier *nil*. We also need a special mechanism for describing the result type of a proper procedure. *Void_type* specifies this case, and in fact is used whenever a result is to be discarded.

For languages like ALGOL 60 and FORTRAN, which have only a fixed number of types, an enumeration similar to *type_class* serves to represent all types. Array types must also specify the number of dimensions, but the element type can be subsumed into the enumeration (e.g. *integer_array_type* or *real_array_type*). Pascal requires additional specifications for the index bounds; in LAX the bounds are expressions whose values do not belong to the static semantics, as illustrated by the rules of Figure 9.8.

Figure 9.9 shows how procedure types are constructed in LAX. (*Bad_symbol* represents a nonexistent identifier.) Because parameter transmission is always by value (reference parameters are implemented by passing a *ref* value as discussed in Section 2.5.3) it is not necessary to give a parameter transmission mechanism. In Pascal or ALGOL 60, however, the transmission mechanism must be included for each parameter. For a language like Ada, in which keyword association of arguments and parameters is possible, the identifiers must be retained also. We retain the parameter identifiers, even though this is not required in LAX, to reduce the number of attributes for the common case of a procedure declaration (A.3.0.8). Here we can use the procedure type attribute both to validate the

rule *type _specification* :: = *'ref' type _specification* .
attribution
  type _specification[1].*repr* ←
    N_mode (*ref _type,type _specification*[2].*repr*);

rule *type _specification* :: = *'ref' array _type* .
attribution
  type _specification.repr ← *N_mode* (*ref _type,array _type.repr*);

rule *array _type* :: = *array* '[' *dimensions* ']' *'of' type _specification* .
attribution
  array _type.repr ←
    N_mode (*arr _type,dimensions.count,type _specification.repr*);

rule *dimensions* :: = .
attribution
  dimensions.count ← 1;

rule *dimensions* :: = *dimensions* ',' .
attribution
  dimensions [1].*count* ← *dimensions* [2].*count* +1;

rule *record _type* :: = *'record' fields 'end'* .
attribution
  record _type.repr ← *N_mode* (*rec _type,fields.definitions*);
condition
  unambiguous (*fields.definitions*);

rule *fields* :: = *field* .

rule *fields* :: = *fields* ';' *field* .
attribution
  fields[1].*definitions* ← *fields*[2].*definitions* & *field.definitions*;

rule *field* :: = *identifier* ':' *type _specification* .
attribution
  field.definitions ←
    N_definition(
      gennum ,
       identifier.sym ,
       object _definition,
       type _specification.repr);

Figure 9.8. Type Definition

rule *type_specification* ::= *'procedure'* *parameter_type_list* *result_type* .
attribution
  type_specification.repr ←
    N_mode (*proc_type,parameter_type_list.definitions,result_type.repr*);

rule *parameter_type_list* ::= .
attribution
  parameter_type_list.definitions ← **nil**;

rule *parameter_type_list* ::= *'(' parameter_types ')'* .

rule *parameter_types* ::= *type_specification* .
attribution
  parameter_types.definitions ←
    N_definition(gennum,bad_symbol,type_definition,type_specification.repr);

rule *parameter_types* ::= *parameter_types ',' type_specification* .
attribution
  parameter_types[1].*definitions* ←
    parameter_types[2].*definitions* &
    N_definition(gennum,bad_symbol,type_definition,type_specification.repr);

Figure 9.9. Procedure Type Definition

type compatibility and to provide the parameter definitions. If we were to remove the parameter identifiers from the procedure type this would not be possible.

When types and definitions are represented by attributes, the complete set of declarations (other than procedure declarations) can, in principle, be deleted from the structure tree to avoid duplicating information both as attributes and as subtrees of the structure tree. Actually, however, this compression of the representation should only be carried out under extreme storage constraints; normally both representations should be retained. The main reason is that expressions (like dynamic array bounds) appearing within declarations cannot be abstracted as attributes because they are not evaluated until the program is executed.

Context-sensitive properties of types lead to several relations that can be expressed as recursive functions over types (objects of type *mode*). These basic relations are:

- *Equivalent*: Two types t and t' are semantically equivalent.
- *Compatible*: Usually an asymmetric relation, in which an object of type t can be used in place of an object of type t'.
- *Coercible*: A type t is coercible to a type t' if it is either compatible with t' or can be converted to t' by a sequence of coercions.

Type equivalence is defined in Section A.3.1 for LAX; this definition is embodied in the procedure *type_equivalent* of Figure 9.10. *Type_equivalent* must be used in all cases where two types should be compared. The direct comparison $t_1 = t_2$ may not yield *true* for equivalent composite types because the pointers contained in the type records may address equivalent types represented by different records.

The test for equivalence of type identifiers is for the identity of the type declarations rather than for the equivalence of types they declare. This reflects the name equivalence rule of Section A.3.1. If structural

```
function type_equivalent (t 1,t 2: mode ): boolean ;
  (* Compare two types for equivalence *)

  function compare_parameters (f 1,f 2: definition_table ): boolean ;
    (* Compare parameter lists for equivalent types *)
    begin (* compare_parameters *)
    if f 1 = nil then compare_parameters : = f 2 = nil
    else if f 2 = nil then compare_parameters : = false
    else
      compare_parameters : =
        type_equivalent (f 1 ↑ .first.object_type,f 2 ↑ .first.object_type ) and
        compare_parameters (f 1 ↑ .rest,f 2 ↑ .rest )
    end; (* compare_parameters *)

  begin (* type_equivalent *)
  if t 1.k < > t 2.k then type_equivalent : = false
  else
    case t 1.k of
      ref_type :
        type_equivalent : = type_equivalent (t 1.target ↑ ,t 2.target ↑ );
      arr_type :
        type_equivalent : =
          t 1.dimension = t 2.dimension and
          type_equivalent (t 1.element ↑ ,t 2.element ↑ );
      rec_type :
        type_equivalent : = false;
      proc_type :
        type_equivalent : =
          compare_parameters (t 1.parameters ,t 2.parameters ) and
          type_equivalent (t 1.result ↑ ,t 2.result ↑ );
      identified_type :
        type_equivalent : = t 1.definition = t 2.definition
      otherwise type_equivalent : = true
      end;
  end; (* type_equivalent *)
```

Figure 9.10. Type Equivalence in LAX

function *coercible* (*t* 1,*t* 2: *mode*): *boolean* ;
  (* Verify that *t* 1 can be coerced to *t* 2 *)
  begin (* *coercible* *)
  if *type_equivalent* (*t* 1,*t* 2) **or** *t* 2.*k* = *void_type* **or** *t* 2.*k* = *bad_type*
  then *coercible* : = *true*
  else
    case *t* 1.*k* **of**
      bad_type : *coercible* : = *true*
      nil_type : *coercible* : = *t* 2.*k* = *ref_type* ;
      int_type : *coercible* : = *t* 2.*k* = *real_type* ;
      ref_type : *coercible* : = *coercible* (*t* 1.*target* ↑ ,*t* 2);
      proc_type : *coercible* : = *t* 1.*parameters* = **nil and** *coercible* (*t* 1.*result* ↑ ,*t* 2)
      otherwise *coercible* : = *false*
    end;
  end; (* *coercible* *)

Figure 9.11. Coercibility in LAX

equivalence is required, as in ALGOL 68, then we must compare the declared types instead. A simple implementation of this comparison leads to infinite recursion for types containing pointers to themselves. The recursion can, however, be stopped as soon as we attempt to compare two types whose comparison has been begun but has not yet terminated. During comparison we therefore hold such pairs in a stack. Since the only types that can participate in infinite recursion are those of class *identified_type,* we enter pairs of *identified_type* types into the stack when we begin to compare them. The next pair is checked against the stack before beginning their comparison; if the pair is found then they are considered to be equivalent and no further comparison of them is required. (If they are not equivalent, this will be detected by the first comparison — the one on the stack.)

Figure 9.10 compares exactly two types. If we wish to group all types of a block, procedure or program into classes of structurally equivalent types then it is better to use the refinement algorithm of Section B.3.2 as generalized in Exercise B.7. This algorithm has the advantage of reducing the number of records that represent types, and therefore the amount of storage required to hold the attributes.

The Pascal Standard proposes name equivalence for all types except sets and subranges, whose equivalence depends upon the equivalence of the base types. In addition, however, it defines the property of type compatibility and relies upon that property for assignments and parameter transmission. Among other things, two array types are compatible if they have the same bounds and compatible element types. Other languages also provide (explicitly or implicitly) a somewhat weaker compatibility relation in addition to the strong type equivalence. There is no separate type compatibility rule in LAX.

The allowable LAX coercions (Section A.4.2) are embodied in the

rule *variable_declaration* $::=$ *identifier* ':' *type_specification* .
attribution
  variable_declaration.definitions ←
    N_definition(
      gennum,
      identifier.sym,
      object_definition,
      N_mode (*ref_type*,*type_specification.repr*));

rule *variable_declaration* $::=$.
  identifier ':' 'array' '[' *bounds* ']' 'of' *type_specification*.
attribution
  variable_declaration.definitions ←
    N_definition(
      gennum,
      identifier.sym,
      object_definition,
      N_mode (
        ref_type,
        N_mode (*arr_type*,*bounds.count*,*type_specification.repr*)));

rule *bounds* $::=$ *bound_pair* .
attribution
  bounds.count $:= 1$;

rule *bounds* $::=$ *bounds* ',' *bound_pair* .
attribution
  bounds[1].*count* $:=$ *bounds*[2].*count* $+ 1$;

rule *identity_declaration* $::=$ *identifier* 'is' *expression* ':' *type_specification* .
attribution
  identity_declaration.definitions ←
    N_definition(
      gennum,
      identifier.sym,
      object_definition,
      type_specification.repr);

Figure 9.12. Variable and Identity Declarations

function *coercible* (Figure 9.11). Note that when the type class of a type is *bad_type* any coercion is allowed. The reason is that this class can only occur as the result of an error. If we did not allow the coercion, the use of an erroneous construct would lead to further (superfluous) error messages.

9.1.3. Declarations Figure 9.12 shows the attribution rules for variable and identity declarations in LAX. A definition is created for each declaration, just as was done for label definitions in Figure 9.3. Note that the variable declaration creates a reference to the given type, while the identity declaration uses that type as it stands. This is because the variable declaration creates 'a variable referring to an undefined value (of the specified type)' (Section A.3.2) and the identity declaration creates 'a new instance of the value (of the specified type)' (Section A.3.3).

The treatment of array variables in Figure 9.12 reflects the requirements of Section A.3.2. We construct the array type based only on the dimensionality and element type. The bounds must be integer expressions, but they are to be evaluated at execution time.

Type declarations introduce apparent circularities into the declaration

rule *type_specification* :: = *identifier* .
attribution
    type_specification.repr ← *N_mode* (*unidentified_type,identifier.sym*);

a) Reference to a type identifier

rule *type_declaration* :: = '*type*' *identifier* '=' *record_type* .
attribution
    type_declaration.definitions ←
      N_definition(*gennum,identifier.sym ,type_definition,record_type.repr*);

rule *declaration* :: = *variable_declaration* .

rule *declaration* :: = *identity_declaration* .

rule *declaration* :: = *type_declaration* .

rule *declarations* :: = *declarations* ';' *declaration* .
attribution
    declarations [1].*definitions* ←
      declarations [2].*definitions* & *declaration.definitions*;

rule *block* :: = '*declare*' *declarations* '*begin*' *statements* '*end*' .
attribution
    declarations.environment ←
      complete_env (
        declarations.definitions,
        declarations.definitions & *statements.definitions* & *block.environment*) &
      statements.definitions &
      block.environment ;
    statements.environment ← *declarations.environment* ;
condition
    unambiguous (*declarations.definitions* & *statements.definitions*);

b) Completing the type declarations

Figure 9.13. Type Declarations

function *identify_type* (*s* : *symbol* ; *e* : *definition_table*): *mode* ;
  (* Find the type defined by an identifier *)
  begin (* *identify_type* *)
  if *e* = **nil then** *identify_type* : = *N_mode* (*bad _type*)
  else with *e* ↑, *first* **do**
   if *s* < > *ident* **then** *identify_type* : = *identify_type* (*s* ,*rest*)
   else if *def.k* < > *type_definition* **then** *identify_type* : = *N_mode* (*bad _type*);
   else *identify_type* : = *N_mode* (*identified_type* ,*uid*)
  end; (* *identify_type* *)

Figure 9.14. Type Identification

process: The definition of an identifier must be known in order to define
that identifier. One obvious example, the declaration **type** *t* = **record** *x* :
real ; *p* : **ref** *t* **end**, was mentioned in Section 8.1. Another is the fact that the
analysis process discussed in Section 9.1.1 assumes we can construct
definitions for all identifiers in a range and then form an environment for
that range. Unfortunately the definition of a variable identifier includes its
type, which might be specified by a type identifier declared in the same
range. Hence the environment must be available to obtain the type. We
solve the problem in three steps, as shown in Figure 9.13, using the
unidentified_type and *identified_type* variants of *mode* :

1. Collect all of the type declarations of a range into one attribute, of type
   definition_table . Any type identifiers occurring in the corresponding
   types are not yet identified, but are given by the *unidentified_type* variant.
2. As soon as step (1) has been completed, transform the entire attribute to
   another *definition_table* in which each *unidentified_type* has been replaced by an *identified_type* that identifies the proper definition. This
   transformation uses the environment inherited by the range as well as the
   information present in the type declarations.
3. Incorporate the newly-created *definition_table* into the range's environment, and then process all of the remaining declarations (none of which
   are type declarations).

Complete_env is a recursive function that traverses the definitions seeking
unidentified types. Whenever one is found, *identify_type* (Figure 9.14) is
used to obtain the current definition of the type identifier. Note that
identify_type must use a unique representation of the definition, not the
definition itself, corresponding to the type identifier. The reason is that, if
types involve recursive references, we cannot construct any of the definitions
until we have constructed all of them! (Remember that attributes are not
variables, so it is not possible to construct an 'empty' definition and then fill
it in later.)

9.1.4. Expressions and Statements The *a priori* type (*primode*) of an
expression is a synthesized attribute, and describes the type with which a

result is computed; the *a posteriori* type (*postmode*) is an inherited attribute, and describes the type required by the context. If these two types are different then a sequence of coercion operations must be used during execution to convert the value from one to the other.

The a posteriori type of a particular expression may or may not depend upon its a priori type. If the expression is an operand of an operator indication like +, which can stand for several operations (e.g. integer addition, real addition), then its *postmode* depends upon the *primode* attributes of both operands. If, on the other hand, the expression is an array index in LAX then *postmode* is *integer* independent of the expression's *primode*.

Some constructs, like the LAX *clause,* may not yield a result of the same type every time they are executed. This does not lead to difficulty when the construct appears in a context where the a posteriori type is fixed, because each part of the construct simply inherits the fixed *postmode*. When the a posteriori type depends upon the a priori types of the operands, however, we

```
function base_type (t : mode ): mode ;
   (* Remove all levels of reference and procedure call from a type *)
   begin (* base_type *)
   if t.k =ref_type then base_type : = base_type (t.target ↑ )
   else if t.k =proc_type then
      if t.parameters < >nil then base_type : = t
      else base_type : = base_type (t.result ↑ )
   else base_type : = t
   end; (* base_type *)


function balance (t 1,t 2: mode ): mode ;
   (* Obtain the representative a priori type of t1,t2 *)
   begin (* balance *)
   if coercible (t 1,t 2) then balance : = t 2
   else if coercible (t 2,t 1) then balance : = t 1
   else if coercible (t 1,base_type (t 2)) then
      case t 2.k of
         ref_type : balance : = balance (t 1,t 2.target ↑ );
         proc_type : balance : = balance (t 1,t 2.result ↑ )
      end
   else if coercible (t 2,base_type (t 1)) then
      case t 1.k of
         ref_type : balance : = balance (t 1.target ↑ ,t 2);
         proc_type : balance : = balance (t 1.result ↑ ,t 2)
      end
   else N_mode (void_type );
   end; (* balance *)
```

Figure 9.15. Balancing in LAX

need a type t to serve as a 'model a priori type' in place of the result types $t_1, \ldots, t_n$. This type is obtained by *balancing*: A set of types $t_1, \ldots, t_n$, $n > 1$ can be balanced to a type t if each t_i is coercible to t, and there is no type t' coercible to t such that each t_i is coercible to t'.

For LAX (and most other languages) balancing is commutative and 'associative' (Exercise 9.11), so that we may restrict ourselves to the case $n = 2$ (Figure 9.15). Three facts were used in constructing *balance*:

- If t_1 is coercible to but not equivalent to t_2, t_2 is not coercible to t_1.
- If not voided, the result has the same base type (type after all references and procedures have been removed) as one of the operands.
- If t_1 is coercible to the base type of t_2 but not to t_2 itself, the result type is a dereferencing and/or deproceduring of t_2.

If LAX types t_1 and t_2 are coerced to an a posteriori type t', then the type *balance*(t_1, t_2) always appears as an intermediate step. This may not be true in other languages, however. In ALGOL 68, for example, *balance*(*integer*,*real*) = *real* but both types can be coerced to *union* (*integer*,*real*) and in this case *integer* is not coerced to *real* first.

Figure 9.16 illustrates the use of balancing. In addition to the attributes

type
    case_selectors = ↑ *cs_element* ;
    cs_element = **record** *first*: *integer* ; *rest* : *case_selectors* **end**;

a) Type of label_values

rule *case_clause* ::= '*case*' *expression* '*of*' *cases* '*else*' *statement_list* '*end*' .
attribution
    clause.primode ← *balance* (*cases.primode*,*statement_list.primode*);
    expression.postmode ← *N_mode* (*int_type*);
condition
    values_unambiguous (*cases.label_values*);

rule *cases* ::= *case* .

rule *cases* ::= *cases* '//' *case* .
attribution
    cases[1].*primode* ← *balance* (*cases*[2].*primode*,*case.primode*);
    cases[1].*label_values* ← *cases*[2].*label_values* & *case.label_values* ;

rule *case* ::= *case_label* ':' *statement_list* .
attribution
    case.label_values ← *case_label.value* ;

b) Attribution rules

Figure 9.16. Case Clauses

primode and *postmode*, this example uses *label_values* (synthesized, type *case_selectors*). *Postmode* is simply passed through from top to bottom, so we follow our convention of not writing these transfers explicitly. *Label_values* collects the values of all case labels into a list so we can check that no label has occurred more than once (Section A.4.5).

Note that there is no **condition** checking coercibility of the resulting a priori type of the case clause to the a posteriori type. Similarly, the a priori type of the selecting expression is not checked against its a posteriori type in these rules. Such tests appear only in those rules where the a priori type is determined by considerations other than balancing or transfer from adjacent nodes.

Figure 9.17 illustrates some typical attribution rules for *primode* and *postmode* in expressions. Table A.2 requires that the left operand of an assignment be a reference, and Section A.4.2 permits only dereferencing coercions of the left operand. Thus the assignment rule invokes *deproc* (Figure 9.18) to obtain an a posteriori type for the name. Note that there is no guarantee that the type obtained actually *is* a reference, so additional checks are needed. *Coercible* (Figure 9.11) is invoked to verify that the a priori type of the assignment itself can be coerced to the a posteriori type required by the context in which the assignment appears. As can be seen from the remainder of Figure 9.17, this check is made every time an object is created.

Assignment is the only dyadic operator in Table A.2 whose left and right operands have different types. In all other cases, the types of the operands must be the same. The attribution rules for *comparison* show how *balance* can be used in this case to obtain a candidate operand type. The two rules for *eqop* illustrate placement of additional requirements upon this candidate.

The attribution for a simple name sets the a priori type to the type specified by the identifier's definition, and must also verify (via *coercible*) that the a priori type satisfies the requirements of the context as specified by the a posteriori type. Field selection is a bit trickier. Section A.4.4 states that the name preceding the the dot may yield either an object or a reference to an object. This requirement, which also holds for index selection, is embodied in *one_ref* (Figure 9.18). Note that the environment in which the field identifier is sought is that of the record type definition, not the one in which the field selection appears. We must therefore write the transfer of the environment attribute explicitly. Finally, the type yielded by the field selection is a reference if and only if the object yielded by the name to the left of the dot was a reference (Section A.4.4).

Figure 9.19 shows how the field definitions of the record are obtained. Section A.3 requires that every record type be given a name. The declaration process described in Figures 9.13 and 9.14 guarantees that if this name is associated with an *identified_type*, the type definition will actually be in the current environment. Moreover, the type definition cannot specify anything but a record. Thus *record_env* need not verify these conditions.

rule *assignment* $::=$ *name* $':='$ *expression* .
attribution
  assignment.primode $\leftarrow$ *name.postmode* ;
  name.postmode $\leftarrow$ *deproc* (*name.primode*);
  expression.postmode $\leftarrow$
    if *name.postmode.k* $<>ref\_type$ **then** N_mode (*bad_type*)
    else *name.postmode.target* $\uparrow$;
condition
  coercible (*assignment.primode* ,*assignment.postmode*) **and**
  name.postmode.k $=ref\_type$;

rule *comparison* $::=$ *relation eqop relation* .
attribution
  comparison.primode $\leftarrow$ N_mode (*bool_type*);
  relation [1].*postmode* $\leftarrow$ *eqop.operand* $\_post$;
  eqop.operand $\_pri$ $\leftarrow$ *balance* (*relation* [1].*primode* ,*relation* [2].*primode*);
  relation [2].*postmode* $\leftarrow$ *eqop.operand* $\_post$;
condition
  coercible (*comparison.primode* ,*comparison.postmode*);

rule *eqop* $::=$ $'='$.
attribution
  eqop.operand $\_post$ $\leftarrow$ *deref* (*eqop.operand* $\_pri$);
condition
  eqop.operand $\_post.k$ $<>$ *void* $\_type$;

rule *eqop* $::=$ $'\equiv'$.
attribution
  eqop.operand $\_post$ $\leftarrow$ *deproc* (*eqop.operand* $\_pri$);
condition
  eqop.operand $\_post.k$ $=ref\_type$;

rule *name* $::=$ *name* $'.'$ *identifier_use* .
attribution
  name [1].*primode* $\leftarrow$
    if *identifier_use.current* $\_definition<>object\_definition$ **then**
      N_mode (*bad_type*)
    else if *name* [2].*postmode.k* $=ref\_type$ **then**
      N_mode (*ref* $\_type$,*identifier_use.current* $\_definition.object\_type$)
    else *identifier_use.current* $\_definition.object$ $\_type$;
  name [2].*postmode* $\leftarrow$ *one* $\_ref$ (*name* [2].*primode*);
  name [2].*environment* $\leftarrow$ *name* [1].*environment* ;
  identifier_use.environment $\leftarrow$
    if *deref* (*name* [2].*postmode*).*k* $<>$ *identified_type* **then nil**
    else *record* $\_env$ (*deref* (*name* [2].*postmode*).*definition* ,*name* [1].*environment*);
condition
  coercible (*name* [1].*primode* ,*name* [1].*postmode*) **and**
  identifier_use.current $\_definition.k$ $=object\_definition$;

Figure 9.17. Determining A Priori and A Posteriori Types

function *deproc* (*t* : *mode*): *mode* ;
  (* Remove all levels of procedure call from a type *)
  begin (* *deproc* *)
  if *t.k* < >*proc _type* **then** *deproc* : = *t*
  else if *t.parameters* < >**nil then** *deproc* : = *t*
  else *deproc* : = *deproc* (*t.result* ↑)
  end; (* *deproc* *)

function *deref* (*t* : *mode*): *mode* ;
  (* Remove all levels of reference from a type *)
  begin (* *deref* *)
  if *t.k* < >*ref _type* **then** *deref* : = *t*
  else *deref* : = *deref* (*t.target* ↑);
  end; (* *deref* *)

function *one _ref* (*t* : *mode*): *mode* ;
  (* Remove all but one level of reference from a type *)
  begin (* *one _ref* *)
  case *t.k* **of**
    ref _type :
      if *t.target* ↑ .*k* < >*arr _type* **and** *t.target* ↑ .*k* < >*rec _type* **then**
        one _ref : = *one _ref* (*t.target* ↑)
      else *one _ref* : = *t* ;
    proc _type :
      if *t.parameters* < >**nil then** *one _ref* : = *t*
      else *one _ref* : = *one _ref* (*t.result* ↑)
    otherwise
      one _ref : = *t*
    end;
  end; (* *one _ref* *)

Figure 9.18. Type Transformations in LAX

function *record _env* (*i* : *integer* ; *e* : *definition_table*): *definition_table* ;
  (* Obtain the field definitions of a record type
    On entry-
      t = type for which the fields are sought
      e = environment containing the type definition
  *)
  begin (* *record _env* *)
  if *e* ↑ .*first.uid* < >*i* **then** *record _env* : = *record _env* (*i* ,*e* ↑ .*rest*)
  else *record _env* : = *e* ↑ .*first.defined_type.fields*;
  end; (* *record _env* *)

Figure 9.19. Obtaining a Record's Field Definitions

In most programming languages the specification of the operator and the a posteriori types of the operands uniquely determines the operation to be carried out, but usually no *operation* attribute appears in the language description itself. The reason is that semantic analysis does not make any further use of the operation, and the operation determined by the semantic analysis may be either an over- or underspecification for code generation purposes. For example, the distinction between integer and real assignment is usually an overspecification because only the length of the object being assigned is of interest. On the other hand, a record assignment operator is an underspecification because the code generator must decide between a load/store sequence, a block transfer and a closed subroutine on the basis of the record size.

The situation is different for languages like ALGOL 68 and Ada, in which a user may define operations. There the semantic analyzer must identify the operations, and there is scarcely any distinction between operators and functions of one or two operands. Which operations or functions are implemented with closed subprograms and which with open sequences of instructions is a decision made by the code generator.

Operator identification for Ada depends not only upon the a priori types of the operands, but also upon the a posteriori type of the result. There is no coercion, so the a priori and a posteriori types must be compatible, but on the other hand the constant 2 (for example) could have any of the types 'short integer', 'integer' and 'long integer'. Thus both the operand types and the result types must be determined by analysis of the tree.

Each operand and result is given one inherited and one synthesized attribute, each of which is a set of types. We begin at the leaves of the tree and compute the possible (a priori) types of each operand. Moving up the tree, we specify the possible operations and result types based upon the possible combinations of operand types and the operator indication. Upon arriving at the root of the tree for the expression we have a synthesized attribute for every node giving the possible types for the value of this node. Moving down the tree, these type sets are now further restricted: An inherited attribute, a subset of the previous synthesized attribute, is computed for each node. It specifies the set of types permitted by the use of this value as an operand in operations further up the tree. At the beginning of the descent, the previously-computed set of possible result types at the root is used as the inherited attribute of the root. If this process leads to a unique type for every node of the tree, i.e. if the inherited attribute is always a singleton set, then the operations are all specified; otherwise at least one operator (and hence the program) is semantically ambiguous and hence illegal.

Because LAX is an expression-oriented language, statements and statement-like constructs (*statement_list, iteration, loop,* etc.) also have *primode* and *postmode* attributes. Most rules involving these constructs simply transfer those attributes. Figure 9.20 shows rules that embody the conditions given in Sections A.2.4 through A.2.6.

rule *statements* $::=$ *statements* ';' *statement* .
attribution
   statements [1].*primode* ← *statement.primode* ;
   statements [2].*postmode* ← *N_mode* (*void_type*);
   statement.postmode ← *statements* [1].*postmode* ;

rule *iteration* $::=$ *'while'* *expression* *loop* .
attribution
   iteration.primode ← *N_mode* (*void_type*);
   expression.postmode ← *N_mode* (*bool_type*);
   loop.postmode ← *N_mode* (*void_type*);
condition
   iteration.postmode.k $=$ *void_type* ;

rule *iteration* $::=$ *'for'* *identifier* *'from'* *expression* *'to'* *expression* *loop* .
attribution
   iteration.primode ← *N_mode* (*void_type*);
   expression [1].*postmode* ← *N_mode* (*int_type*);
   expression [2].*postmode* ← *N_mode* (*int_type*);
   loop.environment ←
      N_definition(*gennum,identifier.sym,object_definition,N_mode* (*int_type*)) &
      iteration.environment ;
   loop.postmode ← *N_mode* (*void_type*);
condition
   iteration.postmode.k $=$ *void_type* ;

rule *jump* $::=$ *'goto'* *identifier_use* .
attribution
   jump.primode ← *N_mode* (*void_type*);
condition
   jump.postmode.k $=$ *void_type* **and**
   (*identifier_use.corresponding_definition.k* $=$ *label_definition* **or**
     identifier_use.corresponding_definition.k $=$ *unknown_definition*);

Figure 9.20. A Priori and A Posteriori Types in Statements

9.2. Implementation of Semantic Analysis

If we have fully specified the semantic analysis with an attribute grammar and auxiliary functions, the implementation consists of the following steps:

- Derive the abstract syntax for the structure tree.
- Derive the attribution algorithms as discussed in Section 8.2.
- Derive the attribute storage layout as discussed in Section 8.3.
- Code the attribution rules and auxiliary functions.

As we noted in connection with Figure 4.2, the distinction between the concrete and abstract syntax is that groups of symbols appearing in the former are really different names for a single construct of the latter, and hence chain rules that simply transform one of these symbols into another are omitted. The abstract syntax is derived from the attribute grammar by identifying symbols whose attributes are the same, and deleting all rules whose attribution consists solely of transfers.

We extract the context-free syntax directly from the attribute grammar for input to a parser generator. The only thing missing is the connection point specifications, which can be attached systematically as discussed in Section 7.1.1. If a rule does not belong to the abstract syntax, no connection points are attached to it. Thus the parser uses the concrete syntax for its analysis of the token sequence, but produces a connection sequence that is a linearization of a structure tree obeying the abstract syntax.

The result of the attribution algorithm specification leads to the choice of analysis technique: multi-pass, ordered, etc. As with the selection of a parsing technique discussed in Chapter 7, this choice depends primarily upon the experience of the compiler writer and the availability of tools for automated processing. Tools are indispensable if ordered grammars are to be used; the evaluation sequence for multi-pass grammars can be obtained by hand. Further, the available memory plays a role. Roughly the same amount of memory suffices to store the attributes for any method, if intermediate attributes are suitably overlaid. In the case of multi-pass evaluation, however, the algorithm and attribution rules can be segmented and overlaid so that only the relevant part is required during each pass.

The storage layout of the attributes is fixed last, based upon the discussion in Section 8.3.2. As noted there, particular attention must be paid to the interaction among attribute representation, algorithms and formulation of the attribution rules. Often one can influence the entire behavior of the semantic analysis through small (in terms of content) variations in the attribute representation or attribution rules. For example, a one-pass attribution for languages like Pascal is usually not obtained at first, but only after some modification of the original specification. This is not surprising, since the language description discussed in Section 9.1 aims above all for a correct rendition of the language properties and does not consider implementability.

One of the most common attributes in the structure tree is the environment, which allows us to determine the meaning of an identifier at a given point in the program. In the simplest case, for example in several machine-oriented languages, each identifier has exactly one definition in the program. The definition entry can then be reached directly via a pointer in the symbol table. In fact, the symbol and definition table can be integrated into a single table in this case.

Most languages permit an identifier to have several meanings. Figure 9.21 shows a definition table organization that provides access to the current definition for an identifier, given its symbol table entry, in constant time:

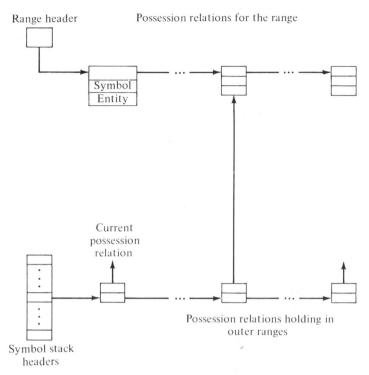

Note : 'Entity' is a pointer to a definition.

Figure 9.21. A Definition Table Structure

The symbol table entry points to a stack of elements, the first of which contains a pointer to the current possession, and the current possession points to the definition. But this access is exactly the *current_definition* function of Figure 9.1c. Thus Figure 9.21 allows us to implement *current_definition* without using any list search at all. The access time is essentially the same as that in the simple case of the previous paragraph; only two additional memory accesses (to follow the possession pointer contained in the stack and the definition pointer contained in the possession) are required.

At first glance, it may seem that there is too much indirection in Figure 9.21. Why does the stack element contain a pointer to the possession instead of a pointer to the definition? Why does the possession contain a pointer to the definition instead of the definition itself? The answers to these questions become clear if we examine the operations that take place on entry to and exit from a range, when the set of currently-valid declarations changes and the definition table must be updated to reflect these changes.

When a range is entered, the stack for each identifier defined in the range must be pushed down and an entry describing the definition valid in this range placed on top. Conversely, the stack for each identifier defined in a range must be popped when leaving that range. To simplify the updating, we represent the range by a linear list of elements specifying a symbol table entry and a corresponding definition as shown at the top of Figure 9.21. This gives constant-time access to the stacks to be pushed or popped, and means that the amount of time required to enter or leave a range is linear in the number of identifiers having definitions in it.

We use a pointer to the definition rather than the definition itself in the range list because many identifiers in different ranges may refer to the same definition. (For example, in Pascal many type identifiers might refer to the same complex record type.) By using a pointer we avoid having to store multiple copies of the definition itself, and also we simplify equality tests on definitions.

We stack a pointer to the appropriate range list entry instead of stacking the range list entry itself because it is possible to enter a range and then enter it again before leaving it. (Figure 9.22 is a Pascal fragment that has this property. The statement **with** $j \uparrow$ enters the range of the record type *one*; the range will be left at the end of that statement. However, the nested statement **with** $h \uparrow$ also enters the same range!) When a range is entered twice without being left, its definitions are stacked twice. If the (single) range list entry were placed on the stack twice, a cycle would be created and the compiler would fail.

Finally, we stack a pointer to the range list entry rather than a pointer to the definition to cater for languages (such as COBOL and PL/1) that allow partial qualification: In a field selection the specification of the containing record may be omitted if it can be determined unambiguously. (This assumes that, in contrast to LAX, exactly one object exists for each record

```
type
  one = record f : integer ; g :  ↑ two end;
  two = record f : boolean ; h :  ↑ one end;
var
  j :  ↑ one ;
  . . .

with j ↑ do
  begin
    . . .

  with g ↑ do
    begin
      . . .

    with h ↑ do
      begin
        . . .

      end
    end
  end;
```

Figure 9.22. Self-Nesting Ranges

type. In other words, the concepts of record and record type merge.)

Figure 9.23 illustrates the problem of partial qualification, using an example from PL/1. Each qualified name must include sufficient identifiers to resolve any ambiguity within a single block; the reference is unambiguous if either or both of the following conditions hold:

- The reference gives a valid qualification for exactly one declaration.
- The reference gives the complete qualification for exactly one declaration.

Most of the references in Figure 9.23 are unambiguous because the first of these conditions holds. The Q in $W=Q$, however, gives a valid qualification for either the major structure or the field $Q.X.Q$; it is unambiguous because it gives the *complete* qualification of the major structure. References Z and $Q.Z$ in procedure B would be ambiguous.

In order to properly analyze Figure 9.23, we must add three items of structural information to each possession relation in Figure 9.21: The *level* is the number of identifiers in a fully-qualified reference to the entity possessed. If the level is greater than 1, *containing_structure* points to the possession relation for the containing structure. In any case, the range to which the possession belongs must be specified. Figure 9.24 shows the pos-

```
A:    PROCEDURE;
      DECLARE
         1 W ,
         . . . ;
B:    PROCEDURE;
      DECLARE
         P,
         1 Q,
             2 R,
                 3 Z,
             2 X,
                 3 Y,
                 3 Z,
                 3 Q;
         Y = R.Z;              /* Q.X.Y from B, Q.R.Z from B */
         W = Q, BY NAME;       /* W from A, major Q from B */
         C:   PROCEDURE
              DECLARE Y,
                  1 R,
                      2 Z;
              Z = Q.Y          /* R.Z from C, Q.X.Y from B */
              X = R, BY NAME;  /* Q.X from B, R from C */
              END C;
         END B;
      END A;
```

Figure 9.23. Partial Qualification

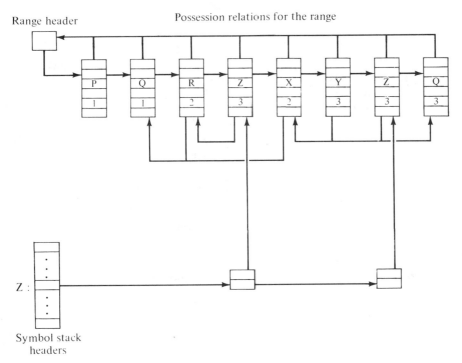

Figure 9.24. Range Specification Including Structure

session relations for procedure B of Figure 9.23. Note that this range contains two valid possession relations for Q and two for Z. The symbol stack entries for Z have been included to show that this results in two stack entries for the same range.

A reference is represented by an array of symbols. The stack corresponding to the *last* of these is scanned, and the test of Figure 9.25 applied to each possession relation. When a relation satisfying the test is found, no further ranges are tested; any other relations for the same symbol within that range must be tested, however. If more than one relation in a range satisfies the test, then the reference is ambiguous unless the level of one of the relations is equal to the number of symbols in the reference.

A definition table module might provide the following operations:

- *New_range ()range* : Establish a new range.
- *Add_possession (symbol,definition,range)*: Add a possession relation to a given range.
- *Enter_range (range)*: Enter a given range.
- *Leave_range* : Leave the current range.
- *Current_definition(symbol)definition*: Identify the definition corresponding to a given identifier at the current point in the program.
- *Definition_in_range (symbol,range)definition*: Identify the definition corresponding to a given identifier in a given range.

```
type
  possession = record
    range :  ↑ range _header ;
    next :  ↑ possession ;
    possessing _symbol : symbol ;
    possessed _entity : entity ;
    level : integer ;
    containing _structure :  ↑ possession
    end;
  symbol _array = array [1..max_qualfiers] of symbol ;

function test (qualifier: symbol _array ; i : integer ; p : possession ): boolean ;
  (* Check a qualified reference
     On entry-
       qualifier = reference to be checked
       i = number of symbols in the reference
       p = possession to be checked
     If the reference describes the possession then on exit-
       test = true
     Else on exit-
       test = false
  *)
  label 1;
  begin (* test *)
  test : = true ;
  while i < p.level do
    begin
    if qualifier[i ] = p.possessing _symbol then
      begin
      i : = i − 1;
      if i = 0 then goto 1;
      end;
    p : = p.containing _structure
    end;
  if i = p.level then
    while qualifier[i ] = p.possessing _symbol do
      begin
      i : = i − 1;
      if i = 0 then goto 1;
      p : = p.containing _structure
      end;
  test : = false
1: end; (* test *)
```

Figure 9.25. Test for Partially Qualified Reference

The first two of these operations are used to build the range lists. The next three have been discussed in detail above. The last is needed for field selection in languages such as Pascal and LAX. Recall the treatment of field selection in Figure 9.17. There the environment in which the field identifier was sought consisted *only* of the field identifiers defined in the record yielded by *name*. This is exactly the function of *definition_in_range*. If we were to enter the range corresponding to the record and then use *current_definition*, we would not achieve the desired effect. If the identifier sought were not defined in the record's range, but was defined in an enclosing range, the latter definition would be found!

Unfortunately, *definition_in_range* must perform a search. (Actually, the search is slightly cheaper than the incorrect implementation outlined in the previous paragraph.) It might linearly search the list of definitions for the range representing the record type. This technique is advantageous if the number of fields in the record is not too large. Alternatively, we could associate a list of pairs (record type, pointer to a definition entry for a field with this selector) with each identifier and search that. This would be advantageous if the number of record types in which an identifier occurred was, on the average, smaller than the number of fields in a record.

9.3. Notes and References

Many language definitions use context-free syntax rules to indicate properties that are more easily checked with attribute computations. The compiler designer should not slavishly follow the language definition in this regard; checks should be apportioned between the context-free rules and attribution rules on the basis of simplicity.

In many compilers the semantic analysis is not treated as a separate task but as a by-product of parsing or code generation. The result is generally that the static semantic conditions are not fully verified, so erroneous programs are sometimes accepted as correct. We have taken the view here that semantic analysis is the fundamental target-independent task of the compiler, and should be the controlling factor in the development of the analysis module.

Many of the techniques presented here for describing specific language facilities were the result of experience with attribute grammars for PEARL [DIN 1980], Pascal [Kastens 1982] and Ada [Uhl 1982] developed at the Universität Karlsruhe. The representation of arbitrarily many types by lists was first discussed in conjunction with ALGOL 68 compilers [Peck 1971]. Koster [1969] described the recursive algorithm for ALGOL 68 mode equivalence using this representation.

The attribution process for Ada operator identification sketched in Section 9.1.4 is due to Persch and his colleagues [1979, 1980]. Baker [1982] has proposed a similar algorithm that computes attributes containing pointers to the operator nodes that must be identified. The advantage claimed by the author is that if the nodes can be accessed randomly, this means that a complete second traversal is unnecessary. Operator identification cannot be considered in isolation, however. It is not at all clear that a second complete traversal will not be required by other attribution, giving us the operator identification 'for free'. This illustrates the importance of constructing the *complete* attribute grammar without regard to number of traversals, and then processing it to determine the overall evaluation order.

Most authors combine the symbol and definition tables into a single 'symbol table' [Gries 1971, Bauer 1976, Aho 1977]. Separate tables appear in descriptions of multi-pass compilers and serve above all to reduce the main storage requirements [Naur 1964a]; the literature on ALGOL 68 [Peck 1971] is an exception. In his description of a multi-pass compiler for 'sequential Pascal', Hartmann [1977] separates the tables both to reduce the storage requirement and simplify the compiler structure.

The basic structure of the definition table was developed for ALGOL 60 [Randell 1964, Grau 1967, Gries 1971]. We have refined this structure to allow it to handle record types and incompletely-qualified identifiers [Busam 1971]. An algebraic specification of a module similar to that sketched at the end of Section 9.2 was given by Guttag [1975, 1977].

EXERCISES

9.1. Determine the visibility properties of Pascal labels. Write attribution rules that embody these properties. Treat the prohibition against jumping into a compound statement as a restriction on the visibility of the label *definition* (as opposed to the label *declaration*, which appears in the declaration part of the block).

9.2. Write the function *current _ definition* (Figure 9.1c).

9.3. Write the function *unambiguous* (Figure 9.2a).

9.4. Note that Figure 9.5 requires additional information: the implicit type of an identifier. Check the FORTRAN definition to find out how this information is determined. How would you make it available in the attribute grammar? Be specific, discussing the role of the lexical analyzer and parser in the process.

9.5. [Sale 1979] Give attribution rules and auxiliary functions to verify the definition before use constraint in Pascal. Assume that the environment is being passed along the text, as illustrated by Figure 9.4.

   a. Add a *depth* field to the definition record, and provide attribution rules that set this field to the static nesting depth at which the definition occurred.

   b. Add attribution rules that check the definition depth at each use of an identifier. Maintain a list of identifiers that have been used at a depth greater than their definition.

   c. When an identifier is defined, check the list to ensure that the identifier has not previously been used at a level greater than or equal to the current level when it was defined at a level less than the current level.

   d. Demonstrate that your rules correctly handle Figure 9.6.

9.6. What extensions to the environment attribute are required to support modules as defined in MODULA2?

9.7. Extend the representation of LAX types to handle enumerated types and records with variants, described as in Pascal.

9.8. Develop type representations analogous to Figure 9.7 for FORTRAN, ALGOL 60 and Ada.

9.9. Modify the procedure *type_equivalent* to handle the following alterations in the LAX definition:
   a. Structural type equivalence similar to that of ALGOL 68 is specified instead of the equivalence of A.3.1.
   b. Union types $union(t_1, \ldots, t_n)$ similar to those of ALGOL 68. The sequence of types is arbitrary and $union(t_1, union(t_2, t_3)) = union(union(t_1, t_2), t_3) = union(t_1, t_2, t_3)$.

9.10. Consider the case clause described in Figure 9.16.
   a. Formulate a procedure *value_unambiguous* to verify the uniqueness of the case labels.
   b. Alter the attribution rules to check the uniqueness at each label.
   c. Alter the attribution rules and extend the *value_unambiguous* procedure so that the labels may be constants of an enumerated type (see Exercise 9.7).

9.11. Prove the following relations for types t_1, t_2 and t_3, using the coercion rules defined in A.4.1:
   a. $balance(t_1, t_2) = balance(t_2, t_1)$
   b. $balance(balance(t_1, t_2), t_3) = balance(t_1, balance(t_2, t_3))$

9.12. Suppose that we chose to use the definition table discussed in Section 9.2 for a LAX compiler.
   a. [Guttag 1975, 1977] The definition table module operations were stated as operations of a package, with 'definition table' as an implied parameter. Restate them as operations of an abstract data type, making this dependence explicit.
   b. Two abstract data types, *range* and *definition_table*, are involved in this module. Which of the attributes in the LAX rules discussed in this chapter will be of type *range*, and which of type *definition_table*?
   c. Replace the computations of the attributes you listed in (b) with computations involving the operations of the definition table module. Does this change affect the traversal strategy?
   d. Given the modified rules of (c), do any of the attributes you listed in (b) satisfy the conditions for implementation as global variables? As global stacks? How do your answers to these questions bear upon the implementation of the definition table as a package vs. an abstract data type?

9.13. Develop definition tables for BASIC, FORTRAN, COBOL and Pascal.

9.14. Add the use before definition check of Exercise 9.5 to the definition table of Figure 9.21.

9.15. Give a detailed explanation of the problems encountered when analyzing Figure 9.22 if possession relation entries are stacked directly.

9.16. How must a Pascal definition table be set up to handle the *with* statement? (Hint: Build a stack of *with* expressions for each record type.)

9.17. Show the development during compilation of the definition table for the program of Figure 9.23 by giving a sequence of snapshots.

CHAPTER 10
Code Generation

The code generator creates a target tree from a structure tree. This task has, in principle, three subtasks:

- Resource allocation: Determine the resources that will be required and used during execution of instruction sequences. (Since in our case the resources consist primarily of registers, we shall speak of this as register allocation.)
- Execution order determination: Specify the sequence in which the descendants of a node will be evaluated.
- Code selection: Select the final instruction sequence corresponding to the operations appearing in the structure tree under the mapping discussed in Chapter 3.

In order to produce code optimum under a cost criterion that minimizes either program length or execution time, these subtasks must be intertwined and iterated. The problem is NP-complete even for simple machine architectures, which indicates that in practice the cost will be exponential in the number of structure tree nodes. In view of the simple form of the expressions that actually occur in programs, however, it is usually sufficient to employ linear-cost algorithms that do not necessarily produce the optimum code in all cases.

The approach taken in this chapter is to first map the source-language objects onto the memory of the target machine. An estimate of register usage is then made, and the execution order determined on the basis of that estimate. Finally, the behavior of the target machine is simulated during an execution-order traversal of the structure tree, driving the code selection and register assignment. The earlier estimate of register usage must guarantee that all register requirements can actually be met during the final traversal. The code may be suboptimal in some cases because the final register assignment cannot affect the execution order.

The computation graph discussed in Section 4.1.3 is implicit in the execution-order structure tree traversal. Chapter 13 will make the computation graph explicit, and discuss optimizing transformations that can be applied to it. If a compiler writer follows the strategies of Chapter 13, some of the optimization discussed here becomes redundant. Nevertheless, the three code generation subtasks introduced above remain unchanged.

Section 10.1 shows how the memory map is built up, starting with the storage requirements for elementary objects given by the implementor in the mapping specification of Section 3.4. We present the basic register usage estimation process in Section 10.2, and show how additional attributes can be used to improve the generated code. Target machine simulation and code selection are covered in Section 10.3.

10.1. Memory Mapping

Memory mapping determines the size and (relative) address of each object. In the process, it yields the sizes and alignments for all target types and the relative addresses of components of composite objects. This information is used to find access paths during the code selection and, in the case of static allocation, to generate storage reservation requests to the assembly module. It also constitutes most of the information needed to construct the type templates discussed in Section 3.3.3, if these are required.

The storage mapping process begins with elementary objects whose sizes and alignments are known. These are combined, step-by-step, into larger aggregates until an object is created whose base address cannot be determined until run time. We term such an object *allocatable*. Examples of allocatable objects are activation records and objects on the heap. Objects are characterized during this aggregation process by their size and relative address within the containing object. The sum of the base address determined at run time and the sequence of relative addresses of aggregates in which an object is contained yields the effective address of that object.

When the objects are combined, the compactness (packed/aligned) may be specified. This specification influences not only the relative address of a component, but also its size and the alignment of the composite object: If the source language permits value constraints (e.g. Pascal subranges), then a type can be characterized by both a size (for the unconstrained value set) and a minimum size (taking the constraint into account). For example, in Pascal an object defined to lie in a subrange 0..10 would have a minimum size of 4 (if sizes are expressed in bits) or 1 (if sizes are expressed in bytes) and a size equal to that of an unconstrained integer. When this object is combined with others in a packed composite object, its minimum size is assumed; when the composite object is not packed, the size is used.

The alignment of a composite object that is not packed is the least common multiple of the alignments of its components. When the object is packed, however, no alignment constraint is imposed.

The storage mapping process can, of course, only use objects of known length as components of other objects. As noted in Chapter 3, this means that activation records containing arrays whose bounds are not known until run time must be split into two parts; only the array descriptor is held in the static part. For languages like FORTRAN, in which all objects have fixed size, and in which each procedure is associated with one and only one local storage area, the procedure and its activation record can be combined into a single allocatable object. This object then becomes the basis for planning run-time overlay structure.

Figure 10.1 defines an interface for a memory mapping module. The module is independent of both source language and target machine. It can be used for packing to either the memory cell or the bit, depending upon the interpretation of the types *size* and *location*.

The basic idea of the storage module is that one has *areas* that may grow by accretion of *blocks* (objects of known size). An area whose growth has ceased becomes a block and can itself be added to other areas. Areas may grow either upward or downward in memory, and the packing attribute is specified individually for each area. (Both properties are fixed at the time the area is established.) Each area has a *growth point* that summarizes the current amount of the area's growth. For example, at the beginning of the variant part of a Pascal record, the storage mapping module notes the growth point; for each alternative it resets to that point. Since variants may be nested, the growth points must be saved on stacks (one per area) within the memory mapping module. After all of the alternatives have been specified, the growth point is advanced by the maximum length over all alternatives.

In Pascal, the size and alignment of each variant of a record must be kept so that *new* and *dispose* calls can be handled correctly. This requirement is most easily satisfied by adding two output parameters to both *back* and *combine* (Figure 10.1), making their calling sequences identical to that of *end_area*.

In areas that will become activation records, storage must be reserved for pointers to static and dynamic predecessors, plus the return address and possibly a template pointer. The size and alignment of this information is fixed by the mapping specification, which may also require space for saving registers and for other working storage. It is usually placed either at the beginning of the record or between the parameters and local variables. (In the latter case, the available access paths must permit both negative and positive offsets.) Finally, it is convenient to leave an activation record area open during the generation of code for the procedure body, so that compiler-generated temporaries may be added. Only upon completion of the code

type
   area = ···
   size = ···
   location = ···
   direction = (*up, down*);
   strategy = (*align , pack*);

procedure *new_area* (*d* : *direction* ; *s* : *strategy* ; **var** *a* : *area*);
   (* Establish a new memory area
     On entry -
       d = growth direction for this area
       s = growth strategy for this area
     On exit -
       a specifies the new area
   *)
   ··· ;

procedure *add_block* (*a* : *area* ; *s* : *size*; *alignment* : *integer* ; **var** *l* : *location*);
   (* Allocate a block in an area
     On entry -
       a specifies the area to which the block is to be added
       s = size of the block
       alignment = alignment of the block
     On exit -
       l = relative location of the first cell of the block
   *)
   ··· ;

procedure *end_area* (*a* : *area* ; **var** *s* : *size*; **var** *alignment* : *integer*);
   (* Terminate an area
     On entry -
       a specifies the area to be terminated
     On exit -
       s = size of the resulting block
       alignment = alignment of the resulting block
   *)
   ··· ;

procedure *mark*(*a* : *area*);
   (* Mark the current growth point of an area *)
   ··· ;

procedure *back*(*a* : *area*);
   (* Reset the growth point of an area to the last outstanding mark *)
   ··· ;

procedure *combine* (*a* : *area*);
   (* Erase the last outstanding mark in an area and
    reset the growth point to the maximum of all previous growths
   *)
   ··· ;

Figure 10.1. Memory Mapping Module Interface

selection will the area be closed and the size and alignment of the activation record finally determined.

In principle, the storage module is invoked at the beginning of code generation to fix the length, relative address and alignment of all declared objects and types. For languages like Ada, integration with the semantic analyzer is essential because object size may be interrogated by the program and must be used in verifying semantic conditions. Even in this case, however, we must continue to regard the storage module as a part of the synthesis task of the compiler; only the location of the calls, not the modular decomposition, is changed.

10.2. Target Attribution

In the simplest case we fix the execution order without regard to target machine register allocation. The code selector performs a depth-first, left-to-right traversal of the structure tree that corresponds directly to the postfix form of the expressions. It does not alter the left-to-right evaluation of the operands, since there is no additional information upon which to base such an alteration. If the number of registers available does not suffice to hold the intermediate results while computing the value of an expression then an ad hoc decision is made during the code generation about which intermediate value(s) should be left in memory. In general this strategy leads to greater register requirements and longer code than necessary; hence some planning is recommended. This planning results in computation of additional attributes.

In this section we consider the computation of seven attributes: *Register_count*, *store* and *operand_sequence* are used to determine the execution order, *desire* and *target_labels* provide information about the use of a result, *cost* and *decision* are used to modify the instruction sequence generated from a node. These attributes are evaluated by three distinct kinds of computation, which we treat in the following subsections: Register allocation (Section 10.2.1) is concerned with determining the temporary storage requirements of subtrees and hence the execution order. Targeting (Section 10.2.2) specifies desirable placement of results. Finally, algebraic identities (Section 10.2.3) can be used to obtain equivalent computations having better properties.

10.2.1. Register Allocation   We distinguish *global* register allocation, which holds over an entire procedure, from *local* register allocation, which controls the use of registers within expressions and influences the execution order. Further, we partition the task into *allocation*, by which we plan the register usage, and *assignment*, by which we fix the registers actually used for a specific purpose. Register assignment takes place during code selection, and will be discussed in Section 10.3.1; here we concern ourselves only with allocation.

Global register allocation begins with values specified by the implementation as being held permanently in registers. This might result in the following allocations for the IBM 370:

Register 15: Subprogram entry address
Register 14: Return address
Register 13: Local activation record base address
Register 12: Global activation record base address
Register 11: Base address for constants
Register 10: Code base address
Register 9: Code offset (Section 11.1.3)

Only two registers are allocated globally as activation record bases; registers for access to the activation records of intermediate contours are obtained from the local allocation, as are registers for stack and heap pointers.

Most compilers use no additional global register allocation. Further global allocation might, for example, be appropriate because most of a program's execution time is spent in the innermost loops. We could therefore stretch the register usage considerably and shorten the code if we reserved a fixed number of registers (say, 3) for the most-frequently used values of the innermost loops. The controlled variable of the loop is often one of these values. The simple approach of assigning the controlled variables of the innermost loops to the reserved registers gives very good results in practice; more complex analysis is generally unnecessary.

Upon completion of the global allocation, we must ensure that at least n registers always remain for local allocation. Here n is the maximum number of registers used in a single instruction. (For the IBM 370, $n = 4$ in the MVCL instruction.) A rule of thumb says that we should actually guarantee that $n + 1$ registers remain for local allocation, which allows at least one additional intermediate result or base address to be held in a register.

Pre-planning of local register allocation would be unnecessary if the number of available registers always sufficed for the number of simultaneously-existing intermediate results of an expression. Given a limited number of registers, however, we can guarantee this only for some subtrees. Outside of these, the register requirement is not fixed unambiguously: Altering the sequence of operations may change the number of registers required. Figure 10.2 shows an example.

The general strategy for local register allocation is to seek subtrees evaluable, possibly with rearrangement, using only the number of registers available to hold intermediate results. These subtrees can be coded without additional store instructions. We choose the largest, and generate code to evalu-

$$(x + y) / (a*b + c*d)$$

a) A LAX expression

LE	0,x		LE	2,a
AE	0,y		ME	2,b
LE	2,a		LE	0,c
ME	2,b		ME	0,d
LE	4,c		AER	2,0
ME	4,d		LE	0,x
AER	2,4		AE	0,y
DER	0,2		DER	0,2
(uses 3 registers)			(uses 2 registers)	

b) Two possible IBM 370 implementations

Figure 10.2. Dependence of Register Usage on Evaluation Order

ate it and store the result. All registers are then again available to hold intermediate results in the next subtree.

Consider an expression represented as a structure tree and a machine with n identical registers r_i. The machine's instructions have one of the following forms:

- Load: $r_i := memory\_location$
- Store: $memory\_location := r_i$
- Compute: $r_i := op(v_j, \ldots, v_k)$, where v_h may be either a register or a memory location.

The machine has various computation instructions, each of which requires specific operands in registers and memory locations. (Note that a load instruction can be considered to compute the identity function, and require a single operand in a memory location.)

We say that a program fragment is in *normal form* if it is written as $P_1 J_1 \cdots P_{s-1} J_{s-1} P_s$ such that each J is a store instruction, each P is a sequence containing no store instructions, and all of the registers are free immediately after each store instruction. Let $I_1 \cdots I_n$ be one of the sequences containing no stores. We term this sequence *strongly contiguous* if, whenever I_i is used to compute an operand of I_k ($i < k$) all I_j such that $i \leqslant j < k$ are also used in the computation of operands of I_k. The sequence $P_1 J_1 \cdots P_s$ is in *strong normal form* if P_q is strongly contiguous for all $1 \leqslant q \leqslant s$.

Aho [1976] shows that, provided no operand or result has a size exceeding the capacity of a single register, an optimal program to evaluate an expression tree on our assumed machine can be written in strong normal form. (The criterion for optimality is minimum program length.) Thus to achieve an optimal program it suffices to determine a suitable sequence in which to evaluate the operands of each operator and — in case the register requirements exceed n — to introduce store operations at the proper points. The result can be described in terms of three attributes: *register_count*, *store* and *operand_sequence*. *Register_count* specifies the maximum number of registers needed simultaneously at any point during the computation of the subtree. *Store* is a Boolean attribute that is true if the result of this node must be stored. *Operand_sequence* is an array of integers giving the order in which the operands of the node should be evaluated. A Boolean attribute can be used if the maximum number of operands is 2.

The conditions for a strong normal form stated above are fulfilled on most machines by floating point expressions with single-length operands and results. For integer expressions they generally do not hold, since multiplication of single-length values produces a double-length result and division requires a double-length dividend. Under these conditions the optimal

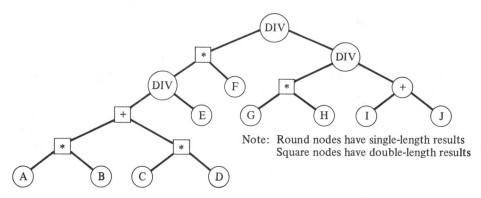

Note: Round nodes have single-length results
Square nodes have double-length results

a) An expression involving single- and double-length values

```
MOV    A,R0    (R0,R1):=A*B
MUL    B,R0
MOV    C,R2    (R2,R3):=C*D
MUL    D,R2
ADD    R3,R1   (R0,R1):=(R0,R1)+(R2,R3)
ADC    R2
ADD    R2,R0
DIV    E,R0    R0:=(R0,R1) DIV E
MOV    G,R2    (R2,R3):=G*H
MUL    H,R2
MOV    I,R1    R1:=I+J
ADD    J,R1
DIV    R1,R2   R2:=(R2,R3) DIV R1
MUL    F,R0    (R0,R1):=R0*F
DIV    R2,R0   R0:=(R0,R1) DIV R2
```

b) An optimal PDP11 program to evaluate (a)

Figure 10.3. Oscillation

instruction sequence may involve 'oscillation'. Figure 10.3a shows a tree that requires oscillation in any optimal program. The square nodes produce double-length values, the round nodes single-length values. An optimal PDP11 program to evaluate the expression appears as Figure 10.3b. The PDP11 is an 'even/odd machine' — one that requires double-length values to be held in a pair of adjacent registers, the first of which has an even register number. No polynomial algorithm that yields an optimal solution in this case is known.

Under the conditions that the strong normal form theorem holds and, with the exception of the load instruction, all machine instructions take their operands from registers, the following register allocation technique leads to minimum register requirements: For the case of two operands with register requirements $k_1 > k_2$, always evaluate the one requiring k_1 registers first. The result remains as an intermediate value in a register, so that while evaluating the other operand, $k_2 + 1$ registers are actually required. Since $k_1 > k_2$ however, the total register requirement cannot exceed k_1.

When $k_1 = k_2$, either operand may be evaluated first. The evaluation of the first operand will still require k_1 registers and the result remains in a register. Thus $k_1 + 1$ registers will be needed to evaluate the second operand, leading to an overall requirement for $k_1 + 1$ registers. If $k_1 = n$ then it is not possible to evaluate the entire expression in the registers available, although either subexpression can be evaluated entirely in registers. We therefore evaluate one operand (usually the second) and store the result. This leaves all n registers free to evaluate the other operand. Figure 10.4 formalizes the computation of these attributes.

If the second operand may be either in a register or in memory we apply

rule *expression* $::=$ *simple_operand* .
attribution
   expression.register_count $\leftarrow$ 1;
   expression.operand_sequence $\leftarrow$ *true*,

rule *expression* $::=$ *expression operator expression* .
attribution
   expression[1].*operand_sequence* $\leftarrow$
     expression[2].*register_count* $>$ *expression*[3].*register_count* ;
   expression[1].*register_count* $\leftarrow$
     if *expression*[2].*register_count* $=$ *expression*[3].*register_count* **then**
       min(*expression*[2].*register_count* $+ 1, n$)
     else max(*expression*[2].*register_count* , *expression*[3].*register_count*) ;
   expression[2].*store* $\leftarrow$ *false*;
   expression[3].*store* $\leftarrow$
     expression[2].*register_count* $= n$ **and**
     expression[3].*register_count* $= n$;

Figure 10.4. Local Register Allocation and Execution Order Determination

the same rules, but begin with simple operands having a *register_count* of 0; further, the left operand count is replaced by max (*expression* [2].*register_count*,1) since the first operand must always be loaded and therefore has a cost of at least one register. Extension to the case in which the second operand *must* be in memory (as for halfword arithmetic on the IBM 370) presents some additional problems (Exercise 10.3). For integer multiplication and division we must take account of the fact that the result (respectively the first operand) requires two registers. The resulting sequence is not always optimal in this case.

Several independent sets of registers can also be dealt with in this manner; examples are general registers and floating point registers or general registers and index registers. The problem of the Univac 1108, in which the index registers and general registers overlap, requires additional thought.

On machines like the PDP11 or Motorola 68000, which have stack instructions in addition to registers or the ability to execute operations with all operands and the result in memory, optimization of the local register allocation is a very difficult problem. The minimum register requirement in these cases is always 0, so that we must include the program length or execution time as cost criteria. The result is that in general memory-to-memory operations are only reasonable if no operands are available in registers, and also the result does not appear in a register and will not be required in one. Operations involving the stack usually have longer execution time than operations of the same length involving registers. On the other hand, the operations to move data between registers and the stack are usually shorter and faster than register-memory moves. As a general principle, then, intermediate results that must be stored because of insufficient registers should be placed on the stack.

10.2.2. Targeting   Targeting attributes are inherited attributes used to provide information about the desired destination of a result or target of a jump.

We use the targeting attribute *desire* to indicate that a particular operand must be in a register of a particular class. If a descendant can arrange to have its result in a suitable register at no extra cost, this should be done. Figure 10.5 gives the attribution rules for expressions containing the four basic arithmetic operations, assuming the IBM 370 as the target machine. This machine requires a multiplicand to be in an odd register, and a dividend to be in a register pair. We therefore target a single-length dividend to the even-numbered register of the pair, so that it can be extended to double-length with a simple shift.

In the case of the commutative operators addition and multiplication, we target both operands to the desired register class. Then if the register allocation can satisfy our preference for the second operand but not the first, we make use of commutativity (Section 10.2.3) and interchange the operands. If neither of the preferences can be satisfied, then an instruction to move the

type *register_class* = (*dont_care*, *even*, *odd*, *pair*);

rule *expression* ::= *expression operator expression* .
attribution
  expression[2].*desire* ←
  case *operator.operator* **of**
    plus, *minus* :
      if *expression*[1].*desire* =*pair* **then** *even*
      else *expression*[1].*desire* ;
    times: *odd* ;
    divided_by : *even*
    end;
  expression[3].*desire* ←
  case *operator.operator* **of**
    plus :
      if *expression*[1].*desire* =*pair* **then** *even*
      else *expression*[1].*desire* ;
    times: *odd* ;
    otherwise *dont_care*
    end;

Figure 10.5. Even/Odd Register Targeting for the IBM 370

information to the proper register will be generated as a part of the coding of the multiplication or division operator. No disadvantages arise from inability to satisfy the stated preference. This example illustrates the importance of the non-binding nature of targeting information. We propagate our desire to *both* branches in the hope it will be satisfied on *one* of them. If it is satisfied on one branch then it is actually spurious on the other, and no cost should be incurred by trying to satisfy it there.

Many Boolean expressions can be evaluated using conditional jumps (Section 3.2.3), and it is necessary to specify the address at which execution continues after each jump. Figure 10.6 shows the attribution used to obtain short-circuit evaluation, in the context of a conditional jump. (If short-circuit evaluation is not permitted by the language, the only change is to delay generation of the conditional jumps until after all operands not containing Boolean operators have been evaluated, as discussed in Section 3.2.3.) Labels (and procedure entry points) are specified by references to target tree elements, for which the assembler must later substitute addresses. Thus the type *assembler_symbol* is defined not by the code generator, but by the assembler (Section 11.1.1).

Given the attribution of Figure 10.6, it is easy to see how code is generated: A conditional jump instruction is produced following the code to evaluate each operand that contains no further Boolean operators (e.g. a relation). The target of the jump is the label that does not immediately follow the operand, and the condition is chosen accordingly. Boolean operator

type *boolean_labels* = **record**
  false_label, true_label : *assembler_symbol* ;
  immediate_successor : *boolean* ;
  end;

rule *conditional_clause* :: =
  'if' boolean_expression 'then' statement_list 'else' statement_list 'end' .
attribution
  boolean_expression.location ← *N_assembler_symbol* ;
  conditional_clause.then_location ← *N_assembler_symbol* ;
  conditional_clause.else_location ← *N_assembler_symbol* ;
  boolean_expression.jump_target ←
    N_boolean_labels (
      conditional_clause.else_location ,
      conditional_clause.then_location ,
      true); (* *true* target follows immediately *)

rule *boolean_expression* :: =
  boolean_expression boolean_operator boolean_expression .
attribution
  boolean_expression[2].*location* ← *boolean_expression*[1].*location* ;
  boolean_expression[3].*location* ← *N_assembler_symbol* ;
  boolean_expression[2].*jump_target* ←
    if *boolean_operator.operator* = *'or'* **then**
      N_boolean_labels (
        boolean_expression[3].*location* ,
        boolean_expression[1].*jump_target.true_label* ,
        false) (* *false* target follows immediately *)
    else (* operator must be **and** *)
      N_boolean_labels (
        boolean_expression[1].*jump_target.false_label* ,
        boolean_expression[3].*location* ,
        true);
  boolean_expression[3].*jump_target* ← *boolean_expression*[1].*jump_target* ;

rule *boolean_expression* :: = *'not' boolean_expression* .
attribution
  boolean_expression[2].*location* ← *boolean_expression*[1].*location* ,
  boolean_expression[2].*jump_target* ←
    N_boolean_labels (
      boolean_expression[1].*jump_target.true_label* ,
      boolean_expression[1].*jump_target.false_label* ,
      not *boolean_expression*[1].*jump_target.immediate_successor*);

Figure 10.6. Jump Targeting for Boolean Expression Evaluation

nodes generate no code at all. Moreover, the execution order is fixed; no use of commutativity is allowed.

10.2.3. Use of Algebraic Identities   The goal of the attribution discussed in Section 10.2.1 was to reduce the register requirements of an
expression, which usually leads to a reduction in the length of the code
sequence. The length of the code sequence can often be reduced further
through use of the algebraic identities summarized in Figure 10.7a. We distinguish two steps in this reduction:

- Reduction of the number of computational instructions.
- Reduction of the number of load instructions.

The number of computational instructions can be reduced by, for example,
using the identities of Figure 10.7a to remove a change of sign or combine it
with a load instruction (unary complement elimination). Load operations
can be avoided by applying commutativity when the right operand of a
commutative operator is already in a register and the left operand is still in
memory. Figures 10.7b-d give a simple example of these ideas.

None of the identities of Figure 10.7a involve the associative or distributive laws of algebra. Computers do not obey these axioms, and hence
transformations based upon them are not safe. Also, if the target machine
uses a radix-complement representation for negative numbers then the iden-

$$x + y = y + x$$
$$x - y = x + (-y) = -(y - x)$$
$$-(-x) = x$$
$$x * y = y * x = (-x)*(-y)$$
$$-(x * y) = (-x)*y = x*(-y)$$

a) Identities for integer and real operands

L	1,x
LNR	1,1
L	2,y
S	2,z
MR	0,2

b) Computation of $(-x)*(y - z)$

L	2,z
S	2,y
L	1,x
MR	0,2

c) Computation of $x*(z - y)$, which is equivalent to (b)

L	1,z
S	1,y
M	0,x

d) Computation of $(z - y)*x$, which is equivalent to (c)

Figure 10.7. Algebraic Identities

tity $-(-x)=x$ fails when x is the most negative representable value, leaving commutativity of addition and multiplication as the only safe identities. As implementors, however, we are free to specify the range of values representable using a given type. By simply stating that the most negative value does not lie in that range, we can use all of the identities listed in Figure 10.7a. This does not unduly constrain the programmer, since its only effect is to make the range symmetric and thus remove an anomaly of the hardware arithmetic. (We normally remove the analogous anomaly of sign-magnitude representation, the negative zero, without debate.)

Although use of algebraic identities can reduce the register requirement, the decisive cost criterion is the code size. Here we assume that every instruction has the same cost; in practical applications the respective instruction lengths must be introduced. Let us also assume, for the moment, a machine that only provides register-register arithmetic instructions. All operands must therefore be loaded into registers before they are used. We shall restrict ourselves to addition, subtraction, multiplication and negation in this example and assume that multiplication yields a single-length result. The basic idea consists of attaching a synthesized attribute, *cost*, to each expression. *Cost* specifies the minimum costs (number of instructions) to compute the result of the expression in its correct and inverse (negated) form. It is determined from the costs of the operation, the operand computations, and any complementing required. An inherited attribute, *decision*, is then computed on the basis of these costs and specifies the actual form (correct or inverse) that should be used.

To generate code for a node, we must know which operation to actually implement. (In general this may differ from the operator appearing in the structure tree.) If the actual operation is not commutative then we have to know whether the operands are to be taken in the order given by the structure tree or not. Finally, we need to know whether the result must be complemented. As shown in Table 10.8, all of this information can be deduced from the structure tree operator and the forms of the operands and result.

The k column of Table 10.8 gives the cost of the operation, including any complementing. This information is used to obtain the minimum costs of the correct and inverse forms of the expression as shown in Figure 10.9: *Best* is invoked with the structure tree operator and the costs of all combinations of operand computations. It tests all of the possibilities, finding the combination of operand forms that minimizes the cost of computing each of the possible result forms. Figure 10.10 gives the attribution rules. Note that the costs assessed to simple operands in Figure 10.10 do not include the cost of a load operation. Loads and stores are completely determined by the local register allocation process for a machine with only register-register instructions.

Let us now consider a machine that has an additional instruction for each binary arithmetic operation. These additional instructions require the left operand value to be in a register and the right operand value to be in

Table 10.8. Unary Complement Elimination

Tree Node	Result Form	Operand Forms	k	Reverse Operands	Negate	Actual Operation	Method
$a+b$	c	cc	1	false	false	plus	$a+b$
		ci	1	false	false	minus	$a-(-b)$
		ic	1	true	false	minus	$b-(-a)$
		ii	2	false	true	plus	$-(-a+(-b))$
	i	cc	2	false	true	plus	$-(a+b)$
		ci	1	true	false	minus	$-b-a$
		ic	1	false	false	minus	$-a-b$
		ii	1	false	false	plus	$-a+(-b)$
$a-b$	c	cc	1	false	false	minus	$a-b$
		ci	1	false	false	plus	$a+(-b)$
		ic	2	false	true	plus	$-(-a+b)$
		ii	1	true	false	minus	$-b-(-a)$
	i	cc	1	true	false	minus	$b-a$
		ci	2	false	true	plus	$-(-a+(-b))$
		ic	1	false	false	plus	$-a+b$
		ii	1	false	false	minus	$-a-(-b)$
$a*b$	c	cc	1	false	false	times	$a*b$
		ci	2	false	true	times	$-(a*(-b))$
		ic	2	false	true	times	$-(-a*b)$
		ii	1	false	false	times	$-a*(-b)$
	i	cc	2	false	true	times	$-(a*b)$
		ci	1	false	false	times	$a*(-b)$
		ic	1	false	false	times	$-a*b$
		ii	2	false	true	times	$-(-a*(-b))$

c means that the sign of the operand is not inverted
i means that the sign of the operand is inverted
k is a typical cost of the operation in instructions

memory. Since the best choice of computation depends upon the operand locations, we must extend Table 10.8 to include this information. Table 10.11 shows such an extension for the integer addition operator. The k column of Table 10.11 includes the cost of a load instruction when both operands are in memory.

We took the operand location as fixed in deriving Table 10.11. This meant, for example, that when the correct left operand was in memory and the inverted right operand was in a register we used the sequence *subtract*, *negate* to obtain the correct value of the expression (Table 10.11, row 7). We could also have used the sequence *load, subtract,* but this would have increased the register requirements. If we allow the unary complement elimination to alter the register requirements then it must be integrated with the local register allocation, increasing the number of attribute dependencies

type
  form = (*correct*, *inverse*);
  combination = (*cc*, *ci*, *ic*, *ii*);
  cost_specification = **array** [*correct..inverse*] **of record**
    length : *integer*;
    operands : *combination*
    end;

function *best* (*op* : *operator*; *kcc*, *kci*, *kic*, *kii* :*integer*): *cost_specification*;
  (* Determine the cheapest combination
    On entry-
      op = Structure tree operator
      kpq = Sum of the operand costs for combination *pq*
    On exit -
      best = Cost of the optimum instructions yielding, respectively, the
        correct and inverted values of the expression
  *)

var
    operand_length : **array** [*ci..ii*] **of** *integer*;
    cost : *cost_specification*;
    next : *integer*;

begin (* *best* *)
operand_length [*ci*] := *kci*;
operand_length [*ic*] := *kic*;
operand_length [*ii*] := *kii*;
for *f* := *correct* **to** *inverse* **do**
  begin
  cost [*f*].*length* := *kcc* + *k* [*op,f,cc*]; *cost* [*f*].*operands* := *cc*;
  for *pq* := *ci* **to** *ii* **do**
    begin
    next := *operand_length* [*pq*] + *k* [*op,f,pq*]; (* *k* from Table 10.8.*)
    if *cost* [*f*].*length* > *next* **then**
      begin
      cost [*f*].*length* := *next*; *cost* [*f*].*operands* := *pq*
      end
    end
  end;
best := *cost*
end; (* *best* *)

Figure 10.9. The Cost Attribute

and possibly requiring a more complex tree traversal. Our approach is
optimal provided that the cost of a load instruction is never less than the cost
of negating a value in a register.

rule *assignment* ::= *name* ':=' *expression* .
attribution
  expression.decision ← *correct* ;

rule *expression* ::= *denotation* .
attribution
  expression.cost ←
    N _cost _specification((* Combination is a dummy value *)
      0, *cc*,   (* Load instruction only *)
      0, *cc*);   (* Negative constant is stored *)

rule *expression* ::= *name* .
attribution
  expression.cost ←
    N _cost _specification((* Combination is a dummy value *)
      0, *cc*,   (* Load instruction only *)
      1, *cc*);   (* Load and complement *)

rule *expression* ::= *expression binary _operator expression* .
attribution
  expression [1].*cost* ←
    best (
      binary _operator.op,
      expression [2].*cost* [*correct*].*length* + *expression* [3].*cost* [*correct*].*length*,
      expression [2].*cost* [*correct*].*length* + *expression* [3].*cost* [*inverse*].*length*,
      expression [2].*cost* [*inverse*].*length* + *expression* [3].*cost* [*correct*].*length*,
      expression [2].*cost* [*inverse*].*length* + *expression* [3].*cost* [*inverse*].*length*);
  expression [2].*decision* ←
    if *expression* [1].*cost* [*expression* [1].*decision*].*operands* **in** *[cc , ci]* **then** *correct*
    else *inverse* ;
  expression [3].*decision* ←
    if *expression* [1].*cost* [*expression* [1].*decision*].*operands* **in** *[cc , ic]* **then** *correct*
    else *inverse* ;

rule *expression* ::= *unary _operator expression* .
attribution
  expression [1].*cost* ←
    best (
      unary _operator.op,
      expression [2].*cost* [*correct*].*length*,
      maxint, *maxint*,   (* *ci , ic* are invalid in this case *)
      expression [2].*cost* [*inverse*].*length*);
  expression [2].*decision* ←
    if *expression* [1].*cost* [*expression* [1].*decision*].*operands* = *cc* **then** *correct*
    else *inverse* ;

Figure 10.10. Unary Complement Costing

Table 10.11. Addition on a Machine with Both Memory and Register Operands

Result Form	Operand Forms	Operand Locations	k	Reverse Operands	Negate	Actual Operation	Method
c	cc	rr	1	false	false	plus	$a+b$
		rm	1	false	false	plus	$a+b$
		mr	1	true	false	plus	$b+a$
		mm	2	false	false	plus	$a+b$
	ci	rr	1	false	false	minus	$a-(-b)$
		rm	1	false	false	minus	$a-(-b)$
		mr	2	true	true	minus	$-(-b-a)$
		mm	2	false	false	minus	$a-(-b)$
	ic	rr	1	true	false	minus	$b-(-a)$
		rm	2	false	true	minus	$-(-a-b)$
		mr	1	true	false	minus	$b-(-a)$
		mm	2	true	false	minus	$b-(-a)$
	ii	rr	2	false	true	plus	$-(-a+(-b))$
		rm	2	false	true	plus	$-(-a+(-b))$
		mr	2	true	true	plus	$-(-b+(-a))$
		mm	3	false	true	plus	$-(-a+(-b))$
i	cc	rr	2	false	true	plus	$-(a+b)$
		rm	2	false	true	plus	$-(a+b)$
		mr	2	true	true	plus	$-(b+a)$
		mm	3	false	true	plus	$-(a+b)$
	ci	rr	1	true	false	minus	$-b-a$
		rm	2	false	true	minus	$-(a-(-b))$
		mr	1	true	false	minus	$-b-a$
		mm	2	true	false	minus	$-b-a$
	ic	rr	1	false	false	minus	$-a-b$
		rm	1	false	false	minus	$-a-b$
		mr	2	true	true	minus	$-(b-(-a))$
		mm	2	false	false	minus	$-a-b$
	ii	rr	1	false	false	plus	$-a+(-b)$
		rm	1	false	false	plus	$-a+(-b)$
		mr	1	true	false	plus	$-b+(-a)$
		mm	2	false	false	plus	$-a+(-b)$

c means that the sign of the operand is not inverted
i means that the sign of the operand is inverted
r means that the value of the operand is in a register
m means that the value of the operand is in memory
k is a typical cost of the operation in instructions

When we apply algebraic identities on a machine with both register-register and register-memory instructions, the local register allocation process should assume that each computational instruction can accept any of its operands either in a register or in memory, and returns its result to a register (the general model proposed in Section 10.2.1). This assumption leads to the proper register requirement, and allows complete freedom in applying the identities. Local register allocation decides the evaluation order of the operands, but leaves open the question of which operand is left and which is right. Algebraic identities, on the other hand, deal with the choice of left and right operands but make no decisions about evaluation order.

10.3. Code Selection

Although the techniques of the previous sections largely determine the shape of the generated code, a number of problems remain open. These include the final assignment of registers and the question of which instructions will actually implement a previously-specified operation: On the IBM 370, for example, can a constant be loaded with an LA instruction or must it be stored as a literal? Does an addition of two addresses require a separate add instruction, or can the addition be carried out during computation of the effective address of the following instruction?

10.3.1. Machine Simulation   The relationship between values computed by the program being compiled and the machine resources that will be used to represent them during execution can be characterized by a sequence of *machine states*. These states form the pre- and post-conditions for the generated instructions. We could include the machine state as an attribute in the structure tree and specify it in advance by attribution rules. This would mean, for example, that we would combine register assignment with local register allocation and thereby specify the final register numbers for operands and results. Such a strategy complicates a number of optimizations, however. Examples are the re-use of intermediate results that remain in registers from previous computations in the same expression, and the delay of store instructions discussed below. Thus we assume that, during the execution-order traversal of the structure tree in which code selection takes place, a machine simulation is used to determine the run-time machine state as closely as possible.

Every value computed by the program and every allocatable resource of the target machine is (conceptually) specified by a *descriptor*. The machine state consists of links between these descriptors, indicating the relationship between the values and the resources representing them at a given point in the execution sequence. Figure 10.12 shows typical descriptor layouts for implementing LAX on the IBM 370.

Constants that might appear in the address field of the instruction, and constants whose values are to be processed further by the code generator, are described by the value class *literal_value*. Other constants, like strings and floating point numbers, will be placed in storage and consequently appear as memory values.

type
  main_storage_access = **record**
    base, *index*; ↑ *value_descriptor*;
    displacement : *internal_int*;
    end;
  value_class = ((* Current access *)
    literal_value,   (* Manipulable integer constant *)
    label_reference,   (* Explicitly-referenced label *)
    procedure_reference,   (* Explicitly-referenced procedure *)
    general_register,   (* Single general register *)
    register_pair,   (* Adjacent even/odd general registers *)
    floating_point_register, (* Single floating point register *)
    memory_address,   (* Pointer to a memory location *)
    memory_value);   (* Contents of a memory location *)
  value_descriptor = **record**
    tmode : *target_type*;
    case *class* : *value_class* **of**
      literal_value :
        (*lval* : *internal_int*);
      label_reference, *procedure_reference*:
        (*code* : *assembler_symbol*;
        environment : ↑ *value_descriptor*);
      general_register, *register_pair*, *floating_point_register* :
        (*reg* : ↑ *register_descriptor*);
      memory_address, *memory_value* :
        (*location* : *main_storage_access*)
    end;
  register_state = ((* Current usage *)
    free,   (* Unused *)
    copy,   (* A copy exists in memory *)
    unique,   (* No other copy available *)
    locked);   (* Not available for assignment *)
  register_descriptor = **record**
    state : *register_state*;
    content : ↑ *value_descriptor*;
    memory_copy : *main_storage_access*;
    end;

Figure 10.12. Descriptors for Implementing LAX on the IBM 370

Label and procedure references are represented by closures (Section 2.5.2), leaving the code location to be defined by the assembler and indicating the proper environment by an execution-time value. Note that this representation is used only for an explicit label or procedure reference; the closure for a label or procedure-type variable or parameter is not known at compile time and must therefore appear as a memory or register value.

The value descriptors of Figure 10.12 contain no information for the storage classes 'program counter' and 'condition code' (Section 3.1.1), since these classes occur only implicitly in IBM 370 instructions. The situation could be different on the PDP11, where explicit assignments to the program counter are possible. Computers like the Motorola 68000 and PDP11, which provide stack instructions, also require information about the storage class 'stack'. The actual representation in the descriptor depends upon how many stacks there are and whether only the top element or also lower elements can be accessed. We restrict ourselves here to two storage classes: 'main storage' and 'registers'. Similar techniques can be used for other storage classes.

When an access function is realizable within a given addressing structure, we say that the accessed object is *addressable* within that structure. If an object required by the computation is not addressable then the code generator must issue instructions to manipulate the state, making it addressable, before it can be used. These manipulations can be divided into two groups, those required by source language concepts and those required by limitations on the addressing structure of the target machine. Implementing a reference with a pointer variable would be an example of the former, while loading a value into an index register illustrates the latter. The exact division between the groups is determined by the structure of the main storage access function implemented in the descriptors. We assume that every non-literal leaf of the structure tree is addressable by this access function. The main storage access function of Figure 10.12 is stated in terms of a base, an index and a displacement. The base refers to an allocatable object (Section 10.1) whose address may, in general, be computed during execution. The index is an integer value computed during execution, while the displacement is fixed at compile time. Index and displacement values are summed to yield the relative address of the accessed location within the allocatable object referred to by the base.

If the access is to statically-allocated storage then the 'allocatable object' to which the accessed object belongs is the entire memory. We indicate this special case by a **nil** base, and the displacement becomes the static address. A more interesting situation arises when the access is to storage in the activation record of a LAX procedure. Figure 10.13a shows a LAX program with five static nesting levels. If we associate activation records only with procedures (Section 3.3.2) then we need consider only three levels. Value descriptors for the three components of the assignment in the body of q could be constructed as shown in Figure 10.13b.

The level array is built into the compiler with an appropriate maximum size. When the compiler begins to translate a procedure, it ensures one value descriptor for each level up to the level of the procedure. Initially, the descriptor at level 1 indicates that the global activation record base address can be found in register 12 and the descriptor at the procedure's level indicates that the local activation record base address can be found in register 13. Base addresses for other activation records can be found by following

declare
a : *integer* ;
procedure *p* ;
  declare
  b : *integer* ;
  procedure *q* (*c* : *integer*); *a* := *b* + *c*
  begin
  b := 1; *q* (2)
  end
begin
p
end

a) A LAX program

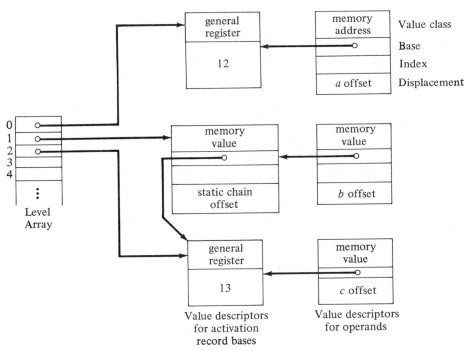

b) Value descriptors for the IBM 370

Figure 10.13. Referencing Dynamic Storage

the static chain, as indicated by the descriptor at level 2. This initial condition is determined by the mapping specification. We are assuming here that the LAX-to-IBM 370 mapping specification makes the global register allocation proposed at the beginning of Section 10.2.1.

When a value descriptor is created for a variable, its base is simply a copy of the level array element corresponding to the variable's static nesting depth. (The program is assumed at level 0 here.) The index field for a simple variable's access function is **nil** (indicated in Figure 10.13b by an empty field) and the displacement is the offset of the variable within the activation record. For array variables, the index field points to the value descriptor of the index, and the displacement is the fictitious offset discussed in Section 3.2.2.

The access function for a value may change as instructions that manipulate the value are generated. For example, suppose that we generate code to carry out the assignment in Figure 10.13a, starting from the machine state described by Figure 10.13b. We might first consider generating a load instruction for b. Unfortunately, b is not addressable; the IBM 370 load instruction requires that the base be in a register. Thus we must first obtain a register (say, general register 1) and load the base address for the activation record at level 2 into it. When this instruction has been generated, we change the value descriptor for the base to have a value class of *general_register* and indicate general register 1. Generation of the load for b is now possible, and the value descriptor for b must be altered to reflect the fact that it is in (say) general register 3.

There is one register descriptor for each register used by the code generator. This includes both the registers controlled by the local register allocation and globally-assigned registers with fixed interpretations. The local register allocation process discussed in Section 10.2.1 schedules movement of values into and out of registers. As we noted at the beginning of the chapter, however, only an *estimate* of the register requirements is possible. The code selection process, working with the machine state description, may be able to reduce the register count below that estimated by the local register allocator. As a consequence, it may be unnecessary to store an intermediate value whose node had been given the *store* attribute. For this reason, we defer the generation of store instructions requested by these attributes in the hope that the register holding the value will not actually be required before the value can be used again. Using this strategy, we may have to free the register 'unexpectedly' in a context where the value descriptor for the value is not directly accessible. This means that the register descriptor of a register containing a value must point to the value descriptor for the contained value. If the register must be freed, a store instruction can be emitted and the value descriptor updated to reflect the current location of the value.

Immediately after a load or store instruction, the contents of a register are a copy of the contents of some memory location. This 'copy' relationship represents a condition that occurs during execution, and to specify it the register descriptor must be able to define a memory access function. This access function is copied into the register descriptor from a value descriptor at the time the two are linked; it might describe the location from which the register was loaded or that to which it was stored. Some care must be exercised in deciding when to establish such a relationship: The code gen-

if *free* registers exist **then** choose one arbitrarily
else if *copy* registers exist **then** choose the least-recently accessed
else
  begin
  choose the least-recently accessed *unique* register;
  allocate a temporary memory location;
  emit a store instruction;
  end;
if chosen register has an associated value descriptor **then**
  de-link the value descriptor;
lock the chosen register;

Figure 10.14. Register Management

erator must be able to guarantee that the value in memory will not be altered by side effects without explicitly terminating the relationship. Use of programmer-defined variables is particularly dangerous because of this requirement, but use of compiler-generated temporaries and activation record bases is safe.

The register assignment algorithm should not make a random choice when asked to assign a register (Figure 10.14). If some register is in state *free*, it may be assigned without penalty. A register whose state is *copy* may be assigned without storing its value, but if this value is needed again it will have to be reloaded. The contents of a register whose state is *unique* must be stored before the register can be reassigned, and a *locked* register cannot be reassigned at all. All globally-allocated registers are locked throughout the simulation. The states of locally-allocated registers change during the simulation; they are always free at a label.

As shown in Figure 10.14, the register assignment algorithm locks a register when it is assigned. The code selection routine requesting the register then links it to the proper value descriptor, generating any code necessary to place the value into the register. If the value is the result of a node with the *store* attribute then the register descriptor state is changed to *unique*. This makes the register available for reassignment, and guarantees that the value will be saved if the register is actually reassigned. When a value descriptor is destroyed, it is first de-linked from any associated register descriptor. The state of the register descriptor is changed to *free* if the register descriptor specifies no memory copy; otherwise it is changed to *copy*. In either case it is available for reassignment without any requirement to store its contents. The local register allocation algorithm of Section 10.2.1 guarantees that the simulator can never block due to all registers being locked.

10.3.2. Code Transformation   We traverse the structure tree in execution order, carrying out a simulation of the target machine's behavior, in order to obtain the final transformation of the structure tree into a sequence of instructions. When the traversal reaches a leaf of the tree, we construct a value descriptor for the object that the leaf represents. When the traversal reaches an interior node, a decision table specific to that kind of node is consulted. There is at least one decision table for every abstract operation, and if the traversal visits the node more than once then each visit may have its own decision table. The condition stubs of these decision tables involve attributes of the node and its descendants.

Figure 10.15 shows a decision table for integer addition on the IBM 370 that is derived from Table 10.11. The condition stub uses the form and location attributes discussed in Section 10.2.3 to select a single column, and the elements of the action stub corresponding to X's in that column are carried out in sequence from top to bottom. These actions are based primarily upon the value descriptors for the operands, but they may interrogate any of the node's attributes. They are basically of two kinds, machine state manipulation and instruction generation, although instructions must often be generated as a side effect of manipulating the machine state.

Four machine state manipulation actions appear in Figure 10.15: $swap(l, r)$ simply interchanges the contents of the value descriptors for the left and right operands. A register is allocated by $lreg(l, desire)$, taking into account the preference discussed in Section 10.2.2. This action also generates an instruction to load the allocated register with the value specified by value descriptor l, and then links that value descriptor to the register

```
Result correct    Y Y Y Y Y Y Y Y Y Y Y Y Y Y Y Y Y Y Y N N N N N N N N N N N N N N N N N N
ℓ correct         Y Y Y Y Y Y Y Y Y N N N N N N N N N N Y Y Y Y Y Y Y Y Y N N N N N N N N N
r correct         Y Y Y Y N N N N Y Y Y Y N N N N Y Y Y Y N N N N Y Y Y Y N N N N Y Y Y N N N
ℓ in register     Y Y N N Y Y N N Y Y N N Y Y N N Y Y N N Y Y N N Y Y N N Y Y N N Y Y N N Y N N
r in register     Y N Y N Y N Y N Y N Y N Y N Y N Y N Y N Y N Y N Y N Y N Y N Y N Y N Y N Y N

swap(ℓ,r)             X       X   X   X X      X          X   X   X X      X       X
ℓreg(ℓ,desire)          X       X       X          X       X          X       X          X
gen(A,ℓ,r)          X X X                       X X X   X X X                           X X X
gen(AR, ℓ,r)        X                       X           X                       X
gen(S, ℓ,r)                 X X X   X X X                           X X X   X X X
gen(SR,ℓ,r)             X       X                               X       X
gen(LCR, ℓ,ℓ)               X       X       X X X X X X X X   X               X
free(r)           X X X X X X X X X X X X X X X X X X X X X X X X X X X X X X X X X X X X
result(ℓ,store)   X X X X X X X X X X X X X X X X X X X X X X X X X X X X X X X X X X X X
```

"correct" means the sign is not inverted
l = value descriptor of the left operand
r = value descriptor of the right operand
$desire$ = $desire$ attribute of the current node
$store$ = $store$ attribute of the current node
AR, A, S, SR and LNR are IBM 370 instructions

Figure 10.15. IBM 370 Decision Table for $+(integer,integer)integer$
Based on Table 10.11

descriptor of the allocated register. After the code to carry out the addition has been generated, registers that might have been associated with the right operand must be freed and the descriptor for the register holding the left operand must be linked to the value descriptor for the result. If the *store* attribute is *true* then the result register descriptor state is set to *unique* ; otherwise it remains locked as discussed in Section 10.3.1.

Figure 10.15 contains one action to generate the RR-format of the add instruction and another to generate the RX-format. A single action could have been used instead, deferring the selection to assembly. The choice between having the code generator select the instruction format and having the assembler select it is made on grounds of convenience. In our case the code generator possesses all of the information necessary to make the selection; for machines with several memory addressing formats this is not always true because the proper format may depend upon the location assigned to an operand by the assembler.

We must stress here a point made earlier: The code selection process, specified by the decision tables and the register assignment algorithm operating on the machine state, produces the final code. All previous attribution prepares for this process, gathering information but making no decisions.

Decision tables occurring in the code generator usually have a comparatively small number of conditions (two to six), and well-known techniques for converting decision tables into programs can be applied to implement them. We can distinguish two essentially different methods: programmed decision trees and realization as data structures. The former method generally leads to long programs with large storage requirements. In the latter case the tables must be interpreted; the storage costs are smaller but the execution time is longer. Because each decision table is used infrequently, we give priority to reduction of memory requirements over shortening of execution time. Mixed-code approaches, based upon the frequency of use of the table, can also be followed. Programmed decision tables are most successful in small, simple compilers. The more cases and attributes that the code generator distinguishes, the more heavily the advantages of a data structure weigh.

To represent the decision tables by data structures we first collect all of the possible actions into a large case statement. The actions can then be represented in the tables by their case selectors. In most cases the tables are (or are close to being) complete, so we can apply a method based upon the idea that the sequence of values for the conditions that characterize the possible cases can be regarded as a mixed-radix number. The lower right quadrant of the decision table (see Figure 10.15) is implemented as a Boolean matrix indexed by the action number (row) and the condition (column). An *X* corresponds to a *true* element, a blank to a *false* element. Instead of using a Boolean matrix, each column could also be coded as a list of the case labels that correspond to the actions which must be carried out.

10.4. Notes and References

The *memory_map* module enters blocks into an area as they are delivered, regardless of whether or not gaps are introduced because of alignment constraints. As noted in Chapter 3, such gaps can often be eliminated or reduced by rearrangement of the components of a composite object. Unfortunately, the problem of obtaining an optimum layout is a variant of the 'knapsack problem' [Miller 1972], which is known to be NP-complete.

The problem of optimal code generation for expression trees has been studied extensively. Proof that the problem is NP-complete was given by Bruno [1976]. Our treatment is derived from those of Bruno and Lassagne [1975] and Aho and Johnson [1976]. The basic method for estimating register usage is due to Sethi and Ullman [1970]. Multi-register machines were discussed by Aho, Johnson and Ullman [1977b], who showed that a polynomial algorithm for optimal code generation could be obtained if double-length values could occupy arbitrary pairs of registers. Unfortunately, most machines restrict double-length values to pairs of adjacent registers, and usually require that the first register of the pair have an even number.

Targeting is a concept that is implicit in the notion of an inherited attribute. Wulf and his students [1975] were the first to make systematic use of targeting under that name, and our discussion of unary complement elimination is based upon their work.

Target attribution is described by an attribute grammar, and hence the semantic analysis and code generation tasks can be interfaced by merging their attribute grammars. If storage constraints require splitting of this combined attribution, the split should be made on the basis of traversals required by the combined attribute grammar. Thus each traversal may be implemented as a pass, and each pass may carry out both semantic analysis and code generation tasks. The specifications of the two tasks remain distinct, however, their merging is an implementation decision that can be carried out automatically.

'Peephole optimization' [McKeeman 1965] uses a machine simulation, and capitalizes upon relationships that arise when certain code fragments are joined together. Wilcox [1971] proposed a code generator consisting of two components, a *transducer* (which essentially evaluates attributes) and a *simulator* (which performs the machine simulation and code selection). He introduced the concepts of value and register descriptors in a form quite similar to that discussed here. Davidson [1980] uses a simulation following a simple code selector based upon a depth-first, left-to-right traversal of the structure tree with no attempt to be clever about register allocation. He claims that this approach is easier to automate, and gives results approaching those of far more sophisticated techniques.

Formulation of the code selection process in terms of decision tables is relatively rare in the literature, although they seem to be the natural vehicle for describing it. A number of authors [Elson 1970, Wilcox 1971, Waite

1974] have proposed special code generator description languages that effectively lead to programmed decision trees. Gries [1971] mentions decision tables, but only in the context of a rather specialized implementation used by the IBM FORTRAN H compiler [Lowry 1969]. This technique, known as 'bit strips', divides the conditions into two classes. Conditions in the first class select a column of the table, while those in the second are substituted into particular rows of the selected column. It is useful only when a condition applies to some (but not all) elements of a row. The technique precludes the use of a bit matrix because it requires each element to specify one of three possibilities (execute, skip and substitute) instead of two.

Glanville and Graham [1978] use SLR(1) parse tables as a data structure implementation of the decision tables; this approach has also been used in the context of LALR(1) parse tables by Jansohn and Landwehr [1982].

EXERCISES

10.1. Complete the definition of the memory mapping module outlined in Figure 10.1 for a machine of your choice.

10.2. Devise a linear algorithm to rearrange the fields of a record to minimize waste space, assuming that the only possible alignments are 1 and 2. (The DEC PDP11 and Intel 8086 have this property.)

10.3. [Aho 1976] Consider an expression tree attributed according to the rules of Figure 10.4.
   a. State an execution-order traversal algorithm that will produce optimum code when arithmetic instructions are emitted at the postfix encounters of interior nodes.
   b. State the conditions under which LOAD and STORE instructions will be emitted during the traversal of (a).
   c. Show that the attribution of Figure 10.4 is inadequate in the case where some arithmetic operations can be carried out *only* by instructions that require one operand in memory.
   d. Show that optimum code can be produced in case (c) if it is possible to create a queue of pointers to the tree and use this queue to guide the execution-order traversal.

10.4. Extend the attribution of Figure 10.4 to handle expression nodes with arbitrary numbers of operands, all of which must be in registers.

10.5. [Bruno 1975] Suppose that the target computer has a stack of fixed depth instead of a set of registers. (This is the case for most floating point chips available for microprocessors.) Show that your algorithm of Exercise 10.4 will still work if extra constraints are placed upon the allowable permutations.

10.6. What changes would you make in your solution to Exercise 10.4 if some of a node's operands had to be in memory and others in registers?

10.7. Show that the attribution rules of Figure 10.6 obey DeMorgan's law, i.e. that either member of the following pairs of LAX expressions leads to the same set of attributes for *a* and *b*:

> **not** (*a* **and** *b*), **not** *a* **or not** *b*
> **not** (*a* **or** *b*), **not** *a* **and not** *b*

10.8. Modify Figure 10.6 for a language that does not permit short-circuit evaluation. What corresponding changes must be made in the execution-order determination?

10.9. [Elson 1970] The PL/1 *LENGTH* function admits optimizations of string expressions analogous to short-circuit evaluation of Boolean expressions: *LENGTH*(*A* | | *B*) becomes *LENGTH*(*A*)+*LENGTH*(*B*). ('| |' is the concatenation operator.) Devise targeting attributes to carry this information and show how they are propagated.

10.10. Show that the unary complement elimination discussed in Section 10.2.3 also minimizes register requirements.

10.11. Extend Table 10.8 to include division.

10.12. Show that the following relation holds for the cost attribute (Figure 10.10) of any expression node:

$$| \ cost\,[correct\,].length - cost\,[inverse\,].length \ | \leqslant L$$

Where L is the length of a negation operator. (This condition must hold for all operations, not just those illustrated in Table 10.8.) What follows from this if register-memory instructions are also allowed?

10.13. What changes would be required in Figure 10.10 for a machine with a 'load negative' instruction that places the negative of a memory value into a register?

10.14. Modify Figure 10.9 for a machine with both register-register and register-memory instructions. Write a single set of attribution rules incorporating the tasks of both Figure 10.4 and Figure 10.10.

10.15. Specify descriptors to be used in implementing LAX on some computer other than the IBM 370. Carefully explain any difference between your specification and that of Figure 10.12.

10.16. Under what circumstances could a LAX code generator link register values to programmer-defined variables? Do you believe that the payoff would justify the analysis required?

10.17. There is no guarantee that the heuristic of Figure 10.14 will produce optimal code. Under what circumstances would the code improve when *unique* registers were chosen before *copy* registers?

10.18. Give, for a machine of your choice, the remaining decision tables necessary to translate LAX trees involving simple integer operands and operators from Table A.2.

CHAPTER 11

Assembly

The task of assembly is to convert the target tree produced by the code generator into the target code required by the compiler specification. This target code may be a sequence of bit patterns to be interpreted by the control unit of the target machine, or it may be text subject to further processing by a link editor or loader. In either case, the assembler must determine operand addresses and resolve any issues left open by the code generator.

Since the largest fraction of the compilers for most machines originate from the manufacturer, the manufacturer's target code format provides a de facto standard that the compiler writer should use: If the manufacturer's representation is abandoned then all access to the software already developed using other compilers, and probably all that will be developed in the future at other installations, is lost. For the same reason, it is best to use manufacturer-supplied link editors and loaders to carry out the external address resolution. Otherwise, if the target code format is extended or changed then we must alter not only the compilers, but also the resolution software that we had developed. We shall therefore assume that the output of the assembly task is a module rather than a whole program, and that external address resolution is to be provided by other software. (If this is not the case, then the encoding process is somewhat simplified.)

Assembly is essentially independent of the source language, and should be implemented by a common module that can be used in any compiler for the given machine. To a large extent, this module can be made machine-independent in design. Regardless of the particular computer, it must be able to resolve operand addresses and encode instructions. The information required by different link editors and loaders does not vary significantly in content. In this chapter we shall discuss the two main subtasks of assembly,

282

internal address resolution and instruction encoding, in some detail. We shall sketch the external address resolution problem briefly in order to indicate the kind of information that must be provided by the compiler; two specific examples of the way in which this information is represented can be found in Chapter 14.

11.1. Internal Address Resolution

Internal address resolution is the process of mapping the target tree onto a block of contiguous target machine memory locations, determining the addresses of all labels relative to the beginning of this block. We begin by assuming that the size of an instruction is fixed, and then show how this assumption can be relaxed. Special problems can arise from particular machine architectures, and we shall briefly discuss a representative example.

11.1.1. Label Value Determination We begin with the structure of the target tree discussed in Section 4.1.4, which can be characterized by the context-free rules of Figure 11.1. The attribution rules in Figure 11.1 gather information from the tree about the relationships among sequences (*origin_env*) and the placement of labels within the sequences (*label_env*). This information is exactly what is found in the 'symbol table' of a conventional symbolic assembler. It can easily be shown that Figure 11.1 is LAG(1), and the single traversal corresponds to 'pass 1' of the conventional assembler. Clearly we could integrate this traversal with the code selection process in an implementation, but it remains conceptually distinct.

The environments are lists whose elements have the types shown in Figure 11.2a. A based origin element specifies an address expression stored as a tree, using linked records of the form shown in Figure 11.2b. This tree actually forms a part of the *origin_env* attribute; it is abstracted from the target tree by rules not shown in Figure 11.1, and delivered as the attribute *expression.expr* in the rule for *sequence* ::= *expression nodes*. We shall assume that all address computations either involve only absolute values or have the form *relative* ± *absolute*; situations requiring more complex calculations can easily be avoided by the compiler.

On the basis of the information in *label_env* and *origin_env*, every label can be assigned a value that is either absolute or relative to the origin of a sequence whose origin class is *arbitrary*. We could simply consider each *arbitrary*-origin sequence as a separate 'module' and terminate the internal address resolution process when the attribution of Figure 11.1 was complete. This is generally not done. Instead, we compute the overall length of each *arbitrary*-origin sequence and concatenate them, restating all but the first as *based*. The concatenated sequences form the *relocatable* portion of the program in which every label can be assigned a relocatable address — an address relative to the single arbitrary origin.

rule *target_tree* :: = *sequences*

rule *sequences* :: =
attribution
  sequences.label_env ← **nil**;
  sequences.origin_env ← **nil**;

rule *sequences* :: = *sequences sequence*
attribution
  sequences[1].*label_env* ←
    sequences[2].*label_env* & *sequence.origin_env* ;
  sequences[1].*origin_env* ←
    sequences[2].*origin_env* & *sequence.origin_env* ;

rule *sequence* :: = *nodes*
attribution
  nodes.base ← *gennum* ;
  sequence.origin_env ←
    N_origin_element (*nodes.base*, *nodes.length*, *arbitrary*)

rule *sequence* :: = *expression nodes*
attribution
  nodes.base ← *gennum* ;
  sequence.origin_env ←
    N_origin_element (*nodes.base*, *nodes.length*, *based*, *expression.expr*);

rule *nodes* :: =
attribution
  nodes.label_env ← **nil**;
  nodes.length ← 0;

rule *nodes* :: = *nodes operation*
attribution
  nodes[1].*length* ← *nodes*[2].*length* + *instr_size* (*operation.instr*);

rule *nodes* :: = *nodes constant*
attribution
  nodes[1].*length* ← *nodes*[2].*length* + *const_size* (*constant.value*);

rule *nodes* :: = *nodes label*
  nodes[1].*label_env* ←
    nodes[2].*label_env* &
    N_label_element (*label.uid*, *nodes*[1].*base*, *nodes*[2].*length*);

Figure 11.1. Target Tree Structure and Attribution

Most programming languages do not offer the user a way to specify an absolute origin, and hence the compiler will create only relocatable target

type
  label_element = **record**
    uid : *integer* ;   (* Unique identification for the label *)
    base : *integer* ;   (* Sequence to which the label belongs *)
    relative_address : *integer*   (* Address of the label in the sequence *)
  end;
  origin_element = **record**
    uid : *integer* ;   (* Unique identification for the sequence *)
    length : *integer*   (* Space occupied by the sequence *)
    case *k* : *origin_class* **of**
      arbitrary : ();
      based : (*origin* : *address_exp*)
  end;

          a) Types used in the environments of Figure 11.1

type
  address_exp = **record**
    case *k* : *expr_class* **of**
      absolute :
        (*value* : *integer_value*);   (* Provided by the constant table *)
      relative :
        (*label* : *integer*);   (* Unique identification of the referenced label *)
      computation :
        (*rator* : (*add* , *sub*);
        right, *left*: ↑ *address_exp*)
  end;

         b) Types used to represent address expressions

          Figure 11.2. The Environment Attributes

code. If a particular implementation does require absolute sequences, there are two ways to proceed. The first is to fix the arbitrary origin and treat the entire program as absolute; the second is to resolve the addresses separately in the absolute and relocatable portions, resolving cross references between them by the methods of Section 11.2. The latter approach can also be taken when the source language allows the programmer to specify that portions of the program reside in read-only memory and others in read-write memory.

11.1.2. Span-Dependent Instructions   The assumption that the size of an instruction is fixed does not hold for all machines. For example, the conditional branch instructions of the PDP11 use a single-byte address and can therefore transfer control a maximum of 127 words back or 128 words forward. If the branch target lies outside of this range then a sequence involving a conditional branch over an unconditional jump must be used. The code generator cannot decide between these two possibilities, and hence it outputs an abstract conditional jump instruction for the assembler to resolve. Clearly the size of the resulting code depends upon the relative locations of the target label and jump instruction. (A simple-minded assembler could always assume the worst case and generate the longest version of the jump.)

A span-dependent instruction can be characterized by its location and the manner in which its length depends upon the label(s) appearing in its operand(s). For example, the length of a jump may depend upon the difference between the location of the jump and the location of its target; in rare cases the length of a constant-setting instruction may depend upon the value of an expression ($LABEL\,1 - LABEL\,2$). In the remainder of this section we shall consider only the former situation, and restrict the operand of the span-dependent instruction to a simple label.

Span-dependence does not change the basic attribution of Figure 11.1, but it requires that an extra attribute be constructed. This attribute, called *mod_list*, consists of linked records whose form is given in Figure 11.3a. *Mod_list* is initialized and propagated in exactly the same way as *label_env*. Elements are added to it at span-dependent instructions as shown in Figure 11.3b. The function *instr_size* returns the *minimum* length of the span-dependent instruction, and this value is used to determine origin values as discussed in Section 11.1.1.

The next step is to construct a *relocation table* that can be consulted whenever a label value must be determined. Each relocation table entry specifies

type
   mod_element = **record**
      base : *integer* ;   (* Sequence in which instruction appears *)
      relative_address : *integer* ; (* Address of the instruction in the sequence *)
      operand : *integer* ;   (* Unique identification for the operand label *)
      instr : *machine_op* ;   (* Characterization of the instruction *)
   end;

a) Type used in mod_list

     rule *nodes* ::= *nodes span_dependent_operation*
     attribution
       nodes[1].*length* ←
        nodes[2].*length* + *instr_size* (*span_dependent_operation.instr*);
       nodes[1].*mod_list* ←
        nodes[2].*mod_list*&
        N_mod_element (
         nodes[1].*base*,
         nodes[2].*length*,
         span_dependent_operation.operand_uid,
         span_dependent_operation.instr);

b) Calculation of mod_list

Figure 11.3. Span-Dependent Instructions

the total increase in size for all span-dependent instructions lying below a given address (relative or absolute). When the label address calculation of Section 11.1.1 indicates an address lying between two relocation table entries, it is increased by the amount specified in the lower entry.

The properties of the span-dependent instructions are embodied in a module that provides two operations:

Too_short (*machine_op* ,*integer*)*boolean* :   Yields *true* if the instruction defined by *machine_op* cannot have its operand at the (signed) distance from the instruction given by the integer.

Lengthen (*machine_op*, *integer*)*integer* :   Updates   the   given *machine_op*, if necessary, so that the instruction defined can have its operand at the (signed) distance given by the integer. Yields the increase in instruction size resulting from the change.

The relocation table is built by the following algorithm:
1. Establish an empty relocation table.
2. Make the first element of *mod_list* current.
3. Calculate the addresses of the span-dependent instruction represented by the current element of *mod_list* and its operand, using the current environments and relocation table.
4. Apply *too_short* to the (signed) distance between the span-dependent instruction and its operand. If the result is *false*, go to step 6.
5. Lengthen the instruction and update the relocation table accordingly. Go to step 2.
6. If elements remain in *mod_list*, make the next element current and go to step 3. Otherwise stop.

This algorithm has running time proportional to n^2 in the worst case (n is the number of span-dependent instructions), even when each span-dependent instruction has more than two lengths.

Span-dependency must be resolved separately in each portion of the program that depends upon a different origin (see the end of Section 11.1.1). If span-dependent instructions provide cross-references between portions based on different origins then either *all* analysis of span-dependence must be deferred to external address resolution or some arbitrary assumption must be made about the cross-referencing instructions. The usual approach is to optimize span-dependent instructions making internal references and use the longest version of any cross-referencing instruction.

11.1.3. Special Problems   The IBM 370 and its imitators have a short address field and do not permit addressing relative to the program counter. This is a design flaw that means the general-purpose registers must be used as base registers to provide addressability within the code sequence. Such addressability is required for two purposes: access to constants and specification of jump targets. The code generator could, as a part of the memory mapping process, map all constants into a contiguous block of memory and determine the number of base registers required to provide addressability for this block. Given our decomposition of the compilation process, however, it is impossible to guarantee that the code generator can allocate the minimum number of base registers needed for jump target specification.

The number of code base registers required for any procedure can be reduced to two, at the cost of increasing the size of a jump instruction from 4 bytes to 8: One of the two registers holds the address of the procedure's first instruction. Any jump target is defined by its address, t, relative to this address. Let $t = 4096q + d$, such that $0 \leqslant d < 4096$ will fit the displacement field of an RX-format instruction. Assuming that the address of the first instruction is in register 10 and the second register allocated for code basing is 9, a jump to t becomes

$$\text{LH} \quad 9,\text{CONS} + 2*q(10)$$
$$\text{BC} \quad \text{MASK},d(9,10)$$

(Here 'CONS' is an array of halfword values for $4096q$ and 'MASK' is the condition code mask defining the branch condition.)

By performing additional analysis of the code sequence, it may be possible to avoid expanding some of the jumps. The value of q (and hence the contents of register 9) is easily determined at every point in the program. If the target of a jump has the same q as is in force at the location of the jump then no expansion is necessary. Effectively, jump becomes a span-dependent instruction. The problem of finding the minimum number of jumps that must be expanded is NP-complete, but a linear algorithm that never shortens a previously-generated jump gives adequate results in practice.

11.2. External Address Resolution

External address resolution combines separately-compiled modules into a complete program or simply a larger module. Component modules may constitute a part of the input text, or may be extracted automatically from one or more libraries. They may have originally been coded in a variety of programming languages, and translated by different compilers. (This last is only possible when all of the compilers produce target code using a common representation.)

We restrict ourselves here to the basic problems of external address resolution and their solution. To do so we must assume a particular code format, but this should in no way be taken as advice that the compiler writer should design his own representation! As noted at the beginning of the chapter, we strongly advocate use of manufacturer-supplied link editors and loaders for external address resolution.

11.2.1. Cross-Referencing   In many respects, external address resolution is analogous to internal address resolution: Each module is a single code sequence with certain locations (usually called *entry points*, although they may be either data or code addresses) distinguished. These locations are analogous to the label nodes in the internal address resolution case. The module may also contain address expressions that depend upon values (usually called *external references*) not defined within that module. These values are analogous to the label references in the internal address resolution case. When the modules are combined, they can be considered to be a list of independent code sequences and all of the techniques discussed in Section 11.1 can be carried over.

There can be some benefit in going beyond the analogy discussed in the previous paragraph, and simply deferring the internal address resolution until all modules have been gathered together. Under those circumstances one could optimize the length of inter-module references as well as intra-module references (Section 11.1.2). We believe that the benefits are not commensurate with the costs, however, since inter-module references should be relatively rare.

Two basic mechanisms are available for establishing inter-module references: *transfer vectors* and *direct substitution*. A transfer vector is best suited to references involving a transfer of control. It is a block of memory, included in each module that contains external references, consisting of one element for each distinct external symbol referenced (Figure 11.4). The internal address resolution process replaces every external reference with a reference to the corresponding element of the transfer vector, and the external address resolution process fills each transfer vector element with the address of the proper entry point. When the machine architecture permits indirect addressing, the initial reference is indirect and may be either a con-

```
procedure ex (x, y : real ): real ;
  var
    a, b : real ;
  begin
  a := sign (x )*sqrt(abs (x ));
  b := sign (y )*sqrt(abs (y ));
  ex := (a − b )/(a + b )
  end; (* ex *)
```

a) External references

abs
sign
sqrt

b) Transfer vector for procedure *ex*

Figure 11.4. Transfer Vectors

trol or a data reference. If the machine does not provide indirect addressing via main memory, the transfer vector address must be loaded into a base register for the access. When the address length permits jumps to arbitrary addresses, we might also place an unconditional jump to the entry point in the transfer vector and implement a call as a call to that transfer vector entry.

Direct substitution avoids the indirection inherent in the transfer vector mechanism: The actual address of an entry point is determined during external address resolution and stored into the instruction that references it. Even with the transfer vector mechanism, direct substitution is required within the transfer vector itself. In the final analysis, we use a transfer vector because it reduces to one the number of changes that must be made when the address of an entry point changes, and concentrates these changes at a particular point in the program. Entry point addresses may change statically, as when a module is newly compiled and bound without altering the program, or they may change dynamically, as when a routine resides in memory temporarily. For example, service routines in an operating system are often 'transient' — they are brought into memory only when needed. The operating system provides a transfer vector, and all invocations of service routines must go via this transfer vector. When a routine is not in memory, its transfer vector entry is replaced by a jump to a loader. Even if the service routines are not transient, a transfer vector is useful: When changes made to the operating system result in moving the service routine entry points, only the transfer vector is altered; there is no need to fix up the external references of all user programs. (Note that in this case the transfer vector is a part of the operating system, not of each module using the operating system as discussed in the previous paragraph. If the vector occupies a fixed location in memory, however, it may be regarded either as part of the module or as part of the operating system.)

In the remainder of this section we shall consider the details of the direct substitution mechanism. As pointed out earlier, this is analogous to internal address resolution. We shall therefore concern ourselves only with the differences between external and internal resolution. These differences lie mainly in the representation of the modules.

A *control dictionary* is associated with each module to provide the following information:

- Length of the module.
- Locations of entry points relative to the beginning of the module.
- Symbols used to denote entry points and external values.
- Fields within the module that represent addresses relative to the beginning of the module.
- Fields within the module that represent external references.

Additional information about the size of external areas may also be carried, to support external static data areas such as FORTRAN COMMON.

The module length, relative entry point addresses and symbols are used to establish an attribute analogous to *label_element*. Note that this requires a traversal of the list of modules, but not of the individual modules themselves. After this attribute is known, the fields representing relative and external addresses must be updated. A relative address is updated by adding the address of the module origin; the only information necessary to characterize the field is the fact that it contains a relative address. One common way of encoding this information is to associate *relocation bits* with the module text. The precise relationship between relocation bits and fields depends upon the machine architecture. For example, on the PDP11 a relative address occurring in an instruction must occupy one word. We might therefore use one relocation bit per word, 1 indicating a relative address. Note that this encoding precludes other placement of relative addresses, and may therefore impose constraints upon the code generator's mapping of data structures to be initialized by the compiler.

To characterize an external reference we must specify the particular external symbol involved in addition to the fact that an external reference occurs in the field. The concept of a relocation bit can be extended to cover the existence of an external reference by adding a third state: For a particular field the possibilities are 'no change', 'relative' and 'external'. The field itself then contains an integer specifying the particular external symbol.

There are two disadvantages to this strategy for characterizing external references. The most important is that it does not permit an address relative to an external symbol, since the field must be used to define the symbol itself. Data references, especially those to external arrays like FORTRAN COMMON, tend to violate this constraint. A second disadvantage is that the number of relocation bits for *every* field is increased, although only a small minority of the fields may actually contain external references. Both disadvantages may be overcome by maintaining a list of all fields containing external references relative to a particular symbol. The field itself contains the relative address and the symbol address is simply added to it, exactly as a relative address is updated. (This same strategy can be used instead of relocation bits for relative addresses on machines whose architectures tend to make relative addresses infrequent; the IBM 370 is an example.)

The result of the cross-referencing process could be a ready-to-run program, with all addresses absolute, or it could be single module with relative addresses, entry points and external references that can be used as input to further linkage steps. In the latter case, the input must specify not only the modules to be linked but also the entry points to be retained after linkage. External references will be retained automatically if and only if they do not refer to entry points of other input modules.

11.2.2. Library Search   A language such as Ada requires that the semantic analyzer verify the correctness of all inter-module references. Thus during assembly all of the modules needed are already known. This is not the case for languages such as FORTRAN. Mathematical subroutines, I/O procedures, environment inquiries and the like are almost always supplied by the installation and placed in a library in target code format. After the first traversal of the input module list, external references not corresponding to entry points may be looked up in this library. If a module in the library has one or more of these symbols as entry points then it is added to the list and processed just as though it had come from the input. Clearly more than one library may be searched in the process of satisfying external references; the particular libraries and order of search are specified by the user.

A library is often quite large, so it would be inefficient to scan all of the modules in a search for entry points. The entry point information is therefore normally gathered into a *catalog* during the process of constructing the library, and only the catalog is examined to select appropriate modules. Since the modules of a library may have a high degree of internal linkage, the catalog should also specify the external symbols referenced by each module. After the modules necessary to satisfy user external references have been determined, a transitive closure operation adds any others required by those already selected.

11.3. Instruction Encoding

After all attributes of target tree nodes have been computed, the information must be converted into target code suitable for execution. This process is similar to the code selection discussed in Section 10.3, but somewhat different specification techniques are appropriate. After discussing an appropriate interface for the target code converter, we shall present an encoding mechanism and a specification language.

11.3.1. Target Code We regard the target code as an abstract data type defined by eight operations:

Module_name (identifier_string): Establish the name of the module being generated.

Module_size (length): Specify the length of the block of contiguous memory locations required for the module being generated.

Entry_point (identifier_string): Establish an entry point to the module being generated.

Set_location (relative_address): Specify the load point at which subsequent target code is to be placed in memory.

Absolute_text (target_text,length): Place encoded target text into memory at the current load point. The *length* argument gives the amount of text to be placed. After the text has been placed, the current load point is the point immediately beyond it.

Internal_reference (*relative_address*): Place an encoded relative address into memory at the current load point. After the address has been placed, the current load point is the point immediately beyond it.

External_reference (*offset,identifier_string*): Place an external reference into memory at the current load point. The *offset* is the address relative to the external symbol *identifier_string*. After the reference has been placed, the current load point is the point immediately beyond it.

These operations provide the information summarized in Section 11.2, and would constitute the interface for a module that actually produced a target code file. Some manufacturer's software may place restrictions upon parameter values, and some may provide facilities (such as repetitions of data values) that cannot be reached via these operations.

Module_name, *module_size* and *entry_point* all provide specific information for the control dictionary. *Set_location* is used to reset the current load point at the beginning of a code sequence. It embodies the 'scatter loading' concept in which the target code is broken up into a number of compact blocks, each of which carries the address at which it is to be placed. These addresses need not be contiguous. We shall consider two specific implementations of this concept in Section 14.2.

Only a small range of length parameters is possible for the *absolute_text* operation on any given machine: There is a fixed set of instruction and instruction fragment lengths, and most constants have a length dependent only upon their type and not upon their value. One notable exception is the string constant, which must be broken into smaller units to be used with the *absolute_text* operation.

There is no length parameter specified for an internal or external reference. On most computers, relative addresses are only useful as operands of a specific length, and hence that length is assumed.

Absolute text, internal references and external references are distinguished because they may be represented in very different ways by the manufacturer's software. For a particular target computer there may even be several operating systems with quite different target code formats. It is therefore wise for the compiler writer to design his target code module according to the abstract data type given here instead of attempting to merge *absolute_text, internal_reference* and *external_reference* into one operation and inserting relocation bits explicitly.

11.3.2. The Encoding Process   Each target tree node represents a label, storage reservation, constant or abstract machine instruction. Label nodes are ignored by the encoding process, and storage reservation nodes simply result in invocations of the *set_location* operation. The remaining nodes must be encoded by invoking one or more of the last three operations defined in the previous section.

Constants may appear as literal values to be incorporated directly into the target code, or they may be components of address expressions. In the latter case, the result of the expression could be used as data or as an operand of an instruction. Literal values must be converted using the internal-to-target conversion operations of the constant table (Section 4.2.2), and then inserted into the target code by *absolute_text*. An address expression is evaluated as outlined in Exercise 11.9. If the result is used as data then the appropriate target code operation is used to insert it; otherwise it is handled by the instruction encoding.

In the simplest case the abstract instructions correspond to unique operation codes of the real machine. In general, however, the correspondence is not so simple: One abstract operation can represent several instructions, or one of several operation codes could be appropriate depending upon the operand access paths. Decisions are thus made during instruction encoding on the basis of the abstract operator and the attributes of the operand(s) just as in the case of code generation.

The basic instruction encoding operations are called *formats*. They are procedures that take sets of values and add them to the target code so that the result is a single instruction. These procedures sometimes correspond to the instruction formats recognized by the target machine's control unit, and hence their name. In many cases, however, the instruction format shows regularities that can be exploited to reduce the number of encoding formats. For example, the five instruction formats of the IBM 370 (Figure 11.5a) might correspond to only three encoding formats (Figure 11.5b).

An instruction is encoded by calling a sequence of one or more format-encoding procedures. The process can be described in a language resembling a normal macro assembly language. Figure 11.6 shows a portion of a description of the IBM 370 instruction encoding cast in this form. Each macro body specifies the sequence of format invocations, using constants or macro parameters (denoted by the character '%' followed by the position of the parameter) as arguments. A separate directive, NAME, is used to associate the macro body with an instruction because many instructions can often use the same encoding procedure. NAME directives may specify an argument, which becomes parameter 0 of the macro. In Figure 11.6 the NAME directive has been used to supply the hexadecimal operation code for each instruction. (A hexadecimal constant begins with a digit and ends with 'H'.) We use the IBM mnemonics to denote the instructions; in practice these macros would be represented by tables and the node type of an abstract operation would appear in place of the symbolic operation code.

Formal parameters of the macros in Figure 11.6 are described by comments. (Strings following ';' on the same line are comments.) The corresponding actual parameters are the operands of the target tree node, and their values will have been established during code generation or address resolution. Note that a 'memory' operand includes its base register but not an index register. Thus the 'FM' format takes a single memory address and encodes it as a base and displacement. This reflects the fact that the index register is assigned by the code generator, while the base register is

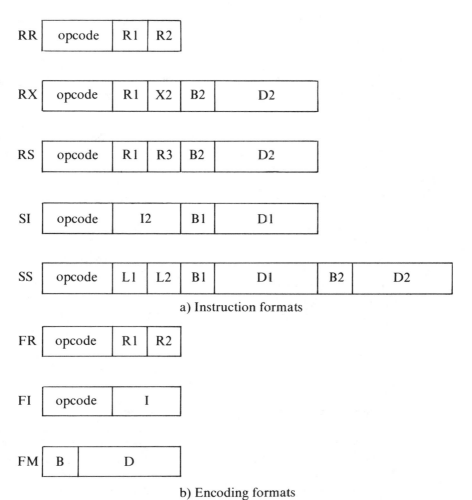

a) Instruction formats

b) Encoding formats

Figure 11.5. IBM 370 Formats

determined during assembly. In other words, the abstract IBM 370 from which these macros were derived did not have the concept of a based access.

Consider the LAX expression $a + b \uparrow [c]$. If a were in register 1, $b \uparrow$ in register 2 and c (multiplied by the appropriate element length) in register 3 then the addition could be performed by a single IBM 370 add instruction with $R1 = 1$, $B2 = 2$, $X2 = 3$ and $D2$ a displacement appropriate to the lower bound of the array being referenced. Given the macros of Figure 11.6, however, this instruction could not be encoded because the abstract machine has no concept of a based access. Clearly one solution to this problem is to give FM two arguments and make the base register explicit in the abstract machine; another is to provide the abstract machine with *two* kinds of memory address: one in the code sequence and the other in data memory.

```
AR    NAME    1AH
SR    NAME    1BH
      MACRO                  ; Register,Register
      FR      %0,%1,%2
      ENDM


A     NAME    5AH
S     NAME    5BH
      MACRO                  ; Register,Memory,Index
      FR      %0,%1,%3
      FM      %2
      ENDM


AP    NAME    0FAH
SP    NAME    0FBH
      MACRO                  ; Memory,Length,Memory,Length
      FR      %0,%2,%4
      FM      %1
      FM      %3
      ENDM
```

Note: Suffix 'H' denotes hexadecimal.

Figure 11.6. IBM 370 Instruction Encoding

We favor the latter solution because these two kinds of memory address are specified differently. The code generator defines the former by a label and the latter by a base register and displacement. The assembler must pick a base register for the former but not the latter. Because of these differences it is probably useful to have distinct target node formats for the two cases.

Figure 11.7 shows a modification of the macros of Figure 11.6 to allow our second solution. In Figure 11.7a the add instruction is associated with *two* macro bodies, and one of the parameters of the first is specified. The specification gives the attribute that the operand must possess if this macro is to be selected. By convention, the macros associated with a given name are checked in the order in which they appeared in the definition; parameters with no specified attributes match anything. Figure 11.7b combines the two bodies, using a conditional to select the proper format invocation. Here the operator '@' is used to select the *attribute* rather than the *value* of the parameter. This emphasizes the fact that there are two components of an operand, attribute and value, which must be distinguished.

What constitutes an attribute of an operand, and what constitutes a value? These questions depend intimately upon the design of the abstract machine and its relationship to the actual target instructions. We shall sketch a specific mechanism for defining and dealing with attributes as an illustration.

```
A    NAME      5AH
S    NAME      5BH
     MACRO     ,LABEL              ; Register,Memory,Index
     FR        %0,%1,%3
     FM1       %2
     ENDM
     MACRO                         ; Register,Base,Index,Displacement
     FR        %0,%1,%3
     FM2       %2,%4
     ENDM
```

a) Selection of different macros

```
A    NAME      5AH
S    NAME      5BH
     MACRO                         ; Either pattern
     FR        %0,%1,%3
     IF        @%2≠ LABEL
     FM1       %2
     ELSE
     FM2       %2,%4
     ENDIF
     ENDM
```

b) Conditional within a macro

Figure 11.7. Two Memory Operand Types

The value and attribute of an operand are arbitrary bit patterns of a specified length. They may be accessed and manipulated individually, using the normal arithmetic and bitwise-logical operators. Any expression yields a value consisting of a single bit pattern. Two expressions may be formed into a value/attribute pair by using the quote operator: $e_1"e_2$. (See Figure 11.8 for examples.) An operand is compatible with a parameter of a macro if the following expression yields *true* :

$$(@operand \textbf{ and } @parameter) = parameter$$

Thus the operand R2 would be compatible with the parameters R2, EVENGR and GENREG in Figure 11.8; it would not be compatible with ODDGR or LABEL. Clearly any operand is compatible with ANY, and it is this object that is supplied when a parameter specification is omitted.

Macro languages similar to the one sketched here have been used to specify instruction encoding in many contexts. Experience shows that they are useful, but if not carefully implemented can lead to very slow processors. It is absolutely essential to implement the formats by routines coded in the implementation language of the compiler. Macros can be interpreted, but the interpretive code must be compact and carefully tailored to the interpretation process. The normal implementation of a macro processor as a string

ANY	SET	0"0	; Any operand
LABEL	SET	10H"10H	; Code sequence memory operand
EVENGR	SET	20H"21H	; Even-numbered general register
ODDGR	SET	21H"21H	; Odd-numbered general register
GENREG	SET	20H"20H	; Any general register
R0	SET	0"20H	; General register 0
R1	SET	1"21H	; General register 1
R2	SET	2"22H	; General register 2
R3	SET	3"23H	; General register 3

a) Symbol definitions

LABEL	= 10H
@LABEL	= 10H
R0 + 1	= 1
@R0-1	= 17H
R1 + @LABEL	= 11H
@R3 **and** @EVENGR	= 21H
@R3 **and** @ODDGR	= 21H

b) Expressions

Figure 11.8. Values and Attributes

manipulator is inadequate. Names should be implemented as a compact set of integers so that access to lists of macro bodies is direct. Since the number of bodies associated with a name is usually small, linear search is adequate. Note that a tradeoff is possible between selection on the basis of the name and selection on the basis of attributes.

As a by-product of the encoding, it is possible to produce a symbolic assembly code version of the program to aid in the debugging and maintenance of the compiler itself. If the macro names are specified symbolically, as in Figures 11.6 and 11.7, these can be used as symbolic operation codes in the listing. The *uid* that appears as an intrinsic attribute of the label nodes can be converted into a normal identifier by prefixing a letter. Only constants need special treatment: a set of target value-to-character conversion procedures must be provided.

11.4. Notes and References

Assembly is seldom provided as a cleanly-separated module that can be invoked by any compiler. Exceptions to this rule are IBSYS [Talmadge 1963] and EMAS [Stephens 1974], both of which contain standard assembly modules. The IBSYS assembler requires the target code tree to reside on a sequential file, while EMAS makes a collection of assembly procedures available as part of the standard library. IBM chose not to follow the IBSYS example in OS/360, probably because of complaints about performance degradation due to the need to explicitly write the target code tree.

The idea of using separate code sequences instead of specific storage reservation nodes in the target tree was discussed by Mealy [1963]. Talmadge [1963] shows how complex addressing relationships among sequences can be implemented. His philosophy was to provide complete flexibility in the assembler (which was written once for each machine) in order to reduce effort that would otherwise be duplicated in every compiler. In practice, it seems that the duplicated effort is generally required to support quality code generation. Thus the complexity does not occur in target code produced by a compiler, but it is often found in symbolic assembly code produced by human programmers.

Several 'meta-assemblers' have been proposed and used to implement symbolic assembly languages. These systems provide mechanisms for specifying the instruction encoding process in terms of formats and macros as discussed in Section 11.3.2. Most of the basic ideas are covered by Graham and Ingerman [1965], but the concept of including attributes in the pattern match does not occur until much later [Language Resources 1981].

The problem of span-dependence has been studied by a number of authors. Our treatment follows that of Hanglberger [1977] and Szymanski [1978], and is specially adapted for use in a compiler. In symbolic assemblers, more complex address expressions may appear and the order of the algorithm may be altered thereby.

EXERCISES

11.1. Complete Figure 11.1 by adding rules to describe address expressions and construct the attribute *expression . expr.*

11.2. [Galler 1964] Consider the problem of mapping storage described by FORTRAN COMMON, DIMENSION, EQUIVALENCE and DATA statements onto a sequence of contiguous blocks of storage (one for each COMMON area and one for local variables).
   a. How can these statements be translated into a target tree of the form discussed in Section 4.2.2 and Figure 11.1?
   b. Will the translation you describe in (a) every produce more than one *arbitrary*-origin sequence? Carefully explain why or why not.
   c. Does your target tree require any processing by the assembler in addition to that described in Section 11.1.1? If so, explain why.

11.3. [Talmadge 1963] Consider the concatenation of all *arbitrary*-origin sequences discussed in Section 11.1.1.
   a. Write a procedure to determine the length of an *arbitrary*-origin sequence.
   b. Write a procedure to scan *origin_env*, finding two *arbitrary*-origin sequences and concatenating them by altering the *origin_element* record for the second.

11.4. Consider the implementation of the span-dependence algorithm of Section 11.1.2.
   a. Show that the algorithm has running time proportional to n^2 in the worst

case, where n is the number of span-dependent instructions.

    b. Define a relocation table entry and write the update routine mentioned in step (5) of the algorithm.

11.5. [Szymanski 1978] Modify the span-dependence analysis to allow target expressions of the form *label* $\pm$ *constant* .

11.6. Consider the code basing problem of Section 11.1.3.

    a. Define any attributes necessary to maintain the state of q within a code sequence, and modify the rules of Figures 11.1 and 11.3 to include them.

    b. Explain how the operations *too_short* and *lengthen* (Section 11.1.2. must be altered to handle this case. Would you prefer to define other operations instead? Explain.

11.7. [Robertson 1979] The Data General Nova has an 8-bit address field, addressing relative to the program counter is allowed, and any address may be indirect. Constants must be placed in the code sequence within 127 words of the instruction that references them. If a jump target is further than 127 words from the jump then the address must be placed in the code sequence as a constant and the jump made indirect. (The size of the jump instruction is the same in either case.)

    a. Give an algorithm for placing constants that takes advantage of any unconditional jumps already present in the code, placing constants after them.

    b. Indicate how the constant blocks might be considered span-dependent instructions, whose size varies depending upon whether or not they contain jump target addresses.

    c. Show that the problem of optimizing the span-dependence in (b) is NP-complete.

11.8. [Talmadge 1963] Some symbolic assemblers provide 'multiple location counters', where each location counter defines a sequence in the sense of Section 11.1.1. Pseudo operations are available that allow the user to switch arbitrarily from one location counter to another.

    a. Show how a target tree could represet arbitrary sequence changes by using internally-generated labels to associate 'pieces' of the same sequence.

    b. Some computers (such as the Control Data Cyber series) have instructions that are smaller than a single memory element, but an address refers only to an entire memory element. How could labels be represented for such a machine? How does the choice of label representation impact the solution to (a)?

    c. What changes to Figure 11.1 would be needed if we chose not to represent arbitrary sequence changes by internally-generated labels, but instead gave every 'piece' of the same sequence the same *uid*?

    d. If we used the representation for sequences suggested in (c), how would the answer to (b) change?

11.9. The ultimate value of an address embedded in the target code must be either a number or a pair (external symbol, number). A number alone may represent either a numeric operand or a relative address.

a. Suppose that A, B and C are labels. What form does the value of $(A+B)-C$ take? Why is $(A+B)+C$ a meaningless address expression?

b. Specify an attribute that could be used to distinguish the cases mentioned in (a).

c. If A were an external symbol, would your answer to (a) change? Would your answer to (b) change? How?

d. Would you allow the expression $(A+B)-(A+C)$, A an external symbol, B and C labels? What form would its value take?

e. Use an attribute grammar to define the language of legal address expressions. Make the value of the expression an attribute of the root.

11.10. [Hedberg 1963] What requirements are placed upon the external address resolution process by FORTRAN COMMON blocks? Quote the FORTRAN standard to support your position, and then explain how these requirements might be satisfied.

11.11. Suppose that the target machine provided an instruction to add an immediate value to a register, but none to subtract an immediate value from a register. The addition is, however, a 2's complement addition so that subtraction can be accomplished by adding the complement of an immediate value. How would you provide the complement of a relative address as an immediate operand?

11.12. [GE 1965] Several utility modules may require the same support functions, but optimizations may arise from integrating these support functions with the utility modules. The result is that several modules may have identical entry points for the support functions but differ in other entry points. Devise a library catalog that will distinguish between *primary* and *secondary* entry points: A module will be selected only if one or more of its primary entry points corresponds to an unsatisfied external reference. Once a module has been selected, however, secondary entry points can be used to satisfy external references. Comment upon any user problems you foresee.

CHAPTER 12

Error Handling

Error handling is concerned with failures due to many causes: errors in the compiler or its environment (hardware, operating system), design errors in the program being compiled, an incomplete understanding of the source language, transcription errors, incorrect data, etc. The tasks of the error handling process are to detect each error, report it to the user, and possibly make some repair to allow processing to continue. It cannot generally determine the cause of the error, but can only diagnose the visible symptoms. Similarly, any repair cannot be considered a *correction* (in the sense that it carries out the user's intent); it merely neutralizes the symptom so that processing may continue.

The purpose of error handling is to aid the programmer by highlighting inconsistencies. It has a low frequency in comparison with other compiler tasks, and hence the time required to complete it is largely irrelevant, but it cannot be regarded as an 'add-on' feature of a compiler. Its influence upon the overall design is pervasive, and it is a necessary debugging tool during construction of the compiler itself. Proper design and implementation of an error handler, however, depends strongly upon complete understanding of the compilation process. This is why we have deferred consideration of error handling until now.

It is perhaps useful to make a distinction between the *correctness* of a system and its *reliability*. The former property is derived from certain assumptions regarding both the primitives upon which the system is based and the inputs that drive it. For example, program verification techniques might be used to prove that a certain compiler will produce correct object programs for all source programs obeying the rules of the source language. This would not be a useful property, however, if the compiler collapsed whenever some illegal source program was presented to it. Thus we are more interested in the reliability of the compiler: its ability to produce useful results under the weakest possible assumptions about the quality of the environment, input data and human operator. Proper error handling techniques contribute to the reliability of a system by providing it with a means for dealing with violations of some assumptions on which its design was based. (Theoretically, of course, this could be regarded simply as a relaxation of those assumptions; pragmatically, techniques for achieving correctness and reliability are quite different.)

We shall begin this chapter by considering some general principles of error handling. A distinction will be made between errors detectable at compilation time and errors whose symptoms do not appear until execution time. The compiler must deal with those in the former class directly, and must provide support for the run-time system that allows it to handle those in the latter class. Section 12.2 further classifies compiler-detected errors, and explains methods of recovering from erroneous input in order to obtain as much diagnostic information as possible from a single run. Support for run-time error handling is considered in Section 12.3.

12.1. General Principles

The class of *detectable errors* is determined by the design of the programming language, not the design of the compiler. An error handler should recognize and repair all detectable errors occurring in a program. Unfortunately, this goal often conflicts with the principle that a correct program should pay nothing for error handling. One compromise is to subdivide the detectable errors into several classes and proceed in a stepwise fashion: The detection of errors in different classes is provided for by distinct options in the compiler or controlled by additional monitoring code during execution.

Almost by definition, error handling involves a mass of special cases and exceptions to rules. It is thus very difficult to provide any sort of clean, theoretical foundation for this aspect of the compilation process. What we shall try to do in this section is to classify errors and outline the broad strategies useful in dealing with these classes.

12.1.1. Errors, Symptoms, Anomalies and Limitations We distinguish between the actual *error* and its *symptoms*. Like a physician, the error handler sees only symptoms. From these symptoms, it may attempt to *diagnose* the underlying error. The diagnosis always involves some uncertainty, so we may choose simply to report the symptoms with no further attempt at diagnosis. Thus the word 'error' is often used when 'symptom' would be more appropriate.

A simple example of the symptom/error distinction is the use of an undeclared identifier in LAX. The use is only a symptom, and could have arisen in several ways:

- The identifier was misspelled on this use.
- The declaration was misspelled or omitted.
- The syntactic structure has been corrupted, causing this use to fall outside of the scope of the declaration.

Most compilers simply report the symptom and let the user perform the diagnosis.

An error is detectable if and only if it results in a symptom that violates the definition of the language. This means that the error handling procedure is dependent upon the language definition, but independent of the particular source program being analyzed. For example, the spelling errors in an identifier will be detectable in LAX (provided that they do not result in another declared identifier) but not in FORTRAN, which will simply treat the misspelling as a new implicit declaration.

Our goal in implementation should be to report each detectable error at the earliest opportunity. If the symptom can be noticed at compile time, then we should do so. Some care must be taken, however, not to report errors *before* their symptoms occur. For example, the LAX expression (1/0) conforms to the syntax and static semantics of the language; the symptom 'division by zero' only occurs when the expression is actually evaluated during execution. It is important that the compiler *not* report an error in this case, even though it might detect the problem (say, while folding constants). The reason is that this expression may never actually be evaluated, and hence the program may not be incorrect at all. (Another possibility is that the programmer is attempting to force an execution-time error, perhaps to check out a new recovery mechanism.)

We shall use the term *anomaly* to denote something that appears suspicious, but that we cannot be certain is an error. Anomalies cannot be derived mechanically from the language definition, but require some exercise of judgement on the part of the implementor. As experience is gained with users of a particular language, one can spot frequently-occurring errors and report them as anomalies before their symptoms arise. An example of such a case is the fragment of ALGOL 60 shown in Figure 12.1a. Since ALGOL 60 treats text following **end** as a comment (terminated by **else**, **end** or ;), there is no inconsistency here. However, the appearance of := in the comment makes one suspicious that the user actually intended the fragment of Figure 12.1b. Many ALGOL 60 compilers will therefore report an anomaly in this case.

Note that a detectable error may appear as an anomaly before its symptoms arise: A LAX compiler could report the expression (1/0) as an anomaly even though its symptoms would not be detected until execution time. Reports of anomalies therefore differ from error reports in that they are simply warnings that the user may choose to suppress.

Anomalies may be reported even though there is no reason whatever to believe that they represent true errors; some compilers are quite prepared to simply comment on the programmer's style. The SIMULA compiler for the Univac 1108, for example, diagnoses Figure 12.1c as poor style because — as in ALGOL 60 — the upper limit of the iteration is evaluated $2n + 1$ times even though its value probably does not change during execution of the loop. Such reports may also be used to call the programmer's attention to nonstandard constructs supported by the particular system on which he is running.

A particular implementation normally places some *limitations* on the language definition, due to the finite resources at its disposal. (Examples include the limitation of finite-precision arithmetic, a limit on the number of identifiers in a program, the number of dimensions in an array or the maximum depth of parentheses in an expression.) Although violations of implementation-imposed constraints are not errors in the sense discussed above, they have the same effect for the user. A major design goal is therefore to minimize the number of such limitations, and to make them as 'reasonable' as possible. They should not be imposed lightly, simply to ease the task of the implementor, but should be based upon a careful analysis of the cost/benefit ratio for user programs.

12.1.2. Responses   We distinguish three possible levels of response to a symptom:

1. Report: Provide the user with an indication that an error has occurred. Specify the symptom, locate its position precisely, and possibly attempt a diagnosis.
2. Recover: Make the state of the process (compilation, execution) consistent and continue in an attempt to find further errors.
3. Repair: On the basis of the observed symptom, attempt a diagnosis of the error. If confident that the diagnosis is correct, make an appropriate alteration in the program or data and continue.

Both the compiler and the run-time system *must* at least report every symp-

end

$i := 1;$

a) A legal fragment of an ALGOL 60 program

end;

$i := 1;$

b) The probable intent of (a)

for $i := 1$ **step** 1 **until** $2*n + 1$

c) A probable inefficiency in SIMULA

Figure 12.1. Anomalies

tom they detect (level 1). Recovery (level 2) is generally provided only by the compiler, while repair may be provided by either. The primary criterion for recovery techniques is that the system must not collapse, since in so doing it may take the error message (and even the precise location of the symptom) with it. There is nothing more frustrating than a job that aborts without telling you why!

A compiler that reports the first symptom detected and then terminates compilation is not useful in practice, since one run would be needed for each symptom. (In an interactive setting, however, it may be reasonable for the compiler to halt at the first symptom, requiring the programmer to deal with it before continuing.) The compiler should therefore recover from almost all symptoms, allowing detection of as many as possible in a single run. Some errors (or restrictions) make it impossible for the compiler to continue; in this case it is best to give a report and terminate gracefully. We shall term such errors *deadly*, and attempt to minimize their number by careful language and compiler design.

Recovery requires that the compiler make some alteration of its state to achieve consistency. This alteration may cause spurious errors to appear in later text that is actually correct. Such spurious errors constitute an *avalanche*, and one of the major design criteria for a recovery scheme is to minimize avalanches. We shall discuss this point in more detail in Section 12.2.

If the compiler is able to diagnose and repair all errors with a high probability of success, then the program could safely be executed to permit detection of further errors. We must, however, be quite clear that a repair is *not* a correction. Much of the early literature on this subject used these terms interchangeably. This has unfortunate connotations, particularly for the novice, indicating that the compiler is capable of actually determining the programmer's intent.

Repair requires some circumspection, since the cost of execution could be very high and the particular nature of the repair could render that execution useless or could cause it to destroy important data files. In general, repair should not be attempted unless the user specifically requests it.

As in the case of recovery, we may classify certain errors as uneconomic or impossible to repair. These are termed *fatal*, and may cause us to refuse to execute the program. If a program containing a fatal error is to be executed, the compiler should produce code to abort the program when the error location is reached.

12.1.3. Communication with the User   The program listing is the primary document linking the user and the compiler. At a minimum, the listing reproduces the source program that the compiler translated; it may also provide indexes and cross-references to data items, labels and procedures. All error reports must indicate the relevant position of the symptom on the listing in addition to describing the symptom.

As indicated in Figure 1.3, the compiler itself should not produce the program listing. A separate *listing editor* uses the original source text and a compiler-generated error report file to create the listing. Each error report specifies the error number and a source text position. The reports are sorted according to source text position either by the compiler or by the listing editor. As the listing editor creates the listing, it inserts the full text of the error message at the error location. A standard format, which causes the message to stand out in the listing, should be used: Special characters, printed in some part of the print line that is normally blank, act as a flag. The position of the symptom is clearly marked, and the remainder of the line contains a brief description. This description should be *readable* (in the user's natural language), *restrained* and *polite*. It should be stated in terms of what the user has done (or not done) rather than in terms of the compiler's internal state. If the compiler has recovered from the error, the nature of the recovery should be made clear so that any resulting avalanche will be understandable.

Ideally, error reports should occur in two places: at the point where the compiler noticed the symptom, and in a summary at the end of the program. By placing a report at the point of detection, the compiler can identify the coordinates of the symptom in a simple manner and spare the programmer the task of switching his attention from one part of the listing to another. The summary report directs the programmer to the point of error without requiring him to scan the entire listing, reducing the likelihood that errors will be missed.

Compiler error reports may be classified into several levels according to severity:

1. Note
2. Comment
3. Warning
4. Error
5. Fatal error
6. Deadly error

Levels 1-3 are reports of anomalies: Notes refer to nonstandard constructs, and are only important for programs that will be transported to other implementations; comments criticize programming style; warnings refer to possible errors. The remaining levels are reports of actual errors or violations of limits. Errors at level 4 can be repaired, fatal errors suppress production of an executable program (but the compiler will recover from them), and deadly errors cause compilation to terminate.

The user should be able to suppress messages below a given severity level. Both the default severity cutoff and the number of reports possible on each level will vary with the design goals of the compiler. A compiler for use in introductory programming courses should probably have a default cutoff of 0 or 1, and produce a plethora of comments and warnings; one for use in a production operation with a single type of computer should probably have a cutoff of 3, and do very little repair. The ability to vary these characteristics is a key component in the adaptability of a compiler.

The programmer's ability to cope with errors seems to be inversely proportional to the *density* of errors. If the error density becomes very large, the compiler should probably abandon the program and let the programmer deal with those errors found so far. (There is always the chance that a job control error has been made, and the 'program' is really a data file or a program in another language!) It is difficult to state a precise criterion for abandonment, but possibly one should consider this response when the number of errors exceeds one-tenth of the number of lines processed and is greater than 10.

The error report file is maintained by a module that provides a single operation:

Error(*position,severity,code*)
  position : The source text position for the message.
  severity : One of the numbers 1-6, as discussed above.
  code : An integer defining the error.

There is no need to supply additional information, such as symbols or context, in the error report. For example, if the symptom is that a particular symbol is undefined, we do not need to include the symbol. This is because the position is located precisely, and the message points directly to the symbol for which there is no definition. Further, the position given by the report need not be the position reached by the lexical analyzer at the time the error was detected. We can retain position information for certain constructs and then use that information later when we have sufficient context to diagnose an error. For example, suppose that a label was declared in a Pascal program and then never used. The error would be diagnosed at the end of the procedure declaring the label, but we would give the position of the declaration in the report and therefore the message 'label never used' would point directly to the declaration.

12.2. Compiler Error Recovery

All errors detected at compile time are detected during analysis of the source program. During program synthesis, we can detect only compiler errors or violations of limits; these are invariably fatal, and do not interest us in this section. Errors detected during analysis can be classified by the analysis task being carried out at the time:

- Lexical. Errors in token formation, such as illegal characters or misspelled keywords.
- Syntactic. Errors in structure formation, such as missing operators or parentheses.

- Semantic. Errors in agreement, such as operands whose types are incompatible with their operator, or undeclared variables.

If recovery is to be achieved, each analysis task must repair the errors it detects and pass a consistent result to the next task. Unfortunately, this repair may be less than perfect; it usually leads to a local repair, rather than a repair in the sense of Section 12.1.2 and often results in detection of related errors by subsequent tasks that have more contextual information.

Any recovery scheme must be based upon redundant information present in the program. The higher the redundancy, the easier and more certain recovery will be. Since the amount of structure available to the error recovery procedure increases significantly from the lexical level to the semantic level, competent semantic error recovery is considerably easier than competent recovery from lexical errors. We shall therefore begin by discussing recovery from semantic errors and work our way back through syntactic errors to lexical errors.

12.2.1. Semantic Errors   Semantic errors are detected when conditions embedded in the attribute grammar of the language yield *false*. Recovery from semantic errors is simply a function of the attribute grammar itself. In Chapter 8 we emphasized the importance of guaranteeing that all attributes are defined under all circumstances, and noted that this implied the introduction of special error values for some attributes.

If the attributes of an item can be determined unambiguously then the compiler can work with the correct attributes after an error has been detected. This occurs in LAX with multiple definitions of an identifier in a range, possibly as a field selector or formal parameter. Operands on the right hand sides of identity declarations and assignments provide another example, as do situations in which the operator fully determines the type of the required operand(s). Finally, we have type declarations for which the storage requirements cannot be determined: **type** t = **record** a : *integer*;b:t **end**.

The recovery is more difficult if several attributes influence the choice, or if the erroneous symbol is not unambiguously determined. Consider the case of a binary operator indication, none of whose associated operators is consistent with the pattern of operand types given. This symptom could result from an error in one of the operand expressions, or from an erroneous operator indication. There is no way to be certain which error has occurred, although the probability of the former is enhanced if *one* of the operands is consistent with some operator associated with the indication. In this case, the choice of operator should be based upon the consistent operand, and might take into account the use of the result. If this choice is not correct, however, spurious errors may occur later in the analysis. To prevent an avalanche in this case, we should carry along the information that a semantic error has been repaired. Further error messages involving type mismatches of this result should then be suppressed.

Another important class of semantic error is the undeclared identifier. We have already noted (Section 12.1.1) that this error may arise in several ways. Clearly we should produce an error message if the problem was that the identifier was misspelled on this use, but if the declaration were misspelled or omitted the messages attached to each use of the variable constitute an avalanche, and should be suppressed.

In order to distinguish between these cases, we might set up a definition table entry for the undeclared identifier specifying as many properties as could be determined from the context of the use. Subsequent occurrences could then be used to refine the properties, but error messages would not be issued unless the properties were inconsistent. This strategy attempts to distinguish the cases on the basis of frequency of use of an identifier: At the first use an error will be reported; thereafter we assume that the declaration is missing or erroneous and do not make further reports. This method works well in practice. It breaks down when the programmer chooses an identifier susceptible to a consistent misspelling, or when the text is entered into the machine by a typist prone to a certain type of error (usually a character transposition or replacement).

The specific details of the consistency check are language dependent. As a concrete example, consider the algorithm used by the Whetstone Compiler for ALGOL 60 [Randell 1964]. (There the algorithm is not used to suppress avalanches, but rather to resolve forward references to declared identifiers in a one-pass compilation.) The Whetstone Compiler created a property set upon the first use of an (as yet) undeclared identifier, with each element specifying a distinct property that could be deduced from local context (Table 12.2). The first three elements of Table 12.2 determine the form of the use, while the remaining nine elements retain information about its context. For each successive occurrence, a new set A' was established and checked for consistency with the old one, A: The union of the two must be

Table 12.2. Identifier Properties in the Whetstone ALGOL Compiler

Property	Meaning
simple	The use takes the form of a simple variable.
array	The use takes the form of an array reference.
proc	The use takes the form of a procedure call.
value	The object may be used in a context where a value is required.
variable	The object is a variable to which assignments can be made.
arithmetic	The object has an arithmetic (i.e. integer or real) value.
Boolean	The object has a Boolean value.
integer	The object has an integer value.
location	The object is either a label or a switch.
normal	The object is not a label, switch or string.
string	The object is a string.
nopar	The object is a parameterless procedure.

identical to either set (e.g. A must be a subset of A' or A' must be a subset of A). If A' is a superset of A, then the new use provides additional information.

Suppose that we encounter the assignment $p := q$ where neither p nor q have been seen before. We deduce that both p and q must have the form of simple variables, and that values could be assigned to each; the type must therefore be real, integer or Boolean. If the assignment $r := p + s$; were encountered later, we could deduce that p must possess an *arithmetic* (i.e. real or integer) value. This use of p is consistent with the former use, and provides additional information. (Note that the same deduction can be applied to q, but this relationship is a bit too devious to pursue.) Figures 12.3a and 12.3b show the sets established for the first and second occurrences of p. If the statement $p[i] := 3$; were now encountered, the union of Figure 12.3c with Figure 12.3b would indicate an inconsistency.

If a declaration is available, we are usually not able to accept additional information about the variable. There is one case in ALGOL 60 (and in many other languages) in which the declaration does not give all of the necessary information: A procedure used as a formal parameter might or might not have parameters of its own, so the declaration does not specify which of the properties {*simple,proc*} should appear (Figure 12.3d). That decision must be deferred until a call of the procedure is encountered.

12.2.2. Syntactic Errors   A syntactic error is one resulting in a program that is not a sentence in the (context-free) language being compiled. Recovery from syntactic errors can change the structure of the program and the entire semantic analysis. (Lexical errors with such far-reaching consequences are considerably rarer.)

Consider the grammar $G = (N, T, P, Z)$ for the source language L. If we think of the elements of T^* as being points in space, we might ask which sentence is 'closest' to the erroneous program. We would then take this sentence as the correct version of the program, and define the error as the

{*simple, value, variable*}

a) Property set for both p and q derived from $p := q$

{*simple, value, variable, arithmetic*}

b) Property set for p derived from $r := p + s$;

{*array, value, variable*}

c) Property set for p derived from $p[i] := 3$;

procedure $x(p)$; **procedure** p;

d) A declaration that leaves properties unspecified

Figure 12.3. Consistency Checks

transformation that carries the correct program into the incorrect one. This approach is called *minimum-distance* correction, and it requires that we define a metric on the T^* space. One way of defining this metric is to regard every transformation as a sequence of elementary transformations, each corresponding to a distance of 1. The usual elementary transformations are:

- Insert one symbol
- Delete one symbol
- Replace one symbol by another

Global minimum-distance correction, which examines the entire program, is currently impractical. Moreover, a minimum-distance correction is often not the best: The minimum-distance correction for an ALGOL 60 statement containing more than one error would be to precede it with **comment**! For ALGOL-like languages simpler methods that can change more symbols are often superior. On the other hand, global minimum-distance correction minimizes avalanches.

The symptom of a syntactic error is termed a *parser-defined* error. Since we parse a program deterministically from left to right, the parser-defined error is the first symbol t such that ω is a head of some string in the language, but ωt is not. For example, the string ω of Figure 12.4a is certainly a head of a legal FORTRAN program, which might continue as shown in Figure 12.4b. If t is the end-of-statement marker, $\#$, then ωt is not the head of any legal program. Hence $\#$ constitutes a parser-defined error. Possible minimum-distance corrections are shown in Figure 12.4d. From the programmer's point of view, the first has the highest probability of being a correct program. This shows that a parser-defined error may not always coincide with the point of the error in the user's eyes. This is especially true for bracketing errors, which are generally the most difficult to repair.

Ad hoc parsing techniques, and even some of the older formal methods,

DO 10 I = J(K,L)

a) A head, ω, of a FORTRAN program

ω) $\#$ χ

b) A possible continuation ($\#$ is end-of-statement)

ω $\#$ χ

c) A parser-defined error

DO 10 I = J,K,L
DO 10 I = J(K,L)

d) Two minimum-distance corrections

Figure 12.4. Syntax Errors

may fail to detect any errors at all in certain strings not belonging to the language. Other approaches (e.g. simple precedence) may delay the point of detection arbitrarily. The LL and LR algorithms will detect the error immediately, and fail to accept t. This not only simplifies the localization of the symptom in the listing, but also avoids the need to process any syntactically incorrect text. Recovery is eased, since the immediate context of the error is still available for examination and alteration.

If $\omega t \chi \in (T^* - L)$ is an erroneous program with parser-defined error t, then to effect recovery the parser must alter either ω or $t\chi$ such that $\omega' t \chi \in L$ or $\omega t' \chi' \in L$. Alteration of ω is unpleasant, since it may involve undoing the effects of connection points. It will also slow the processing of correct programs to permit backtrack when an error is detected. Thus we shall only consider alteration of the erroneous symbol t and the following string χ.

Our basic technique will be to recover from each error by the following sequence of steps:

1. Determine a *continuation*, μ, such that $\omega\mu \in L$.
2. Construct a set of *anchors* $D = \{d \in T \mid \nu$ is a head of μ and $\omega\nu d$ is a head of some string in $L\}$.
3. Find the shortest string $\eta \in T^*$ such that $t\chi = \eta t''\mu', t'' \in D$.
4. Discard η from the input string and insert the shortest string $\nu \in T^*$ such that $\omega\nu t''$ is a head of some string in L.
5. Resume the normal parse.

This procedure can never cause the error recovery process to loop indefinitely, since at least one symbol (t'') of the input string is consumed each time the parser is restarted. Note also that it is never necessary to actually alter the input string during step (2); the parser is simply advanced through the required steps. A dummy symbol of the appropriate kind is created at each symbol connection encountered during this advance.

The sequence of connection points reported by the parser is always *consistent* when this error recovery technique is used. Semantic analysis can therefore proceed without checking for inconsistent input. Generated symbols, however, must be recognized as having arbitrary attributes. This is guaranteed by using special 'erroneous' attribute values as discussed in the previous section.

It is clear from the example of Figure 12.4 that we can make no claim regarding the 'correctness' of the continuation determined during step (1). The quality of the recovery in the eyes of the user depends upon the particular continuation chosen, but it seems unlikely that we will find an algorithm that 'optimizes' this choice at acceptable cost. We therefore advocate a process that can be incorporated into a parser generator and applied automatically without any effort on the part of the compiler writer. The most important benefit is a guarantee that the parser will recover from all syntactic errors, presenting only consistent input to the semantic analyzer. This guarantee cannot be made with ad hoc error recovery techniques.

We begin by designating one production for each nonterminal, such that the set of designated productions contains no recursion. For example, in the production set of Figure 12.5a we would designate the productions listed in Figure 12.5b. (With this example the designation is unique, a condition seldom encountered in larger grammars.) We then reorder the productions for each nonterminal so that the designated production is first, and apply the parser generation algorithms of Chapters 5 and 7. As the transitions of the parsing automata are derived, certain of them are *marked*. When an error occurs during the parse, we choose a valid continuation by allowing the parsing automaton to carry out the marked transitions until it reaches its final state. No input is read during this process, but at each step the set of input symbols that could be accepted is added to the set of anchors.

Construction 5.23, as modified in Section 7.2.1 for strong LL(1) gram-

$$P = \{ \quad Z \to E\#,$$
$$E \to FE',$$
$$E' \to +FE', E' \to \epsilon,$$
$$F \to i, F \to (E)\}$$

a) Productions of the grammar

$$Z \to E\#$$
$$E \to FE'$$
$$E' \to \epsilon$$
$$F \to i$$

b) Designated productions

$${}^*q_0i \to q_1q_2i, q_0(\to q_1q_2(,$$
$${}^*q_1 \to \epsilon,$$
$${}^*q_2i \to q_3q_4i, q_2(\to q_3q_5(,$$
$${}^*q_3\# \to q_6q_7\#, q_3) \to q_6q_7), q_3+ \to q_6q_8+,$$
$${}^*q_4i \to q_9,$$
$${}^*q_5(\to q_{10},$$
$${}^*q_6 \to \epsilon,$$
$${}^*q_7 \to \epsilon,$$
$${}^*q_8+ \to q_{11},$$
$${}^*q_9 \to \epsilon,$$
$${}^*q_{10}i \to q_{12}q_2i, q_{10}(\to q_{12}q_2(,$$
$${}^*q_{11}i \to q_{13}q_4i, q_{11}(\to q_{13}q_5(,$$
$${}^*q_{12}) \to q_{14},$$
$${}^*q_{13}\# \to q_{15}q_7\#, q_{13}) \to q_{15}q_7), q_{13}+ \to q_{15}q_8+,$$
$${}^*q_{14} \to \epsilon,$$
$${}^*q_{15} \to \epsilon$$

c) The transitions of the parsing automaton (compare Figure 7.5)

Figure 12.5. Adding Error Recovery to an LL(1) Parser

mars, was used to generate the automaton of Figure 12.5c. The transitions were marked as follows (marked transitions are preceded by an asterisk in Figure 12.5c):

- Any transition introduced by step 3 or step 4 of the construction was marked.
- The elements of H in step 5' are listed in the order discussed in the previous paragraph. The *first* transition $q\omega \rightarrow qh[1]\omega$ of a group introduced by step 5' was marked.

To see the details of the recovery, consider the erroneous sentence $i + \#$. Figure 12.6a traces the actions of the automaton up to the point at which the error is detected. The continuation is traced in Figure 12.6b. Note that the input is simply ignored, and the stack is updated as though the parser were reading symbols that caused it to make the marked transition. At each step, all terminal symbols that could be accepted are added to D. Figure 12.6c shows the remainder of the recovery. No symbols are deleted from the input string, since $\#$ is in the set of anchors. The parser now follows the continuation again, generating any terminal symbols needed to cause it to make the marked transitions. When it reaches a point where the first symbol of

$$q_0 i + \#$$
$$q_1 q_2 i + \#$$
$$q_1 q_3 q_4 i + \#$$
$$q_1 q_3 q_9 + \#$$
$$q_1 q_3 + \#$$
$$q_1 q_6 q_8 + \#$$
$$q_1 q_6 q_{11} \#$$

a) Parse to the point of error detection

$$q_1 q_6 q_{11} \qquad D = \{i\ (\}$$
$$q_1 q_6 q_{13} q_4$$
$$q_1 q_6 q_{13} q_9$$
$$q_1 q_6 q_{13} \qquad D = \{i\ (\#\ )+\}$$
$$q_1 q_6 q_{15} q_7$$
$$q_1 q_6 q_{15}$$
$$q_1 q_6$$
$$q_1$$

b) Continuation to the final state

$$q_1 q_6 q_{11} \#$$
$$q_1 q_6 q_{13} q_4 \#$$
$$q_1 q_6 q_{13} q_9 \# \qquad i \text{ is generated by } q_4 i \rightarrow q_9$$
$$q_1 q_6 q_{13} \# \qquad \text{the normal parse may now continue}$$

c) Continuation to the resume point

Figure 12.6. Recovery Using Figure 12.5c

the input string can be accepted, the normal parse resumes.

Let us now turn to the LR case. Figure 12.7a shows a left-recursive grammar for the same language as that defined by the grammar of Figure 12.5a. The designated productions are 1, 3 and 4. If we reorder productions 2 and 3 and then apply Construction 5.33, we obtain the states of Figure 12.7b. The situations are given in the order induced by the ordering of the productions and the mechanics of Construction 5.33. Figure 12.7c shows the transition table of the automaton generated from Figure 12.7b, incorporating shift-reduce transitions. The marked transition in each state (indicated by a prime) was the first shift, reduce or shift-reduce transition generated in that state considering the situations in order.

An example of the LR recovery is given in Figure 12.8, using the same

$$(1)\ Z \rightarrow E\#$$
$$(2)\ E \rightarrow E + F, \quad (3)\ E \rightarrow F$$
$$(4)\ F \rightarrow i, \quad\quad (5)\ F \rightarrow (E)$$

a) The grammar

```
0:  Z →.E ; #              4:  F →(.E) ; # +)
    E →.F ; # +                E →.F ; )+
    E →.E+F ; # +              E →.E+F ; )+
    F →.i ; # +                F →.i ; )+
    F →.(E) ; # +              F →.(E) ; )+

1:  Z →E. ; #              5:  E →E+.F ; # +)
    E →E.+F ; # +              F →.i ; # +)
                               F →.(E) ; # +)
2:  E →F. ; # +)
                           6:  F →(E.) ; # +)
3:  F →i. ; # +)               E →E.+F ; )+

                           7:  E →E+F. ; # +)

                           8:  F →(E). ; # +)
```

b) States of the Automaton

	i	(	)	+	#	E	F
0	-4′	4	.	.	.	1	-3
1	.	.	.	5	*1′		
4	-4′	4	.	.	.	6	-3
5	-4′	4	.	.	.		-2
6	.	.	-5′	5	.		

c) The transition function for the parser

Figure 12.7. Error Recovery in an LR(0) Parser

$$q_0 i +)i\#$$
$$q_0 q_1 +)i\#$$
$$q_0 q_1 q_5)i\#$$

a) Parse to the point of error detection

$$q_0 q_1 q_5 \quad D = \{ i \ (\}$$
$$q_0 q_1 \quad D = \{ i \ (\ + \ \# \ \}$$

b) Continuation to the final state

$$q_0 q_1 q_5 i\# \quad \text{the normal parse may now continue}$$

c) Continuation to the resume point

Figure 12.8. LR Error Recovery

format as Figure 12.6. The erroneous sentence is $i +)i\#$. In this case,) does not appear in the set of anchors and is therefore deleted.

One obvious question raised by use of automatic syntactic error recovery is that of providing meaningful error reports for the user. Fortunately, the answer is also obvious: Describe the repair that was made! This description requires one error number per token class (Section 4.1.1) to report insertions, plus a single error number to report deletions. Since token classes are usually denoted by a finite type, the obvious choice is to use the ordinal of the token class as the error number to indicate that a token of that class has been inserted.

Missing or superfluous closing brackets always present the danger that avalanches will occur because brackets are inserted in (globally) unsuitable places. For this reason we must take cognizance of error recovery when designing the grammar. In particular, we wish to make bracketed constructs 'visible' as such to the error recovery process. Thus the grammar should be written to ensure that closing brackets appear in the anchor sets for any errors that could cause them to be deleted from the input string. This condition guarantees that an opening bracket will not be deleted by mistake and lead to an avalanche error at the matching closing bracket. It is easy to see that the grammar of Figure 12.5a satisfies the condition, but that it would not if F were defined as follows:

$$F \rightarrow i, F \rightarrow (F',$$
$$F' \rightarrow E)$$

12.2.3. Lexical Errors The lexical analyzer recognizes two classes of lexical error: Violations of the regular grammar for the basic symbols and illegal characters not belonging to the terminal vocabulary of the language or, in languages with stropping conventions, misspelled keywords.

Violations of the regular grammar for the basic symbols ('structural' errors), such as the illegal LAX floating point number $.E2$, are recovered in essentially the same way as syntax errors. Characters are not usually deleted from the input string, but insertions are made as required to force the lexical analyzer to either a final state or a state accepting the next input character. If a character can neither form part of the current token, nor appear as the first character of *any* token, then it must be discarded. A premature transition to a final state can make two symbols out of one, usually resulting in syntactic avalanche errors. A third possibility is to skip to a symbol terminator like 'space' and then return a suitable symbol determined in an ad hoc manner. This is interesting because in most languages lexical errors occur primarily in numbers, where the kind of symbol is known.

Invalid characters are usually deleted without replacement. Occasionally these characters are returned to the parser so it can give a more informative report. This behavior violates the important basic principle that each analysis task should cope with its own errors.

When keywords are distinguished by means of underlines or bracketed by apostrophes, the compiler has sufficient information available to attempt a more complete recovery by checking for certain common misspellings. If we restrict ourselves to errors consisting of single-character substitutions, insertions, omissions or transpositions then the length of the basic symbol cannot change by more than one character. For each erroneous symbol there exists a (relatively small) set of correct keywords that are identical to it if one of these errors occurred.

If a spelling-correction algorithm is used, it should form a distinct module that tests a pair of strings to determine whether they are equivalent under one of the four transformations listed in the previous paragraph. The two strings should be in a standard form, chosen to speed the test for equivalence. This module can be used in other cases also, such as to check whether an undefined identifier is misspelled. The spelling-correction algorithm should not be required to scan a list of candidate strings, since different callers will generate candidates in different ways.

The decision to provide spelling correction usually has far-reaching effects on the compiler data structures: Searches for additional candidates to test against a misspelled word often have a pattern different from the normal accesses. This entails additional linkage, as well as the additional information to facilitate 'quick checks'. Such increases in data storage violate our previously-stated principle that an error-free program should not be required to pay for error recovery.

12.3. Run-Time Errors

During execution of a program, the values of the data objects obey certain restrictions and relationships, so that the operations of the program can be carried out. Most relationships result either implicitly or explicitly from the language definition or implementation restrictions. When the validity of these relationships cannot be determined from the context during compilation, they can be tested at run time with the help of the hardware or by code generated by the compiler. If such a test fails, then a symptom of a run-time error has been detected.

Examples of such relationships are given in Figure 12.9. Since $c**2$ cannot be less than 0, the compiler could prove that both the first and the third assertions in Figure 12.9b hold; in the case of $1+c**2 \neq 0$, however, this would be costly. Frequently the first assertion will be tested again at run time (and consequently the test could be omitted at compile time), because the computation and test of the storage mapping function is done by a standard library routine.

A run-time error report should give the symptom and location in the source program. The compiler must therefore provide at least the information needed by the run-time system to locate the symptom of the error. If a more exact description or a diagnosis of the cause of the error is required, the compiler must prepare additional information about the neighborhood of the error and its dynamic environment. Debugging aids (like traces and snapshots) require similar information from the compiler's symbol and definition tables.

In this section we shall not consider run-time error handling in detail. Our concern will be with the information that the compiler must provide to the run-time system to make competent error handling possible.

a : **array** [1:4, 1:4] **of** *real* ;
$\cdots$
$b := a[3, i]/(1+c**2)$

a) A LAX fragment

$$1 \leqslant 3 \leqslant 4$$
$$1 \leqslant i \leqslant 4$$
$$1+c**2 \neq 0$$

b) Relationships implied by the LAX definition and (a)

$$J = K * L$$

c) A FORTRAN statement

$$|K| < 2^{48}$$

d) Relationship implied by the
Control Data 6000 FORTRAN implementation and (c)

$$\text{ASSERT } m = n$$

e) Relationship explicitly stated by the programmer

Figure 12.9. Implicit and Explicit Relationships

12.3.1. Static Error Location   In order to specify the exact location of an error in the program, it must be possible to determine from the instruction position, z, the position, $f(z)$, of the corresponding source text in the program listing. This requires us to establish an appropriate coordinate system for the listing. The lines of the listing are usually chosen as the basis for this coordinate system, and are numbered in ascending order of appearance to facilitate location of a position in the program. The numbers may be chosen in various ways: One of the simplest is to use the address of the first instruction generated by the source line. (This numbering, like others discussed below, may contain gaps.) The contents of the location counter provides a direct reference to the program line if the compiler produces absolute code. If the compiler produces relocatable code and the final target program is drawn from several sources, then the conversion $f(z)$ first requires identification of the (separately compiled) program unit by means of a *load map* produced when the units are linked. This map gives the absolute address of each program unit. The relative address appearing on the listing is obtained by subtracting the starting address from the address of the erroneous instruction.

If the compiler has used several areas for instructions (Section 11.1.4), the monotonicity of the (relative) addresses is no longer guaranteed and we must use arbitrary *sequence numbers*. These numbers could be provided by the programmer himself or supplied by the compiler. In the latter case the number could be incremented for each line or for each construct of a given class (for example, assignments).

When arbitrary sequence numbers are used, the compiler must either store $f(z)$ in tabular form accessible to the run-time system or insert instructions into the target program to place the current sequence number into some specified memory location. If a table is given in a file, a relationship between the table and the program must be established by the run-time system; no further cost is incurred. In the second case all information is held within the program and a run-time overhead in both time and space is implied.

The line number, and even the position within the line, can be given for each instruction if a table is used. For dynamic determination of line numbers, the line number must be set in connection with a suitable syntactic unit of the source program. The instructions making up an assignment, for example, do not always occur in the order in which they appear in the source program. This is noticeable when the assignment is spread over several source lines. Of course the numbering need only be updated at those syntactic units that might fail; it may be omitted for the empty statement in ALGOL 60, for example.

12.3.2. Establishing the Dynamic Environment   Run-time errors usually lead to symptoms that can be described quite simply. Diagnosis of the error from these symptoms is considerably more difficult than diagnosis of compile time errors because it must take account of the dynamic environment of the error: the values of data objects being manipulated and the path by which control arrived at the failure point. Most of this information can be recovered from the contents of the memory at the failure point; the only difficulty lies in establishing the correct relationship to the source program. For this purpose, the compiler should at least provide sufficient information in the source program listing to enable the programmer to locate every data object in a printout of the memory contents. This information, in conjunction with that discussed in Section 12.3.1, we shall term *cross-reference information*; if it exists in tabular form, these tables are *cross-reference tables*.

Analysis of a memory dump is always tedious. In order to provide a more convenient specification of the data objects, the compiler could generate templates similar to those needed to support garbage collection (Section 3.3.3). These templates can then be used by a run-time support routine to print the object in a suitable form. Templates may be incorporated into the compiled program or written on an auxiliary file. Extra storage is required by the former approach, cooperation of the loader and the operating system by the latter.

A symbolic dump describes a single state of the computation—it is a 'snapshot' of the program's execution. In order to achieve a full understanding of the symptom we often need information about how the program reached the failure point. There are two aspects of this execution history, the *call hierarchy*, which specifies the procedures whose invocation has not yet ended, and the *jump history*, which defines the path taken through the procedures.

The call hierarchy is embodied in the current state as a chain of procedure activation records. In order to represent it we extend the symbolic dump by attaching the procedure name and point of call to each procedure's activation record. (The former is obtained from the cross-reference tables, the latter from the return address.)

The jump history, represented by the addresses of successful jumps, cannot be obtained from the environment of the symptom. It must be stored explicitly during execution. Either the compiler must generate specific instructions for this purpose, or the hardware must store the addresses of successful jumps automatically (EDSAC 2 [Barron 1963] and the Siemens 7000 series are examples of such machines). The relevance of the jump history diminishes with the 'age' of the jumps; to save memory we would therefore retain only the most recent jump addresses. In some debugging systems for machine-oriented languages the number 4 is chosen, EDSAC 2 chose 41 and the Siemens 7000 chose 64. Loops rapidly fill the jump history with useless information. It is thus better to store a sequence of identical jumps as a single address with a cycle count. Cycles of length 2 can be represented in a similar manner, but recognition of longer cycles does not seem worthwhile.

In a language like LAX, which provides a variety of control structures, source programs will usually contain no jumps at all. The jump history is thus understandable only if the sequence of source language constructs that created it can be recovered. For this purpose one can use the cross-referencing techniques of Section 12.3.1, augmented with information about the kind of jump (conditional, case clause, repetition of a loop, etc.) The source language constructs need be determined from the cross-reference tables only when the dump actually occurs, and then only for the jumps appearing in the jump history.

We must always be aware of the possibility that the state of the memory may have been corrupted by the error, and that inconsistencies may be present that could cause the analysis routines to loop or make further errors. During the output of a symbolic dump or jump history all information must be carefully examined for consistency. The compiler may provide redundant information, for example special bit patterns in particular places, to aid in this process.

12.3.3. Debugging Aids A program can be tested by following its progress to normal termination or to some unusual event. This can be done by tracing the jump addresses and/or procedure calls, tracing the values of certain data objects, or taking selective symbolic dumps. When working interactively, one can insert breakpoints to halt execution and permit examination and resetting of variables. The program can then be restarted at a specified point, possibly after alteration of the call hierarchy. All of these techniques require the support of the compiler as discussed in Sections 12.3.1 and 12.3.2.

All supervision mechanisms other than those specific to interactive execution can be provided by modification and recompilation of the program. With large programs this is quite costly; in addition, the modification can cause unrecognized side effects in the program's behavior. By concentrating the facilities in a test system independent of the compiler, this problem can be avoided. Such a solution increases the demands on the cross-reference tables, since the test system is now in the position of having to use them to modify the target program. If the same test system is to be used for several languages, then the structure and contents of the cross-reference tables becomes a standard interface for all compilers.

12.4. Notes and References

The user orientation of the error handling (understandable error reports, suppression of avalanches, run-time information in terms of the source program), and the principle that the cost of preventive tests should be as small as possible, obviously represent the main problems of error handling today. Koster [1972] gives a good overview of the demands placed upon the error handler. The implementation of PL/C [Conway 1973] represents an attempt at extensive error recovery.

Lyon [1974] gives an algorithm for global minimum-distance correction that requires $O(n^2)$ space and $O(n^3)$ time to correct an n-symbol input string. Theoretical results [Peterson 1972] indicate that improvement of these bounds is highly unlikely. A backtracking method for global repair of syntactic errors is given by Levy [1975]; our approach is based upon some ideas of Irons [1963b] that were applied to top-down parsers by Gries [1971]. Röhrich [1978, 1980] formalized these ideas and extended them to LR parsers. The use of recovery sequences as error messages first appeared in the SP/k compiler [Holt 1977].

Damerau [1964] has observed that over 80% of all spelling errors in a particular retrieval system consisted of single-character substitutions, insertions, omissions or transpositions. This observation serves as the basis for most spelling correction algorithms, of which the one described by Morgan [1970] is typical.

Dynamic updating of a variable containing a line number may consume significant resources. Brinch-Hansen [1975] notes that up to 25% of the generated code for a Sequential Pascal program may be devoted to line number bookkeeping. Kruseman-Aretz [1971] considers how this overhead can be minimized in the context of ALGOL 60, and Klint [1979] suggests that the information be obtained from a static analysis of the program rather than being maintained dynamically.

Symbolic dumps in source language terms have been available since the early sixties. The papers by Seegmüller [1963] and Bayer [1967] summarize the information the compiler must provide to support them. Other descriptions of this information can be found in the literature on symbolic debugging packages [Hall 1975, Pierce 1974, Satterthwaite 1972, Balzer 1969, Gaines 1969].

EXERCISES

12.1. Define the class of detectable errors for some language available at your installation. Which of these are detected at compile time? At run time? Are any of the detectable errors left undetected? Have you made any such errors in your programming?

12.2. We have classified the LAX expression (1/0) as a compile-time anomaly, rather than a compile-time error. Some authors disagree, arguing that if the expression is evaluated at run time it will lead to a failure and that if it can *never* be evaluated then the program is erroneous for other reasons. Write a cogent argument for or against (whichever you prefer) our classification.

12.3. The definition of the programming language Euclid specifies minimum limitations that may be placed on programs by an implementation. For example, the definition requires that any compiler accept expressions having parentheses nested to depth 7, and programs having environments nested to depth 31. The danger of setting such minimum limits is pointed out by Sale [1977], who demonstrates that the requirement for environments nested to depth 31 effectively precludes implementation of Euclid on Burroughs 6700 and 7700 equipment. Comment on the advantages and disadvantages of Euclid approach, indicating the scope of the problem and possible compromise solutions.

12.4. Consider some compiler running at your installation. How are its error messages communicated to the user? If the result gives less information than the model we discussed in Section 12.1.3, argue for or against its adequacy. Were there any constraints on the implementor forcing him to his choice?

12.5. Experiment with some compiler running at your installation, attempting to create an avalanche based upon a semantic error. If you succeed, analyze the cause of the avalanche. Could it have been avoided? How? At what cost to correct programs? If you do not succeed, analyze the cause of your failure. Is the language subject to avalanches from semantic errors? Is the implementation very clever, possibly at some cost to correct programs?

12.6. Under what conditions might a simple precedence analyzer [Gries 1971] delay detection of an error?

12.7. [Röhrich 1980] Give an algorithm for designating productions of a grammar so that there is one production designated for each nonterminal, and the set of designated productions contains no recursion.

12.8. Apply the syntactic error recovery technique of Section 12.2.2 to a recursive descent parser based upon extended BNF (Section 7.2.2).

12.9. Apply both the automaton of Figure 12.5c and that of Figure 12.7c to the string $(i(i + i \#$. Do you feel that the recovery is reasonable?

12.10. [Dunn 1981] Consider the modification of Figure 7.10 to support automatic error recovery.
    a. Assuming that the form of the table entry remained unchanged, how would you incorporate the definition of the continuation into the tables?
    b. Based upon your answer to (a), write procedures *parser_error*, *get_anchor* and *advance_parser* to actually carry out the recovery. These procedures should be nested in *parser* as follows, and *parser* should be modified appropriately to invoke them:
    parser
        parser_error
        get_anchor
        advance_parser
    c. Carefully explain your mechanism for generating symbols. Does it require access to information known only to the lexical analysis module? If so, how do you obtain this information?

12.11. [Morgan 1970] Design an algorithm for checking the equivalence of two strings under the transformations discussed in Section 12.2.3.. How would you interface this algorithm to the analysis process discussed in Chapters 6 and 7? *Be specific!*

12.12. Consider some compiler running at your installation. How is the static location of a run-time error determined when using that compiler? To what extent could the determination be automated without making any change to the compiler? What (if anything) would such automation add to the cost of running a correct program?

12.13. [Kruseman-Aretz 1971] A run-time error-reporting system for ALGOL 60 programs uses a variable *lnc* to hold the line number of the first basic symbol of the smallest statement whose execution has begun but not yet terminated. We wish to minimize the number of assignments to *lnc*. Give an algorithm that decides when assignments to *lnc* must be generated.

12.14. Consider some compiler running at your installation. How is the dynamic environment of a run-time error determined when using that compiler? To what extent could the determination be automated without making any change to the compiler? What (if anything) would such automation add to the cost of running a correct program?

12.15. [Bayer 1967] Consider some language and machine with which you are familiar. Define a reasonable symbolic dump format for that language, and specify the information that a compiler must supply to support it. Give a detailed encoding of the information for the target computer, and explain the cost increase (if any) for running a correct program. ed without making any change to the compiler? What (if anything) would such automation add to the cost of running a correct program?

CHAPTER 13
Optimization

Optimization seeks to improve the performance of a program. A true optimum may be too costly to obtain because most optimization techniques interact, and the entire process of optimization must be iterated until there is no further change. In practice, therefore, we restrict ourselves to a fixed sequence of transformations that leads to useful improvement in commonly-occurring cases. The primary goal is to compensate for inefficiencies arising from the characteristics of the source language, not to lessen the effects of poor coding by the programmer. These inefficiencies are inherent in the concept of a high level language, which seeks to suppress detail and thereby simplify the task of implementing an algorithm.

Every optimization is based upon a cost function, a meaning-preserving transformation, and a set of relationships occurring within some component of the program. Code size, execution time and data storage requirements are the most commonly used cost criteria; they may be applied individually, or combined according to some weighting function.

The boundary between optimization and competent code generation is fuzzy. We have chosen to regard techniques based upon processing of an explicit computation graph as optimizations. A computation graph is implicit in the execution-order traversal of the structure tree, as pointed out at the beginning of Chapter 10, but the code generation methods discussed so far do not require that it ever appear as an explicit data structure. In this chapter we shall consider ways in which a computation graph can be manipulated to improve the performance of the generated code.

Our treatment in this chapter differs markedly from that in the remainder of the text. The nature of most optimization problems makes computationally efficient algorithms highly unlikely, so the available techniques are all heuristic. Each has limited applicability and many are quite complex. Rather than selecting a particular approach and exploring it in detail, we shall try to explain the general tasks and show how they fit together. Citations to appropriate literature will be given along with the discussion. In Section 13.1 we motivate the characteristics of the computation graph and sketch its implementation. Section 13.2 focuses on optimization within a region containing no jumps, while Section 13.3 expands our view to a complete compilation unit. Finally, Section 13.4 gives an assessment of the gains to be expected from various optimizations and the costs involved.

13.1. The Computation Graph

Profitable optimizations usually involve the implementation of data access operations, and hence the target form of these operations should be made explicit before optimization begins. Moreover, many optimizations depend upon the execution order, and others may alter that order. These requirements make the structure tree an unsuitable representation of the program being optimized. In the first place, the structure tree reflects the semantics of the source language and therefore suppresses detail. Secondly, execution-order tree traversals depend upon the values of specified attributes and hence cannot be generated mechanically by the tools of Chapter 8.

Data access operations are often implicit in the target machine code as well: They are incorporated into the access paths of instructions, rather than appearing as separate computations. Because of this, it is difficult to isolate them and discover patterns that can be optimized. The target tree is thus also an unsuitable representation for use by an optimizer.

To avoid these problems, we define the computation graph to have the following properties:

- All source operations have been replaced by (sequences of) operations from the instruction set of the target machine. Coercions appear as machine operations only if they result in code. Other coercions, which only alter the interpretation of the binary representation of a value, are omitted.
- Every operation appears individually, with the appropriate number of operands. Operands are either intermediate results or directly-accessible values. Each value has a specified target type.
- All address computations are explicit.
- Assignments to program variables are separated from other operations.
- Control flow operations are represented by conditional and unconditional jumps.

Although based upon target machine operations, the computation graph is largely machine-independent because the instruction sets of most Von Neumann machines are very similar.

We assume that every operation has no more than one result. To satisfy this assumption, we either ignore any side effects of the machine instruction(s) implementing the operation or we create a sequence of operations making those side effects explicit. In both cases we rely upon subsequent processing to generate the proper instructions. For example, the arithmetic operations of some machines set the condition code as a side effect. We ignore this, producing comparison operators (whose one result is placed in the condition code) where required. Peephole optimization (Section 13.2.3) will remove superfluous comparisons in cases where a preceding arithmetic operation has properly set the condition code. The second approach is used to deal with the fact that on many machines the integer division instruction yields both the quotient and the remainder. Here we create a sequence of two operations for both **div** and **mod**. The first operation in each case is *divmod*; the second is a unary selector, *div* or *mod* respectively, that operates on the result of *divmod*. Common subexpression elimination (Section 13.2.1) will remove any superfluous *divmod* operators.

The atoms of the computation graph are *tuples*. A tuple consists of an operator of the (abstract) target machine and one or more operands, each of which is either a value known to the compiler or the result of a computation described by a tuple. Each appearance of a tuple in the computation graph is called a *program point*, and given an integer index greater than 0.

Let o_1 and o_2 be operands in a computation graph. These operands are *congruent* if they are the same known value, or if they are the results of tuples t_1 and t_2 with the same numbers of operands for which $operator(t_1) = operator(t_2)$ and $operand_i(t_1)$ is congruent to $operand_i(t_2)$ for all i. A unique *operand identifier* is associated with each set of congruent operands, and this identifier is used to denote all of the operands in the set.

Figure 13.1b has 12 program points and 9 distinct tuples. Values known to the compiler have the corresponding source language constructs as their operand identifiers. The full definition of a tuple is given only at its first occurrence; subsequent occurrences are denoted by the operand identifier

$$V.i := aa \uparrow *y + V.j \,; \, aa \uparrow := aa \uparrow + V.j \,;$$

a) A Pascal fragment

$t_1: aa \uparrow$	t_1
$t_2: t_1 \uparrow$	t_2
$t_3: y \uparrow$	t_5
$t_4: t_2 * t_3$	$t_8: t_2 + t_5$
$t_5: V.j \uparrow$	$t_9: t_1 := t_8$
$t_6: t_4 + t_5$	
$t_7: V.i := t_6$	

b) The tuple sequence resulting from (a)

Figure 13.1. Tuples and Operands

alone. Note that each operand identifier denotes a *single* value. For example, $V.j$ is the address of the j field of the record V, relative to the base of the activation record. This value is the sum of the offset of V from the base of the activation record and the offset of j from the base of the record. Both offsets are known to the compiler, and hence the sum is known. Also, contrast the representations of the two assignments. In the first, the target address ($V.i$) is known to the compiler, while in the second it is the content of a pointer variable.

A module very similar to the symbol table acts as a source of unique operand identifiers. By analogy to section 4.2.1, this module provides three operations:

- *initialize*: Enter the standard entities.
- *give_operand_identifier(tuple_spec)operand_identifier*: Obtain the operand identifier for a specified tuple or known value.
- *give_tuple(operand_identifier)tuple_spec*: Obtain the tuple or known value having a specified operand identifier.

Tuple_spec is a variant record capable of describing any tuple or known value. One possible representation would be as two major variants, a value descriptor to specify a known value and an operator plus an array of operand identifiers to specify a tuple.

A *straight-line segment* is a set of tuples, each of which will be executed exactly once whenever the first is executed. A straight-line segment of maximal length is called a *basic block*. The *flow graph* of a compilation unit is a directed graph whose nodes are basic blocks and whose edges specify the possible execution sequences of those basic blocks. We also sometimes consider *extended basic blocks*, which are subtrees of the flow graph. (Extended basic blocks correspond to nested conditional clauses and to the bodies of innermost loops that contain no jumps.)

The value of every tuple depends ultimately upon some set of variables. If the value of any of these variables changes, then the value computed by the tuple will also change. Figure 13.2c is a directed acyclic graph illustrating such dependency for the tuples of Figure 13.2b. A tuple is dependent upon a variable if there is a directed path in the graph from the node corresponding to the variable to the node corresponding to the tuple. When the value of a variable is altered, any previously-computed value of a tuple depending upon that variable becomes invalid. Note that a is treated as a single variable, whose value directly influences the value of t_4 but not the value of t_3.

In general, evaluation of a particular tuple may use some operand values, define some operand values and invalidate some operand values. We can define the following *dependency sets* for each tuple t:

$$U_t = \{o \mid o \text{ is a tuple or program variable operand of } t\}$$
$$D_t = \{o \mid o \text{ is an operand defined by } t\}$$
$$X_t = \{o \mid o \text{ is an operand invalidated by } t\}$$

$$w := a[i]; a[j] := x; z := a[i] + z;$$
a) A Pascal fragment

$t_1: i \uparrow$	$t_6: j \uparrow$	t_1
$t_2: t_1 * 4$	$t_7: t_6 * 4$	t_2
$t_3: a + t_2$	$t_8: a + t_7$	t_3
$t_4: t_3 \uparrow$	$t_9: x \uparrow$	t_4
$t_5: w := t_4$	$t_{10}: t_8 := t_9$	$t_{11}: z \uparrow$
		$t_{12}: t_4 + t_{11}$
		$t_{13}: z := t_{12}$

b) Tuple sequence resulting from (a)

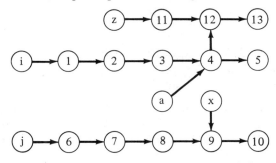

c) Dependency graph for the tuples of (b)

	U	D	X
t_1	$\{\}$	$\{i \uparrow\}$	$\{\}$
t_2	$\{i \uparrow\}$	$\{t_1 * 4\}$	$\{\}$
t_3	$\{t_1 * 4\}$	$\{a + t_2\}$	$\{\}$
t_4	$\{a + t_2\}$	$\{t_3 \uparrow\}$	$\{\}$
t_5	$\{t_3 \uparrow\}$	$\{w \uparrow\}$	$\{\}$
t_6	$\{\}$	$\{j \uparrow\}$	$\{\}$
t_7	$\{j \uparrow\}$	$\{t_6 * 4\}$	$\{\}$
t_8	$\{t_6 * 4\}$	$\{a + t_7\}$	$\{\}$
t_9	$\{\}$	$\{x \uparrow\}$	$\{\}$
t_{10}	$\{a + t_7, x \uparrow\}$	$\{t_8 \uparrow\}$	$\{t_3 \uparrow, t_4 + t_{11}\}$
t_{11}	$\{\}$	$\{z \uparrow\}$	$\{\}$
t_{12}	$\{t_3 \uparrow, z \uparrow\}$	$\{t_4 + t_{11}\}$	$\{\}$
t_{13}	$\{t_4 + t_{11}\}$	$\{z \uparrow\}$	$\{t_4 + t_{11}\}$

d) Dependency sets for the tuples of (b)

Figure 13.2. Analyzing Array References

The rules of the language determine these sets. Figure 13.2d shows the sets
for the tuples of Figure 13.2b.

The effect of an assignment to a pointer variable is similar to, but more extensive than, that of an assignment to an array element. Pointer variables in Pascal or Ada potentially access any anonymous target of any other pointer variable of the same type. In LAX or ALGOL 68, *every* object of the given target type is potentially accessible. A reference parameter of a procedure has the same properties as a LAX or ALGOL 68 pointer in most languages, except that the accessibility is limited to objects outside the current activation record. A procedure call must be assumed to use and potentially modify every variable visible to that procedure, as well as every variable passed to it as a reference parameter.

To construct the computation graph, we apply the storage mapping, target attribution and code selection techniques of Sections 10.1-10.3. These methods yield the tuples in an execution order determined by the target attributes, in particular the register estimate. The only changes lie in the code selection process (Section 10.3), where the abstract nature of the computation graph must be reflected.

A new *value_class, generated,* must be introduced in Figure 10.12. If the *class* of a value descriptor is *generated*, the variant part contains a single *id* field specifying an operand identifier. Decision tables (such as Figure 10.15) do not have tests of operand value class in their condition stubs, nor do they generate different instructions for memory and register operands. The result is a significant reduction in the table size (Figure 13.3). Note that the *gen* routine calls in Figure 13.3 still specify machine operation codes, even though no instruction is actually being produced. This is done to emphasize the fact that the tuple's operator is actually a machine operator. In this case we have chosen 'A' to represent IBM 370 integer addition. A tuple whose operator was A might ultimately be coded using an AR instruction or appear as an access path of an RX-format instruction, but it would never result in (say) a floating add.

The *gen* routine's behavior is controlled by the operator and the operand descriptor classes. When the operands are literal values and the operator is

Result correct	Y	Y	Y	Y	N	N	N	N
ℓ correct	Y	Y	N	N	Y	Y	N	N
r correct	Y	N	Y	N	Y	N	Y	N
$swap(\ell,r)$				X			X	
$gen(A,\ell,r)$	X			X	X			X
$gen(S,\ell,r)$		X	X			X	X	
$gen(LCR,\ell,\ell)$				X	X			

Figure 13.3. Decision Table for +(*integer,integer*) *integer* Based on Figure 10.15

one made available by the constant table, then the specified computation is performed and the appropriate literal value delivered as the result. In this case, nothing is added to the computation graph. Memory operands (either addresses or values) are checked to determine whether they are directly addressable. If not, tuples are generated to produce the specified results. In any case, the value descriptors are altered to class *generated* and an appropriate operand identifier is inserted. Finally a tuple is generated to describe the current operation and the proper operand identifier is inserted into the value descriptor for the left operand.

Although we have not shown it explicitly, part of the input to the *gen* routine specifies the program variables potentially used and destroyed. This information is used to derive the dependency sets. An example giving the flavor of the process can be found in the description of Bliss-11 [Wulf 1975].

13.2. Local Optimization

The simplest approach to optimization is to treat each basic block as a separate unit, optimizing it without regard to its context. A computation graph is built for the basic block, transformed, and used to generate the final machine code. It is then discarded and the next basic block is considered.

Our strategy for optimizing a basic block is to carry out the following steps in the order indicated:

1. *Value Numbering*: Perform a 'symbolic execution' of the block, propagating symbolic values and eliminating redundant computations.
2. *Coding*: Collect access paths for program variables and combine them with operations to form valid target machine instructions, assuming an infinite set of registers.
3. *Peephole Optimization*: Attempt to combine sequences of instructions into single instructions having the same effect.
4. *Register Allocation*: Map the register set resulting from the coding step onto the available target machine registers, generating spill code (code to save and/or restore registers) as necessary.

Throughout this section we assume that all program variables are potentially accessed after the end of the basic block, and that no tuple values are. The latter assumption fails for an expression-oriented language, and in that case we must treat the tuple representing the final value of the expression computed by the block as a program variable. Section 13.3 will consider the more general case occurring as a result of global optimization.

13.2.1. Value Numbering Access computations for composite objects are rich sources of *common subexpressions*. One classic example is the code for the following FORTRAN statement, used in solving three-dimensional boundary value problems:

$$A(I,J,K) = \quad (A(I,J,K-1) + A(I,J,K+1) + $$
$$A(I,J-1,K) + A(I,J+1,K) + $$
$$A(I-1,J,K) + A(I+1,J,K)) \; / \; 6.0$$

The expression $I + d_1 * (J + d_2 * K)$, where d_1 and d_2 are the first two dimensions of A, is generated (in combination with various constants) seven times. The value of this expression cannot change during evaluation of the assignment statement if I, J and K are variables, and hence six of the seven occurrences are redundant.

Value numbering is used to detect and eliminate common subexpressions in a basic block. The general idea is to simulate the computation described by the tuples, generating a new basic block that is no longer than the origi-

invalid := *initialize_vn*;
Set all elements of *PV* to *invalid*;
for *i* := first program point **to** last program point **do**
 if $PV[t_i] = invalid$ **then**
 begin
 $T := evaluate(t_i)$;
 if $T = "v := o"$ **then**
  begin
  if $PV[v \uparrow] \neq PV[o]$ **then**
   begin $V := new\_value(T)$; **for** $tuple \in X_{t_i}$ **do** $PV[tuple] := invalid$ **end**;
  $V := PV[o]$;
  end
 else if $(T \neq "v \uparrow")$ **and** $(T \; occurred \; earlier)$ **then**
  $V :=$ value number of the previous occurrence of T
 else
  begin $V := new\_value(T)$; **for** $tuple \in X_{t_i}$ **do** $PV[tuple] := invalid$ **end**;
 for $tuple \in D_{t_i}$ **do** $PV[tuple] := V$;
 end;

a) The algorithm

Operation	Meaning
initialize_vn : *value_number*	Clear the output block and return the first value number.
evaluate (*tuple*): *tuple*	Create a new tuple by replacing each tuple reference *t* in the argument by $PV[t]$. Return the newly-created tuple.
new_value (*tuple*): *value_number*	Add *tuple* to the output block, associating it with a new value number. Return the new value number.

b) Operations of the output module

Figure 13.4. Value Numbering

nal. In the new basic block, only fetch ($v \uparrow$) and assignment ($v := o$) tuples may appear at more than one program point. Each such occurrence is given a unique identifier, so that every tuple appearing in the new basic block is associated with a distinct identifier. These new identifiers are called *value numbers,* since each denotes a particular value generated by the computation. As the new basic block is being constructed, we use an array to keep track of the value numbers that currently denote the values generated by each tuple. A distinguished value number denotes an unknown value. Figure 13.4 defines the value numbering algorithm, and the example of Figure 13.5 gives the flavor of the process. (Operand identifiers of the form v_i have been used in Figure 13.5c to emphasize the fact that a new set of tuples is being generated, and that the value numbers can be used as operand identifiers.)

Simulation of t_1 requires generation of an assignment, and as a result the value of $a \uparrow$ is known to be 2. Tuple t_2 then has a value known to the compiler; no computation is required in the basic block being generated. No value is known for $X \uparrow$, so v_2 must be generated. When we reach t_7, the

$$a := 2;$$
$$b := a*X + 1;$$
$$a := 2*X;$$
$$c := a + 1 + b;$$

a) A sequence of assignments

Tuple	U	D	X
$t_1: a := 2$	{}	$\{a \uparrow\}$	$\{t_2*t_3, t_4+1, t_2+1, t_9+t_{10}\}$
$t_2: a \uparrow$	{}	$\{a \uparrow\}$	{}
$t_3: X \uparrow$	{}	$\{X \uparrow\}$	{}
$t_4: t_2*t_3$	$\{a \uparrow, X \uparrow\}$	$\{t_2*t_3\}$	{}
$t_5: t_4+1$	$\{t_2*t_3\}$	$\{t_4+1\}$	{}
$t_6: b := t_5$	$\{t_4+1\}$	$\{b \uparrow\}$	$\{t_9+t_{10}\}$
t_3			
$t_7: 2*t_3$	$\{X \uparrow\}$	$\{2*t_3\}$	{}
$t_8: a := t_7$	$\{2*t_3\}$	$\{a \uparrow\}$	$\{t_2*t_3, t_4+1, t_2+1, t_9+t_{10}\}$
t_2			
$t_9: t_2+1$	$\{a \uparrow\}$	$\{t_2+1\}$	{}
$t_{10}: b \uparrow$	{}	$\{b \uparrow\}$	{}
$t_{11}: t_9+t_{10}$	$\{t_2+1, b \uparrow\}$	$\{t_9+t_{10}\}$	{}
$t_{12}: c := t_{11}$	$\{t_9+t_{10}\}$	$\{c \uparrow\}$	{}

b) Tuples and sets for (a)

$v_1: a := 2$	$v_5: b := v_4$
$v_2: X \uparrow$	$v_6: a := v_3$
$v_3: 2*v_2$	$v_7: v_4+v_4$
$v_4: v_3+1$	$v_8: c := v_7$

c) Transformed computation graph

Figure 13.5. Common Subexpression Elimination

value computed by t_3 is known to be v_2. The computation needed in the new basic block is therefore $2*v_2$. But a tuple for this computation will have already been executed, and we have called its result v_3. Thus $2*v_2$ is a common subexpression that may be eliminated. The only result of the simulation is to note that the value of t_7 is v_3.

Execution of t_8 may cause four earlier computations to yield new values if carried out again (the other three elements of X_{t_8} correspond to computations not yet performed). Thus we must treat the old values of those computations as invalid at this point. In addition, the value of $a \uparrow$ is set to v_3 by t_8. The values of t_2, t_9 and t_{10} are known. Finally, t_{11} and t_{12} result in the last two tuples of Figure 13.5c. As can be seen from this example, value numbering recognizes some common subexpressions even when they are written differently in the source program.

In more complex examples than Figure 13.5, the precise identity of the accessed object may not be known. For example, the value of $a[i]$ in Figure 13.2a might be altered even though none of the assignment tuples in the corresponding straight-line segment has $a[i]$ as a target. The analysis uses $X_{t_{10}}$ to account for this phenomenon, yielding the basic block of Figure 13.6. Note that the algorithm correctly recognizes the *address* of $a[i]$ as being a common subexpression.

The last step in the value numbering process is to delete redundant assignments to program variables (such as v_1 in Figure 13.5c) and, as a byproduct, to develop use counts for all of the tuples. Figure 13.7 gives the algorithm. Since each tuple value is defined exactly once, and never used

$$
\begin{array}{l|l|l}
v_1: i \uparrow & v_6: j \uparrow & v_{11}: v_3 \uparrow \\
v_2: v_1 * 4 & v_7: v_6 * 4 & v_{12}: z \uparrow \\
v_3: a + v_2 & v_8: a + v_7 & v_{13}: v_{11} + v_{12} \\
v_4: v_3 \uparrow & v_9: x \uparrow & v_{14}: z := v_{13} \\
v_5: w := v_4 & v_{10}: v_8 := v_9 &
\end{array}
$$

Figure 13.6. Value Numbering Applied to Figure 13.2

for $o \in \underset{t}{\cup} [U_t \cup D_t]$ **do** $USECOUNT[o] := 0$;

for $o \in \{\text{Program variables}\}$ **do** $USECOUNT[o \uparrow] := 1$;

for $i := $ last program point **downto** first program point **do**
  begin
  $c := 0$;
  for $o \in D_{t_i}$ **do**
    begin
    $c := c + USECOUNT[o]$;
    if o is a program variable **then** $USECOUNT[o] := 0$;
    end;
  if $c = 0$ **then** delete tuple t_i
  else for $o \in U_{t_i}$ **do** $USECOUNT[o] := USECOUNT[o] + 1$;
  end;

Figure 13.7. Redundant Assignment Elimination and Use Counting

before it is defined, $USECOUNT[v]$ will give the number of uses of v at the end of the algorithm. The entries for program variables, on the other hand, may not be accurate because they include potential uses by procedures and pointer assignments.

The analysis discussed in this section can be easily generalized to extended basic blocks. Each path through the tree of basic blocks is treated as a single basic block; when the control flow branches, we save the current information in order to continue the analysis on the other branch. Should constant folding determine that the condition of a conditional jump is fixed, we replace this conditional jump by an unconditional jump or remove it. In either case one of the alternatives and the corresponding basic block is superfluous and its code can be deleted. These situations arise most frequently in automatically-generated code, or when the **if** · · · **then** · · · **else** construct, controlled by a constant defined at the beginning of the program, is used for conditional compilation.

To generalize Figure 13.7, we begin by analyzing the basic blocks at the leaves of the extended basic block. The contents of $USECOUNT$ are saved, and analysis restarted on a predecessor block by resetting each element of $USECOUNT$ to the maximum of the saved values for the successors. We cannot guarantee consistency in the use counts by this method, since not all of the use counts must reach their maxima along the same execution path. It turns out, however, that this inconsistency is irrelevant for our purposes.

13.2.2. Coding   The coding process is very similar to that of Section 10.3. We maintain a value descriptor for each operand identifier, and simulate the action of the target computer using these value descriptors as a data base. There is no need to maintain register descriptors, since we are assuming an infinite supply.

Figure 13.8 gives two possible codings of Figure 13.1a for the IBM 370. Our notation for describing the instructions is essentially that of Davidson [1980]: 'R[· · ·]' means 'contents of register · · · ' and 'M[· · ·]' means 'contents of the memory location addressed by · · · '. Register numbers greater than 15 represent 'abstract registers' of the infinite-register machine, while those less than 15 represent actual registers whose usage is prescribed by the mapping specification. (As discussed in Section 10.2.1, register 13 is used to address the local activation record.)

The *register transfer notation* of Figure 13.8 is independent of the target machine (although the particular descriptions of Figure 13.8b are specific to the IBM 370), and is useful for the peephole optimization discussed at the end of this section. Figure 13.8b is not a complete description of the register transfers for the given instructions, but it suffices for the current example. Later we shall show an example that uses a more complete description.

The differences between the left and right columns of Figure 13.8b stem from the choice of the left operand of the multiply instruction, made when the second line was generated. Because the multiply is a two-address instruction, the value of the left operand will be replaced by the value of the result. Wulf [1975] calls this operand the *target path*.

In generating the left column of Figure 13.8b, we used Wulf's criterion: Operand v_2 has a use count greater than 1, and consequently it cannot be destroyed by the operation because it will be needed again. It should not lie on the target path, because then an extra instruction would be needed to copy it. Since v_3 is only used once, no extra instructions are required when it is chosen as the target path. Nevertheless, the code in the right column is two bytes shorter—why? The byte counts for the first six rows reflect the extra instruction required to preserve v_2 when it is chosen as the target path. However, that instruction is an LR rather than an L and thus its cost is only two bytes. It happens that the last use of v_2 involves an operation with two memory operands, one of which must be loaded at a cost of 4 bytes! If the last use involved an operation whose other operand was in a register, we could use an RR instruction for that operation and hence the byte counts of the two codings would be equal.

This example points up the fact that the criteria for target path selection depend strongly upon the target computer architecture. Wulf's criterion is

Tuple	Use count
v_1: aa ↑	2
v_2: v_1 ↑	2
v_3: y ↑	1
v_4: $v_2 * v_3$	1
v_5: $V.j$ ↑	2
v_6: $v_4 + v_5$	1
v_7: $V.i := v_6$	
v_8: $v_2 + v_5$	1
v_9: $v_1 := v_8$	

a) Result of value numbering

R[16] := M[R[13]+aa]	R[16] := M[R[13]+aa]
R[17] := M[R[13]+y]	R[17] := M[R[16]+0]
	R[18] := R[17]
R[17] := R[17]*M[R[16]+0]	R[18] := R[18]*M[R[13]+y]
R[17] := R[17]+M[R[13]+$V.j$]	R[18] := R[18]+M[R[13]+$V.j$]
M[R[13]+$V.i$] := R[17]	M[R[13]+$V.i$] := R[18]
R[18] := M[R[16]+0]	
R[18] := R[18]+M[R[13]+$V.j$]	R[17] := R[17]+M[R[13]+$V.j$]
M[R[16]+0] := R[18]	M[R[16]+0] := R[17]

32 bytes   30 bytes
3 registers   4 registers

b) Two possible codings

Figure 13.8. Coding Figure 13.1 for the IBM 370.

the proper one for the DEC PDP11, but not for the IBM 370.

Figure 13.8b does not account for the fact that the IBM 370 multiply instruction requires the multiplicand to be in an odd register and leaves the product in a register pair. The register allocation process must enforce these conditions in any event, and it does not appear useful to introduce extra notation for them at this stage. We shall treat the problem in detail in Section 13.2.4.

13.2.3. Peephole Optimization   Every tuple of the computation graph corresponds to some instruction of the target machine. It may be, however, that a sequence of several tuples can be implemented as a single instruction. The purpose of peephole optimization is to combine such tuples, reducing the size of the basic block and the number of intermediate values. There are two basic strategies:

- Each instruction of the target machine is defined in terms of register transfers. The optimizer determines the overall register transfer of a group of instructions and seeks a single instruction with the same effects [Davidson 1980].
- A set of patterns describing instruction sequences is developed, and a single instruction associated with each. When the optimizer recognizes a given pattern in the basic block, it performs the associated substitution [Tanenbaum 1982].

Figure 13.9 illustrates register transfer descriptions of PDP11 and IBM 370 instructions; no attempt at completeness has been made in either case. Upper-case identifiers and special characters are matched as they stand, while lower-case identifiers represent generic patterns as indicated. (Note that in Figure 13.9b the description of an add instruction fits both A and AR; there is no need to distinguish these instructions until assembly, when they could be encoded by the technique of Section 11.3.2.) Literal characters in the patterns are chosen simply for their mnemonic value. The optimizer needs no concept of machine operations; optimization is carried out solely on the basis of pattern matching and replacement. Thus the *process* is machine-independent—all machine dependence is concentrated in the register transfer descriptions themselves.

In Section 13.1 we asserted that extra comparisons introduced to allow us to ignore the side effect of condition code setting in arithmetic instructions could easily be removed. The example of Figure 13.10 illustrates the steps involved. (Abstract registers have numbers larger than 7, and we assume that register 5 addresses the local activation record.) Note that the combined effect of the move and compare instructions (Figure 13.10d) is identical to the effect of the move instruction (line 3 of Figure 13.10c). The optimizer discovers this by pattern matching, and replaces the pair (move, compare) by the single move.

A two-instruction 'window' was sufficient to detect the redundant comparison in the example of Figure 13.10. When a computer provides memory updating instructions that are equivalent to simple load/operate/store sequences, the optimizer needs to examine instruction triples rather than pairs. Figure 13.11 shows how an increment instruction is generated. The '···' in Figure 13.11a stands for an arbitrarily complex address expression that appears on both sides of the assignment. This expression is recognized as common during value numbering, and the address it describes appears as an operand identifier (Figure 13.11b).

Davidson and Fraser [1980] assert that windows larger than 3 are not required. Additional evidence for this position comes from Tanenbaum's [1982] table of 123 optimization patterns. Only seven of these were longer than three instructions, and none of the seven resulted in just a single output instruction. Three of them converted addition or subtraction of 2 to two increments or decrements, the other four produced multi-word move instructions from successive single-word moves when the addresses were adjacent. All of these patterns were applied rather infrequently.

The optimizations of Figures 13.10 and 13.11 could be specified by the following patterns if we used the second peephole optimization method mentioned at the beginning of this section:

$$\text{MOV } a,b \quad \text{CMP } a,b \qquad\qquad \Rightarrow \quad \text{MOV } a,b$$
$$\text{MOV } a,b \quad \text{ADD } 1,b \quad \text{MOV } b,a \quad \Rightarrow \quad \text{INC } a$$

Instruction		Register transfers
MOV	s,d	$d:=s$; $\text{CC}:=s?0$
ADD	s,d	$d:=d+s$; $\text{CC}:=d+s?0$
CMP	s,d	$\text{CC}:=s?d$
Bc	l	if $\text{CC}=c$ then $\text{PC}:=l$
INC	d	$d:=d+1$; $\text{CC}:=d+1?0$

d and s match any PDP11 operand address.
c matches any condition.
l matches any label.

a) DEC PDP11

Instruction		Register transfers
L	r,x	$r:=x$;
A	r,x	$r:=r+x$; $\text{CC}:=r+x?0$
C	r,x	$\text{CC}:=r?x$
Bc	l	if $\text{CC}=c$ then $\text{PC}:=l$

r matches any register.
x matches any RX-format operand.
c matches any condition.
l matches any label.

b) IBM 370

Figure 13.9. Register Transfer Descriptions.

$$a := b + c \, ; \text{ if } a > 0 \text{ then goto } L \, ;$$

a) A straight-line segment involving local variables

$$t_1 : b \uparrow$$
$$t_2 : c \uparrow$$
$$t_3 : t_1 + t_2$$
$$t_4 : a := t_3$$
$$t_5 : t_3 \& 0$$
$$t_6 : JGT(t_5) \, L$$

b) The tuple sequence for (a) after value numbering

R[8] := M[R[5]+b]; CC := M[R[5]+b]?0;
R[8] := R[8]+M[R[5]+c]; CC := R[8]+M[R[5]+c]?0;
M[R[5]+a] := R[8]; CC := R[8]?0;
CC := R[8]?0;
if CC = GT **then** PC := L;

c) Register transfers for instructions implementing (b)

R[8] := M[R[5]+b];
R[8] := R[8]+M[R[5]+c];
M[R[5]+a] := R[18];
CC := R[8]?0;
if CC = GT **then** PC := L;

d) After eliminating redundant transfers from (c)

M[R[5]+a] := R[8]; CC := R[8]?0;

e) The combined effect of lines 3 and 4 in (d)

Figure 13.10. Comparison.

Any finite-state pattern matching technique, such as that of Aho and Corasick [1975], can be modified to efficiently match patterns such as these. (Modification is required to guarantee that the item matching the first occurrence of a or b also matches subsequent occurrences.) A complete description of a particular algorithm is given by Ramamoorthy and Jahanian [1976].

As indicated earlier, an extensive set of patterns may be required. (Tanenbaum and his coauthors [1982] give a representative example.) The particular set of patterns that will prove useful depends upon the source language, compiler code generation and optimization strategies, and target machine. It is developed over time by examining the code output by the compiler and recognizing areas of possible improvement. There is never any guarantee that significant optimizations have not been overlooked, or that useless patterns have not been introduced. On the other hand, the processing is significantly faster than that for the first method because it is unnecessary to 'rediscover' the patterns for each pair of instructions.

$$\cdots := \cdots + 1$$

a) Incrementing an arbitrary location

$t_i : t_j \uparrow$ t_j is the address $\cdots$
$t_k : t_i + 1$ Increment the value
$t_l : t_j := t_k$ Store the result

b) The tuple sequence for (a) after value numbering

$$R[8] := M[R[9]];$$
$$R[8] := R[8] + 1;$$
$$M[R[9]] := R[8];$$

c) Registers transfers for (b) after redundant transfer elimination

$$M[R[9]] := M[R[9]] + 1;$$

d) The overall effect of (c)

Figure 13.11. Generating an Increment.

13.2.4. Local Register Allocation   The classical approach to register allocation determines the register assignment 'on the fly' as the final code is being output to the assembler. This determination is based upon attributes calculated by previous traversals of the basic block, and uses value descriptors to maintain the state of the allocation. We solve the register pair problem by computing a size and alignment for each abstract register. (Thus the abstract register becomes a block in the sense of Section 10.1.) In the right column of Figure 13.8b, R[16] and R[17] each have size 1 and alignment 1 but R[18] has size 2 and alignment 2 because of its use as a multiplicand. Other machine-specific attributes may be required. For example, R[16] is used as a base register and thus cannot be assigned to register 0 on the IBM 370.

A register assignment algorithm similar to that described in Section 10.3.1 can be used. The only modification lies in the choice of a register to free. In Figure 10.14 we chose the least-recently accessed register; here we should choose the one whose next access is furthest in the future. (Belady [1966] has shown this strategy to be optimal in the analogous problem of determining which page to replace in a virtual memory system.) We can easily obtain this information at the same time we compute the other attributes mentioned in the previous paragraph. Note that all of the attributes used in register allocation must be computed after peephole optimization; the peephole optimizer, by combining instructions, may alter some of the attribute values.

Figure 10.14 makes use of a register state *copy* that indicates existence of a memory copy of the register content. If it has been necessary to spill a register then the assignment algorithm knows that it is in the *copy* state. However, as the example of Figure 13.8 shows, a register (e.g. R[16]) may be in the copy state because it has been loaded from a memory location whose content will not be altered. In order to make use of this fact, we must guarantee that no side effect will invalidate the memory copy. The necessary information is available in the sets D and X associated with the original tuples, and must be propagated by the value numbering and coding processes.

When we are dealing with a machine like the IBM 370, the algorithm of Figure 10.14 should make an effort to maximize the number of available pairs by appropriate choice of a free register to allocate. Even when this is done, however, we may reach a situation in which no pair is free but at least two registers are free. We can therefore free a pair by freeing one register, and we might free that register by moving its content to the second free register at a cost of two bytes. If the state of one of the candidate registers is *copy*, then it can be freed at a cost of two bytes if and only if its next use is the proper operand of an RR instruction (either operand if the operation is commutative). It appears that we cannot lose by using an LR instruction. However, suppose that the value being moved must ultimately (due to other conflicts) be saved in memory. In that case, we are simply paying to postpone the inevitable! We conclude that the classical strategy cannot be guaranteed to produce an optimum assignment on a machine with double-length results.

13.3. Global Optimization

Code is ultimately produced by the methods discussed in Section 13.2, one basic block at a time. The purposes of global optimization are to perform global rearrangement of the computation graph and to provide contextual information at the basic block boundaries. For example, in Section 13.2 we assumed that all program variables were potentially accessed after the end of each basic block. Thus the algorithm of Figure 13.7 initialized *USECOUNT*[v] to 1 for all program variables v. A global analysis of the program might show, however, that there was no execution path along which certain of these variables were used before being reset. *USECOUNT*[v] could be initialized to 0 for those variables, and this might result in eliminating more tuples.

We shall first sketch the process by which information is collected and disseminated over the computation graph, and then discuss two common global transformations. The last section considers ways of allocating registers globally, thus increasing register utilization and avoiding mismatches at basic block boundaries.

It is important to emphasize that none of the algorithms discussed in Section 13.2 should precede global optimization. Papers appearing in the literature often combine value numbering with the original generation of tuples, but doing so may prevent global optimization by destroying congruence of tuples in different basic blocks.

13.3.1. Global Data Flow Analysis The information derived by global data flow analysis consists of sets defined at particular program points. Two types of set may be interesting: a set of operand identifiers and a set of program points. For example, we might define a set $LIVE(b)$ at the end of each basic block b as the set of operand identifiers that were used after the end of b before being reset. This set could then be used in initializing $USECOUNT$ as discussed above.

Sets of program points are useful when we need to find all the uses of an operand that could be affected by a particular definition of that operand, and vice-versa. Global constant propagation is a good example of this kind of analysis. As the computation graph is being built, we accumulate a list of all of the program points at which an operand is given a constant value. During global data flow analysis we define a set $USES(o,p)$ at each program point p as the set of program points potentially using the value of o defined at p. Similarly, a set $DEFS(o,p)$ is the set of program points potentially defining the value of operand o used at program point p. For each element of the list of constant definitions, we can then find all of the potential uses. For each potential use, in turn, we can find all *other* potential definitions. If all definitions yield the same constant then this constant can be substituted for the operand use in question. Finally, if we substitute constants for *all* operand uses in a tuple then the tuple can be evaluated and its program point added to the list. The process terminates when the list is empty.

For practical reasons, global data flow analysis is carried out in two parts. The first part gathers information within a single basic block, summarizing it in sets defined at the entry and/or exit points. This drastically reduces the number of sets that must be processed during the second part, which propagates the information over the flow graph. The result of the second part is then again sets defined at the entry and/or exit points of basic blocks. These sets are finally used to distribute the information within the block. A complete treatment of the algorithms used to propagate information over the flow graph is beyond the scope of this book. Kennedy [1981] gives a good survey, and Hecht [1977] covers the subject in depth.

As an example, consider the computation of $LIVE(b)$. We characterize the flow graph for this computation by two sets:

$PRED(b) = h - h$ is an immediate predecessor of b in the flow graph
$SUCC(b) = h - h$ is an immediate successor of b in the flow graph

An operand is then live on exit from a block b if it is used by any block in $SUCC(b)$ before it is either defined or invalidated. Moreover, if a block $h \in SUCC(b)$ neither defines nor invalidates the operand, then it is live on exit from b if it is live on exit from h. Symbolically:

$$LIVE(b) = \bigcup_{h \in SUCC(b)} [IN(h) \cup THRU(h) \cap LIVE(h)] \qquad (1)$$

$IN(h)$ is the set of operand identifiers used in h before being defined or invalidated, and $THRU(h)$ is the set of operand identifiers neither defined nor invalidated in h.

We can solve the system of set equations (1) iteratively as shown in Figure 13.12. This algorithm is $O(n^2)$, where n is the number of basic blocks: At most $n-1$ executions of the **repeat** statement are needed to make a change in a basic block b available to another arbitrary basic block b'. The actual number of iterations depends upon the sequence in which the basic blocks are considered and the complexity of the program. For programs without explicit jumps the cost can be reduced to two iterations, if the basic blocks are ordered so that inner loops are processed before the loops in which they are contained.

Computation of the sets $USES(o,p)$ and $DEFS(o,p)$ provides a more complex example of global flow analysis. We begin by computing $REACHES(b)$, the set of program points that define values valid at the entry point of basic block b. Let $DEF(b)$ be the set of program points within b whose definitions remain valid at the end of b, and let $VALID(b)$ be the set of program points whose definitions are not changed or invalidated in b. $REACHES(b)$ is then defined by:

$$REACHES(b) = \bigcup_{h \in PRED(b)} [DEF(h) \cup VALID(h) \cap REACHES(h)] \quad (2)$$

Note the similarity between (1) and (2). It is clear that essentially the same algorithm can be used to solve both sets of equations. Similar systems of equations appear in most global data flow analysis problems, and one can show that a particular problem can be handled by a standard algorithm

```
for all basic blocks b do
   begin
   IN(b): = ∅; THRU(b) : = {all operand identifiers};
   for i : = last program point of b downto first program point of b do
      begin
      IN(b): = (IN(b) − D_{t_i} − X_{t_i}) ∪ U_{t_i};
      THRU(b): = THRU(b) − D_{t_i} − X_{t_i}
      end;
   LIVE(b): = ∅
   end;
repeat
   changed : = false;
   for all basic blocks b do
      begin
      old : = LIVE(b);
      LIVE(b): =   ∪   [IN(h) ∪ THRU(h) ∩ LIVE(h)];
                h ∈ SUCC(b)
      changed : = changed or (LIVE(b) ≠ old);
      end;
   until not changed;
```

Figure 13.12. Computation of $LIVE(b)$.

simply by showing that the sets and rules for combining them at junctions satisfy the axioms of the algorithm.

The computation of $DEF(b)$ and $VALID(b)$ is described in Figure 13.13a. It uses auxiliary sets $DF(o)$ which specify, for each operand identifier o, the program points whose definitions of o reach the ends of the basic blocks containing those program points. Once $DEF(b)$ and $VALID(b)$ are known for every basic block, $REACHES(b)$ can be com-

```
C: array [operand_identifier] of program_point;

for all operand identifiers o do DF(o):= ∅;
for all basic blocks b do
  begin
  for all operand identifiers o do C[o]:=0;
  for i:=first program point of b to last program point of b do
    begin
    for o ∈X_t(i) do C[o]:=0;
    for o ∈D_t(i) do C[o]:=i;
    end;
  DEF(b):= ∅;
  for all operand identifiers o do
    if C[o]≠0 then
      begin
      DEF(b):=DEF(b)∪{C[o]};
      DF(o):=DF(o)∪{C[o]};
      end;
  end;
for all basic blocks b do
  begin
  VALID(b):= ∅;
  for all operand identifiers o do
    if o ∈THRU(b) then VALID(b):=VALID(b)∪DF(o);
  end;
```

a) Computation of $DEF(b)$ and $VALID(b)$

```
TR:=REACHES(b);
for i:= first program point of b to last program point of b do
  begin
  DEFS(i,o):= ∅;
  for o ∈U_t(i) do DEFS(i,o):=TR∩DF(o);
  for o ∈D_t(i)∪X_t(i) do TR:=TR−DF(o);
  for o ∈D_t(i) do TR:=TR∪{i};
  end;
```

b) Computation of $DEFS(p,o)$

Figure 13.13. Computing a Set of Program Points.

puted by solving the system of set equations (2). Finally, a simple scan (Figure 13.13b) suffices to define $DEFS(p,o)$ at each program point. $USES(p,o)$ is computed by scanning the entire program and, for each tuple p that uses o, adding p to $USES(q,o)$ for every $q \in DEFS(p,o)$.

13.3.2. Code Motion The address expression for $a[i,j]$ in the Pascal value remains unchanged. The second implementation of Figure 13.14b shows how we can move the computation, with the assignment, forming an *epilogue* to the conditional. This *code motion* transformation reduces the code size but leaves the execution time unchanged. In the third implementation of Figure 13.14b we have moved a computation whose value does not change in the inner loop to the *prologue* of that loop. Here the execution time is reduced and the code size is increased slightly.

A key consideration in code motion is *safety*: The transformation is allowed when the transformed program will deliver the same result as the original, and will terminate abnormally only if the original would have terminated abnormally. (Note that the abnormal termination may occur in a different place.) In Figure 13.14, the value of i **div** k does not change in the inner loop. Moving that computation to the prologue of the inner loop would be unsafe, however, because if k were zero the transformed program would terminate abnormally and the original would not.

We can think of code motion as a combination of insertions and deletions. An insertion is safe if the expression being inserted is *available* at the point of insertion. An expression is available at a given point if it has been computed on every path leading to that point and none of its operands have been altered since the last computation. Clearly the program's result will not be changed by the inserted code if the inserted expression is available, and if the inserted code were to terminate abnormally then the original program would have terminated abnormally at one of the earlier computations. This argument guarantees the safety of the first transformation in Figure 13.14b. We first insert the address computation and assignment to $a[i,j]$, making it an epilogue of the conditional. The original computations in the two branches are then redundant and may be removed.

The second transformation in Figure 13.14b involves an insertion where the inserted expression is not available, but where it is *anticipated*. An expression is anticipated at a given point if it appears on every execution path leaving that point and none of its operands could be altered between the point in question and the first computation on each path. In our example, $(i-1)*n$ is anticipated in the prologue of the j loop, but i **div** k is not. Therefore it is safe to insert the former but not the latter. Once the insertion has been made, the corresponding computation in the epilogue of the conditional is redundant because its value is available.

Let $AVAIL(b)$ be the set of operand identifiers available on entry to basic block b and $ANTIC(b)$ be the set of operand identifiers anticipated on exit from b. These sets are defined by the following systems of equations:

```
for i := 1 to n do
  for j := 1 to n do
    if j > k then a[i,j]:= 0 else a[i,j]:= i div k ;
```

a) A Pascal fragment

(142 bytes)
```
        LA   R0,1
        C    R0,n(R13)
        BH   ENDI
        B    BODI
INCI  A    R0,=1
BODI  ST   R0,i(R13)
        C    R0,n(R13)
        BH   ENDJ

        B    BODJ
INCJ  A    R0,=1
BODJ  ST   R0,j(R13)
        C    R0,k(R13)
        BNH  ELSE
        SR   R1,R1
        L    R3,i(R13)
        S    R3,=1
        M    R2,n(R13)
        A    R3,j(R13)
        SLA  R3,2
        ST   R1,a-4(R3,R13)
        B    ENDC
ELSE  L    R0,i(R13)
        SRDA R0,32
        D    R0,k(R13)
        L    R3,i(R13)
        S    R3,=1
        M    R2,n(R13)
        A    R3,j(R13)

        SLA  R3,2
        ST   R1,a-4(R3,R13)
ENDC  L    R0,j(R13)
        C    R0,n(R13)
        BL   INCJ
ENDJ  L    R0,i(R13)
        C    R0,n(R13)
        BL   INCI
ENDI
```

(118 bytes)
```
        LA   R0,1
        C    R0,n(R13)
        BH   ENDI
        B    BODI
INCI  A    R0,=1
BODI  ST   R0,i(R13)
        C    R0,n(R13)
        BH   ENDJ

        B    BODJ
INCJ  A    R0,=1
BODJ  ST   R0,j(R13)
        C    R0,k(R13)
        BNH  ELSE
        SR   R1,R1

        B    ENDC
ELSE  L    R0,i(R13)
        SRDA R0,32
        D    R0,k(R13)
ENDC  L    R3,i(R13)
        S    R3,=1
        M    R2,n(R13)
        A    R3,j(R13)

        SLA  R3,2
        ST   R1,a-4(R3,R13)
        L    R0,j(R13)
        C    R0,n(R13)
        BL   INCJ
ENDJ  L    R0,i(R13)
        C    R0,n(R13)
        BL   INCI
ENDI
```

(120 bytes)
```
        LA   R0,1
        C    R0,n(R13)
        BH   ENDI
        B    BODI
INCI  A    R0,=1
BODI  ST   R0,i(R13)
        C    R0,n(R13)
        BH   ENDJ
        L    R5,i(R13)
        S    R5,=1
        M    R4,n(R13)
        B    BODJ
INCJ  A    R0,=1
BODJ  ST   R0,j(R13)
        C    R0,k(R13)
        BNH  ELSE
        SR   R1,R1

        B    ENDC
ELSE  L    R0,i(R13)
        SRDA R0,32
        D    R0,k(R13)

ENDC  L    R3,j(R13)
        AR   R3,R5
        SLA  R3,2
        ST   R1,a-4(R3,R13)
        L    R0,j(R13)
        C    R0,n(R13)
        BL   INCJ
ENDJ  L    R0,i(R13)
        C    R0,n(R13)
        BL   INCI
ENDI
```

b) IBM 370 implementations

Figure 13.14. Code Motion.

$$AVAIL(b) = \bigcap_{h \in PRED(b)} [OUT(h) \cup THRU(h) \cap AVAIL(h)]$$

$$ANTIC(b) = \bigcap_{h \in SUCC(b)} [ANLOC(h) \cup THRU(h) \cap ANTIC(h)]$$

Here $OUT(b)$ is the set of operand identifiers defined in b and not invalidated after their last definition, and $ANLOC(b)$ is the set of operand identifiers for tuples computed in b before any of their operands are defined or invalidated.

The main task of the optimizer is to find code motions that are safe and *profitable* (reduce the cost of the program according to the desired measure). Wulf [1975] considers '$\alpha - \omega$' code motions that move computations from branched constructs to prologues and epilogues. (The center column of Figure 13.14 illustrates an ω motion; an α motion would have placed the computation of $a[i,j]$ before the compare instruction.) He also discusses the fragment of Figure 13.14a is common to both branches of the conditional statement, although there is no path from one to the other over which the movement of invariant computations out of loops, as illustrated by the right column of Figure 13.14. If loops are nested, invariant code is moved out one region at a time. Morel and Renvoise [1979] present a method for moving a computation directly to the entrance block of the outermost strongly-connected region in which it is invariant.

13.3.3. Strength Reduction   Figure 13.15 gives yet another implementation of Figure 13.14a for the IBM 370. The code is identical to that of the right-hand column of Figure 13.14b, except that the expression $(i - 1)*n$ has been replaced by an initialization and increment of R5. It is easy to see that in both cases the sequence of values taken on by R5 is 0, n, $2n$, $3n$,... This *strength reduction* transformation reduces the execution time, but its effect on the code size is unpredictable.

Allen [1981] gives an extensive catalog of strength reductions. The major improvement in practice comes from simplifying access to arrays, primarily multidimensional arrays, within loops. We shall therefore consider only strength reductions involving expressions of this kind. All of these transformations are based upon the fact that multiplication is distributive over addition.

Let S be a strongly-connected component of the computation graph. A *region constant* is an expression whose value is unchanged in S, and an *induction value* is one defined only by tuples having one of the following forms:

$$j \pm k$$
$$-j$$
$$i := j$$
$$i \uparrow$$

Here j and k are either induction values or region constants and i is an *induction variable*. The set of induction values is determined by assuming that *all* values defined in the region are induction values, and then deleting those that do not satisfy the conditions [Cocke 1977]. The induction values in Figure 13.16 are I, t_2, t_3 and t_7.

To perform a strength reduction transformation on Figure 13.16, we define a variable V_1 to hold the value t_9. An assignment must be made to

```
        LA      R0,1
        C       R0,n(R13)
        BH      ENDI
        SR      R5,R5              (i − 1)*n  initially 0
        B       BODI
INCI    A       R0,=1
        A       R5,=n              Increment (i − 1)*n
BODI    ST      R0,i(R13)
        LA      R0,1
        C       R0,n(R13)
        BH      ENDJ
        B       BODJ
INCJ    A       R0,=1
BODJ    ST      R0,j(R13)
        C       R0,k(R13)
        BNH     ELSE
        SR      R1,R1
        B       ENDIF
ELSE    L       R0,i(R13)
        SRDA    R0,32
        D       R0,k(R13)
ENDIF   L       R3,j(R13)
        AR      R3,R5
        SLA     R3,2
        ST      R1,a-4(R3,R13)
        L       R0,j(R13)
        C       R0,n(R13)
        BL      INCJ
ENDJ    L       R0,i(R13)
        C       R0,n(R13)
        BL      INCI
ENDI
        (118 bytes)
```

Figure 13.15. Strength Reduction Applied to Figure 13.14b.

this variable prior to entering the strongly-connected region, and at program points where t_9 has been invalidated and yet t_2*d_1 is anticipated. For example, t_9 is invalidated by t_8 in Figure 13.16, and yet t_2*d_1 is anticipated at that point. An assignment $V_1:=t_2*d_1$ should therefore be inserted just before l_2. Since t_2 is the value of $I \uparrow$, $I:=t_7$; $V_1:=t_2*d_1$ is equivalent to $V_1:=(t_2+1)*d_1$; $I:=t_7$. Using the distributive law, and recalling the invariant that V_1 always holds the value of t_9 ($= t_2*d_1$), this sequence can be written as $V_1:=V_1+d_1$; $I:=t_7$. Figure 13.17 shows the result of the transformation, after appropriate decomposition into tuples.

We could now apply exactly the same reasoning to Figure 13.17, noting

for $i := 1$ **to** n **do** $a[j,i] := a[k,i] + a[m,i]$;

a) A Pascal fragment

	$t_1: i := 1$	$l_2:$ t_2	t_2
	$t_2: i \uparrow$	$t_9: t_2 * d_1$	t_9
	$t_3: n \uparrow$	$t_{10}: k \uparrow$	$t_{21}: j \uparrow$
	$t_4: t_2 ? t_3$	$t_{11}: t_{10} + t_9$	$t_{22}: t_{21} + t_9$
	$t_5: JGT(t_4)\, l_3$	$t_{12}: t_{11} * 4$	$t_{23}: t_{22} * 4$
	$t_6: JMP\, l_2$	$t_{13}: a + t_{12}$	$t_{24}: a + t_{23}$
$l_1:$	t_2	$t_{14}: t_{13} \uparrow$	$t_{25}: t_{24} := t_{20}$
	$t_7: t_2 + 1$	t_2	t_2
	$t_8: i := t_7$	t_9	t_3
		$t_{15}: m \uparrow$	t_4
		$t_{16}: t_{15} + t_9$	$t_{26}: JLT(t_4)\, l_1$
		$t_{17}: t_{16} * 4$	$l_3:$
		$t_{18}: a + t_{17}$	
		$t_{19}: t_{18} \uparrow$	
		$t_{20}: t_{14} + t_{19}$	

b) Computation graph for (a)

Figure 13.16. Finding Induction Values.

	t_1	$l_2:$ t_{28}	t_{28}
	t_2	t_{10}	t_{21}
	t_3	$t_{31}: t_{10} + t_{28}$	$t_{40}: t_{21} + t_{28}$
	t_4	$t_{32}: t_{31} * 4$	$t_{41}: t_{40} * 4$
	t_5	$t_{33}: a + t_{32}$	$t_{42}: a + t_{41}$
	$t_{27}: V_1 := d_1$	$t_{34}: t_{33} \uparrow$	$t_{43}: t_{42} := t_{39}$
	t_6	t_{28}	t_2
$l_1:$	$t_{28}: V_1 \uparrow$	t_{15}	t_3
	$t_{29}: t_{28} + d_1$	$t_{35}: t_{15} + t_{28}$	t_4
	$t_{30}: V_1 := t_{29}$	$t_{36}: t_{33} * 4$	t_{26}
	t_2	$t_{37}: a + t_{36}$	$l_3:$
	t_7	$t_{38}: t_{37} \uparrow$	
	t_8	$t_{39}: t_{34} + t_{38}$	

Figure 13.17. Figure 13.16b After One Strength Reduction.

that V_1, t_{28}, t_{29}, t_{31}, t_{35} and t_{40} are now induction values. The obvious variables then hold t_{32}, t_{36} and t_{41}. Unfortunately, none of these variables have simple recurrence relations. Four more variables, to hold $t_{28} * 4$, $t_{10} * 4$, $t_{15} * 4$ and $t_{21} * 4$ must be defined. Although tedious, the process is straightforward; a complete algorithm is given by Allen [1981].

As can be seen from this simple example, the number of variables introduced grows rapidly. Many of these variables will later be eliminated because their functions have been effectively taken over by other variables.

This is the case after further processing of Figure 13.17, where the function of V_1 is taken over by the variable implementing $t_{28}*4$. In fact, the program variable I can be omitted in this loop if the test for termination is changed to use one of the derived induction variables.

Clearly strength reduction must precede code motion. The strength reduction process generates many extra tuples that are constant within the strongly connected region and hence should be moved to its prologue. It is also clear that strength reduction must be iterated if it is to be effective. The proliferation of derived induction variables, with concomitant initialization and incrementing, may cause a significant increase in code size. Thus strength reduction is strictly an execution time optimization, and usually involves a time/space tradeoff. Scarborough and Kolsky [1980] advocate judicious preprocessing of subscript expressions in an effort to reduce the growth due to strength reduction.

13.3.4. Global Register Allocation

As discussed in Section 13.2.4, local register allocation considers each basic block in isolation. Values that live across basic block boundaries are generally program variables, and are stored in memory. Thus it is unnecessary to retain values in registers from one basic block to the next. The global optimizations discussed so far alter this condition. They tend to increase the number of operands whose lifetimes include more than one basic block, and if such operands must be kept in memory then much of the advantage is lost. It is absolutely essential that we take a more global view in allocating registers in order to minimize the number of additional fetch, store and copy register instructions.

Most global register allocation strategies allow program variables to compete equally for registers with other operands. Some care must be taken, however, since program variables may be accessible over paths that are effectively concealed from the compiler. It is probably best to exclude program variables from the allocation when such paths are available. As indicated in Section 13.1, this is a property of the source language and the necessary restrictions will vary from compiler to compiler.

Day [1970] discusses the general register allocation problem and gives optimal solutions for the basic strategies. These solutions provide standards for measuring the effectiveness of heuristics, but are themselves too expensive for use in a production compiler. Two faster, non-optimal procedures are also discussed. All of these algorithms assume a homogeneous set of registers. Late in the paper, Day mentions that the problem of register pairs might be solved by running the allocation twice. The first run would be given only the values that must be assigned to one register of a pair (or both). Input to the second run would include all items, but attach a very high profit to each assignment made by the first run.

One of the problems with global register allocation is the large number of operands that must be considered. In spite of the previous global optimizations, the majority of these operands have lifetimes contained within a basic block. We would like to perform the expensive global allocation procedure on only those operands whose lifetimes cross a basic block boundary, allocating the remainder by the cheaper methods of Section 13.2.4. If we do this, however, we run the risk of allocating *all* registers globally and hence generating very poor local code. Beatty [1974] suggests that we divide the local register allocation process into two phases, determining the *number* of registers required ('allocation') and deciding *which* registers will be used ('assignment'). The requirements set by the first phase are used in determining global register usage, and then the unclaimed registers are assigned in each basic block individually.

All data items that live across basic block boundaries are initially assumed to be in memory, but all instructions that can take either register or memory operands are assumed to be in their register-register form. Explicit loads and stores are inserted where required, and the processes of Sections 13.2.1-13.2.3 are carried out. The methods of Section 13.2.4 are applied to determine the number of registers required locally. With this information, a global analysis [Beatty 1974] is used to guide *load-store motion* (code motion involving only the loads and stores of operands live across basic block boundaries) and global register assignment. As the assignment proceeds, some (but not necessarily all) loads and stores will become redundant and be deleted. When the global analysis is complete, we apply the allocation of Section 13.2.4 to assign local registers.

Real computers usually have annoying asymmetries in register capability that wreak havoc with uniform register allocation schemes. It is necessary to provide a mechanism for incorporating such asymmetries in order to avoid having to exclude certain registers from the allocation altogether. One allocation scheme [Chaitin 1981, Chaitin 1982] that avoids the problem is based on graph coloring (Section B.3.3). The constraints on allocation are expressed as an *interference graph*, a graph with one node for each register, both abstract and actual. An edge connects two nodes if they *interfere* (i.e. if they exist simultaneously). Clearly all of the machine registers interfere with each other. In the left column of Figure 13.8, R[17] and R[18] do not interfere with each other, although they both interfere with R[16]; all abstract registers interfere with each other in the right column. If there are n registers, a register assignment is equivalent to an n-coloring (Section B.3.3) of the interference graph.

Many asymmetry constraints are easily introduced as interferences. For example, any abstract register used as a base register on the IBM 370 interferes with machine register 0. Similarly, we can solve a part of the multiplication problem by making the abstract multiplicand interfere with every even machine register and defining another abstract register that interferes with every odd machine register and every abstract register that exists during the multiply. This guarantees that the multiplicand goes into an odd register and that an even register is free, but it does not guarantee that the multiplicand and free register form a pair.

The coloring algorithm [Chaitin 1981] used for this problem differs from that of Section B.3.3 because the constraints are different: There we are trying to find the minimum number of colors, assuming that the graph is fixed; here we are trying to find an n-coloring, and the graph can be changed to make that possible. (Spilling a value to memory removes some of the interferences, changing the graph.) Any node with fewer than n interferences does not affect the coloring, since there will be a color available for it regardless of the colors chosen for its neighbors. Thus it (and all edges incident upon it) can be deleted without changing whether the graph can be n-colored. If we can continue to delete nodes in this manner until the entire graph disappears, then the original was n-colorable. The coloring can be obtained by adding the nodes back into the graph in the reverse order of deletion, coloring each as it is restored.

If the coloring algorithm encounters a node with n or more interferences, it must make a decision about which node to spill. A separate table is used to give the cost of spilling each register, and the register is chosen for which cost/(incident edges) is as small as possible. Some local intelligence is included: When a computation is local to a basic block, and no abstract register lifetimes end between its definition and last use, the cost of spilling it is set to infinity. The cost algorithm also accounts for the facts that some computations can be redone instead of being spilled and reloaded, and that if the source or target of a register copy operation is spilled then that operation can be deleted. It is possible that a particular spill can have negative cost!

Unfortunately, the introduction of spill code changes the conditions of the problem. Thus, after all spill decisions are made, the original program is updated with spill code and the allocation re-run. Chaitin claims that the second iteration usually succeeds, but it may be necessary to insert more spill code and try again. To reduce the likelihood of multiple iterations, one can make the first run with $n-k$ registers instead of n registers.

13.4. Efficacy and Cost

We have discussed a number of transformations in this chapter. Do they provide an improvement commensurate with the cost of performing them? In some sense this is a meaningless question, because it is too broad. Each user has a definition of 'commensurate', which will vary from one program to another. The best we can do is to try to indicate the costs and benefits of some of the techniques we have discussed and leave it to the compiler writer to strike, under pressure from the marketplace, a reasonable balance.

By halving the code size required to implement a language element that accounts for 1% of a program we reduce the code size of that program by only 0.5%, which certainly does not justify a high compilation cost. Thus it is important for the compiler writer to know the milieu in which his compiler will operate. For example, elimination of common subexpressions, code motion and strength reduction might speed up a numerical computation solving a problem in linear algebra by a factor of 2 or 3. The same optimizations often improve non-numeric programs by scarcely 10%. Carter's [1982] measurements of 95,000 lines of Pascal, primarily non-numeric code, shows that the compiler would typically be dealing with basic blocks containing 2-4 assignments, 10-15 tuples and barely 2 common subexpressions!

Static analysis does not, of course, tell the whole story. Knuth [1971b] found in his study of FORTRAN that less than 4% of a program generally accounts for half of its running time. This phenomenon was exploited by Dakin and Poole [1973] to implement an interactive text editor as a mixture of interpreted and directly-executed code. Their measurements showed that in a typical editing session over 97% of the execution involved less than 10% of the code, and more than half of the code was never used at all. Finally, Knuth discovered that over 25% of the running times of the FORTRAN programs he profiled was spent performing input/output.

Actual measurements of optimization efficacy and cost are rare in the literature, and the sample size is invariably small. It is thus very difficult to draw general conclusions. Table 13.18 summarizes a typical set of measurements [Cocke 1980]. PL/1L, an experimental optimizing compiler for a PL/1-like language, was run over each of four programs several times. A different level of optimization was specified for each compilation of a given program, and measurements made of the compilation time, code space used for the resulting object program, and execution time of the resulting object program on a set of data. At every level the compiler allocated registers globally by the graph coloring algorithm sketched in Section 13.3.4. No other optimizations were performed at the 'None' level. The 'Local' optimizations were those discussed in Section 13.2.1, and the 'Global' optimizations were those discussed in Sections 13.3.1 through 13.3.3. It is not clear what (if any) peephole optimization was done, although the global register allocation sup-

Table 13.18 Evaluation of PL/1L [Cocke 1980]

Measure		Ratios		
		Local/None	Global/None	Global/Local
Compilation time	Min.	0.8	1.0	1.2
	Avg.	0.9	1.4	1.4
	Max.	1.0	1.6	1.6
Code space	Min.	0.42	0.38	0.89
	Avg.	0.54	0.55	1.02
	Max.	0.69	0.66	1.19
Execution time	Min.	0.32	0.19	0.58
	Avg.	0.50	0.42	0.82
	Max.	0.72	0.61	0.94

posedly deleted redundant comparisons following arithmetic operations by treating the condition code as another allocatable register [Chaitin 1981].

The reduction in compilation time for local optimization clearly illustrates the strong role that global register allocation played in the compilation time figures. Local optimization reduced the number of nodes in the interference graph, thus more than covering its own cost. One of the test programs was also compiled by the standard optimizing PL/1 compiler in a bit less than half of the time required by the PL/1L compiler. OPT=0 was selected for the PL/1 compiler, and local optimization for the PL/1L compiler. This ratio changed slightly in favor of the PL/1 compiler (0.44 to 0.38) when OPT=2 and 'global' were selected. When the same program was rewritten in FORTRAN and compiled using FORTRAN H, the ratios OPT=0/local and OPT=2/global were almost identical at 0.13. (Section 14.2.3 discusses the internals of FORTRAN H.)

In the late 1970's, Wulf and his students attempted to quantitatively evaluate the size of the object code produced by an optimizing compiler. They modeled the optimization process by the following equation:

$$K(C,P) = K_u(C,P) \times \prod_i O_i(C)$$

$K(C,P)$ is the cost (code space) of program P compiled with compiler C, and K_u is the corresponding unoptimized cost. Each $O_i(C)$ is a measure of how effectively compiler C applies optimization i to reduce the code size of a typical program, assuming that all optimizations $1, \ldots, i-1$ have already been done. They were never able to validate this model to their satisfaction, and hence the work never reached publication. They did, however, measure the factors $O_i(C)$ for Bliss-11 [Wulf 1975] (Table 13.19).

We have considered optimizations 1 and 4 of Table 13.19 to precede formation of the computation graph; the remainder of 1-6 constitute the local

Table 13.19 Optimization Factors for Bliss-11 [Wulf 1975]

Index	Description	Factor
1	Evaluating constant expressions	0.938
2	Dead code elimination	0.98
3	Peephole optimization	0.88
4	Algebraic laws	0.975
5	CSE in statements	0.987
6	CSE in basic blocks	0.973
7	Global CSE	0.987
8	Global register allocation	0.975
9	Load/store motion	0.987
10	Cross jumping	0.972
11	Code motion	0.985
12	Strength reduction	-

optimizations of Section 13.2. Thus the product of these factors (roughly 0.76) should approximate the effect of local optimization alone. Similarly, the product of factors 7-12 (roughly 0.91) should approximate the additional improvement due to global optimization. Comparing this latter figure with the last column of Table 13.15 shows the deleterious effect of strength reduction on code space discussed in Section 13.3.3.

The first column of Table 13.18 shows a code size improvement significantly better than 0.76, implying that the PL/1L compiler generates poorer initial code than Bliss-11, leaving more to be gained by simple optimizations. This should not be taken as a criticism. After all, using a sophisticated code generator with an optimizer is a bit like vacuuming the office before the cleaning crew arrives! Davidson and Fraser [1980] take the position that code generation should be trivial, producing instructions to simulate a simple stack machine on an infinite-register analog of the target computer. They then apply the optimizations of Section 13.2, using a fragment bounded by labels (i.e. a path in an extended basic block) in lieu of a basic block.

EXERCISES

13.1. Show how the dependency sets would be derived when building a computation graph that represents a LAX program for a target machine of your choice.

13.2. Assume that the FORTRAN assignment statement

$$A(I,J,K) = \quad (A(I,J,K-1)+A(I,J,K+1)+$$
$$A(I,J-1,K)+A(I,J+1,K)+$$
$$A(I-1,J,K)+A(I+1,J,K))/6.0$$

constitutes a single basic block.
a. Write the initial tuple sequence for the basic block.
b. Derive a new tuple sequence by the algorithm of Figure 13.4a.
c. Code the results of (b), using register transfers that describe the instructions of some machine with which you are familiar.

13.3. Give an example, for some machine with which you are familiar, of a common subexpression satisfying each of the following conditions. If this is impossible for one or more of the conditions, carefully explain why.
a. Always cheaper to recompute than save.
b. Never cheaper to recompute than save.
c. Cheaper to recompute iff it must be saved in memory.

13.4. Explain how the first method of peephole optimization described in Section 13.2.3 could be used to generate patterns for the second. Would it be feasible to combine the two methods, backing up the second with the first? Explain.

13.5. Assume that the register management algorithm of Figure 10.14 is to be used in an optimizing compiler. Define precisely the conditions under which all possible changes in register state will occur.

13.6. Show how the D and X sets are propagated through the value numbering and coding processes to support the decisions of Exercise 13.5, as described in Section 13.2.4.

13.7. Give examples of safe code motions in which the following behavior is observed:

    a. The transformed program terminates abnormally in a different place than the original, but with the same error.

    b. The transformed program terminates abnormally in a different place than the original, with a different error.

13.8. Consider a Pascal **for** statement with integer constant bounds. Assume that the lower bound is smaller than the upper bound, which is smaller than *maxint*. Instead of using the schema of Figure 3.10c, the implementor chooses the following:

$$i := e_1; t := e_3;$$
$$l_1: \quad \cdots \qquad\qquad (* \text{ Body of the loop } *)$$
$$i := i + 1;$$
$$\textbf{if } i \leqslant t \textbf{ then goto } l_1;$$

    a. Explain why no strength reduction can be carried out in this loop.

    b. Suppose that we ignore the explanation of (a) and carry out the transformation anyway. Give a specific example in which the transformed program terminates abnormally but the original does not. Restrict the expressions in your example to those arising from array subscript calculations. Your array bounds must be reasonable (i.e. arrays with *maxint* elements

CHAPTER 14
Implementing the Compiler

In earlier chapters we have developed a general framework for the design of a compiler. We have considered how the task and its data structures could be decomposed, what tools and strategies are available to the compiler writer, and what problems might be encountered. Given a source language, target machine and performance goals for the generated code we can design a translation algorithm. The result of the design is a set of module specifications.

This chapter is concerned with issues arising out of the implementation of these specifications. We first discuss the decisions that must be made by the implementors and the criteria that guide these decisions. Unfortunately, we can give no quantitative relationship between decisions and criteria! Compiler construction remains an art in this regard, and the successful compiler writer must simply develop a feel for the inevitable compromises. We have therefore included three case studies of successful compilers that make very different architectural decisions. For each we have tried to identify the decisions made and show the outcome.

14.1. Implementation Decisions

Many valid implementations can generally be found for a set of module specifications. In fact, an important property of a module is that it hides one or more implementation decisions. By varying these decisions, one obtains different members of a 'family' of related programs. All of the members of such a family carry out the same task (defined by the module specifications) but generally satisfy different performance criteria. In our case, we vary the pass structure and data storage strategies of the compiler to satisfy a number of criteria presented in Section 14.1.1. Despite this variation, however, the module specifications remain unchanged. This point is an extremely important one to keep in mind, especially since many implementation languages provide little or no support for the concept of a module as a distinct entity. With such languages it is very easy to destroy the modular decomposition during development or maintenance, and the only protection one has against this is eternal vigilance and a thorough understanding of the design.

14.1.1. Criteria *Maintainability*, *performance* and *portability* are the three main criteria used in making implementation decisions. The first is heavily influenced by the structure of the program, and depends ultimately on the quality of the modular design. Unfortunately, given current implementation languages, it is sometimes necessary to sacrifice some measure of maintainability to achieve performance goals. Such tradeoffs run counter to our basic principles. We do not lightly recommend them, but we recognize that in some cases the compiler will not run at all unless they are made. We do urge, however, that all other possibilities be examined before such a decision is taken.

Performance includes memory requirements, secondary storage requirements and processing time. Hardware constraints often place limits on performance tradeoffs, with time the only really free variable. In Sections 14.1.2 and 14.1.3 we shall be concerned mainly with tradeoffs between primary and secondary storage driven by such constraints.

Portability can be divided into two sub-properties often called *rehostability* and *retargetability*. Rehosting is the process of making the compiler itself run on a different machine, while retargeting is the process of making it generate code for a different machine. Rehostability is largely determined by the implementation language and the performance tradeoffs that have been made. Suppose, for example, that we produce a complete design for a Pascal compiler, specifying all modules and interfaces carefully. If this design is implemented by writing a FORTRAN program that uses only constructs allowed by the FORTRAN standard, then there is a good chance of its running unchanged on a wide variety of computers. If, on the other hand, the design is implemented by writing a program in assembly language for the Control Data Cyber series then running it on another machine would involve a good deal of effort.

Even when we fix both the design and the implementation language, performance considerations may affect rehostability. For example, consider the use of bit vectors (say as parser director sets or error matrices, or as code generator decision table columns) when the implementation language is Pascal. One possible representation is a set, another is a packed array of Boolean. Unfortunately, some Pascal implementations represent all sets with the same number of bits. This usually precludes large sets, and the bit vectors must be implemented as arrays of sets or packed arrays of Boolean.

Other implementations only pack arrays to the byte level, thus making a packed array of Boolean eight times as large as it should be. Clearly when the compiler is rehosted from a machine with one of these problems to a machine with the other, different implementations of bit vectors may be needed to meet performance goals.

Neither of the situations in the two previous paragraphs affected the *design* (set of modules and interfaces). Rehostability is thus quite evidently a property of the implementation. Retargetability, on the other hand, is more dependent upon the design. It requires a clean separation between the analysis and synthesis tasks, since the latter must be redesigned in order to retarget the compiler. If the target machine characteristics have been allowed to influence the design of the analysis task as well as the synthesis task, then the redesign will be more extensive. For example, suppose that the design did not contain a separate constant table module. Operations on constants were carried out wherever they were needed, following the idiosyncrasies of the target machine. Retargeting would then involve redesign of every module that performed operations on constants, rather than redesign of a single module.

Although the primary determinant of retargetability is the design, implementation may have an effect in the form of tradeoffs between modularity and performance that destroy the analysis/synthesis interface. Such tradeoffs also degrade the maintainability, as indicated at the beginning of this section. This should not be surprising, because retargeting a compiler is, after all, a form of maintenance: The behavior of the program must be altered to fit changing customer requirements.

14.1.2. Pass Structure   It often becomes obvious during the design of a compiler that the memory (either actual or virtual) available to a user on the host machine will not be sufficient for the code of the compiler and the data needed to translate a typical program. One strategy for reducing the memory requirement is analogous to that of a dentist's office in which the patient sits in a chair and is visited in turn by the dentist, hygienist and x-ray technician: The program is placed in the primary storage of the machine and the phases of the compiler are 'passed by the program', each performing a transformation of the data in memory. This strategy is appropriate for systems with restricted secondary storage capability. It does not require that intermediate forms of the program be written and then reread during compilation; a single read-only file to hold the compiler itself is sufficient. The size of the program that can be compiled is limited, but it is generally possible to compile programs that will completely fill the machine's memory at execution time. (Source and intermediate encodings of programs are often more compact than the target encoding.)

Another strategy is analogous to that of a bureau of motor vehicles in which the applicant first goes to a counter where application forms are handed in, then to another where written tests are given, and so on through the eye test, driving test, cashier and photographer: The compiler 'passes over the program', repeatedly reading and writing intermediate forms, until the translation is complete. This strategy is appropriate for systems with secondary storage that can support several simultaneously-open sequential files. The size of the program that can be compiled is limited by the filing system rather than the primary memory. (Of course primary memory will limit the *complexity* of the program as discussed in Chapter 1.)

Either strategy requires us to decompose the compilation into a sequence of transformations, each of which is completed before the next is begun. One fruitful approach to the decomposition is to consider relationships between tasks and large data structures, organizing each transformation around a single data structure. This minimizes the information flow between transformations, narrowing the interfaces. Table 14.1 illustrates the process for a typical design. Each row represents a transformation. The first column gives the central data structure for the tasks in the second column. It participates in *only* the transformation corresponding to its row, and hence no two of these data structures need be held simultaneously.

Our second strategy places an extra constraint upon the intermediate representations of the program: They must be linear, and each will be processed sequentially. The transformations are carried out by *passes*, where a pass is a single scan, in either direction, of a linear intermediate representation of the program. Each pass corresponds to a traversal of the structure tree, with forward passes corresponding to depth-first, left-to-right traversals and backward passes corresponding to depth-first, right-to-left traversals. Under this constraint we are limited to $AAG(n)$ attribution; the attribute dependencies determine the number of passes and the tasks carried out in each. It is never necessary to build an explicitly-linked structure tree unless we wish to change traversals. (An example is the change from a depth-first, left-to-right traversal of an expression tree to an execution-order traversal based upon register counts.)

The basic Pascal file abstraction is a useful one for the linear intermediate

Table 14.1 Decomposition via Major Data Structures

Data Structure	Tasks	Reference
Symbol table	Lexical analysis	Chapter 6
Parse table	Parsing	Chapter 7
Definition table	Name analysis	Chapter 9
	Semantic analysis	Chapter 9
	Memory mapping	Section 10.1
	Target attribution	Section 10.2
Decision tables	Code selection	Section 10.3
Address table	Assembly	Chapter 11

representations of the program. A module encapsulates the representation, providing an element type and a single *window* variable of that type. Operations are available to empty the sequence, add the content of the window to the sequence, get the first element of the sequence into the window, get the next element of the sequence into the window, and test for the end of the sequence. This module acts as a 'pipeline' between the passes of the compiler, with each operating directly on the window. By implementing the module in different ways we can cause the communicating passes to operate as coroutines or to interact via a file.

While secondary storage is larger than primary storage, constraints on space are not uncommon. Moreover, a significant fraction of the passes may be I/O-bound and hence any reduction in the size of an intermediate representation will be reflected directly in the compilation time. Our communication module, if it writes information to a file, should therefore encode that information carefully to avoid redundancy. In particular, the element will usually be a variant record and the communication module should transmit only the information present in the stated variant (rather than always assuming the largest variant). Further compression may be possible given a knowledge of the meanings of the fields. For example, in the token of Figure 4.1 the line number field of *coordinates* changes only rarely, and need be included only when it does change. The fact that the line number is present can be encoded by the classification field in an obvious way. Because most tokens are completely specified by the classification field alone, this optimization can reduce the size of a token file by 30%.

14.1.3. Table Representation   We have seen how the requirements for table storage are reduced by organizing each pass around a table and then discarding that table at the end of the pass. Further reduction can be based upon the restricted lifetime of some of the information contained in the table. For example, consider a block-structured language with a left-to-right attribute grammar (such as Pascal). The definition table entries for the entities declared locally are not used after the range in which those entities were declared has been left. They can therefore be thrown away at that point.

Pascal is admittedly a simple case, but even in languages with more complex attribute relationships definition table entities are only accessed during processing of a program fragment. One purpose of the definition table is to abstract information from the program, making it more accessible during processing. This purpose can only be served if the entry is, in fact, accessed. Thus it is often reasonable to destroy definition table entries when the fragment in which they are accessed has been left, and re-create them when that fragment is entered again.

A table entry can only be destroyed if its information is no longer needed, can be recomputed from other information, or can be stored in the structure tree in a position where it can be recovered before it is needed next. The last condition is most easily satisfied if forward and backward passes alternate, but it can also occur in other situations. We shall see several examples of this 'distribution' of attribute information in Section 14.2.1.

Unfortunately, many implementation languages do not support freeing of storage. Even for those where it is nominally supported, the implementation is often poor. The compiler writer can avoid this problem by managing his own dynamic storage, only making requests for storage allocation and never returning storage to the system. The basic strategy for a block-structured language is quite simple: All storage allocated for a given table is held in a single one-way list. A pointer indicates the most-recently delivered element. When a program fragment that will add elements to the table is entered, this pointer is remembered; when the fragment is left, its value is restored. If a new element is needed then the pointer of the current element is checked. If it is *nil,* storage allocation is requested and a pointer to the resulting block placed in the current element. In any case the pointer to the most-recently delivered element is advanced along the list. Thus the list acts like a stack, and its final length is the maximum number of entries the table required at one point in the compilation.

The disadvantage of this strategy is that the storage requirements are those that would obtain if all tables in each pass reached their maximum requirement simultaneously. Often this is not the case, and hence larger programs could have been accommodated if storage for unused entries had been returned to the operating system.

Every pass that manipulates constant values must include the necessary operations of the abstract data type *constant_table* discussed in Section 4.2.2. *Constant_table* defines an internal representation for each type of value. This representation can be used as an attribute value, but any manipulation of it (other than assignment) must be carried out by constant table operations. We pointed out in Section 4.2.2 that the internal representation might simply describe an access function for a data structure within the constant table module. This strategy should be used carefully in a multipass compiler to avoid broadening the interface between passes: The extra data structure should usually not be retained intact and transmitted from one pass to the next via a separate file. Instead, *all* of the information about a constant should be added to the linearized form of the attributed structure tree at an appropriate point. The extra data structure is then reconstituted as the linearized tree is read in.

The string table is a common exception to the approach suggested above. Careful design of the compiler can restrict the need for string table access to two tasks: lexical analysis and assembly. (This is true even though it may be used to store literal strings and strings representing the fractions of floating point numbers as well as identifiers.) Thus the string table is often written to a separate file at the completion of lexical analysis. It is only retrieved during assembly when the character representations of constants must be converted to target code, and identifiers must be incorporated into external symbol dictionaries.

14.2. Case Studies

We have discussed criteria for making implementation decisions and indicated how the pass structure and table representation are affected by such decisions. This section analyzes three compilers, showing the decisions made by their implementors and the consequences of those decisions. Our interest is to explore the environment in which such decisions are made and to clarify their interdependence. We have tried to choose examples that illustrate the important points, and that have been used routinely in a production setting. Pragmatic constraints such as availability of design or maintenance documentation and understandability of the compiler itself were also influential.

14.2.1. GIER ALGOL   This compiler implements ALGOL 60 on GIER, a machine manufactured by Regnecentralen, Copenhagen. The decision to develop the compiler was taken in January, 1962 and the final product was delivered in February, 1963. It implemented all of ALGOL 60 except integer labels, arrays as value parameters, and **own** arrays. The compiler was intended to run on a minimum GIER configuration consisting of 1024 40-bit words of 8.8 microsecond core memory and a 128,000 word drum (320 tracks of 40 words each).

Previous experience with ALGOL compilers led the designers to predict a code size of about 5000 words for the GIER compiler. They chose to organize the compiler as a sequence of passes over linearized representations of the program. Each intermediate representation consists of a sequence of 10-bit bytes. The interpretation of this sequence depends upon the passes accessing it; it is a unique encoding of a specific data structure. Use of relatively small, uniform units improves the efficiency of the encoding and allows the implementors to use common basic I/O routines for all passes. The latter consideration is perhaps most important for compilers implemented in machine code. As we indicated in Section 14.1.2, however, a multi-pass compiler is often I/O bound and hence specially tailored machine code I/O routines might result in a significant performance improvement. We should emphasize that such a decision should only be made on the basis of careful measurement, but the implementor should make it possible by an appropriate choice of representation.

Assuming that about half of the core memory would be used for code in each pass, simple arithmetic shows that 10 passes will be required. This value was not taken as a target to be met, but merely as an indication of the number to be expected. Passes were generally organized around major data structures, with the additional proviso that large tables should be combined with simple code and vice-versa.

Table 14.2 shows the final structure, using the descriptions given by Naur [1964a] and the corresponding tasks discussed in this book.

Lexical analysis is divided into two passes in order to satisfy the code size/table size relationship mentioned in the last paragraph: Since up to 510 identifiers are allowed, and there is no restriction on identifier length, it is clear that the maximum possible space must be made available for the symbol table. Thus the remainder of the lexical analysis was placed in another pass. Here we have a decision that should be validated by measurements made on the running compiler. In the final system, each pass had 769 words of core memory available (the remainder was occupied by the control code). Pass 1 used 501 words of program and 132 words of data, plus a 40-word buffer for long character strings; pass 2 used 89 words for program and 62 words for data. Unless the pass 1 code could be reduced significantly by using a different algorithm or data structure, or the allowance of 510 identifiers was found to be excessive, the decision to split the two tasks stands.

Note the interdependence of the decisions about representation of tokens and form of the intermediate code. A 10-bit byte allows values in the range [0,1023]. By using the subrange [512,1022] for identifiers, one effectively combines the *classification* and *symbol* fields of Figure 4.1. Values less than 512 classify non-identifier tokens, in most cases characterizing them com-

Table 14.2 Pass Structure for the GIER ALGOL Compiler

Pass	Task(s)	Description
1	Lexical analysis	Analysis and check of hardware representation. Conversion to reference language. Strings are assembled.
2	Lexical analysis	Identifier matching. In the output, each distinct identifier is associated with an integer between 512 and 1022.
3	Syntactic analysis	Analysis and check of delimiter structure. Delimiters of multiple meaning are replaced by distinctive delimiters. Extra delimiters are inserted to facilitate later scanning.
4		Collection of declarations and specifications at the **begin** of blocks and in procedure headings. Rearrangements of procedure calls.
5	Name analysis Storage mapping	Distribution of identifier descriptions. Storage allocation for variables.
6	Semantic analysis	Check the types and kinds of identifiers and other operands. Conversion to reverse polish notation.
7	Code generation	Generation of machine instructions for expressions. Allocation of working variables.
8	Assembly	Final addressing of the program. Segmentation into drum tracks. Production of final machine code.
9		Rearrangement of the program tracks on the drum

pletely. Only constants need more than a single byte using this scheme, and we know that constants occur relatively infrequently. Interestingly, only string constants are handled in pass 1. Those whose machine representations do not exceed 40 bits are replaced by a marker byte followed by 4 bytes holding the representation. Longer strings are saved on the drum and replaced in the code by a marker byte followed by 4 bytes giving the drum track number and relative address. In the terminology of Section 4.2.2, the constant table has separate fixed-length representations for long and short strings. Numeric constants remain in the text as strings of bytes, one corresponding to each character of the constant.

Pass 3 performs the normal syntactic analysis, and also converts numeric and logical constants to a flag byte followed by 4 bytes giving the machine representation. Again in the terminology of Section 4.2.2, the internal and target representations of numeric constants are identical. (The flag byte simply serves as the *classification* field of Figure 4.1; it is not part of the constant itself.) Naur's description of the compiler strongly suggests that parsing is carried out by the equivalent of a pushdown automaton while the lexical analysis of pass 1 is more ad-hoc. As we have seen, numeric constants can be handled easily by a pushdown automaton. The decision to process numeric and logical constants in pass 3 rather than in pass 1 was therefore probably one of convenience.

The intermediate output from pass 3 consists of the unchanged identifiers and constants, and a transformed set of delimiters that precisely describe the program's structure. It is effectively a sequence of connection point numbers and tokens, with the transformed delimiters specifying structure connections and each identifier or constant specifying a single symbol connection plus the associated token.

Attribute flow is generally from declaration to use. Since declaration may follow use in ALGOL 60, reverse attribute flow may occur. Pass 4 is a reverse pass that collects all declarative information of a block at the head of the block. It merely simplifies subsequent processing.

In pass 5, the definition table is actually distributed through the text. Each identifier is replaced by a 4-byte group that is the corresponding definition table entry. It gives the kind (e.g. variable, procedure), result type, block number, relative address and possibly additional information. Thus GIER ALGOL does not abstract entities as proposed in Section 4.2.3, but deposits the necessary information at the leaves of the structure tree. This example emphasizes the fact that possessions and definitions are separate. GIER ALGOL uses possessions virtually identical to those discussed in connection with Figure 9.21 to control placement of the attributes during pass 5, but it has no explicit definition table at all.

Given the attribute propagation performed by passes 4 and 5, the attribution of pass 6 is LAG(1). This illustrates the interaction between attribute flow and pass structure. Given an attribute grammar, we must attempt to partition the relationships and semantic functions so that they fall into separable components that can be fit into the overall implementation model. This partitioning is beyond the current state of the art for automatic generators. We can only carry out the partitioning by hand and then use analysis tools based upon the theorems of Chapter 8 to verify that we have not made any mistake.

Address calculations are carried out during both pass 7 and pass 8. Backward references are resolved by pass 7; pass 8 is backward over the program, and hence can trivially resolve forward references. Literal pooling is also done during pass 7. All of the constants used in the code on one drum track appear in a literal pool on that track.

14.2.2. Zurich Pascal The first Pascal compiler was developed during the years 1969-71 for Control Data 6000 series hardware at the Institut für Informatik, Eidgenössische Technische Hochschule, Zürich. Changes were made in Pascal itself as a result of experience with the system, and a new implementation was begun in July, 1972. This project resulted in a family of two compilers, Pascal-P and Pascal-6000, having a single overall design. Pascal-P is a portable compiler that produces code for a hypothetical stack computer; the system is implemented by writing an interpreter for this machine. Pascal-6000 produces relocatable binary code for Control Data 6000 series machines. The two compilers were completed in March, 1973 and July, 1974 respectively. Descendants of these two compilers comprised the bulk of the Pascal implementations in existence in 1982, ten years after their development was initiated.

Written in Pascal itself, the Zürich compilers have a one-pass, recursive descent architecture that reflects the freedom from storage constraints afforded by the Control Data machine. 6000 series processors permit a user direct access to 131,072 60-bit words of 1 microsecond core memory. Even the more common configuration installed at the time Zürich Pascal was developed provided each user with a maximum of about 40,000 words. (This is almost 60 times the random-access memory available for the GIER ALGOL compiler.)

Pascal provides no linguistic mechanisms for defining packages or abstract data types, and hence all explicit modules in the compilers are procedures or variables. The effect of a package must be obtained by defining one or more variables at a given level and providing a collection of procedures to manipulate them. Encapsulation can be indicated by comments, but cannot be enforced. Similarly, an abstract data type is implemented by defining a type and providing procedures to manipulate objects of that type. Lack of linguistic support for encapsulation encourages the designer to consider a program as a single, monolithic unit. Control of complexity is still essential, however, and leads to an approach known as *stepwise refinement*. This technique is particularly well-suited to the development of recursive descent compilers.

Stepwise refinement is subtly different from modular decomposition as a

Table 14.3 Development Steps for the Zürich Pascal Compilers

Step	Task(s)	Description
1	Lexical analysis Syntactic analysis	Syntax analysis for syntactical-ly correct programs
2	Syntactic error recovery	Treatment of syntactic errors
3	Semantic analysis	Analysis of the declarations
4	Semantic analysis	Treatment of declaration errors
5	Memory mapping	Address allocation
6	Code selection Assembly	Code generation
7	Optimization	Local improvement of the gen-erated code

design methodology. Instead of dividing the problem to be solved into a number of independent subproblems, it divides the solution into a number of development steps. A painter uses stepwise refinement when he first sketches the outlines of his subject and then successively fills in detail and adds color; an automobile manufacturer uses modular decomposition when he combines engine, power train and coachwork into a complete product. Table 14.3 lists the development steps used in the Zürich Pascal project, with the descriptions given by Ammann [1975] and the corresponding tasks discussed in this book.

The overall structure of the compiler was established in step 1; Figure 14.4 shows this structure. Each line represents a procedure, and nesting is indicated by indentation. At this step the procedure bodies had the form discussed in Section 7.2.2, and implemented an EBNF description of the language.

Lexical analysis is carried out by a single procedure that follows the outline of Chapter 6. It has no separate scanning procedures, and it incorporates the constant table operations for conversion from source to internal form. Internal form and target form are identical. No internal-to-target operators are used, and the internal form is manipulated directly via normal Pascal operations.

There is no symbol table. Identifiers are represented internally as packed arrays of 10 characters—one 60-bit word. If the identifier is shorter than 10 characters then it is padded on the right with spaces; if it is longer then it is truncated on the right. (We have already deplored this strategy for a language whose definition places no constraints upon identifier length.) Although the representation is fixed-length, it still does not define a small enough address space to be used directly as a pointer or table index. Name analysis therefore requires searching and, because there may be duplicate identifiers in different contexts, the search space may be larger than in the case of a symbol table. Omission of the symbol table does not save much storage because most of the symbol table lookup mechanism must be included in the name analysis.

Syntactic error recovery is carried out using the technique of Section 12.2.2. A minor modification was needed because the stack is not accessible when an error is detected: Each procedure takes an anchor set as an argument. This set describes the anchors *after* reduction of the nonterminal corresponding to the procedure. Symbols must be added to this set to represent anchors within the production currently being examined. Of course all of the code to update the anchors, check for errors, skip input symbols and advance the parse was produced by hand. This augmentation of the basic step 1 routines constituted step 2 of the compiler development.

```
basic symbol
program
       block
                constant
                type
                       simple type
                       field list
                label declaration
                constant declaration
                type declaration
                variable declaration
                procedure declaration
                       parameter list
                body
                       statement
                              selector
                              variable
                              call
                              expression
                                     simple expression
                                            term
                                                   factor
                              assignment
                              compound statement
                              goto statement
                              if statement
                              case statement
                              while statement
                              repeat statement
                              for statement
                              with statement
```

Figure 14.4. The Structure of the Zürich Pascal Compilers.

The basic structure of Figure 14.4 remained virtually unchanged; common routines for error reporting and skipping to an anchor were introduced, with the former preceding the basic symbol routine (so that lexical errors could be reported) and the latter following it (so that the basic symbol routine could be invoked when skipping).

Step 3 was concerned with building the environment attribute discussed in Section 9.1.1. Two record types, *identrec* and *structrec,* were added to the existing compiler. The environment is a linked data structure made up of records of these types. There is one *identrec* per declared identifier, and those for identifiers declared in the same range are linked as an unbalanced binary tree. An array of pointers to tree roots constitutes the definition of the current addressing environment. Three of the definition table operations discussed in Section 9.2 (add a possession to a range, search the current environment, search a given range) are implemented as common routines while the others are coded in line. Entering and leaving a range are trivial operations, involving pointer assignment only, while searching the current environment is complex. This is exactly the opposite of Figure 9.21, which requires complex behavior on entry to and exit from a range with simple access to the current environment. The actual discrepancy between the two techniques is reduced, however, when we recall that the Zürich compiler does not perform symbol table lookups.

Each *identrec* carries attribute information as well as the linkages used to implement the possession table. Thus the possessions and definitions are combined in this implementation. The type attribute of an identifier is represented by a pointer to a record of type *structrec,* and there is one such record for every defined type. Certain types (as for example scalar types) are defined in terms of identifiers and hence a *structrec* may point to an *identrec.* The *identrec* contains an extra link field, beyond those used for the range tree, to implement lists of identifiers such as scalar constants, record fields and formal parameters.

The procedures of Figure 14.4 can be thought of as carrying out a depth-first, left-to-right traversal of the parse tree even though that tree never has an explicit incarnation. Since only one pass is made over the source program, the attribution rules must meet the LAG(1) condition. They were simply implemented by Pascal statements inserted into the procedures of Figure 14.4 at the appropriate points. Thus at the conclusion of step 3 the bodies of these procedures still had the form of Section 7.2.2, but contained additional Pascal code to calculate the environment attribute. As discussed in Section 8.3.2, attribute storage optimization led to the representation of the environment attribute as a linked, global data structure rather than an item stored at each parse tree node. The interesting part of the structure tree is actually represented by the hierarchy of activation records of the recursive descent procedures. Attribute values attached to the nodes are stored as values of local variables of these procedures.

During step 4 of the refinement the remainder of the semantic analysis was added to the routines of Figure 14.4. This step involved additional attribution and closely followed the discussion of Chapter 9. Type definitions were introduced for the additional attributes, global variables were declared for those attributes whose storage could be optimized, and local variables were declared for the others. The procedures of Figure 14.4 were augmented by the Pascal code for the necessary attribution rules, and functions were added to implement the recursive attribute functions.

Ammann [1975] reports that steps 1-4 occupied a bit more than 6 months of the 24-month project and accounted for just over 2000 of the almost 7000 lines in Pascal-6000. Steps 5 and 6 for Pascal-P were carried out in less than two and a half months and resulted in about 1500 lines of Pascal, while the corresponding numbers for Pascal-6000 were thirteen months and 4000 lines. Step 7 added another three and a half months to the total cost of Pascal-6000, while increasing the number of lines by less than 1000.

The abstract stack computer that is the target for the Pascal-P compiler is carefully matched to Pascal. Its elementary operators and data types are those of Pascal, as are its memory access paths. There are special instructions for procedure entry and exit that provide exactly the effect of a Pascal procedure invocation, and an indexed jump instruction for implementing a case selection. Code generation for such a machine is clearly trivial, and we shall not consider this part of the project further.

Section 10.1 describes storage allocation in terms of *blocks* and *areas*. A block is an object whose size and alignment are known, while an area is an object that is still growing. In Pascal, blocks are associated with completely-defined types, whereas areas are associated with types in the process of definition and with activation records. Thus Pascal-6000 represents blocks by means of a *size* field in every *structrec*. The actual form of this field varies with the type defined by the *structrec*; there is no uniform *size* attribute like that of Figure 10.1. Because of the recursive descent architecture and the properties of Pascal, the lifetime of an area coincides with the invocation of one of the procedures of Figure 14.4 in every case. For example, an area corresponding to a record type grows only during an invocation of the field list procedure. This means that the specification of an area can be held in local variables of a procedure. Step 5 added these local variable declarations and the code to process area growth to the procedures of Figure 14.4. The *size* field was also added to *structrec* in this step.

Step 6 was the first point at which a 'foreign' structure—the structure of the target machine—appeared. This refinement was thus the first that added a significant number of procedures to those of Figure 14.4. The added procedures effectively act as modules for simulation and assembly.

As we pointed out earlier, no explicit structure tree is ever created by Pascal-6000. This means that the structure tree cannot be decorated with target attributes used to determine an improved execution order and then traversed according to this execution order for code selection. Pascal-6000 thus computes no target attributes other than the value descriptors of Section

10.3.1. They are used in conjunction with a set of register descriptors and register allocation operations to perform a machine simulation exactly as discussed in Section 10.3.1. The recursive descent architecture once again manifests itself in the fact that global storage is provided for only one value descriptor. Most value descriptors are held as local variables of procedures appearing in Figure 14.4, with the global variable describing the 'current' value—the one that would lie at the 'top of the stack'.

The decision tables describing code selection are hand-coded as Pascal conditionals and case statements within the analysis procedures. Code is generated by invoking register allocation procedures, common routines such as *load* and *store,* and assembly interface procedures from Table 14.5.

The first four operations of Table 14.5 assemble target code sequentially; Pascal-6000 does not have the concept of separate sequences discussed in Section 11.1.1. A 'location counter' holds the current relative address, which may be accessed by any routine and saved as a label. The third operand of a 30-bit instruction may be either an absolute value or a relative address, and *gen*30 has a fourth parameter to distinguish these cases. Forward references are handled by *ins,* which allows a relative address to be stored at a given position in the code already assembled.

In keeping with the one-pass architecture, Pascal-6000 retains all of the code for a single procedure. The assembly 'module' is initialized when the 'body' procedure (Figure 14.4) is invoked, and a complete relocatable deck is output at the end of this invocation to finalize the 'module'. Pascal-6000 uses Control Data's standard relocatable binary text as its target code, in keeping with our admonition at the beginning of Section 11.2. We shall discuss the layout of that text here in some detail as an illustration; another example, the IBM 370 object module, will be given at the end of the next section.

A *relocatable subprogram* is a logical record composed of a sequence of *tables* (Figure 14.6), which are simply blocks of information with various purposes. The first word of each table contains an identifying code and

Table 14.5 Pascal-6000 Assembly Operations

Procedure	Description
noop	Force code alignment to a word boundary
*gen*15	Assemble a 15-bit instruction
*gen*30	Assemble a 30-bit instruction
*gen*60	Assemble a 60-bit constant
searchextid	Set up an external reference
ins	Satisfy a given forward reference
lgohead	Output PIDL and ENTR
lgotext	Output TEXT
lgoend	Output XFER and LINK

specifies the number of additional 60-bit words in the table. As with any record, a relocatable subprogram may be preceded by a *prefix* table containing arbitrary information (such as the date compiled, version of the compiler, etc.), but the first component of the subprogram proper is the *program identification and length (PIDL)* table. PIDL is conventionally followed by an *entry point (ENTR)* table that associates entry point symbols with the locations they denote (Section 11.2.1), but in fact the loader places no constraints on either the number or the position(s) of any tables other than PIDL.

The body of the subprogram is made up of *TEXT* tables. Each TEXT table specifies a block of up to 15 words, the first of which should be loaded at the specified address. Four relocation bits are used for each text word (hence the limit of 15 text words). References to external symbols are not indicated by the relocation bits, which only distinguish absolute and signed relative addresses. External references are specified by *LINK* tables: For each external symbol, a sequence of operand field definitions is given. The loader will *add* the address of the external symbol to each of the fields so defined. Thus a call of *sqrt*, for example, would appear in the TEXT table as an RJ (*return jump*) instruction with the absolute value 0 as its operand. This 0-field would then be described in a LINK table by one of the operand field definitions following the symbol *sqrt*. When the loader had determined the address of *sqrt* it would add it to the 0-field, thus changing the instruction into RJ *sqrt*. There is no restriction on the number of LINK tables, the number of times a symbol may appear or the number of field definitions that may follow a single symbol. As shown in Figure 14.6, each field definition occupies 30 bits, each symbol occupies 60 bits, and a symbol may be split between words.

The *transfer (XFER)* table is conventionally associated with a main program. It gives the entry point to which control is transferred after the loader has completed loading the program. Again, however, the loader places no restriction on the number of XFER tables or the subprograms with which they are associated. An XFER table is ignored if its start symbol begins with a space, or if a new XFER whose start symbol does *not* begin with a space is encountered. The only requirement is that, by the time the load is completed, a start symbol that is an entry point of some loaded subprogram has been specified.

Internal and external references, either of which may occur in a 30-bit instruction, are represented quite differently in the target code. This is reflected at the assembly interface by the presence of *searchextid*. When a 30-bit instruction is emitted, *gen* 30 checks a global pointer. If it is not *nil* then it points to an external symbol, and *gen* 30 adds the target location of the current instruction's third operand to a list rooted in that symbol. This list will ultimately be used by *lgoend* to generate a LINK table. The global pointer checked by *gen* 30 is set by *searchextid* and cleared to *nil* by *gen* 30. When the code generator emits a 30-bit instruction containing an external

reference it therefore first invokes *searchextid* with the external identifier and
then invokes *gen* 30 with the absolute value 0 as the third operand. Section
11.3.1 gives an alternative strategy.

14.2.3. IBM FORTRAN H   The major design goal for FORTRAN H
was production of efficient object code. IBM began development of the
compiler in 1963, using FORTRAN as the implementation language on the
7094. The initial version was used to compile itself for System/360, producing over half a million 8-bit bytes of code. Running on System/360, the
compiler optimized itself, reducing its size by about 25%. It was then rewritten to take advantage of language extensions permitting efficient bit manipulation and introducing a form of record access. This reduced compilation
time by about 35% and allowed the compiler to compile itself on a 262,140
byte configuration. Major development of FORTRAN H was completed in
1967, but modification and enhancement has been a continuous process
since then. The details presented in this section correspond to release 17 of
the compiler [IBM 1968].

The entire program unit being compiled is held in main storage by the

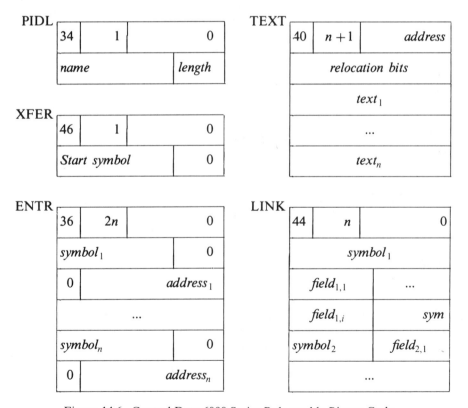

Figure 14.6. Control Data 6000 Series Relocatable Binary Code.

FORTRAN H compiler. This is done to simplify the optimizer, which accesses the program text randomly and rearranges it. It does imply limitations on the size of a compilable unit, but such limitations are less serious for FORTRAN than for ALGOL 60 or Pascal because the language design supports separate compilation of small units.

As shown in Table 14.7, the compiler has five major phases. Code for these phases is overlaid, with a total of 13 overlay segments. A maximum of about 81,000 bytes of code is actually in the memory at any one time (this maximum occurs during phase 20), and the minimum storage in which a compilation can be carried out is about 89,000 bytes.

FORTRAN is a rather unsystematic language, and Phase 10 reflects this. The unit of processing is a complete statement, which is read into a buffer, packed to remove superfluous spaces, and then classified. Based upon the classification, ad hoc analysis routines are used to deal with the parts of the statement. All of these routines have similar structures: They scan the statement from left to right, extracting each operand and making an entry for it in the definition table if one does not already exist, and building a linear list of operator/operand pairs. The operator of the pair is the operator that *preceded* the operand; for the first pair it is the statement class. An operand is represented by a pointer to the definition table plus its type and kind (constant, simple variable, array, etc.) The type and kind codes are also in the definition table entry, and are retained in the list solely to simplify access.

Phase 10 performs only a partial syntactic analysis of the source program.

Table 14.7 Phase Structure of the IBM FORTRAN H Compiler

Phase	Task(s)	Description
10	Lexical analysis Syntactic analysis Semantic analysis	Convert source text to operator-operand pairs and information table entries. Detect syntactic errors.
15	Syntactic analysis Semantic analysis Memory mapping Target attribution	Convert operator-operand pairs to quadruples. Operator identification and consistency checks. Convert constants and assign relative addresses to constants, variables and arrays.
20	Target attribution Optimization	Eliminate common subexpressions, perform live/dead analysis and strength reduction, and move constant expressions out of loops. Assign registers and determine the sizes of code blocks. Optimize jump targets.
25	Code selection Assembly	Convert quadruples into System/360 machine code. Create an object module.
30	Error reporting	Record appropriate messages for errors encountered during previous phases.

It does not determine the tree structure within a statement, but it does extract the statement number and classify some delimiters that have multiple meaning. For example, it replaces '(' by 'left arithmetic parenthesis', 'left subscript parenthesis' or 'function parenthesis' as appropriate.

Name analysis is rudimentary in FORTRAN because the meaning of an identifier is independent of the structure of a program unit. This means that no possessions are required, and the symbol and definition tables can be integrated without penalty. Symbol lookup uses a simple linear scan of the chained definition table entries, but the organization of the chains is FORTRAN-specific: There is one ordered chain for each of the six possible identifier lengths, and each chain is doubly-linked with the header pointing to the center of the chain. Thus a search on any chain only involves half the entries. (The header is moved as entries are added to a chain, in order to maintain the balance.) Constants, statement numbers and common block names also have entries in the definition table. Three chains are used for constants, one for each allowable length (4, 8 or 16 bytes), and one each for statement numbers and common block names.

The only semantic analysis done during Phase 10 is 'declaration processing'. Type, dimension, common and equivalence statements are completely processed and the results summarized in the definition table. Because FORTRAN does not require that identifiers be declared, attribute information must also be gathered from applied occurrences. A minor use of the attribute information is in the classification of left parentheses (mentioned above), because FORTRAN does not make a lexical distinction between subscript brackets and function parentheses.

Phase 15 completes the syntactic analysis, converting the lists of operator/operand pairs to lists of quadruples where appropriate. Each quadruple consists of an operator, a target type and three pointers to the definition table. This means that phase 15 also creates a definition table entry for every anonymous intermediate result. Such 'temporary names' are treated exactly like programmer-defined variables in subsequent processing, and may be eliminated by various optimizations. The quadruples are chained in a *correct* (but not necessarily *optimum*) execution order and gathered into basic blocks.

Semantic analysis is also completed during phase 15, with all operator identification and consistency checking done as the quadruples are built. The target type is expressed as a *general* type (logical, integer, real) plus an *operand* type (short, long) for each operand and for the result.

The syntactic and semantic analysis tasks of phase 15 are carried out by an overlay segment known as *PHAZ15*, which also gathers defined/used information for common subexpression and dead variable analysis. This information is stored in basic block headers as discussed in Chapter 13. Finally, *PHAZ15* links the basic block headers to both their predecessors and their successors, describing the flowgraph of the program and preparing for dominance analysis.

CORAL is the second overlay segment of phase 15, which carries out the memory mapping task. The algorithm is essentially that discussed in Section 10.1, but its only function is to assign addresses to constants and variables (in other words, to map the activation record). There are no variant records, but equivalence statements cause variables to share storage. By convention, the activation record base is in register 13. The layout of the activation record is given in Figure 14.8. It is followed immediately by the code for the program unit. (Remember that storage allocation is static in FORTRAN.) The size of the save area (72 bytes) and its alignment (8) are fixed by the implementation, as is the size of the initial contents for register 12 (discussed below). Storage for the computed GOTO tables and the parameter lists have already been allocated storage by Phase 10. CORAL allocates storage for constants first, then for simple variables and then for arrays. Local variables and arrays mentioned in equivalence statements come next, completing this part of the activation record. Finally the common blocks specified by the program unit are mapped as separate areas.

System/360 access paths limit the maximum displacement to 4095. When a larger displacement is generated during CORAL processing, the compiler defines an adcon variable—a new activation record base—and resets the displacement to 0. The adcon is entered into the definition table and treated as a normal variable for further processing. CORAL does not place either adcons or temporaries into the activation record at this time, because they may be deleted during optimization.

Phase 20 assigns operands to registers. If the user has specified optimization level 0, the compiler treats the machine as having one accumulator, one base register and one register for specifying jump addresses (Table 14.9). Machine simulation (Section 10.3.1) is used to avoid redundant loads and stores, but no change is made in the execution order of the quadruples. Attributes are added to the quadruples, specifying the register or base register used for each operand and for the result.

Level 1 optimization makes use of a pool of general-purpose registers, as shown in Table 14.9. Register 13 is always reserved as the base of the

Save area
Initial contents for register 12
Branch tables for computed GOTO's
Parameter lists
Constants and local variables
Address values ('adcons')
Namelist dictionaries
Compiler-generated temporaries
Label addresses

Figure 14.8. FORTRAN H Activation Record.

activation record. A decision about whether to reserve some or all of registers 9-12 is made on the basis of the number of quadruples output by phase 15. This statistic is available prior to register allocation, and it predicts the size of the subprogram code. Once the register pool is fixed, phase 20 performs local register assignment within basic blocks and global assignment over the entire program unit. Again, the order of the quadruples is unchanged and attributes giving the registers used for each operand or memory access path are added to the quadruples.

Common subexpression elimination, live/dead analysis, code motion and strength reduction are all performed at optimization level 2. The register assignment algorithms used on the entire program unit at level 1 are then applied to each loop of the modified program, starting with the innermost and ending with the entire program unit. This guarantees that the register assignment within an inner loop will be determined primarily by the activity of operands within that loop, whereas at level 1 it may be influenced by operand activity elsewhere in the program.

The basic implementation used for a branch is to load the target address of the branch into a register and then execute an RR-format branch instruction. This requires an adcon for every basic block whose first instruction is a

Register	Assignment at optimization level 0	1,2
0	Operands and results	Operands and results
1		
2	Not used	
3		
4		
5	Branch addresses Selected logical operands	
6	Operands representing index values	
7	Base addresses	
8	Not used	
9		Code bases or operands and results
10		
11		
12	Adcon base	
13	Activation record base	
14	Computed GOTO Logical results of comparisons	Operands and results
15	Computed GOTO	

Table 14.9. General-Purpose Register Assignment by FORTRAN H

branch target. If a register already happened to hold an address less than 4096 bytes lower than the branch target, however, both the load and the adcon would be unnecessary. A single RX-format branch instruction would suffice. Thus the compiler reserves registers to act as code bases. To understand the mechanism involved, we must consider the layout of information in storage more carefully.

We have already seen that phase 15 allocates activation record storage for constants and programmer-defined variables, generating adcons as necessary to satisfy the displacement limit of 4095. When register allocation is complete, all adcons and temporary variables that have not been eliminated are added to the activation record. The adcons must all be directly addressable, since they must be loaded to provide base addresses for memory access. If they are not all within 4095 bytes of the activation record base then the reserved register 12 is assumed to contain either the address of the first adcon or (*base address of the activation record* +4096), whichever is larger. It is assumed that the number of adcons will never exceed 1024 (although this is theoretically possible, given the address space of System/360) and hence all adcons will be directly accessible via either register 12 or register 13. (Note that a fail-safe decision to reserve register 12 can be made on the basis of the phase 15 output, without regard to the number of quadruples.)

If the number of quadruples output from phase 15 is large enough, register 11 will be reserved and initialized to address the 4096th byte beyond that addressed by register 12. Similarly, for a larger number of quadruples, register 10 will be reserved and initialized to an address 4096 larger than register 11. Finally, register 9 will be reserved and initialized for an even larger number of quadruples. Phase 20 can calculate the maximum possible address of each basic block. Those lying within 4096 bytes of one of the reserved registers are marked with the register number and displacement. The adcon corresponding to the basic block label is then deleted. (These deletions, plus the ultimate shortening of the basic blocks due to optimization of the branch instructions, can never invalidate the addressability conditions on the basic blocks.)

The branch optimization described in the previous paragraphs is carried out only at optimization levels 1 and 2. At optimization level 0 the basic implementation is used for all branches.

Phase 25 uses decision tables to select the proper sequence of machine instructions. The algorithm is basically that of Section 10.3.2, except that the action stub of the decision table is simply a sequence of instruction templates. Actions such as *swap* and *lreg* (Figure 10.15) have already been carried out during phase 20. There is conceptually one table for every quadruple operator. Actually, several tables are associated with families of operators, and the individual operator modifies the skeletons as they are extracted. The condition is selected by a 4-bit *status*, which may have somewhat different meanings for different operators. It is used as an index to select the proper column of the table, which in turn identifies the templates to be used in implementing the operator.

FORTRAN H generates System/360 object modules, which are sequences of 80-character card images (Figure 14.10). Each card image is output by a normal FORTRAN formatted write statement. The first byte contains 2, which is the communication control character STX (*start of text*). All other fields left blank in Figure 14.10 are unused. Columns 2-4 and 73-80 contain alphanumeric information as indicated, with the serial number

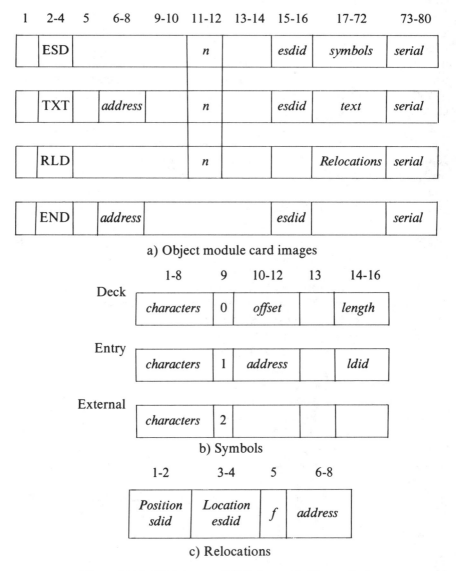

Figure 14.10. IBM System/360 Relocatable Binary Code.

consisting of a four-character deck identifier and a four-digit sequence number. The remaining columns simply contain whatever character happens to have the value of the corresponding byte as its EBCDIC code. Thus 24-bit (3-byte) addresses occupy three columns and halfword (2-byte) integers occupy two columns. Even though the length field n has a maximum value of 56, it occupies a halfword because System/360 has no byte arithmetic.

Comparing Figure 14.10 with Figure 14.6, we see that essentially the same elements are present. END optionally carries a transfer address, thus subsuming XFER. ESD plays the roles of both PIDL and ENTR, and also specifies the symbols from LINK. Its purpose is to describe the characteristics of the *control sections* associated with global symbols, and to define short, fixed-length representations (the *esdid*'s) for those symbols. The *esdid* in columns 15-16 identifies a deck or external; only one symbol of these types may appear on an ESD card. Entry symbols identify the control sections to which they belong (*ldid*), and therefore they may be placed on any ESD card where space is available.

RLD provides the remaining function of LINK, and also that of the relocation bits in TEXT. Each item of relocation information modifies the field at the absolute location specified in the *position esdid* and *address* by either adding or subtracting the value identified by the *relocation esdid*. Byte f determines whether the value will be added or subtracted, and also specifies the width of the field being modified (which may be 1, 2, 3 or 4 bytes). If a sequence of relocations involve the same *esdid*'s then these specifications are omitted from the second and subsequent relocations. (The rightmost bit of f is 1 if the following relocation does not specify *esdid*'s, 0 otherwise.)

The decision to use relocation bits on the Control Data machine and the RLD mechanism on System/360 reflects a fundamental difference in the instruction sets: 30-bit instructions on the 6000 Series often reference memory directly, and therefore relocatable addresses are common in the text. On System/360, however, all references to memory are via values in registers. Only the adcons are relocatable and therefore relocatable addresses are quite rare in the text.

14.3. Notes and References

Most implementation decisions are related to performance in one way or another, and must either be made on the basis of hard data or validated on that basis when the compiler is running. It is well known that performance problems are elusive, and that most programmers have incorrect ideas about the source of bottlenecks in their code. Measurement of critical parameters of the compiler as it is running is thus imperative. These parameters include the sizes of various data structures and the states of various allocation and lookup mechanisms, as well as an execution histogram [Waite 1973b].

The only description of GIER ALGOL in the open literature is the paper by Naur [1964] cited earlier, but a very similar compiler for a variant of Pascal was discussed in great detail by Hartmann [1977].

Ammann [1975] gives an excellent account in German of the development of Zürich Pascal, and partial descriptions are available in English [Ammann 1974, Ammann 1977].

In addition to the Program Logic Manual [IBM 1968], descriptions of FORTRAN H have been given by Lowry [1969] and Scarborough [1980]. These treatments concentrate on the optimization performed by Phase 20, however, and give very little information about the compiler as a whole.

APPENDIX A

The Sample Programming Language LAX

In this Appendix we define the sample programming language LAX (*LA*nguage e*X*ample), upon which the concrete compiler design examples in this book are based. LAX illustrates the fundamental problems of compiler construction, but avoids uninteresting complications.

We shall use *extended Backus-Naur form* (*EBNF*) to describe the form of LAX. The differences between EBNF and normal BNF are:

- Each rule is terminated by a period.
- Terminal symbols of the grammar are delimited by apostrophes. (Thus the metabrackets '<' and '>' of BNF are superfluous.)
- The following abbreviations are permitted:

Abbreviation	Meaning
$X ::= \alpha(\beta)\gamma$.	$X ::= \alpha Y\gamma$. $Y ::= \beta$.
$X ::= \alpha[\beta]\gamma$.	$X ::= \alpha\gamma \mid \alpha(\beta)\gamma$.
$X ::= \alpha u +\gamma$.	$X ::= \alpha Y\gamma$. $Y ::= u \mid Yu$.
$X ::= \alpha u^*\gamma$.	$X ::= \alpha[u +]\gamma$.
$X ::= \alpha \mid \mid t$.	$X ::= \alpha(t\alpha)^*$.

Here α, β and γ are arbitrary right-hand sides of rules, Y is a symbol that does not appear elsewhere in the specification, u is either a single symbol or a parenthesized right-hand side, and t is a terminal symbol.

For a more complete discussion of EBNF see Section 5.1.4.

The axiom of the grammar is *program*. EBNF rules marked with an asterisk in this Appendix are included to aid in the description of the language, but they do not participate in the derivation of any sentence. Thus they define useless nonterminals in the sense of Chapter 5.

A.1. Basic Symbols

A.1.0.1   *   *basic_symbol* ::= *identifier* | *denotation* | *delimiter* .

A.1.0.2   *identifier* ::= *letter* (['_'] *letter* | *digit*)* .

A.1.0.3   *letter* ::= 'a' | 'b' | 'c' | 'd' | 'e' | 'f' | 'g' | 'h' | 'i'
          | 'j' | 'k' | 'l' | 'm' | 'n' | 'o' | 'p' | 'q' | 'r'
          | 's' | 't' | 'u' | 'v' | 'w' | 'x' | 'y' | 'z' .

A.1.0.4   *digit* ::= '0' | '1' | '2' | '3' | '4' | '5' | '6' | '7' | '8' | '9' .

A.1.0.5   *denotation* ::= *integer* | *floating_point* .

A.1.0.6   *integer* ::= *digit* + .

A.1.0.7   *floating_point* ::= *digit* + *scale* | *digit* * '.' *digit* + [*scale*] .

A.1.0.8   *scale* ::= 'e' ['+' | '−'] *integer* .

A.1.0.9   *   *delimiter* ::= *special* | *keyword* .

A.1.0.10 *   *special* ::= '+' | '−' | '*' | '/' | '<' | '>' | '=' | '↑'
          | ':' | ';' | '.' | ',' | '(' | ')' | '[' | ']'
          | '//' | ':=' | '≡' .

A.1.0.11 *   *keyword* ::= 'and' | 'array' | 'begin' | 'case'
          | 'declare' | 'div' | 'do' | 'else' | 'end'
          | 'for' | 'from' | 'goto' | 'if' | 'is'
          | 'loop' | 'mod' | 'new' | 'not' | 'of' | 'or'
          | 'procedure' | 'record' | 'ref' | 'then' | 'to'
          | 'type' | 'while' .

A.1.0.12 *   *comment* ::= '(*' *arbitrary* '*)' .

Note: *arbitrary* does not contain '*)'

An identifier is a freely-chosen representation for a type, label, object, procedure, formal parameter or field selector. It is given meaning by a construct of the program. The appearances at which an identifier is given a meaning are called *defining occurrences* of that identifier. All other appearances of the identifier are called *applied occurrences*.

Integer and floating point denotations have the usual meaning.

Keywords are reserved identifiers that can only be used as indicated by the rules of the EBNF specification. We have used boldface type to represent keywords in the book only to enhance readability. This convention is not followed in the grammar, where the keywords are simply strings to be processed.

Comments, spaces and newlines may not appear within basic symbols. Two adjacent basic symbols must be separated by one or more comments, spaces or newlines unless one of the basic symbols is a *special*. Otherwise comments, spaces and newlines are meaningless.

An upper case letter is considered to be equivalent to the corresponding lower case letter.

A.2. Program Structure

A.2.0.1   *program* :: = *block* .

A.2.0.2   * *range* :: =
       block | *statement_list* | *iteration* | *record_type* | *procedure* .

A.2.0.3   *block* :: = *'declare'* (*declaration* | | *';'*) *'begin'*
       (*statement* | | *';'*) *'end'* .

A.2.0.4   *statement_list* :: = *statement* | | *';'* .

A.2.0.5   *statement* :: = *label_definition** (*expression* | *iteration* | *jump*) .

A.2.0.6   *label_definition* :: = *identifier* *':'* .

A.2.0.7   *iteration* :: = *'while'* *expression* *loop*
       | *'for'* *identifier* *'from'* *expression* *'to'* *expression* *loop* .

A.2.0.8   *loop* :: = *'do'* *statement_list* *'end'* .

A.2.0.9   *jump* :: = *'goto'* *identifier* .

See Section A.3 for declarations, record types and procedures, and Section A.4 for expressions.

A.2.1. Programs   A program specifies a computation by describing a sequence of actions. A computation specified in LAX may be realized by any sequence of actions having the same effect as the one described here for the given computation. The meaning of constructs that do not satisfy the rules given here is undefined. Whether, and in what manner, a particular implementation of LAX gives meaning to undefined constructs is outside the scope of this definition.

Before translation, a LAX program is embedded in the following block, which is then translated and executed:

declare standard_declarations begin program end

The standard declarations provide defining occurrences of the predefined identifiers given in Table A.1. These declarations cannot be expressed in LAX.

Table A.1 Predefined Identifiers

Identifier	Meaning
boolean	Logical type
false	Falsity
integer	Integer type
nil	Reference to no object
real	Floating point type
true	Truth

A.2.2. Visibility Rules   The text of a range, excluding the text of ranges nested within it, may contain no more than one defining occurrence of a given identifier. Every applied occurrence of an identifier must *identify* some defining occurrence of that identifier. Unless otherwise stated, the defining occurrence D identified by an applied occurrence A of the identifier I is determined as follows:

1. Let R be the text of A, and let B be the block in which the LAX program is embedded.
2. Let R' be the smallest range properly containing R, and let T be the text of R' excluding the text of all ranges nested within it.
3. If T does not contain a defining occurrence of I, and R' is not B, then let R be R' and go to step (2).
4. If T contains a defining occurrence of I then that defining occurrence is D.

Identifier is a defining occurrence in the productions for *label_definition* (A.2.0.6), *iteration* (A.2.0.7), *variable_declaration* (A.3.0.2), *identity_declaration* (A.3.0.7), *procedure_declaration* (A.3.0.8), *parameter* (A.3.0.10), *type_declaration* (A.3.0.12) and *field* (A.3.0.14). All other instances of *identifier* are applied occurrences.

A.2.3. Blocks   The execution of a block begins with a *consistent renaming*: If an identifier has defining occurrences in this block (excluding all blocks nested within it) then those defining occurrences and all applied occurrences identifying them are replaced by a new identifier not appearing elsewhere in the program.

After the consistent renaming, the declarations of the block are executed in the sequence they were written and then the statements are executed as described for a statement list (Section A.2.4). The result of this execution is the result of the block. The extent of the result of a block must be larger than the execution of that block.

A.2.4. Statement Lists   Execution of a statement list is begun by executing the first statement in the list. The remaining statements in the list are then executed in the sequence in which they were written unless the sequence is altered by executing a jump (Section A.2.6). If a statement is followed by a semicolon then its result (if any) is discarded when its execution is finished. The result of the last statement in a statement list is the result of the statement list; if the last statement does not deliver a result then the statement list does not deliver a result.

A.2.5. Iterations   The iteration

while *expression* **do** *statement_list* **end**

is identical in meaning to the conditional clause:

if *expression* **then**

statement _list ;

while *expression* **do** *statement _list* **end**

end

The iteration

for *identifier* **from** *initial _value* **to** *final _value* **do** *statement _list* **end**

is identical in meaning to the block:

declare *a* : *integer* ; *b* : *integer*
begin
a : = *initial _value* ; *b* : = *final _value* ;
if not (*a* > *b*) **then**
  declare *identifier* **is** *a* : *integer* **begin** *statement _list* **end**;
  while *a* < *b* **do**
    a : = *a* + 1;
    declare *identifier* **is** *a* : *integer* **begin** *statement _list* **end**
    end (* *while* *)
  end (* *if* *)
end

Here *a* and *b* are identifiers not appearing elsewhere in the program.
An iteration delivers no result.

A.2.6. Labels and Jumps If an identifier has an applied occurrence in a jump then the defining occurrence identified must be in a label definition. A jump breaks off the execution of the program at the point of the jump, and resumes execution at the labelled expression, iteration or jump.

A jump delivers no result.

A.3. Declarations

A.3.0.1   *declaration* :: = *variable _declaration*
                | *identity _declaration*
                | *procedure _declaration*
                | *type _declaration* .
A.3.0.2   *variable _declaration* :: = *identifier* ':' *type_specification*
                | *identifier* ':'
                    'array' '[' (*bound _pair* | | ',') ']' 'of' *type _specification* .
A.3.0.3   *type _specification* :: = *identifier*
                 | 'ref' *type _specification*
                 | 'ref' *array _type*
                 | *procedure _type* .
A.3.0.4   *bound _pair* :: = *expression* ':' *expression* .

A.3.0.5   *array_type* ::= *'array' '[' ',' '*' ']' 'of' type_specification* .
A.3.0.6   *procedure_type* ::=
             'procedure' [*'('* (*type_specification* | | *','*) *')'*] [*result_type*] .
A.3.0.7   *identity_declaration* ::=
             identifier 'is' expression ':' type_specification .
A.3.0.8   *procedure_declaration* ::= *'procedure' identifier procedure* .
A.3.0.9   *procedure* ::= [*'('* (*parameter* | | *';'*) *')'*]
             [*result_type*] *';' expression* .
A.3.0.10   *parameter* ::= *identifier ':' type_specification* .
A.3.0.11   *result_type* ::= *':' type_specification* .
A.3.0.12   *type_declaration* ::= *'type' identifier '=' record_type* .
A.3.0.13   *record_type* ::= *'record'* (*field* | | *';'*)*'end'*
A.3.0.14   *field* ::= *identifier ':' type_specification* .
A.3.0.15   * *type* ::= *type_specification* | *array_type* | *procedure_type* .

See Section A.4 for Expressions.

A.3.1. Values, Types and Objects   *Values* are abstract entities upon which operations may be performed, *types* classify values according to the operations that may be performed upon them, and *objects* are the concrete instances of values that are operated upon. Two objects are *equal* if they are instances of the same value. Two objects are *identical* if references (see below) to them are equal. Every object has a specified *extent*, during which it can be operated upon. The extents of denotations, the value *nil* (see below) and objects generated by *new* (Section A.4.3) are unbounded; the extents of other objects are determined by their declarations.

The predefined identifiers *boolean, integer* and *real* represent the types of truth values, integers and floating point numbers respectively. Values of these types are called *primitive values*, and have the usual meanings.

An instance of a value of type **ref** *t* is a *variable* that can *refer to* (or contain) an object of type *t*. An assignment to a variable changes the object to which the variable refers, but does not change the identity of the variable. The predefined identifier *nil* denotes a value of type **ref** *t*, for arbitrary *t. Nil* refers to no object, and may only be used in a context that specifies the referenced type *t* uniquely.

Values and objects of array and record types are composite. The immediate components of an array are all of the same type, and the simple selectors are integer tuples. The immediate components of a record may be of different types, and the simple selectors are represented by identifiers. No composite object may have a component of its own type.

Values of a procedure type are specifications of computations. If the result type is omitted, then a call of the procedure yields no result and the procedure is called a *proper procedure*; otherwise it is called a *function procedure*.

If two types consist of the same sequence of basic symbols and, for every identifier in that sequence, the applied occurrences in one type identify the same defining occurrence as the applied occurrences in the other, then the two types are the same. In all other cases, the two types are different.

A.3.2. Variable Declarations

A variable referring to an undefined value (of the specified type) is created, and the identifier represents this object. The extent of the created variable begins when the declaration is executed and ends when execution of the smallest range containing the declaration is complete.

If the variable declaration has the form

$$identifier : t$$

then the created variable is of type **ref** t, and may refer to any value of type t. If, on the other hand, it has the form

$$identifier : \textbf{array } [l_1:u_1, \ldots, l_n:u_n] \textbf{ of } t$$

then the created variable is of type **ref** *array_type,* and may only refer to values having the specified number of immediate components. The type of the array is obtained from the *variable_declaration* by deleting '*identifier:*' and each bound pair $e_1:e_2$; **array** $[l_1:u_1, \ldots, l_n:u_n]$ **of** t specifies an array of this type with $(u_1 - l_1 + 1) * \cdots * (u_n - l_n + 1)$ immediate components of type t. The bounds l_i and u_i are integers with $l_i \leqslant u_i$.

A.3.3. Identity Declarations

A new instance of the value (of the specified type) resulting from evaluation of the expression is created, and the identifier represents this object. If the expression yields an array or reference to an array, the new instance has the same bounds. The extent of the created object is identical to the extent of the result of the expression.

A.3.4. Procedure Declarations

A new instance of the value (of the specified procedure type) resulting from copying the basic symbol sequence of the *procedure* is created, and the identifier represents this object. The extent of the created object begins when the declaration is executed and ends when execution of the smallest block containing the declaration is complete.

Evaluation of the *expression* of a function procedure must yield a value of the given *result_type.*

The procedure type is obtained from the *procedure_declaration* by deleting '*identifier*' and '; *expression*', and removing '*identifier :*' from each parameter.

A.3.5. Type Declarations

The identifier represents a new record type defined according to the given specification.

A.4. Expressions

A.4.0.1   *expression* ::= *assignment* | *disjunction* .

A.4.0.2   *assignment* ::= *name* ':=' *expression* .

A.4.0.3   *disjunction* ::= *conjunction* | *disjunction* 'or' *conjunction* .

A.4.0.4   *conjunction* ::= *comparison* | *conjunction* 'and' *comparison* .

A.4.0.5   *comparison* ::= *relation* [*eqop relation*] .

A.4.0.6   *eqop* ::= '=' | '≡' .

A.4.0.7   *relation* ::= *sum* [*relop sum*] .

A.4.0.8   *relop* ::= '<' | '>' .

A.4.0.9   *sum* ::= *term* | *sum addop term* .

A.4.0.10   *addop* ::= '+' | '−' .

A.4.0.11   *term* ::= *factor* | *term mulop factor* .

A.4.0.12   *mulop* ::= '*' | '/' | 'div' | 'mod' .

A.4.0.13   *factor* ::= *primary* | *unop factor* .

A.4.0.14   *unop* ::= '+' | '−' | 'not' .

A.4.0.15   *primary* ::= *denotation* | *name* | '(' *expression* ')'
      | *block* | *clause* .

A.4.0.16   *name* ::= *identifier*
      | *name* '.' *identifier*
      | *name* '[' (*expression* | | ',') ']'
      | *name* '↑'
      | 'new' *identifier*
      | *procedure_call* .

A.4.0.17   *procedure_call* ::= *name* '(' (*argument* | | ',') ')' .

A.4.0.18   *argument* ::= *expression* .

A.4.0.19   *clause* ::= *conditional_clause*
      | *case_clause* .

A.4.0.20   *conditional_clause* ::= 'if' *expression* 'then'
       statement_list 'end'
      | 'if' *expression* 'then' *statement_list*
      'else' *statement_list* 'end' .

A.4.0.21   *case_clause* ::=
      'case' *expression* 'of'
      (*case_label* ':' *statement_list* | | '//')
      'else' *statement_list* 'end' .

A.4.0.22   *case_label* ::= *integer* .

A.4.1. Evaluation of Expressions This grammar ascribes structure to an expression in the usual way. Every subexpression (*assignment, disjunction, conjunction*, etc.) may be evaluated to yield a value of a certain type. The operands of an expression are evaluated collaterally unless the expression is a *disjunction* or a *conjunction* (see Section A.4.3). Each operator indication denotes a set of possible operations, with the particular one meant in a given

Table A.2 Operator Identification

Indication	Operand Type Left	Right	Result Type	Operation
:=	ref *t*	*t*	ref *t*	assignment
or	boolean	boolean		disjunction
and	boolean	boolean		conjunction
==	ref *t*	ref *t*	boolean	identity
=	*m*	*m*		equality
<				less than
>				greater than
+	*a*	*a*		addition
−			*a*	subtraction
*				multiplication
div	integer	integer	integer	division
mod				remainder
/	real	real	real	division
not		boolean	boolean	complement
+		*a*	*a*	no operation
−				negation

Here *t* denotes any type, *m* denotes any non-reference type and *a* denotes integer or real type.

context being determined by the operand types according to Table A.2. When the type of value delivered by an operand does not satisfy the requirements of a operation, a *coercion sequence* can be applied to yield a value that does satisfy the requirements. Any ambiguities in the process of selecting computations and coercions is resolved in favor of the choice with the shortest total coercion sequence length.

It must be possible to determine an operation for every operator indication appearing in a program.

A.4.2. Coercions The context in which a language element (statement, argument, expression, operand, name as a component of an indexed object, procedure call, etc.) appears may permit a stated set of types for the result of that element, prescribe a single type, or require that the result be discarded. When the a priori type of the result does not satisfy the requirements of the context, coercion is employed. The coercion consists of a sequence of coercion operations applied to the result. If several types are permitted by the context then the one leading to the shortest coercion sequence will be selected.

Coercion operations are:

- *Widen*: Convert from integer to floating point.
- *Deprocedure*: Invoke a parameterless procedure (see Section A.4.5). This is the only coercion that can be applied to the left-hand side of an assignment.
- *Dereference*: Replace a reference by the object to which it refers. Dereferencing may also be specified explicitly by using the content operation (see Section A.4.4). *Nil* cannot be dereferenced.
- *Void*: Discard a computed value. If the value to be discarded is a parameterless procedure or a reference to such a procedure, the procedure must be invoked and its result (if any) discarded.

A.4.3. Operations An assignment causes the variable yielded by the left operand to refer to a new instance of the value yielded by the right operand. The result of the assignment is the reference yielded by the left operand. Assignments to *nil* are not permitted, nor are assignments of references or procedures in which the extent of the value yielded by the right operand is smaller than the extent of the reference yielded by the left operand. Assignment of composite objects is carried out by collaterally assigning the components of the value yielded by the right operand to the corresponding components of the reference yielded by the left operand. For array assignments, the reference and value must have the same number of dimensions and corresponding dimensions must have the same numbers of elements.

The expression *a* **or** *b* has the meaning **if** *a* **then** *true* **else** *b*
The expression *a* **and** *b* has the meaning **if** *a* **then** *b* **else** *false*.
The expression **not** *a* has the meaning **if** *a* **then** *false* **else** *true*.
Identity yields *true* if the operand values are identical variables.

Equality has the usual meaning. Composite values are equal if each element of one is equal to the corresponding element of the other. Arrays can only be equal if they have the same dimensions, each with the same number of elements. Procedure values are equal if they are identical.

Relational operators for integer and real types are defined as usual.

The arithmetic operators +, - (unary and binary), *, / have the usual meaning as long as the values of all operands and results lie in the permitted range and division by zero does not occur. **div** (integer division) and **mod** (remainder) are defined only when the value of the right operand is not 0. Their results are then the same as those of the following expressions:

$$i \ \mathbf{div} \ j \ = \ \begin{cases} - \left\lfloor \left| \dfrac{i}{j} \right| \right\rfloor & \text{if } \dfrac{i}{j} < 0 \\[2ex] \left\lfloor \dfrac{i}{j} \right\rfloor & \text{otherwise} \end{cases}$$

$$i \ \mathbf{mod} \ j \ = \ (i - (i \ \mathbf{div} \ j) * j)$$

Here $|x|$ is the magnitude of x and $\lfloor x \rfloor$ is the largest integer not larger than x.

A.4.4. Names Identifiers name objects of specified types created by declarations. If an applied occurrence of an identifier is a name then the defining occurrence identified by it may not be in a type definition, label definition or selector specification.

In the field selection *name.identifier* the name must (possibly after coercion) yield a record or reference to a record. The record type must contain a *field* that provides a defining occurrence of the identifier, and it is this defining occurrence which is identified by *identifier*. If the name yields a record then the result of the field selection is the value of the field selected; otherwise the result of the field selection is a reference to this field.

In the index selection *name*$[j_1, \ldots, j_n]$ the name must (possibly after coercion) yield an n-dimensional array or a reference to an n-dimensional array. The name and subscript expressions j_i are evaluated collaterally. If the name yields an array then the result of the index selection is the value of the element selected; otherwise the result of the index selection is a reference to this element.

In the content operation *name* $\uparrow$ the name must (possibly after coercion) yield a variable. The result of the content operation is the value referred to.

The generator **new** t yields a new variable that can reference objects of type t.

A.4.5. Procedure Calls In the procedure call $p(a_1, \ldots, a_n)$ the name p must (possibly after coercion) yield an object of procedure type having n parameters ($n \geqslant 0$). The name p and argument expressions a_i are evaluated collaterally. Let $P = (p_1, \ldots, p_n)$: *expression* be the result of evaluating the name, and let r_i be the result of evaluating a_i. The procedure call is then evaluated as follows (*copy rule*):

1. If $n = 0$ then the procedure call is replaced by (*expression*), otherwise the procedure call is replaced by the block

   declare p_1 *is* $r_1 : t_1; \cdots ; p_n$ *is* $r_n : t_n$ **begin** *expression* **end**

2. The block (or parenthesized expression) is executed. If it is not left by a jump, the result is coerced to the result type of P (or voided, in the case of a proper procedure).
3. As soon as execution is completed, possibly by a jump, the substitution of step 1 is reversed (i.e. the original call is restored).

The value yielded by the coercion in step (2) is the result of the procedure call.

A.4.6. Clauses The *expression* in a conditional clause must deliver a Boolean result. If this result is *true* then the first statement list will be exe-

cuted and its result will be taken as the result of the conditional clause; otherwise the second statement list will be executed and its result will be taken
as the result of the conditional clause. The first alternative of a one-sided
conditional clause, in which the second alternative is omitted, is voided.

The expression in a case clause must deliver an integer result. When the
value of the expression is i and one of the case labels is $i,$ the statement list
associated with that case label will be executed and its result will be taken as
the result of the case clause; otherwise the statement list following *else* will
be executed and its result will be taken as the result of the case clause. All
case labels in a case clause must be distinct.

The component statement lists of a clause must be *balanced* to ensure that
the type of the result yielded is the same regardless of which alternative was
chosen. Balancing involves coercing the result of each component statement
list to a common type. If there is no one type to which all of the result types
are coercible then all the results are voided. When the type returned by the
clause is uniquely prescribed by the context then this type is chosen as the
common result type for all alternatives. If the context of the expression is
such that several result types are possible, the one leading to the smallest
total number of coercions is chosen.

APPENDIX B
Useful Algorithms for Directed Graphs

The directed graph is a formalism well-suited to the description of syntactic derivations, data structures and control flow. Such descriptions allow us to apply results from graph theory to a variety of compiler components. These results yield standard algorithms for carrying out analyses and transformations, and provide measures of complexity for many common tasks. In this appendix we summarize the terminology and algorithms most important to the remainder of the book.

B.1. Terminology

Definition B.1. A *directed graph* is a pair (K,D), where K is a finite, nonempty set and D is a subset of $K \times K$. The elements of K are called the *nodes* of the graph, and the elements of D are the *edges*.

Figure B.1a is a directed graph, and Figure B.1b shows how this graph might be represented pictorially.

In many cases, a *label function*, f, is defined on the nodes and/or edges of a graph. Such a function associates a *label*, which is an element of a finite, nonempty set, with each node or edge. We then speak of a graph with node or edge labels. The labels serve as identification of the nodes or edges, or indicate their interpretation. This is illustrated in Figure B.1b, where a function has been provided to map K into the set $\{1,2,3,4\}$.

Definition B.2. A sequence $(k_0, \ldots, k_n)$ of nodes in a directed graph (K,D), $n \geqslant 1$, is called a *path of length n* if $(k_{i-1}, k_i) \in D$, $i = 1, \ldots, n$. A path is called a *cycle* if $k_0 = k_n$.

$$K = \{1,2,3,4\}$$
$$D = \{(1,2),(1,3),(4,4),(2,3),(3,2),(3,4)\}$$

a) The components of the graph

b) Pictorial representation

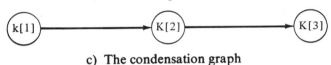

c) The condensation graph

Figure B.1. A Directed Graph.

An edge may appear more than once in a path: In the graph of Figure B.1, the sequence of edges (2,3), (3,2), (2,3), (3,4), (4,4), (4,4) defines the path (2,3,2,3,4,4,4) of length 6.

Definition B.3. Let (K,D) be a directed graph. Partition K into equivalence classes K_i such that nodes u and v belong to the same class if and only if there is a cycle to which u and v belong. Let D_i be the subset of edges connecting pairs of nodes in K_i. The directed graphs (K_i,D_i) are the *strongly connected components* of (K,D).

The graph of Figures B.1a and B.1b has three strongly connected components:

$$K_1 = \{1\}, D_1 = \{\ \}$$
$$K_2 = \{4\}, D_2 = \{(4,4)\}$$
$$K_3 = \{2,3\}, D_3 = \{(2,3),(3,2)\}$$

Often we deal with graphs in which all nodes of a strongly connected component are identical with respect to some property of interest. When dealing with this property, we can therefore replace the original graph with a graph having one node for each strongly connected component.

Definition B.4. Let $P = \{K_1, \ldots, K_n\}$ be a partition of node set of a directed graph (K,D). The *reduction of* (K,D) with respect to the partition P is the directed graph (K',D') such that $K' = \{k_1, \ldots, k_n\}$ and $D' = \{(k_i,k_j) \mid i \neq j$, and (u,v) is an element of D for some $u \in K_i$ and $v \in K_j\}$.

We term the subsets K_i of an (arbitrary) partition *blocks*. The reduction with respect to strongly connected components is the *condensation graph*.

The condensation graph of Figure B.1b is shown in Figure B.1c. Since every cycle lies wholly within a single strongly connected region, the condensation graph has no cycles.

Definition B.5. A *directed acyclic graph* is a directed graph that contains no cycles.

Definition B.6. A directed acyclic graph is called a *tree with root k_0* if for every node $k \neq k_0$ there exists exactly one path $(k_0, \ldots, k)$.

These two special classes of graphs are illustrated in Figure B.2.

If a tree has an edge (k,k'), we say that k' is a *child* of k and k is the *parent* of k'. Note that Definition B.6 permits a node to have any number of children. Because the path from the root is unique, however, every node $k \neq k_0$ has exactly one parent. The root, k_0, is the only node with no parent. A tree has at least one *leaf*, which is a node with no children. If there is a path in a tree from node k to node k', we say that k' is a *descendant* of k and k is an *ancestor* of k'.

Definition B.7. A tree is termed *ordered* if, for every node, a linear order is defined on the children of that node.

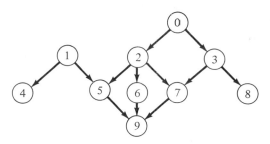

a) A directed acyclic graph

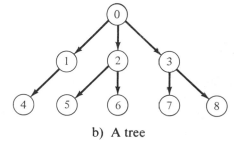

b) A tree

Figure B.2. Special Cases of Directed Graphs.

If we list the children of a node k' in an ordered tree, we shall always do so in the sense of the ordering; we can therefore take the enumeration as the ordering. The first child of k' is also called the *left child*; the child node that follows k in the order of successors of k' is called the *right sibling* of k. In Figure B.2b, for example, we might order the children of a node according to the magnitude of their labels. Thus 1 would be the left child of 0, 2 would be the right sibling of 1, and 3 the right sibling of 2. 3 has no right siblings and there is no relationship between 6 and 7.

In an ordered tree, the paths leaving the root can be ordered lexicographically: Consider two paths $x = (x_0, \ldots, x_m)$ and $y = (y_0, \ldots, y_n)$ with $m \leqslant n$ and $x_0 = y_0$ being the root. Because both paths begin at the root, there exists some $i \geqslant 0$ such that $x_j = y_j, j = 0, \ldots, i$. We say that $x < y$ either if $i = m$ and $i < n$, or if $x_{i+1} < y_{i+1}$ according to the ordering of the children of x_i ($= y_i$). Since there is exactly one path from the root to any node in the tree, this lexicographic ordering of the paths specifies a linear ordering of all nodes of the tree.

Definition B.8. A *cut* in a tree (K,D) is a subset, C, of K such that for each leaf $k_m \in (K,D)$ exactly one element of C lies on the path $(k_0, \ldots, k_m)$ from the root k_0 to that leaf.

Examples of cuts in Figure B.2b are $\{0\}$, $\{1,2,3\}$, $\{1,2,7,8\}$ and $\{4,5,6,7,8\}$.

In an ordered tree, the nodes of a cut are linearly-ordered on the basis of the ordering of all nodes. When we describe a cut in an ordered tree, we shall always write the nodes of that cut in the sense of this order.

Definition B.9. A *spanning forest* for a directed graph (K,D) is a set of trees $\{(K_1,D_1), \ldots, (K_n,D_n)\}$ such that the K_i's partition K and each D_i is a (possibly empty) subset of D.

All of the nodes of a directed graph can be visited by traversing the trees of some spanning forest. The spanning forest used for such a traversal is often the one corresponding to a *depth-first search*:

```
procedure depth_first_search(k:node );
    begin mark k as having been visited;
        for each immediate successor k' of k do
            if k' has not yet been visited then depth_first_search(k')
    end;( *depth_first_search *)
```

To construct a spanning forest, this procedure is applied to an arbitrary unvisited node and repeated so long as such nodes exist.

A depth-first search can also be used to number the nodes in the graph:

Definition B.10. A *depth-first numbering* is a permutation $(k_1, \ldots, k_n)$ of the nodes of a directed graph (K,D) such that k_1 is the first node visited by a particular depth-first search, k_2 the second and so forth.

Once a spanning forest $\{(K_1,D_1),...,(K_n,D_n)\}$ has been defined for a graph (K,D) the set D can be partitioned into four subsets:

- *Tree edges*, elements of $D_1 \cup \cdots \cup D_n$.
- *Forward edges*, (k_p,k_q) such that k_p is an ancestor of k_q in some tree K_i, but (k_p,k_q) is not an element of D_i.
- *Back edges*, (k_q,k_p) such that either k_p is an ancestor of k_q in some tree K_i or $p = q$.
- *Cross edges*, (k_p,k_q) such that k_p is neither an ancestor nor a descendant of k_q in any tree K_i.

These definitions are illustrated by Figure B.3. Figure B.3b shows a spanning forest and depth-first numbering for the graph of Figure B.3a. The forest has two trees, whose roots are nodes 1 and 7 respectively. All edges appearing in Figure B.3b are tree edges. In Figure B.3a, (1.4) is a forward edge, (3,2) and (6,6) are back edges, and (5,3), (6,4) and (6,5) are cross edges.

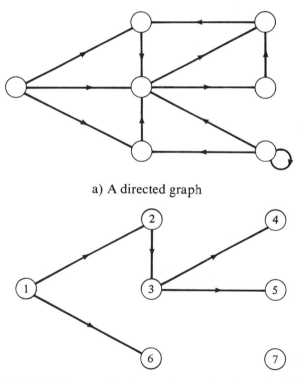

a) A directed graph

b) A depth-first numbering and spanning forest for (a)

Figure B.3. Depth-First Numbering.

B.2. Directed Graphs as Data Structures

Directed graphs can be implemented as data structures in different ways. It can be shown that the efficiency of graph algorithms depends critically upon the representation chosen, and that some form of list is usually the appropriate choice for applications in compilers. We shall therefore use the abstract data type of Figure B.4 for the algorithms described in this Appendix.

```
module graph(n,e:public integer);
  (* Representation of a directed graph
    n = Number of nodes in the graph
    e = Maximum number of edges in the graph
  *)
  var
    node : array [1..n] of record inward,outward,next_in,next_out : integer end;
    edge : array [1..e] of record head,tail,next_in,next_out : integer end;
    i,edge_count : integer ;
  procedure next_succ (n,e : integer ): integer ;
    (* Obtain the next successor of a node
      On entry -
        n = Node for which a successor is desired
        e = First unexplored edge
    *)
    begin (* next_succ *)
    if e =0 then next_succ :=0
    else begin node[n].next_out := =edge[e].next_out ;
      next_succ := =edge[e].tail end;
    end; (* next_succ *)
  procedure next_pred (n,e : integer ): integer ;
    (* Obtain the next predecessor of a node
      On entry -
        n = Node for which a predecessor is desired
        e = First unexplored edge
    *)
    begin (* next_pred *)
    if e =0 then next_pred :=0
    else begin node[n].next_in := =edge[e].next_in ;
      next_pred := =edge[e].head end;
    end; (* next_pred *)
  public procedure define_edge (hd,tl : integer );
    begin (* define_edge *)
    edge_count := =edge_count +1; (* edge_count ⩽ maximum not tested *)
    with edge[edge_count] do
      begin
      head := =hd ; tail := =tl ; next_in := =node[tl].inward ;
      next_out := =node[hd].outward
```

```
        end;
    node [hd ].outward : = node [tl ].inward : = edge_count ;
    end; ( * define_edge *)
public function first_successor (n : integer ): integer ;
    begin first_successor : = next_succ (n,node [n ].outward ) end;
public function next_successor (n : integer ): integer ;
    begin next_successor : = next_succ (n,node [n ].next_out ) end;
public function first_predecessor (n : integer ): integer ;
    begin first_predecessor : = next_pred (n,node [n ].inward ) end;
public function next_predecessor (n : integer ): integer ;
    begin next_predecessor : = next_pred (n,node [n ].next_in ) end;
begin ( * graph *)
for i : = 1 to n do with node [i ] do
    inward : = outward : = next_in : = next_out : = 0;
edge_count : = 0
end; ( * graph *)
```

Figure B.4. Abstract Data Type for a Directed Graph.

A directed graph is instantiated by a variable declaration of the following form:

g: graph (node_count,max_edges);

The structure of the graph is then established by a sequence of calls $g.define\_edge(\cdots)$. Note that the module embodies only the structure of the graph; further properties, such as node or edge labels, must be stored separately.

A directed graph that is a tree can, of course, be represented by the abstract data type of Figure B.4. In this case, however, a simpler representation (Figure B.5) could also be used. This simplification is based upon the fact that any node in a tree can have at most one parent. Note that the edges do not appear explicitly, but are implicit in the node linkage. The abstract data structure is set up by instantiating the module with the proper number of nodes and then invoking *define_edge* once for each edge to specify the nodes at its head and tail. If it is desired that the order of the sibling list reflect a total ordering defined on the children of a node, then the sequence of calls on *define_edge* should be the *opposite* of this order.

A partition is defined by a collection of *blocks* (sets of nodes) and a membership relation *node* ∈ *block* The representation of the partition must be carefully chosen so that operations upon it may be carried out in constant time. Figure B.6 defines such a representation.

When a partition module is instantiated, its block set is empty. Blocks may be created by invoking *new_block*, which returns the index of the new block. This block has no members initially. The procedure *add_node* is used to make a given node a member of a given block. Since each node can be a member of only one block, this procedure must delete the given node from the block of which it was previously a member (if such exists).

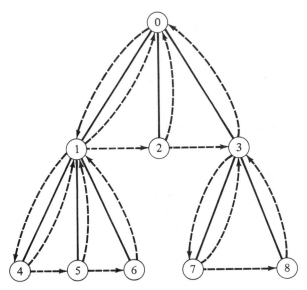

Solid lines represent tree edges. Dashed lines represent actual links maintained by the tree module.

a) Pictorial representation

```
module tree(n:public integer);
   (* Representation of a tree
      n = Number of nodes in the tree
   *)
var
   node : array [1..n] of record parent,child,sibling : integer end;
   i : integer;
public procedure define_edge (hd,tl : integer );
   begin (* define_edge *)
   with node [tl] do
      begin parent : = hd ; sibling : = node [hd ].child end;
   node [hd ].child : = tl ;
   end; (* define_edge *)
public function parent (n : integer ): integer ;
   begin parent : = node [n ].parent end;
public function child (n : integer ): integer ;
   begin child : = node [n ].child end;
public function sibling (n : integer ): integer ;
   begin sibling : = node [n ].sibling end;
begin (* tree *)
for i : = 1 to n do with node [i ] do parent : = child : = sibling : = 0;
end; (* tree *)
```
b) Abstract data type

Figure B.5. Simplification for a Tree.

module *partition*(*n*:**public** *integer*);
(* Representation of a partition on of a set of *n* nodes *)

var
  p : **array**[0..2*n*] **of record** *member,last,next* : *integer* **end**;
  i,number _of_blocks,next _node _state : *integer* ;

public function *block_count:integer*;
  begin *block _count* : = *number _of_blocks* **end**;

public function *new_block:integer*;
  begin *new _block* : = *number _of_blocks* : = *number _of_blocks* +1 **end**;

public   procedure *add_node*(*node,block:integer*);
  begin (* *add _node* *)
  with *p* [*node*] **do**
    begin
    if *member* ≠ 0 **then** (* Remove *node* from its previous block *)
      begin
      p [*member*].*member* : = *p* [*member*].*member* − 1;
      p [*last*].*next* : = *next* ; *p* [*next*].*last* : = *last* ;
      end;
    member : = *block* ;
    p [*block* +*n*].*member* : = *p* [*block* +*n*].*member* +1;
    last : = *member* ; *next* : = *p* [*block* +*n*].*next* ;
    p [*last*].*next* : = *p* [*next*].*last* : = *node* ;
    end;
  end; (* *add _node* *)

public function *block_containing*(*node:integer*):*integer*;
  begin *block _containing* : = *p* [*node*].*member* **end**;

public function *node_count*(*block:integer*):*integer*;
  begin *node _count* : = *p* [*block* +*n*].*member* **end**;

public function *first_node*(*block:integer*):*integer*;
  begin *first_node* : = *next _node _state* : = *p* [*block* +*n*].*next* **end**;

public function *next_node:integer*;
  begin (* *next _node* *)
  if *next _node _state* =0 **then** *next _node* : =0
  else *next _node* : = *next _node _state* : = *p* [*next _node _state*].*next* ;
  end; (* *next _node* *)

begin (* *partition* *)
for *i* : = 1 **to** 2*n* **do with** *p* [*i*] **do** *member* : = *last* : = *next* : =0;
number _of_blocks : = *next _node _state* : =0;
end; (* *partition* *)

Figure B.6. Abstract Data Type for a Partition.

The status of a partition can be determined by invoking
number_of_blocks, block_containing, node_count, first_node and *next_node*. If
a node does not belong to any block, then *block_containing* returns 0;
otherwise it returns the number of the block of which the node is a member.
Application of the function *node_count* to a block yields the number of
nodes in that block. The procedures *first_node* and *next_node* work together
to access all of the members of a block: A call of *first_node* returns the first
member of a specific block. (If the block is empty then *first_node* returns 0.)
Each subsequent invocation of *next_node* returns the next member of that
block. When all members have been accessed, *next_node* returns 0.

The membership relation is embodied in a doubly-linked list. Each node
specifies the block of which it is a member, and each block specifies the
number of members. Figure B.6 uses a single array to store both node and
block information. This representation greatly simplifies the treatment of
the doubly-linked list, since the *last* and *next* fields have identical meanings
for node and block entries. The *member* field specifies the number of
members in a block entry, but the block of which the node is a member in a
node entry. For our problems, the number of partitions can never exceed
the number of nodes. Hence the array is allocated with twice as many elements as there are nodes in the graph being manipulated. (Element 0 is
included to avoid zero tests when accessing the *next* element in a node list.)
The first half of the array is indexed by the node numbers; the second half is
used to specify the blocks of the partition. Note that the user is not aware of
this offset in block indices because all necessary translation is provided by
the interface procedures.

B.3. Partitioning Algorithms

In this section we discuss algorithms for partitioning the node set of a graph
according to three criteria that are particularly important in compiler construction: strong connectivity, compatibility of a partition and a function,
and nonadjacency. All of the algorithms are defined in terms of the
representations presented in Section B.2.

B.3.1. Strongly Connected Components We begin the determination
of the strongly connected components of a directed graph by using a depth-
first search to obtain a spanning forest and a corresponding depth-first
numbering of the nodes. Suppose that k_z is the first node (in the depth-first
numbering) that belongs to a strongly connected component of the graph.
Then, by construction, all other nodes of the component must belong to the
spanning forest subtree, T_z, whose root is k_z. We term k_z the *root* of the
strongly connected component (with respect to the given spanning forest).
Every node, k, of T_z either belongs to the strongly connected component
with root k_z or it belongs to a subtree T_x of T_z, with root k_x, and k_x is the

root of another strongly connected compcnent. (It is possible that $k = k_x$.) These notions are illustrated by Figure B.1: Node 2 is the root of a strongly-connected component of Figure B.1. The only other node in this component is 3, which is a descendant of 2 in the spanning forest subtree rooted at 2. This subtree has three nodes. Nodes 2 and 3 belong to the strongly-connected region, and node 4 is the root of a strongly-connected region containing only itself.

There must be a path from the root of a strongly-connected component to itself. Let k_z be the root, and suppose that the path contained a node $k < k_z$. If this were the case then k would be an ancestor of k_z in the tree, contradicting the hypothesis that k_z is the root of the strongly-connected region. This observation is the basis for recognizing a strongly-connected region: During the depth-first search that numbers the nodes of the spanning forest, we keep track of the lowest-numbered ancestor reachable from a node. (We assume that a node is reachable from itself.) As we back out of the search, we check each node to see whether any ancestors are reachable from it. If not, then it is the root of a strongly-connected component.

The algorithm makes use of a fixed-depth stack (Figure B.7) for holding nodes. (No node is ever stacked more than once, and hence the stack depth

```
module fixed_depth_stack ( public maximum_depth : integer );
   ( * Representation of a stack no deeper than maximum_depth *)

var
   stack : array [1..maximum_depth ] of integer ;
   i ,top : integer ;

public procedure push(n:integer);
   begin stack [n ]: = top ; top : = n  end;

public procedure pop:integer;
   var n : integer ;
   begin n : = top ; top : = stack [n ]; stack [n ]: = 0; pop : = n  end;

public function member(n:integer):boolean;
   begin member: = stack [n ] ≠ 0 end;

public function empty:boolean;
   begin empty: = top < 0 end;

begin ( * fixed_depth_stack *)
for i : = 1 to maximum_depth do stack [i ]: = 0;
top : = − 1;
end; ( * fixed_depth_stack *)
```

Figure B.7. Abstract Data Type for a Fixed-Depth Stack.

can never exceed the number of nodes.) The crucial property of this module is that it provides a constant-time test to discover whether a node is on the stack.

Figure B.8 gives the complete algorithm for identifying strongly connected components. Note that *strongly_connected_components* has a graph as a parameter. This is not a variable declaration, so no new graph is instan-

```
procedure strongly_connected_components ( g : graph ; p : partition );
   ( * Make p define the strongly-connected components of g *)

   var
      lowlink : array [1..g.n ] of integer ;
      i,counter,root : integer ;
      s : fixed_depth_stack( g.n );

   procedure depth_first_search(node : integer );
      var
         serial,k,b,w : integer ;
      begin ( * depth_first_search *)
      serial : = lowlink [node ]: = counter : = counter +1;
      s.push (node );
      k : = g.first_successor (node );
      while k ≠ 0 do
         begin
         if lowlink [k ]=0 then depth_first_search (k ));
         if s.member(k ) then lowlink [node ]: = min (lowlink [node ]lowlink [k ]);
         k : = g.next_successor (node )
         end;
      if lowlink [node ]= serial then
         begin
         b : = p.new_block ;
         repeat s.pop (w ); p.add_node (w,b ) until w = node ;
         end
      end; ( * depth_first_search *)

begin ( * strongly_connected_components *)
for i : = 1 to g.n do lowlink [i ]: =0;
counter : = 0; root : = 1;
while counter ≠ g.n do
   begin
   while lowlink [root ] ≠ 0 do root : = root +1;
   depth_first_search(root );
   end;
end; ( * strongly_connected_components *)
```

Figure B.8. Partitioning Into Strongly Connected Components.

tiated. The value of the parameter is a *reference* to the argument graph; the argument graph is not copied into the procedure.

The algorithm traverses the nodes of the graph in the order of a depth-first numbering. Each activation of *depth_first_search* corresponds to a single node of the graph. *Lowlink*[*i*] specifies the lowest-numbered (in the depth-first numbering) node reachable from node *i*. (The *lowlink* array is also used to indicate the nodes not yet visited.) The fixed-depth stack contains all nodes from which it is possible to reach an ancestor of the current node. Note that all access to a node is in terms of its index in the graph g; the index of a node in the depth-first numbering appears only in *lowlink* and the local variable *serial* of *depth_first_search*.

B.3.2. Refinement Consider a graph (K,D) and a partition $P = \{P_p, \ldots, P_k\}$ of Q with $m \geqslant 2$. We wish to find the partition $R = \{R_1, \ldots, R_r\}$ with smallest r such that:

- Each R_k is a subset of some P_j ('R is a refinement of P')
- If a and b are elements of R_k then, for each $(a,x) \in D$ and $(b,y) \in D$, x and y are elements of some one R_m ('R is compatible with D').

The state minimization problem discussed in Section 6.2.2 and the determination of structural equivalence of types from Section 9.1.2 can both be cast in this form.

The obvious strategy for making a refinement is to check the successors of all nodes in a single element of the current partition. This element must be split if two nodes have successors in different elements of the partition. To obtain the refinement, split the element so that these two nodes lie in different elements. The refined partition is guaranteed to satisfy condition (1). The process terminates when no element must be split. Since a partition in which each element contains exactly one node must satisfy condition (2), the process of successive refinement must eventually terminate. It can be shown that this algorithm is quadratic in the number of nodes.

By checking predecessors rather than successors of the nodes in an element, it is possible to reduce the asymptotic behavior of the algorithm to $O(n \log n)$, where n is the number of nodes. This reduction is achieved at the cost of a more complex algorithm, however, and may not be worthwhile for small problems. In the remainder of this section we shall discuss the $O(n \log n)$ algorithm, leaving the simpler approach to the reader (Exercise B.6).

The refinement procedure of Figure B.9 accepts a graph $G = (K,D)$ and a partition $\{P_1, \ldots, P_m\}$ of K with $m \geqslant 2$. The elements of D correspond to a mapping $f : K \to K$ for which (k,k') is an element of D if $f(k) = k'$. *Refine* inspects the inverse mappings $f^{-1}(P_j)$. A set P_k must be split into two subsets if and only if $P_k \cap f^{-1}(P_j)$ is nonempty for some j, and yet P_k is not a subset of $f^{-1}(P_j)$. The two subsets are then $P'_k = (P_k \cap f^{-1}(P_j))$ and $P''_k = P_k - P'_k$. This split must be carried out once for every P_j. If P_j

contributes to the splitting of P_k and is itself split later, both subsets must again be used to split other partitions.

The first step in each execution of the *split* procedure is to construct the inverse of block P_j. Next the blocks P_k for which $P_k \cap f^{-1}(P_j)$ is nonempty but P_k is not a subset of $f^{-1}(P_j)$ are split and the smaller of the two components is returned to the stack of blocks yet to be considered.

Figure B.10 defines an abstract data type that can be used to represent $f^{-1}(P_j)$. When *inverse* is instantiated, it represents an empty set. Nodes are added to the set by invoking *inv_node*. After all nodes belonging to *inverse*(j) have been added to the set, we wish to consider exactly those

```
procedure refine(p : partition; f : graph);
    (* Make p be the coarsest partition compatible with p and f *)

var
    pending : fixed_depth_stack (f.n);
    i : integer;

procedure split (block : integer);
    var
        inv : inverse (f,block,p);  (* Construct the inverse of block *)
        b,k,n : integer;
    begin (* split *)
    k := inv.next_block;
    while k ≠ 0 do
        begin  (* Pₖ ∪ f⁻¹ (block) ≠ ø but not Pₖ ⊆ f⁻¹ (block) *)
        b := p.new_block;
        while (n := inv.common_node) ≠ 0 do p.add_node (n,b);
        if pending.member (k) or (p.element_count(k) > p.element_count(b))
        then pending.push (b)
        else pending.push (k)
        k := inv.next_block;
        end
    end; (* split *)

begin (* refine *)
for i := 1 to p.block_count do pending.push (i);
repeat pending.pop (i); split (i) until pending.empty
end; (* refine *)
```

Figure B.9. Refinement Algorithm.

module *inverse* (*f* : *graph* ; *b* : *integer* ; *p* : *partition*);
 (* Representation of $f^{-1}(b)$ with respect to partition *p* *)
var
 node : **array** [1..*f.n*] **of** *integer* ;
 block : **array** [1..*p.block_count*] **of record** *first_node,link,count:integer* **end**;
 i ,*j*,*block_list*,*node_list* : *integer* ;
public procedure *inv_node*(*n:integer*);
 var *b* : *integer* ;
 begin (* *inv_node* *)
 b : = *p.block_containing* (*n*);
 with *block* [*b*] **do**
  begin
  if *count* = 0 **then begin** *link* : = *block_list* ; *block_list* : = *b* **end**;
  node [*n*]: = *first_node* ; *first_node* : = *n* ;
  count : = *count* + 1
  end
 end; (* *inv_node* *)
public function *next_block:integer*;
 begin (* *next_block* *)
 while *block_list* $\neq$ 0 **and**
  block [*block_list*].*count* = *p.node_count* (*block_list*) **do**
  block_list : = *block* [*block_list*].*link* ;
 if *block_list* = 0 **then** *next_block* : = 0
 else
  begin
  next_block : = *block_list*
  with *block* [*block_list*] **do**
   begin *node_list* : = *first_node* ; *block_list* : = *link* **end**;
  end
 end; (* *next_block* *)
public function *common_node:integer*);
 begin (* *common_node* *)
 if *node_list* = 0 **then** *common_node* : = 0
 else begin *common_node* : = *node_list* ; *node_list* : = *node* [*node_list*] **end**
 end; (* *common_node* *)
begin (* *inverse* *)
for *i* : = 1 **to** *p.block_count* **do with** *block* [*i*] **do** *first_node* : = *count* : = 0;
block_list : = 0; *i* : = *p.first_node* (*b*);
while *i* $\neq$ 0 **do**
 begin
 j : = *f.first_predecessor* (*i*);
 while *j* $\neq$ 0 **do begin** *inv_node* (*j*); *j* : = *f.next_predecessor* (*j*) **end**;
 i : = *p.next_node* ;
 end
end; (* *inverse* *)

Figure B.10. Abstract Data Type for an Inverse.

blocks that contain elements of *inverse* (*j*) but are not themselves subsets of *inverse* (*j*). The module allows us to obtain a block satisfying these constraints by invoking *next_block*. (If *next_block* returns 0, no more such blocks exist.) Once a block has been obtained, successive invocations of *common_node* yield the elements common to that block and *inverse* (*j*). Note that each of the operations provided by the abstract data type requires constant time.

B.3.3. Coloring   The problem of minimizing the number of rows in a parse table can be cast as a problem in graph theory as follows: Let each row correspond to a node. Two nodes k and k' are *adjacent* (connected by edges (k,k') and (k',k)) if the corresponding rows are incompatible and therefore cannot be combined. We seek a partition of the graph such that no two adjacent nodes belong to the same block of the partition. The rows corresponding to the nodes in a single block of the partition then have no incompatibilities, and can be merged. Clearly we would like to find such a partition having the smallest number of blocks, since this will result in maximum compression of the table.

This problem is known in graph theory as the *coloring* problem, and the minimum number of partitions is the *chromatic number* of the graph. It has been shown that the coloring problem is NP-complete, and hence we seek algorithms that efficiently approximate the optimum partition.

Most approximation algorithms are derived from backtracking algorithms that decide whether a given number of colors is sufficient for the specified graph. If such an algorithm is given a number of colors equal to the number of nodes in the graph then it will never need to backtrack, and hence all of the mechanism for backtracking can be removed. A good backtracking algorithm contains heuristics designed to prune large portions of the search tree, which, in this case, implies using as few colors as possible for trial colorings. But it is just these heuristics that lead to good approximations when there is no backtracking!

A general approach is to make the most constrained decisions first. This can be done by sorting the nodes in order of decreasing incident edge count. The first node colored has the maximum number of adjacent nodes and hence rules out the use of its color for as many nodes as possible. We then choose the node with the most restrictive constraint on its color next, resolving ties by taking the one with most adjacent nodes. At each step we color the chosen node with the lowest possible color.

Figure B.11 gives the complete coloring algorithm. We assume that g contains no cycles of length 1. (A graph with cycles of length 1 cannot be colored because some node is adjacent to itself and thus, by definition, must have a different color than itself.) First we partition the nodes according to number of adjacencies, coloring any isolated nodes immediately. Because

```
procedure coloring (g : graph ; p : partition );
  ( * Make p define a coloring of g  *)
  var
    sort : partition ( g.n );
    choice : array [1..g.n ] of integer ;
    available : array [1..g.n,1..g.n ] of boolean ;
    i,j,k,uncolored,min_choice,node,color : integer ;
  begin ( * coloring  *)
  for i : = 1 to g.n do
    begin
    j : = sort.new_block ;
    choice[i] : = g.n;
    for j : = 1 to g.n do available [i,j ] : = true ;
    end;
  uncolored : = 0;
  for i : = 1 to g.n do
    if g.first_successor (i ) = 0 then p.add_node (i,1)
    else
      begin
      j : = 1; while g.next_successor ≠ 0 do j : = j +1;
      sort.add_block (i,j )
      end;
  for i : = 1 to uncolored do
    begin
    min_choice : = g.n +1;
    for j : = g.n downto 1 do
      begin
      k : = sort.first_node ( j );
      while k ≠ 0 do
        begin
        if choice [k ] < min_choice then
          begin node : = k ; min_choice : = choice [k ] end;
        k : = sort.next_node ;
        end
      end;
    sort.add_node (node,g.n );
    color : = 1; while not available [color,node ] do color : = color +1;
    p.add_node (node,color );
    j : = g.first_successor (node );
    while j ≠ 0 do
      begin
      if available [color,j ] then
        begin available [color,j ] : = false; choice [j ] : = choice [j ] − 1 end;
      j : = g.next_successor (node );
      end
    end
  end; ( * coloring  *)
```

Figure B.11. Coloring Algorithm.

of our assumptions, block *g.n* of *sort* must be empty. The coloring loop then scans the nodes in order of decreasing adjacency count, seeking the most restrictive choice of colors. This node is then assigned the lowest available color, and that color is made unavailable to all of the node's neighbors. Note that we mark a node as having been colored by moving it to block *g.n* of the *sort* partition.

B.4. Notes and References

For further information about graph theory, the interested reader should consult the books by Berge [1962] or Harary [1969].

The representations of graphs and partitions discussed in Section B.2 are chosen to have the least impact on the complexity of the algorithms that follow. Further insight into the rationale underlying these representations can be obtained from the book by Aho, Hopcroft and Ullman [1974]. Both the algorithm for identifying strongly connected components and the partitioning algorithm are drawn from this book.

Proofs of the NP-completeness of the graph coloring problem are given by Karp [1972] and Aho [1974]. It can also be shown that most approximation algorithms perform poorly on particular graphs. Johnson [1974] demonstrates that each of the popular algorithms has an associated class of graphs for which the ratio of the approximate to the true chromatic number grows linearly with the number of vertices. Further work by Garey and Johnson [1976] indicates that it is unlikely that any fast algorithm can guarantee good approximations to the chromatic number. The algorithm presented in Section B.3.3 has been proposed by a number of authors [Wells 1971, Dürre 1973, Brelaz 1979]. It has been incorporated into an LALR(1) parser generator [Dencker 1977] and has proven satisfactory in practice. Further experimental evidence in favor of this algorithm has also been presented by Dürre [1973].

EXERCISES

B.1. The graph module of Figure B.4 is unpleasant when the number of edges is not known at the time the module is instantiated: If *e* is not made large enough then the program will fail, and if it is made too large then space will be wasted.

    a. Change the module definition so that the array *edge* is not present. Instead, each edge should be represented by a record allocated dynamically by *define_edge*.

    b. What is the lifetime of the edge storage in (a)? How can it be recovered?

B.2. Modify the module of Figure B.5 to save space by omitting the *parent* field of each node. Provide access to the parent via the *sibling* pointer of the last child.

What additional information is required? If the two versions of the module were implemented on a machine with which you are familiar, would there be any difference in the actual storage requirements for a node? Explain.

B.3. Consider the partition module of Figure B.6.
   a. Show that if array p is defined with lower bound 1, execution of *add_node* may abort due to an illegal array reference. How can this error be avoided if the lower bound is made 1? Why is initialization of $p[0]$ unnecessary?
   b. What changes would be required if we wished to remove a node from *all* blocks by using *add_node* to add it to a fictitious block 0?
   c. Under what circumstances would the use of *first_node* and *next_node* to scan a block of the partition be unsatisfactory? How could this problem be overcome?

B.4. Explain why the elements of *stack* are initialized to 0 in Figure B.7 and why the *pop* operation resets the element to 0. Could *top* be set to 0 initially also?

B.5. Consider the application of *strongly_connected_components* to the graph of Figure B.3a. Assume that the indexes of the node in the graph were assigned 'by column': The leftmost node has number 1, the next three have numbers 2-4 (from the top) and the rightmost three have numbers 5-7. Also assume that the lists of edges leaving a node are ordered clockwise from the 12 o'clock position.
   a. Show that the nodes will be visited in the order given by Figure B.3b.
   b. Give a sequence of snapshots showing the procedure activations and the changes in *lowlink*.
   c. Show that the algorithm partitions the graph correctly.

B.6. Consider the refinement problem of Section B.3.2.
   a. Implement a Boolean procedure *split(block)* that will refine *block* according to the successors of its nodes: If all of the successors of nodes in *block* lie in the same block of p, then *split(block)* returns *false* and p is unchanged. Otherwise, suppose that the successors of nodes in *block* lie in n distinct blocks, $n > 1$. Add $n - 1$ blocks to p and distribute the nodes of *block* among *block* and these new blocks on the basis of their successor blocks. *Split(block)* returns *true* in this case.
   b. Implement *refine* as a loop that cycles through the blocks of p, applying *split* to each. Repeat the loop so long as any one of the applications of *split* yields *true*. (Note that for each repetition of the loop, the number of blocks in p will increase by at least one.)

B.7. Consider the problem of structural equivalence of types discussed in Section 9.1.2. We can solve this problem as follows:
   a. Define a graph, each of whose nodes represents a single type. There is an edge from node k_1 to node k_2 if type k_1 'depends upon' type k_2. One type 'depends upon' another if its definition uses that type. For example, if k_1 is declared to be of type **ref** k_2 then k_1 'depends upon' k_2.)
   b. Define a partition that groups all of the 'similarly defined' types. (Two types are 'similarly defined' if their type definitions have the same structure, ignoring any type specifications appearing in them. For example, **ref** k_1 and **ref** k_2 are 'similarly defined'.)

   c. Apply the refinement algorithm of Section B.3.2.

      Assume that array types are 'similarly defined' if they have the same dimen-
      sions, and record types are 'similarly defined' if they have the same field
      identifiers in the same order. Apply the procedure outlined above to the
      structural equivalence problem of Exercise 2.2.

B.8. Consider the problem of state minimization discussed in Section 6.2.2. The
     state diagram is a directed graph with node and edge labels. It defines a func-
     tion $f(i,s)$, where i is an input symbol selected from the set of edge labels and
     s is a state selected from the set of node labels.

   a. Assume that the state diagram has been completed by adding an error state,
      so that there is an edge for every input symbol leaving every node. Define a
      three-block partition on the graph, with the error state in one block, all final
      states in the second and all other states in the third. Consider the edges of
      the state diagram to define a set of functions, f_i, one per input symbol.
      Show that the states of the minimum automaton correspond to the nodes of
      the reduction (Definition 3.3) of the state diagram with respect to the
      refinement of the three block partition compatible with all f_i.

   b. Show that Definition B.1 permits only a single edge directed from one
      specific node to another. Is this limitation enforced by Figure B.4? If so,
      modify Figure B.4 to remove it.

   c. Modify Figure B.4 to allow attachment of integer edge labels.

   d. Modify Figure B.9 to carry out the refinement of a graph with edge labels,
      treating each edge label as a distinct function.

   e. Modify the result of (d) to make completion of the state diagram unneces-
      sary: When a particular edge label is missing, assume that its destination is
      the error state.

Bibliography

We have repeatedly stressed the need to derive information about a language from the definition of that language rather than from particular implementation manuals or textbooks describing the language. In this book, we have used the languages listed below as sources of examples. For each language we give a reference that we consider to be the 'language definition'. Any statement that we make regarding the language is based upon the cited reference, and does not necessarily hold for particular implementations or descriptions of the language found elsewhere in the literature.

Ada—The definition of Ada was still under discussion when this book went to press. We have based our examples upon the version described by Ichbiah [Ichbiah 1980].

ALGOL 60—[Naur 1963]

ALGOL 68—[Wijngaarden 1975]

BASIC—Almost every equipment manufacturer provides a version of this language, and the strongest similarity among them is the name. We have followed the standard for 'minimal BASIC' [ANSI 1978a].

COBOL—[ANSI 1968]

Euclid—[Lampson 1977]

FORTRAN—We have drawn examples from both the 1966 [ANSI 1966] and 1978 [ANSI 1978b] standards. When we refer simply to 'FORTRAN', we assume the 1978 standard. If we are pointing out differences, or if the particular version is quite important, then we use 'FORTRAN 66' and 'FORTRAN 77' respectively. (Note that the version described by the 1978 standard is named 'FORTRAN 77', due to an unforeseen delay in publication of the standard.)

LIS—[Ichbiah 1974]

LISP—The examples for which we use LISP depend upon its applicative nature, and hence we rely upon the original description [McCarthy 1960] rather than more modern versions.

MODULA2—[Wirth 1980]

Pascal—Pascal was in the process of being standardized when this book went to press. We have relied for most of our examples on the User Manual and Report [Jensen 1974], but we have also drawn upon the draft standard [Addyman 1980]. The examples from the latter have been explicitly noted as such.

SIMULA—[Dahl 1970]

SNOBOL4—[Griswold 1971]

ACM 1961
    ACM Compiler Symposium 1960. *Communications of the ACM* 4(1), 3-84 (1961).

ANSI 1966
    FORTRAN. American National Standards Institute, New York, X3.9-1966, 1966.

ANSI 1968
    COBOL. American National Standards Institute, New York, X3.23-1968, 1968.

ANSI 1978a
    Minimal BASIC. American National Standards Institute, New York, X3.60-1978, 1978.

ANSI 1978b
    FORTRAN. American National Standards Institute, New York, X3.9-1978, 1978.

Addyman 1980
    Addyman, A. M. A Draft Proposal for Pascal. *SIGPLAN Notices* 15(4), 1-66 (1980).

Aho 1972
    Aho, A. V. and J. D. Ullman. *The Theory of Parsing, Translation and Compiling*. Prentice-Hall, Englewood Cliffs, NJ, 1972.

Aho 1974
    Aho, A. V., J. E. Hopcroft, and J. D. Ullman. *The Design and Analysis of Computer Algorithms*. Addison-Wesley, Reading, Ma, 1974.

Aho 1975
    Aho, A. V. and M. J. Corasick. Efficient String Matching: An Aid to Bibliographic Search. *Communications of the ACM* 18(6), 333-340 (1975).

Aho 1976
    Aho, A. V. and S. C. Johnson. Optimal Code Generation for Expression Trees. *Journal of the ACM* 23(3), 488-501 (1976).

Aho 1977a

Aho, A. V. and J. D. Ullman. *Principles of Compiler Design*. Addison-Wesley, Reading, Ma, 1977.

Aho 1977b

Aho, A. V., S. C. Johnson, and J. D. Ullman. Code Generation for Machines with Multiregister Operations. *Journal of the ACM,* 21-28 (1977).

Allen 1981

Allen, F. E., J. Cocke, and K. Kennedy. Reduction of Operator Strength. In Muchnick, S. S. and N. D. Jones (Eds.) *Program Flow Analysis: Theory and Applications*. Prentice-Hall, Englewood Cliffs, NJ, 1981, pp. 79-101.

Ammann 1974

Ammann, U. The Method of Structured Programming Applied to the Development of a Compiler. In *Proceedings of the International Computing Symposium 1973*. North-Holland, Amsterdam, 1974, pp. 94-99.

Ammann 1975

Ammann, U. Die Entwicklung eines PASCAL-Compilers nach der Methode des Strukturierten Programmierens. Eidgenössische Technische Hochschule Zürich, Zürich, Ph.D. Thesis, 1975.

Ammann 1977

Ammann, U. On Code Generation in a PASCAL Compiler. *Software - Practice and Experience* 7, 391-423 (1977).

Anderson 1973

Anderson, T., J. Eve, and J. J. Horning. Efficient LR(1) Parsers. *Acta Informatica* 2, 12-39 (1973).

Asbrock 1979

Asbrock, B. Attribut-Implementierung und - Optimierung für Attributierte Grammatiken. Fakultät für Informatik, Universität Karlsruhe, Karlsruhe, FRG, Diplomarbeit, 1979.

Baker 1982

Baker, T. P. A One-Pass Algorithm for Overload Resolution in Ada. *ACM Transactions on Programming Languages and Systems* 4(4), 615-649 (1982).

Balzer 1969

Balzer, R. M. EXDAMS - Extendable Debugging and Monitoring System. *AFIPS Conference Proceedings* 34, 567-580 (1969).

Banatre 1979

Banatre, J. P., J. P. Routeau, and L. Trilling. An Event-Driven Compiling Technique. *Communications of the ACM* 22(1), 34-42 (1979).

Barron 1963

Barron, D. W. and D. F. Hartley. Techniques for Program Error Diagnosis on EDSAC2. *Computer Journal* 6, 44-49 (1963).

Barth 1977

Barth, J. M. Shifting Garbage Collection Overhead to Compile Time.

Communications of the ACM 20(7), 513-518 (1977).

Bauer 1976
Bauer, F. L. and J. Eickel (Eds.) *Compiler Construction - An Advanced Course.* (Lecture Notes in Computer Science 21) Springer-Verlag, Heidelberg, FRG, 1976.

Bayer 1967
Bayer, R., D. Gries, M. Paul, and H. Wiehle. The ALCOR ILLINOIS 7090/7094 Post Mortem Dump. *Communications of the ACM* 10(12), 804-808 (1967).

Beatty 1974
Beatty, J. C. Register Assignment Algorithm for Generation of Highly Optimized Object Code. *IBM Journal of Research and Development* 18(1), 20-39 (1974).

Belady 1966
Belady, L. A. A Study of Replacement Algorithms for a Virtual Storage Computer. *IBM Systems Journal* 5(2), 613-640 (1966).

Bell 1974
Bell, J. R. A Compression Method for Compiler Precedence Tables. In Rosenfeld, J. L. (Ed.) *Information Processing 74.* North-Holland, Amsterdam, 1974, pp. 359-362.

Berge 1962
Berge, C. *The Theory of Graphs and Its Applications.* Wiley, New York. 1962.

Bochmann 1976
Bochmann, G. V. Semantic Evaluation from Left to Right. *Communications of the ACM* 19(2), 55-62 (1976).

Borowiec 1977
Borowiec, J. *Pragmatics in a Compiler Production System.* (Lecture Notes in Computer Science 47) Springer-Verlag, Heidelberg, FRG, 1977.

Brelaz 1979
Brelaz, D. New Methods to Color the Vertices of a Graph. *Communications of the ACM* 22(4), 251-256 (1979).

Brinch-Hansen1975a
Brinch-Hansen, P. and A. C. Hartmann. *Sequential Pascal Report.* California Institute of Technology, Pasadena, Ca, 1975.

Brown 1977
Brown, W. S. A Realistic Model of Floating-Point Computation. In Rice, J. R. (Ed.) *Mathematical Software III.* Academic Press, New York, 1977, pp. 343-360.

Brown 1981
Brown, W. S. A Simple But Realistic Model of Floating-Point Computation. Bell Telephone Laboratories, Murray Hill, NJ, Computing Science Technical Report 83, 1981.

Bruno 1975
    Bruno, J. L. and T. Lassagne. The Generation of Optimal Code for
    Stack Machines. *Journal of the ACM* 22(3), 382-396 (1975).
Bruno 1976
    Bruno, J. L. and R. Sethi. Code Generation for a One-Register
    Machine. *Journal of the ACM* 23(3), 382-396 (1976).
Busam 1971
    Busam, V. A. On the Structure of Dictionaries for Compilers. *SIG-
    PLAN Notices* 6(2), 287-305 (1971).
Carter 1982
    Carter, L. R. *An Analysis of Pascal Programs.* UMI Research Press, Ann
    Arbor, Mi, 1982.
Cercone 1982
    Cercone, N., M. Kraus, and J. Boates. Lexicon Design Using Perfect
    Hash Functions. *SIGSOC Bulletin* 13(2), 69-78 (1982).
Chaitin 1981
    Chaitin, G. J., M. A. Auslander, A. K. Chandra, J. Cocke, M. E. Hop-
    kins, and P. W. Markstein. Register Allocation via Coloring. *Computer
    Languages* 6, 47-57 (1981).
Chaitin 1982
    Chaitin, G. J. Register Allocation & Spilling via Coloring. *SIGPLAN
    Notices* 17(6), 98-105 (1982).
Chomsky 1956
    Chomsky, N. Three Models for the Description of Language. *IRE
    Transactions on Information Theory* IT-2, 113-124 (1956).
Cichelli 1980
    Cichelli, R. J. Minimal Perfect Hash Functions Made Simple. *Com-
    munications of the ACM* 23(1), 17-19 (1980).
Clark 1977
    Clark, D. W. and C. C. Green. An Empirical Study of List Structure in
    LISP. *Communications of the ACM* 20(2), 78-87 (1977).
Cocke 1977
    Cocke, J. and K. Kennedy. An Algorithm for Reduction of Operator
    Strength. *Communications of the ACM* 20(11), 850-856 (1977).
Cocke 1980
    Cocke, J. and P. W. Markstein. Measurement of Code Improvement
    Algorithms. In Lavington, S. H. (Ed.) *Information Processing 80.*
    North-Holland, Amsterdam, 1980, pp. 221-228.
Cody 1980
    Cody, W. J. and W. M. Waite. *Software Manual for the Elementary
    Functions.* Prentice-Hall, Englewood Cliffs, NJ, 1980.
Conway 1973
    Conway, R. and T. R. Wilcox. Design and Implementation of a Diag-
    nostic Compiler for PL/1. *Communications of the ACM* 16(3), 169-179
    (1973).

DIN 1980
Programmiersprache PEARL. Beuth-Verlag, DIN 66253, 1980.

Dahl 1970
Dahl, O., B. Myrhaug, and K. Nygaard. *SIMULA 67 Common Base Language*. Norwegian Computing Center, Oslo, S-22, 1970.

Dakin 1973
Dakin, R. J. and P. C. Poole. A Mixed Code Approach. *Computer Journal* 16(3), 219-222 (1973).

Damerau 1964
Damerau, F. A Technique for Computer Detection and Correction of Spelling Errors. *Communications of the ACM* 7(3), 171-176 (1964).

Davidson 1980
Davidson, J. W. and C. W. Fraser. The Design and Application of a Retargetable Peephole Optimizer. *ACM Transactions on Programming Languages and Systems* 2(2), 191-202 (1980).

Day 1970
Day, W. H. E. Compiler Assignment of Data Items to Registers. *IBM Systems Journal* 9(4), 281-317 (1970).

DeRemer 1969
DeRemer, F. L. Practical Translators for LR(k) Languages. Massachusetts Institute of Technology, Cambridge, Ma, MAC-TR-65, 1969.

DeRemer 1971
DeRemer, F. L. Simple LR(k) Grammars. *Communications of the ACM* 14(7), 453-460 (1971).

DeRemer 1974
DeRemer, F. L. Lexical Analysis. In Bauer, F. L. and J. Eickel (Eds.) *Compiler Construction - An Advanced Course*. (Lecture Notes in Computer Science 21) Springer-Verlag, Heidelberg, FRG, 1974, pp. 109-120.

Dencker 1977
Dencker, P. Ein Neues LALR-System. Institut für Informatik, Universität Karlsruhe, Karlsruhe, FRG, Diplomarbeit, 1977.

Deutsch 1976
Deutsch, L. P. and D. G. Bobrow. An Efficient, Incremental, Automatic Garbage Collector. *Communications of the ACM* 19, 522-526 (1976).

Dijkstra 1960
Dijkstra, E. W. Recursive Programming. *Numerische Mathematik* 2, 312-318 (1960).

Dijkstra 1963
Dijkstra, E. W. An ALGOL 60 Translator for the X1. *Annual Review in Automatic Programming* 3, 329-345 (1963).

Dürre 1973
Dürre, K. An Algorithm for Coloring the Vertices of an Arbitrary Graph. In Deussen, P. (Ed.) *2. Jahrestagung der Gesellschaft für Infor-*

matik Karlsruhe, 1972. (Lecture Notes in Economics and Mathematical Systems 78) Springer-Verlag, Heidelberg, FRG, 1973, pp. 82-89.

Dunn 1974
Dunn, R. C. Design of a Higher-Level Language Transput System. University of Colorado, Boulder, Co, Ph.D. Thesis, 1974.

Dunn 1981
Dunn, R. C. and W. M. Waite. *SYNPUT*. Department of Electrical Engineering, University of Colorado, Boulder, Co, 1981.

Elson 1970
Elson, M. and S. T. Rake. Code-Generation Technique for Large Language Compilers. *IBM Systems Journal* 9(3), 166-188 (1970).

Fang 1972
Fang, I. FOLDS, a Declarative Formal Language Definition System. Stanford University, Stanford, Ca, Ph.D. Thesis, 1972.

GE 1965
GE-625/635 General Loader Reference Manual. General Electric Company, Phoenix, Az, CPB-1008B, 1965.

Gaines 1969
Gaines, R. S. The Debugging of Computer Programs. Princeton University, Princeton, NJ, Ph.D. Thesis, 1969.

Galler 1964
Galler, B. A. and M. J. Fischer. An Improved Equivalence Algorithm. *Communications of the ACM* 7(5), 301-303 (1964).

Gallucci 1981
Gallucci, M. A. SAM/SAL. An Experiment Using an Attributed Grammar. University of Colorado, Boulder, Co, Ph.D. Thesis, 1981.

Ganzinger 1978
Ganzinger, H. Optimierende Erzeugung von Ubersetzerteilen aus implementierungsorientierten Sprachbeschreibungen. Technische Universität München, München, FRG, Ph.D. Thesis, 1978.

Garey 1976
Garey, M. S. and D. S. Johnson. The Complexity of Near-Optimal Graph Coloring. *Journal of the ACM* 23(1), 43-49 (1976).

Giegerich 1979
Giegerich, R. Introduction to the Compiler Generating System MUG2. Institut für Mathematik und Informatik, Technische Universität München, München, FRG, TUM-INFO 7913, 1979.

Glanville 1978
Glanville, R. S. and S. L. Graham. A New Method for Compiler Code Generation. In *Conference Record of the Fifth ACM Symposium on Principles of Programming Languages*. Association for Computing Machinery, New York, 1978, pp. 231-240.

Goos 1978
Goos, G. and U. Kastens. Programming Languages and the Design of Modular Programs. In Hibbard, P. and S. Schuman (Eds.) *Constructing*

Quality Software. North-Holland, Amsterdam, 1978, pp. 153-186.
Gordon 1979
Gordon, M. J. C. *The Denotational Definition of Programming Languages. An Introduction.* Springer-Verlag, Heidelberg, FRG, 1979.
Graham 1965
Graham, M. L. and P. Z. Ingerman. An Assembly Language for Reprogramming. *Communications of the ACM* 8(12), 769-773 (1965).
Grau 1967
Grau, A. A., U. Hill, and H. Langmaack. *Translation of ALGOL 60.* Springer-Verlag, Heidelberg, FRG, 1967.
Gries 1971
Gries, D. *Compiler Construction for Digital Computers.* Wiley, New York, 1971.
Griffiths 1973
Griffiths, M. Relationship Between Definition and Implementation of a Language. In Bauer, F. L. (Ed.) *Advanced Course on Software Engineering.* (Lecture Notes in Economics and Mathematical Systems 81) Springer-Verlag, Heidelberg, FRG, 1973, pp. 76-110.
Griswold 1971
Griswold, R. E., J. F. Poage, and I. P. Polonsky. *The SNOBOL4 Programming Language.* Prentice-Hall, Englewood Cliffs, NJ, 1971.
Griswold 1972
Griswold, R. E. *The Macro Implementation of SNOBOL4.* W. C. Freeman and Co., San Francisco, 1972.
Guttag 1975
Guttag, J. The Specification and Application to Programming of Abstract Data Types. Computer Systems Research Group, University of Toronto, Toronto, CSRG-59, 1975.
Guttag 1977
Guttag, J. Abstract Data Types and the Development of Data Structures. *Communications of the ACM* 20(6), 396-404 (1977).
Habermann 1973
Habermann, A. N. Critical Comments on the Programming Language Pascal. *Acta Informatica* 3, 47-58 (1973).
Hall 1975
Hall, A. D. FDS. A FORTRAN Debugging System Overview and Installers Guide. Bell Telephone Laboratories, Murray Hill, NJ, Computing Science Technical Report 29, 1975.
Hangelberger 1977
Hangelberger, P. Ein Algorithmus zur Lösung des Problems der kurzen Sprünge. *Elektronische Rechenanlagen* 19, 68-71 (1977).
Harary 1969
Harary, F. *Graph Theory.* Addison-Wesley, Reading, Ma, 1969.
Hartmann 1977
Hartmann, A. C. *A Concurrent Pascal Compiler for Minicomputers.*

(Lecture Notes in Computer Science 50) Springer-Verlag, Heidelberg, FRG, 1977.

Hecht 1977

Hecht, M. S. *Flow Analysis of Computer Programs*. Elsevier North-Holland, New York, 1977.

Hedberg 1963

Hedberg, R. Design of an Integrated Programming and Operating System Part III. The Expanded Function of the Loader. *IBM Systems Journal* 2, 298-310 (1963).

Hill 1976

Hill, U. Special Run-Time Organization Techniques for ALGOL 68. In Bauer, F. L. and J. Eickel (Eds.) *Compiler Construction - An Advanced Course*. (Lecture Notes in Computer Science 21) Springer-Verlag, Heidelberg, FRG, 1976, pp. 222-252.

Hoare 1973

Hoare, C. A. R. and N. Wirth. An Axiomatic Definition of the Programming Language PASCAL. *Acta Informatica* 3, 335-355 (1973).

Holt 1977

Holt, R. C., D. B. Wortman, D. T. Barnard, and J. R. Cordy. SP/k: A System for Teaching Computer Programming. *Communications of the ACM* 20(5), 301-309 (1977).

Housden 1975

Housden, R. J. W. On string Concepts and their Implementation. *Computer Journal* 18(2), 150-156 (1975).

Hunt 1975

H. B. Hunt, T. G. Szymanski, and J. D. Ullman. On the Complexity of LR(k) Testing. In *Conference Record of the Second ACM Symposium on Principles of Programming Languages*. Association for Computing Machinery, 1975, pp. 137-148.

IBM 1968

IBM System/360 Operating System FORTRAN IV (H) Compiler Program Logic Manual. IBM Corporation, Y28-6642-3, 1968.

ICC 1962

Symbolic Languages in Data Processing. Gordon and Breach, New York, 1962.

Ichbiah 1974

Ichbiah, J. D., J. P. Rissen, J. C. Heliard, and P. Cousot. The System Implementation Language LIS, Reference Manual. CII Honeywell-Bull, Louveciennes, France, Technical Report 4549 E/EN, 1974.

Ichbiah 1980

Ichbiah, J. D. *Ada Reference Manual*. (Lecture Notes in Computer Science 106) Springer-Verlag, Heidelberg, FRG, 1980.

Irons 1961

Irons, E. T. A Syntax-Directed Compiler For ALGOL 60. *Communications of the ACM* 4(1), 51-55 (1961).

Irons 1963a

Irons, E. T. Towards More Versatile Mechanical Translators. In *Experimental Arithmetic, High Speed Computing and Mathematics*. (Proceedings of Symposia in Applied Mathematics 15) American Mathematical Society, Providence, RI, 1963, pp. 41-50.

Irons 1963b

Irons, E. T. An Error Correcting Parse Algorithm. *Communications of the ACM* 6(11), 669-673 (1963).

Jazayeri 1975a

Jazayeri, M., W. F. Ogden, and W. C. Rounds. On the Complexity of the Circularity Test for Attribute Grammars. In *Conference Record of the Second ACM Symposium on Principles of Programming Languages*. Association for Computing Machinery, New York, 1975, pp. 119-129.

Jazayeri 1975b

Jazayeri, M. and K. G. Walter. Alternating Semantic Evaluator. In *Proceedings of the ACM National Conference*. Association for Computing Machinery, New York, 1975, pp. 230-234.

Jazayeri 1977

Jazayeri, M. and D. P. Pozefsky. Algorithms for Efficient Evaluation of Multi-pass Attribute Grammars Without a Parse Tree. Department of Computer Science, University of North Carolina, Chapel Hill, NC, TP77-001, 1977.

Jazayeri 1981

Jazayeri, M. A Simpler Construction Showing the Intrinsically Exponential Complexity of the Circularity Problem for Attribute Grammars. *Journal of the ACM* 28(4), 715-720 (1981).

Jensen 1974

Jensen, K. and N. Wirth. *PASCAL User Manual and Report*. (Lecture Notes in Computer Science 18) Springer-Verlag, Heidelberg, FRG, 1974.

Johnson 1974

Johnson, D. S. Worst Case Behavior of Graph Coloring Algorithms. In *Proceedings of the Fifth Southeastern Conference on Combinatorics, Graph Theory and Computing*. Utilitas Mathematica Publishing, Winnipeg, Canada, 1974, pp. 513-523.

Johnson 1968

Johnson, W. L., J. H. Porter, S. I. Ackley, and D. T. Ross. Automatic Generation of Efficient Lexical Processors Using Finite State Techniques. *Communications of the ACM* 11(12), 805-813 (1968).

Johnston 1971

Johnston, J. B. Contour Model of Block Structured Processes. *SIGPLAN Notices* 6(2), 55-82 (1971).

Joliat 1973

Joliat, M. L. On the Reduced Matrix Representation of LR(k) Parser Tables. University of Toronto, Toronto, Ph.D. Thesis, 1973.

Joliat 1974
> Joliat, M. L. Practical Minimization of LR(k) Parser Tables. In Rosenfeld, J. L. (Ed.) *Information Processing 74*. North-Holland, Amsterdam, 1974, pp. 376-380.

Jones 1971
> Jones, C. B. and P. Lucas. Proving Correctness of Implementation Techniques. In Engeler, E. (Ed.) *Symposium on Semantics of Algorithmic Languages*. (Lecture Notes in Mathematics 188) Springer-Verlag, Berlin, 1971, pp. 178-211.

Karp 1972
> Karp, R. M. Reducibility Among Combinatorial Problems. In Miller, R. E. and J. W. Thatcher (Eds.) *Complexity of Computer Computations*. Plenum Press, New York, 1972, pp. 85-104.

Kastens 1976
> Kastens, U. Systematische Analyse semantischer Abhänigkeiten. In *Programmiersprachen*. (Informatik Fachberichte 1) Springer-Verlag, Heidelberg, FRG, 1976, pp. 19-32.

Kastens 1980
> Kastens, U. Ordered Attribute Grammars. *Acta Informatica* 13(3), 229-256 (1980).

Kastens 1982
> Kastens, U., B. Hutt, and E. Zimmermann. *GAG: A Practical Compiler Generator*. (Lecture Notes in Computer Science 141) Springer-Verlag, Heidelberg, FRG, 1982.

Kennedy 1976
> Kennedy, K. and S. K. Warren. Automatic Generation of Efficient Evaluators for Attribute Grammars. In *Conference Record of the Third ACM Symposium on Principles of Programming Languages*. Association for Computing Machinery, New York, 1976, pp. 32-49.

Kennedy 1979
> Kennedy, K. and J. Ramanathan. A Deterministic Attribute Grammar Evaluator Based on Dynamic Sequencing. *ACM Transactions on Programming Languages and Systems* 1, 142-160 (1979).

Kennedy 1981
> Kennedy, K. A Survey of Data Flow Analysis Techniques. In Muchnick, S. S. and N. D. Jones (Eds.) *Program Flow Analysis: Theory and Applications*. Prentice-Hall, Englewood Cliffs, NJ, 1981, pp. 5-54.

Klint 1979
> Klint, P. Line Numbers Made Cheap. *Communications of the ACM* 22(10), 557-559 (1979).

Knuth 1962
> Knuth, D. E. History of Writing Compilers. *Computers and Automation* 11, 8-14 (1962).

Knuth 1965
> Knuth, D. E. On the Translation of Languages from Left to Right.

Information and Control 8(6), 607-639 (1965).

Knuth 1968a

Knuth, D. E. Semantics of Context-Free Languages. *Mathematical Systems Theory* 2(2), 127-146 (1968).

Knuth 1968b

Knuth, D. E. *Fundamental Algorithms*. (The Art of Computer Programming 1) Addison-Wesley, Reading, Ma, 1968.

Knuth 1969

Knuth, D. E. *Seminumerical Algorithms*. (The Art of Computer Programming 2) Addison-Wesley, Reading, Ma, 1969.

Knuth 1971a

Knuth, D. E. Semantics of Context-free Languages: Correction. *Mathematical Systems Theory* 5, 95-96 (1971).

Knuth 1971b

Knuth, D. E. An Empirical Study of FORTRAN Programs. *Software - Practice and Experience* 1, 105-133 (1971).

Knuth 1973

Knuth, D. E. *Sorting and Searching*. (The Art of Computer Programming 3) Addison-Wesley, Reading, Ma, 1973.

Koster 1969

Koster, C. H. A. On Infinite Modes. *SIGPLAN Notices* 4(3), 109-112 (1969).

Koster 1971

Koster, C. H. A. Affix Grammars. In Peck, J. E. L. (Ed.) *ALGOL 68 Implementation*. North-Holland, Amsterdam, 1971, pp. 95-109.

Koster 1973

Koster, C. H. A. Error Reporting, Error Treatment and Error Correction in ALGOL Translation. Part 1. In Deussen, P. (Ed.) *2. Jahrestagung der Gesellschaft für Informatik Karlsruhe, 1972*. (Lecture Notes in Economics and Mathematical Systems 78) Springer-Verlag, Heidelberg, FRG, 1973.

Koster 1974

Koster, C. H. A. Using the CDL Compiler-Compiler. In Bauer, F. L. and J. Eickel (Eds.) *Compiler Construction - An Advanced Course*. (Lecture Notes in Computer Science 21) Springer-Verlag, Berlin, 1974, pp. 366-426.

Kruseman-Aretz 1971

Kruseman-Aretz, F. E. J. On the Bookkeeping of Source-Text Line Numbers During the Execution Phase of ALGOL 60 Programs. In *MC-25 Informatica Symposium*. (Mathematical Centre Tracts 37) Mathematisch Centrum, Amsterdam, 1971, pp. 6.1-6.12.

Lalonde 1972

Lalonde, W. R., E. S. Lee, and J. J. Horning. An LALR(k) Parser Generator. In Freiman, C. V. (Ed.) *Information Processing 71*. North-Holland, Amsterdam, 1972, pp. 513-518.

Lampson 1977
    Lampson, B. W., J. J. Horning, R. L. London, J. G. Mitchell, and G. L.
    Popek. Report on the Programming Language Euclid. *SIGPLAN
    Notices* 12(2), 1-79 (1977).

Landin 1964
    Landin, P. J. The Mechanical Evaluation of Expressions. *Computer
    Journal* 6(4), 308-320 (1964).

Landwehr 1982
    Landwehr, R., H. Jansohn, and G. Goos. Experience With an
    Automatic Code Generator Generator. *SIGPLAN Notices* 17(6), 56-66
    (1982).

Langmaack 1971
    Langmaack, H. Application of Regular Canonical Systems to Gram-
    mars Translatable from Left to Right. *Acta Informatica* 1, 111-114
    (1971).

Language Resources 1981
    *Language Resources Pascal System BL/M-86 Binding Language
    Specification*. Language Resources Inc., Boulder, Co, 1981.

Lecarme 1974
    Lecarme, O. and G. V. Bochmann. A (Truly) Usable and Portable
    Compiler Writing System. In Rosenfeld, J. L. (Ed.) *Information Pro-
    cessing 74*. North-Holland, Amsterdam, 1974, pp. 218-221.

Lesk 1975
    Lesk, M. E. Lex — A Lexical Analyzer Generator. Bell Telephone
    Laboratories, Murray Hill, NJ, Computing Science Technical Report
    39, 1975.

Levy 1975
    Levy, J. Automatic Correction of Syntax-Errors in Programming
    Languages. *Acta Informatica* 4, 271-292 (1975).

Lewis 1969
    Lewis, P. M. and R. E. Stearns. Property Grammars and Table
    Machines. *Information and Control* 14(6), 524-549 (1969).

Lewis 1974
    Lewis, P. M., D. J. Rosenkrantz, and R. E. Stearns. Attributed Transla-
    tions. *Journal of Computer and System Sciences* 9(3), 279-307 (1974).

Liskov 1974
    Liskov, B. and S. Zilles. Programming with Abstract Data Types. *SIG-
    PLAN Notices* 9(4), 50-59 (1974).

Lowry 1969
    Lowry, E. S. and C. W. Medlock. Object Code Optimization. *Com-
    munications of the ACM* 12(1), 13-22 (1969).

Lucas 1969
    Lucas, P. and K. Walk. On the Formal Description of PL/I. *Annual
    Review in Automatic Programming* 6(3), 105-181 (1969).

Lyon 1974
Lyon, G. Syntax-Directed Least-Error Analysis for Context-Free Languages: A Practical Approach. *Communications of the ACM* 17(1), 3-14 (1974).

McCarthy 1960
McCarthy, J. Recursive Functions of Symbolic Expressions and their Computation by Machine, Part 1. *Communications of the ACM* 3(4), 184-195 (1960).

McClure 1972
McClure, R. M. An Appraisal of Compiler Technology. *AFIPS Conference Proceedings* 40, 1-9 (1972).

McIlroy 1974
McIlroy, M. D. ANS FORTRAN Charts. Bell Telephone Laboratories, Murray Hill, NJ, Computing Science Technical Report 13, 1974.

McKeeman 1965
McKeeman, W. M. Peephole Optimization. *Communications of the ACM* 8(7), 443-444 (1965).

McLaren 1970
McLaren, M. D. Data Matching, Data Alignment and Structure Mapping in PL/I. *SIGPLAN Notices* 5(12), 30-43 (1970).

Mealy 1963
Mealy, G. H. A Generalized Assembly System. Rand Corporation, Santa Monica, Ca, RM-3646-PR, 1963.

Miller 1972
Miller, R. E. and J. W. Thatcher (Eds.) *Complexity of Computer Computations*. Plenum Press, New York, 1972.

Mock 1958
Mock, O., J. Olsztyn, J. Strong, T. B. Steel, A. Tritter, and J. Wegstein. The Problem of Programming Communications with Changing Machines: A Proposed Solution. *Communications of the ACM* 1(2), 12-18 (1958).

Morel 1979
Morel, E. and C. Renvoise. Global Optimization by Suppression of Partial Redundancies. *Communications of the ACM* 22(11), 96-103 (1979).

Morgan 1970
Morgan, D. L. Spelling Correction in System Programs. *Communications of the ACM* 13, 90-94 (1970).

Morris 1978
Morris, F. L. A Time- and Space-Efficient Garbage Compaction Algorithm. *Communications of the ACM* 21(8), 662-665 (1978).

Morrison 1982
Morrison, R. The String as a Simple Data Type. *SIGPLAN Notices* 17(3), 46-52 (1982).

Moses 1970
  Moses, J. The Function of **function** in LISP. *SIGSAM Bulletin* , 13-27
  (1970).
Naur 1963
  Naur, P. Revised Report on the Algorithmic Language ALGOL 60.
  Communications of the ACM 6(1), 1-17 (1963).
Naur 1964
  Naur, P. The Design of the GIER ALGOL Compiler. *Annual Review in
  Automatic Programming* 4, 49-85 (1964).
Pager 1974
  Pager, D. On Eliminating Unit Productions from LR(k) Parsers. In
  Loeckx, J. (Ed.) *Automata, Languages and Programming*. (Lecture
  Notes in Computer Science 14) Springer-Verlag, Heidelberg, FRG,
  1974, pp. 242-254.
Palmer 1974
  Palmer, E. M., M. A. Rahimi, and R. W. Robinson. Efficiency of a
  Binary Comparison Storage Technique. *Journal of the ACM* 21(3),
  376-384 (1974).
Parnas 1972
  Parnas, D. L. On the Criteria to be Used in Decomposing Systems Into
  Modules. *Communications of the ACM* 15(12), 1053-1058 (1972).
Parnas 1976
  Parnas, D. L. On the Design and Development of Program Families.
  IEEE Transactions on Software Engineering SE-2(1), 1-9 (1976).
Peck 1971
  Peck, J. E. L. (Ed.) *ALGOL 68 Implementation*. North-Holland,
  Amsterdam, 1971.
Persch 1980
  Persch, G., G. Winterstein, M. Dausmann, and S. Drossopoulou. Over-
  loading in Preliminary Ada. *SIGPLAN Notices* 15(11), 47-56 (1980).
Peterson 1972
  Peterson, T. G. Syntax Error Detection, Correction and Recovery in
  Parsers. Stevens Institute of Technology, Hoboken, NJ, Ph.D. Thesis,
  1972.
Pierce 1974
  Pierce, R. H. Source Language Debugging on a Small Computer.
  Computer Journal 17(4), 313-317 (1974).
Pozefsky 1979
  Pozefsky, D. P. Building Efficient Pass-Oriented Attribute Grammar
  Evaluators. University of North Carolina, Chapel Hill, NC, Ph.D.
  Thesis, 1979.
Quine 1960
  Quine, W. V. O. *Word and Object*. Wiley, New York, 1960.
Räihä 1977
  Räihä, K. and M. Saarinen. An Optimization of the Alternating

Semantic Evaluator. *Information Processing Letters* 6(3), 97-100 (1977).

Räihä 1978

Räihä, K., M. Saarinen, E. Soisalon-Soininen, and M. Tienari. The Compiler Writing System HLP (Helsinki Language Processor). Department of Computer Science, University of Helsinki, Helsinki, Finland, Report A-1978-2, 1978.

Räihä 1980

Räihä, K. Bibliography on Attribute Grammars. *SIGPLAN Notices* 15(3), 35-44 (1980).

Ramamoorthy 1976

Ramamoorthy, C. V. and P. Jahanian. Formalizing the Specification of Target Machines for Compiler Adaptability Enhancement. In *Proceedings of the Symposium on Computer Software Engineering*. Polytechnic Institute of New York, New York, 1976, pp. 353-366.

Randell 1964

Randell, B. and L. J. Russell. *ALGOL 60 Implementation*. Academic Press, London, 1964.

Richards 1971

Richards, M. The Portability of the BCPL Compiler. *Software - Practice and Experience* 1, 135-146 (1971).

Ripken 1977

Ripken, K. Formale Beschreibung von Maschinen, Implementierungen und Optimierender Machinecoderzeugung Aus Attributierten Programmgraphen. Technische Universität München, München, FRG, Ph.D. Thesis, 1977.

Röhrich 1978

Röhrich, J. Automatic Construction of Error Correcting Parsers. Universität Karlsruhe, Karlsruhe, FRG, Interner Bericht 8, 1978.

Röhrich 1980

Röhrich, J. Methods for the Automatic Construction of Error Correcting Parsers. *Acta Informatica* 13(2), 115-139 (1980).

Robertson 1979

Robertson, E. L. Code Generation and Storage Allocation for Machines with Span-Dependent Instructions. *ACM Transactions on Programming Languages and Systems* 1(1), 71-83 (1979).

Rosen 1967

Rosen, S. *Programming Systems and Languages*. McGraw-Hill, New York, 1967.

Rosenkrantz 1970

Rosenkrantz, D. J. and R. E. Stearns. Properties of Deterministic Top-Down Grammars. *Information and Control* 17, 226-256 (1970).

Ross 1967

Ross, D. T. The AED Free Storage Package. *Communications of the ACM* 10(8), 481-492 (1967).

Rutishauser 1952
Rutishauser, H. *Automatische Rechenplanfertigung bei Programm-gesteuerten Rechenmaschinen.* (Mitteilungen aus dem Institut für Angewandte Mathematik der ETH-Zürich 3) Birkhäuser, Basel, 1952.

Sale 1971
Sale, A. H. J. The Classification of FORTRAN Statements. *Computer Journal* 14, 10-12 (1971).

Sale 1977
Sale, A. H. J. Comments on 'Report on the Programming Language Euclid'. *SIGPLAN Notices* 12(4), 10 (1977).

Sale 1979
Sale, A. H. J. A Note on Scope, One-Pass Compilers, and Pascal. *Pascal News* (15), 62-63 (1979).

Salomaa 1973
Salomaa, A. *Formal Languages.* Academic Press, New York, 1973.

Samelson 1960
Samelson, K. and F. L. Bauer. Sequential Formula Translation. *Communications of the ACM* 3(2), 76-83 (1960).

Satterthwaite 1972
Satterthwaite, E. Debugging Tools for High Level Languages. *Software - Practice and Experience* 2, 197-217 (1972).

Scarborough 1980
Scarborough, R. G. and H. G. Kolsky. Improved Optimization of FORTRAN Object Programs. *IBM Journal of Research and Development* 24(6), 660-676 (1980).

Schulz 1976
Schulz, W. A. Semantic Analysis and Target Language Synthesis in a Translator. University of Colorado, Boulder, Co, Ph.D. Thesis, 1976.

Seegmüller 1963
Seegmüller, G. Some remarks on the Computer as a Source Language Machine. In Popplewell, C. M. (Ed.) *Information Processing 1962.* North-Holland, Amsterdam, 1963, pp. 524-525.

Sethi 1970
Sethi, R. and J. D. Ullman. The Generation of Optimal Code for Arithmetic Expressions. *Journal of the ACM* 17(4), 715-728 (1970).

Steele 1977
Steele, G. L. Arithmetic Shifting Considered Harmful. *SIGPLAN Notices* 12(11), 61-69 (1977).

Stephens 1974
Stephens, P. D. The IMP Language and Compiler. *Computer Journal* 17, 216-223 (1974).

Stevens 1974
Stevens, W. P., G. J. Myers, and L. L. Constantine. Structured Design. *IBM Systems Journal* 2, 115-139 (1974).

Stevenson 1981
    Stevenson, D. A Proposed Standard for Binary Floating-Point Arith-
    metic. *Computer* 14(3), 51-62 (1981).
Szymanski 1978
    Szymanski, T. G. Assembling Code for Machines with Span-
    Dependent Instructions. *Communications of the ACM* 21(4), 300-308
    (1978).
Talmadge 1963
    Talmadge, R. B. Design of an Integrated Programming and Operating
    System Part II. The Assembly Program and its Language. *IBM Systems
    Journal* 2, 162-179 (1963).
Tanenbaum 1976
    Tanenbaum, A. S. *Structured Computer Organization.* Prentice-Hall,
    Englewood Cliffs, NJ, 1976.
Tanenbaum 1978
    Tanenbaum, A. S. Implications of Structured Programming for
    Machine Architecture. *Communications of the ACM* 21(3), 237-246
    (1978).
Tanenbaum 1982
    Tanenbaum, A. S., H. v. Staveren, and J. W. Stevenson. Using
    Peephole Optimization on Intermediate Code. *ACM Transactions on
    Programming Languages and Systems* 4(1), 21-36 (1982).
Tennent 1981
    Tennent, R. D. *Principles of Programming Languages.* Prentice-Hall
    International, London, 1981.
Tienari 1980
    Tienari, M. On the Definition of an Attribute Grammar. In *Semantics-
    Directed Compiler Generation.* (Lecture Notes in Computer Science 94)
    Springer-Verlag, Heidelberg, FRG, 1980, pp. 408-414.
Uhl 1982
    Uhl, J., S. Drossopoulou, G. Persch, G. Goos, M. Dausmann, G.
    Winterstein, and W. Kirchgässner. *An Attribute Grammar for the
    Semantic Analysis of Ada.* (Lecture Notes in Computer Science 139)
    Springer-Verlag, Heidelberg, FRG, 1982.
Waite 1973a
    Waite, W. M. *Implementing Software for Non-Numerical Applications.*
    Prentice-Hall, Englewood Cliffs, NJ, 1973.
Waite 1973b
    Waite, W. M. A Sampling Monitor for Applications Programs.
    Software - Practice and Experience 3(1), 75-79 (1973).
Waite 1974
    Waite, W. M. Code Generation. In Bauer, F. L. and J. Eickel (Eds.)
    Compiler Construction - An Advanced Course. (Lecture Notes in Com-
    puter Science 21) Springer-Verlag, Berlin, 1974, pp. 302-332.

Waite 1977
Waite, W. M. Janus. In Brown, P. J. (Ed.) *Software Portability*. Cambridge University Press, Cambridge, 1977, pp. 277-290.

Wegbreit 1972
Wegbreit, B. A Generalised Compactifying Garbage Collector. *Computer Journal* 15, 204-208 (1972).

Wegner 1972
Wegner, P. The Vienna Definition Language. *Computing Surveys* 4(1), 5-63 (1972).

Wells 1971
Wells, M. B. *Elements of Combinatorial Computing*. Pergamon Press, Oxford, 1971.

Wijngaarden 1975
Wijngaarden, A. v., B. J. Mailloux, J. E. L. Peck, C. H. A. Koster, M. Sintzoff, C. H. Lindsey, L. G. L. T. Meertens, and R. G. Fisker. Revised Report on the Algorithmic Language ALGOL 68. *Acta Informatica* 5, 1-236 (1975).

Wilcox 1971
Wilcox, T. R. Generating Machine Code for High-Level Programming Languages. Computer Science Department, Cornell University, Ithaca, NY, Ph.D. Thesis, 1971.

Wilhelm 1977
Wilhelm, R. Baum Transformatoren: Ein Vergleich mit Baum-Transduktoren und Aspekte der Implementierung. Technische Universität München, München, FRG, Ph.D. Thesis, 1977.

Wirth 1980
Wirth, N. Modula-2. Eidgenössische Technische Hochschule, Zürich, Bericht 36, 1980.

Wulf 1975
Wulf, W. A., R. K. Johnsson, C. B. Weinstock, and S. O. Hobbs. *The Design of an Optimizing Compiler*. American Elsevier, New York, 1975.

Index

Texts and Monographs in Computer Science